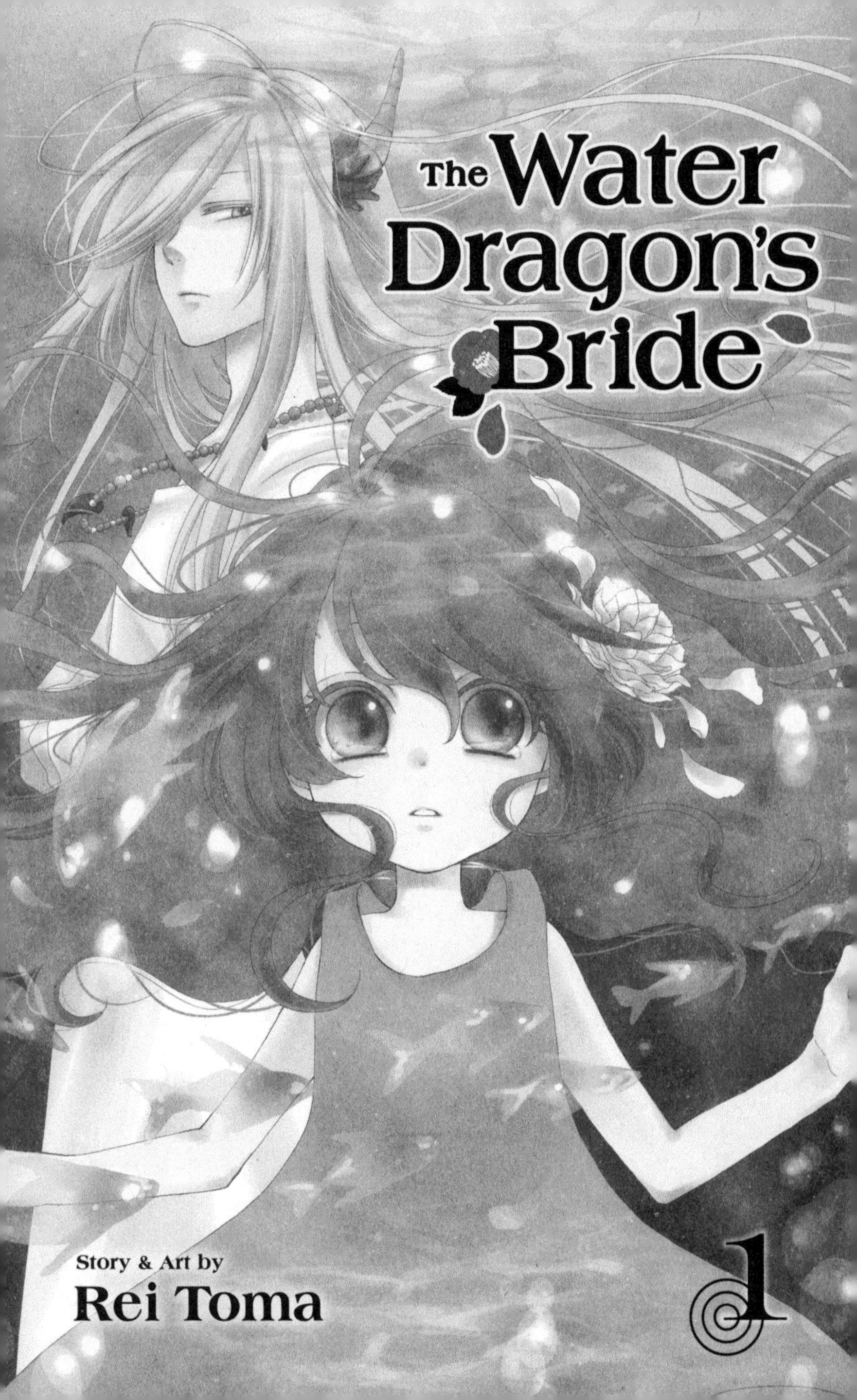
The Water Dragon's Bride
Story & Art by
Rei Toma
1

The Water Dragon's Bride

1

CONTENTS

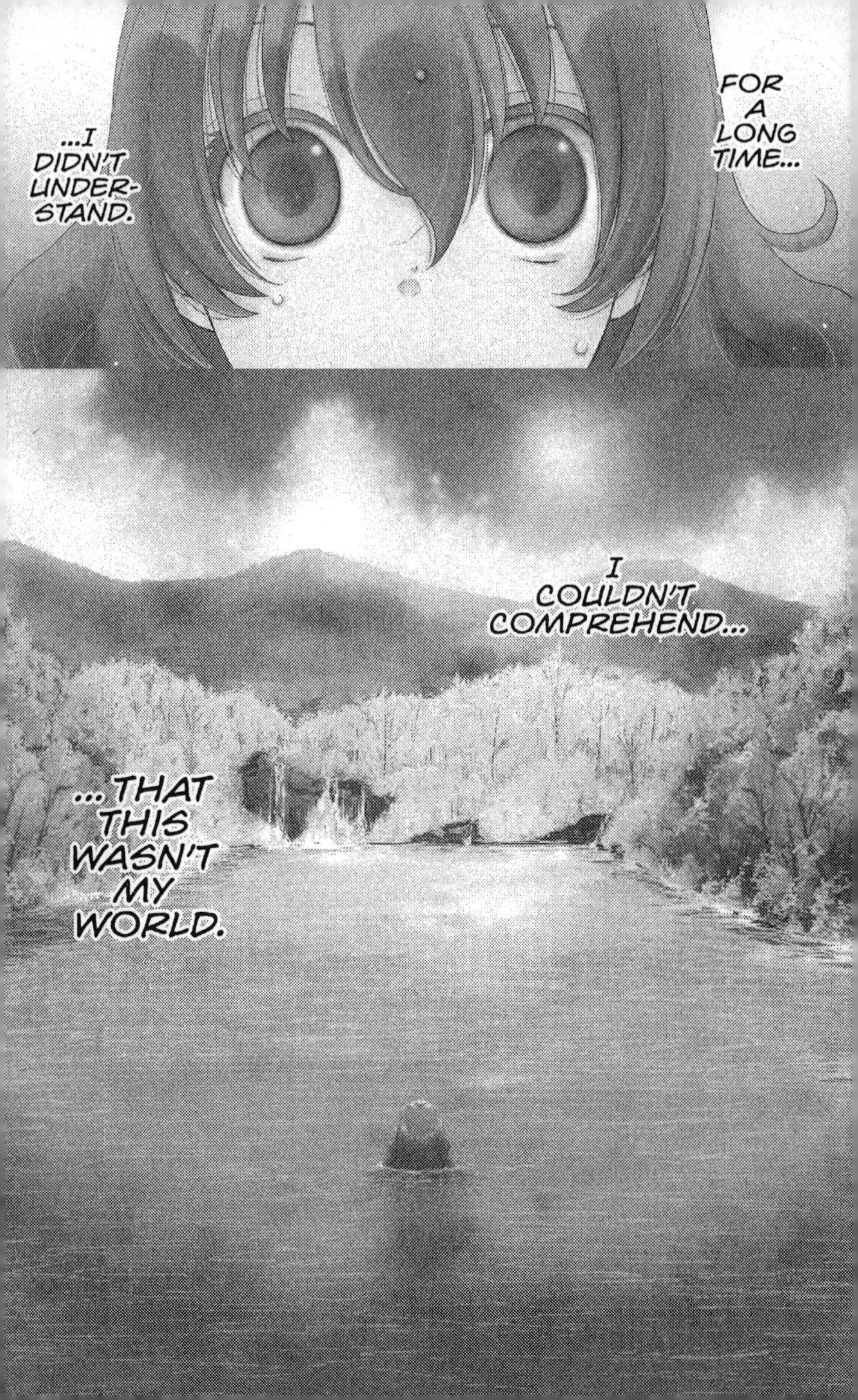
FOR A LONG TIME...
...I DIDN'T UNDER-STAND.
I COULDN'T COMPREHEND...
...THAT THIS WASN'T MY WORLD.

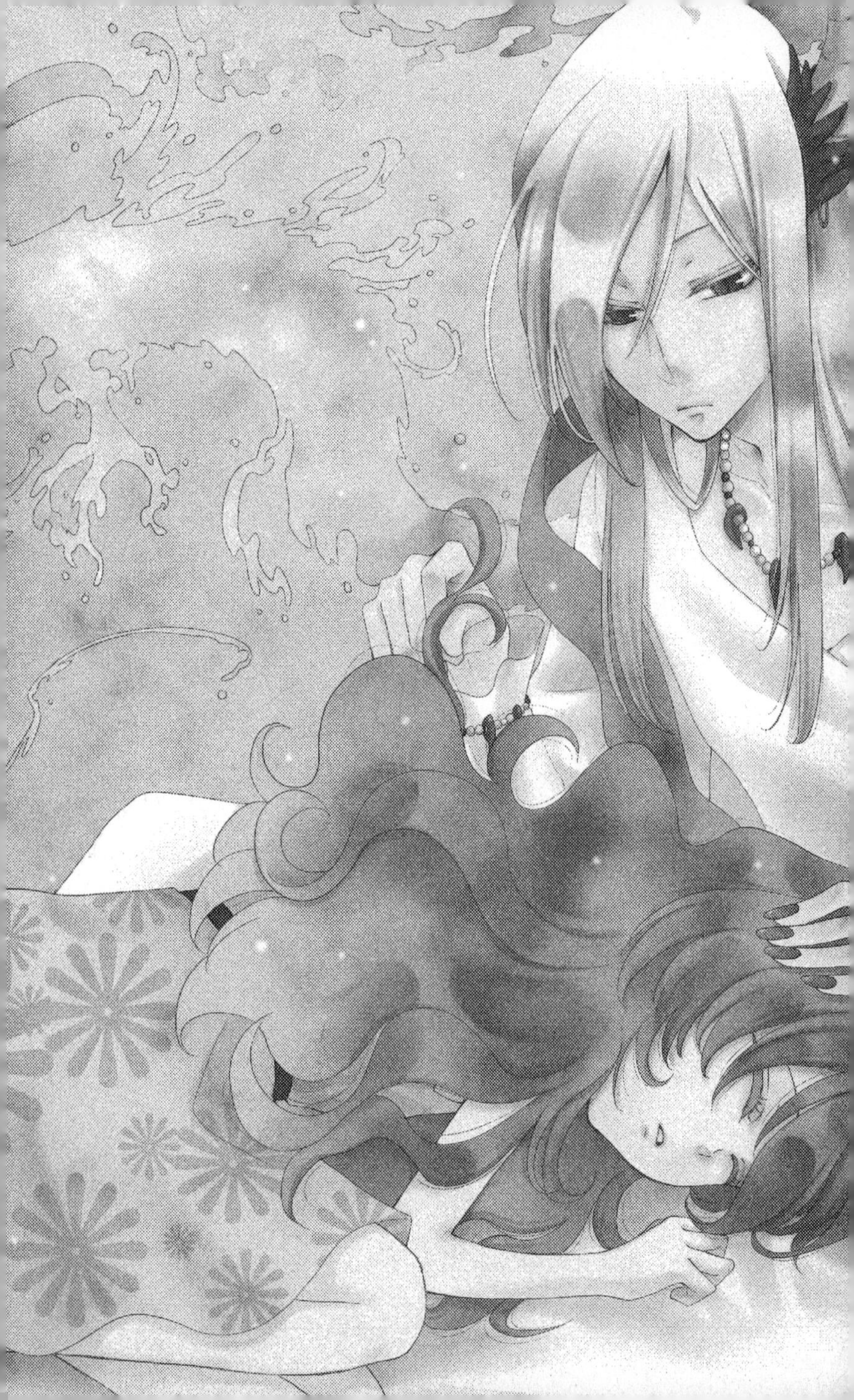

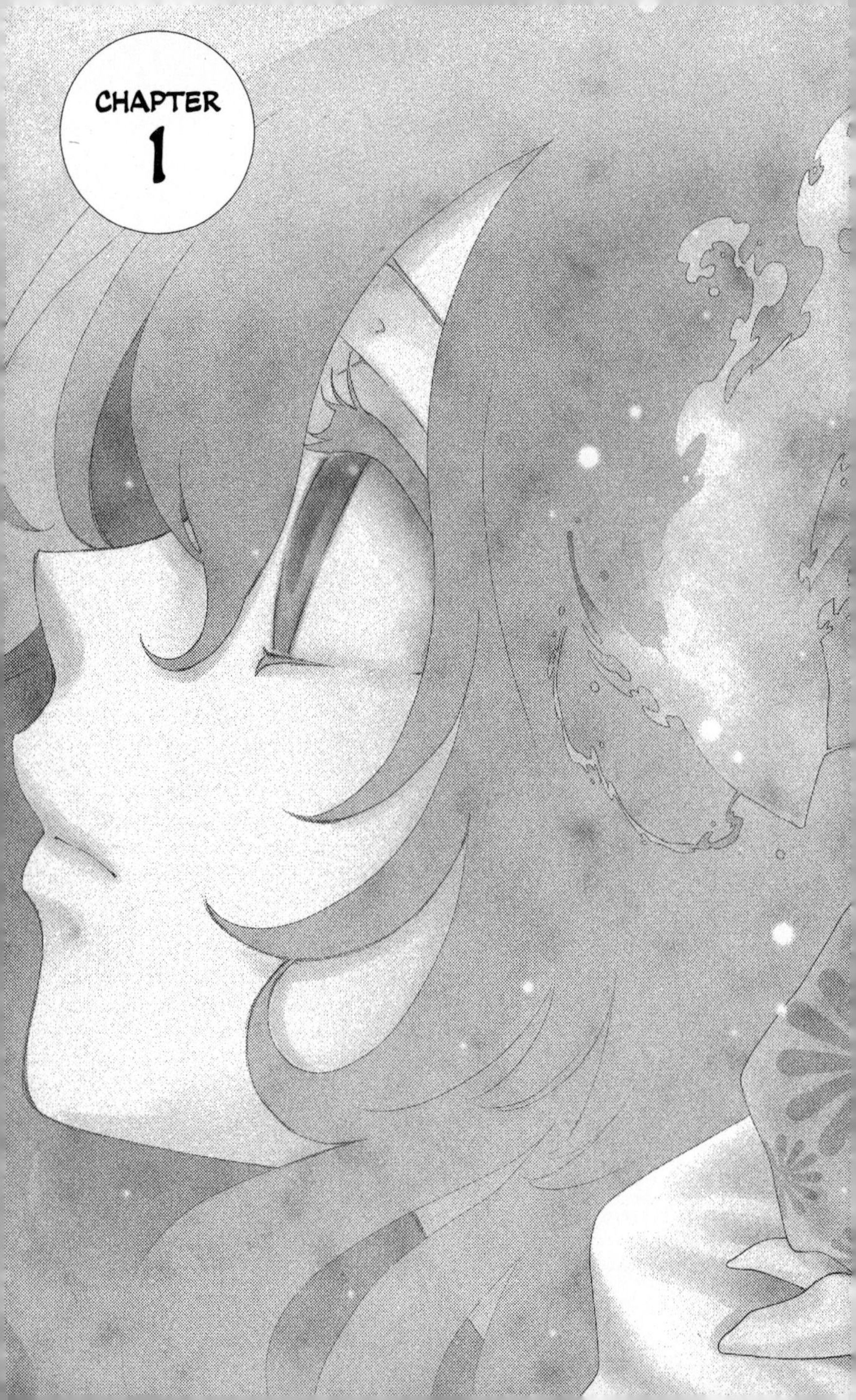
CHAPTER
1

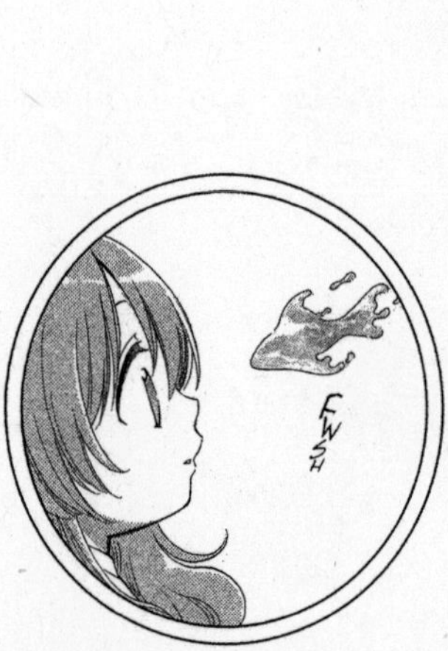
FWSH

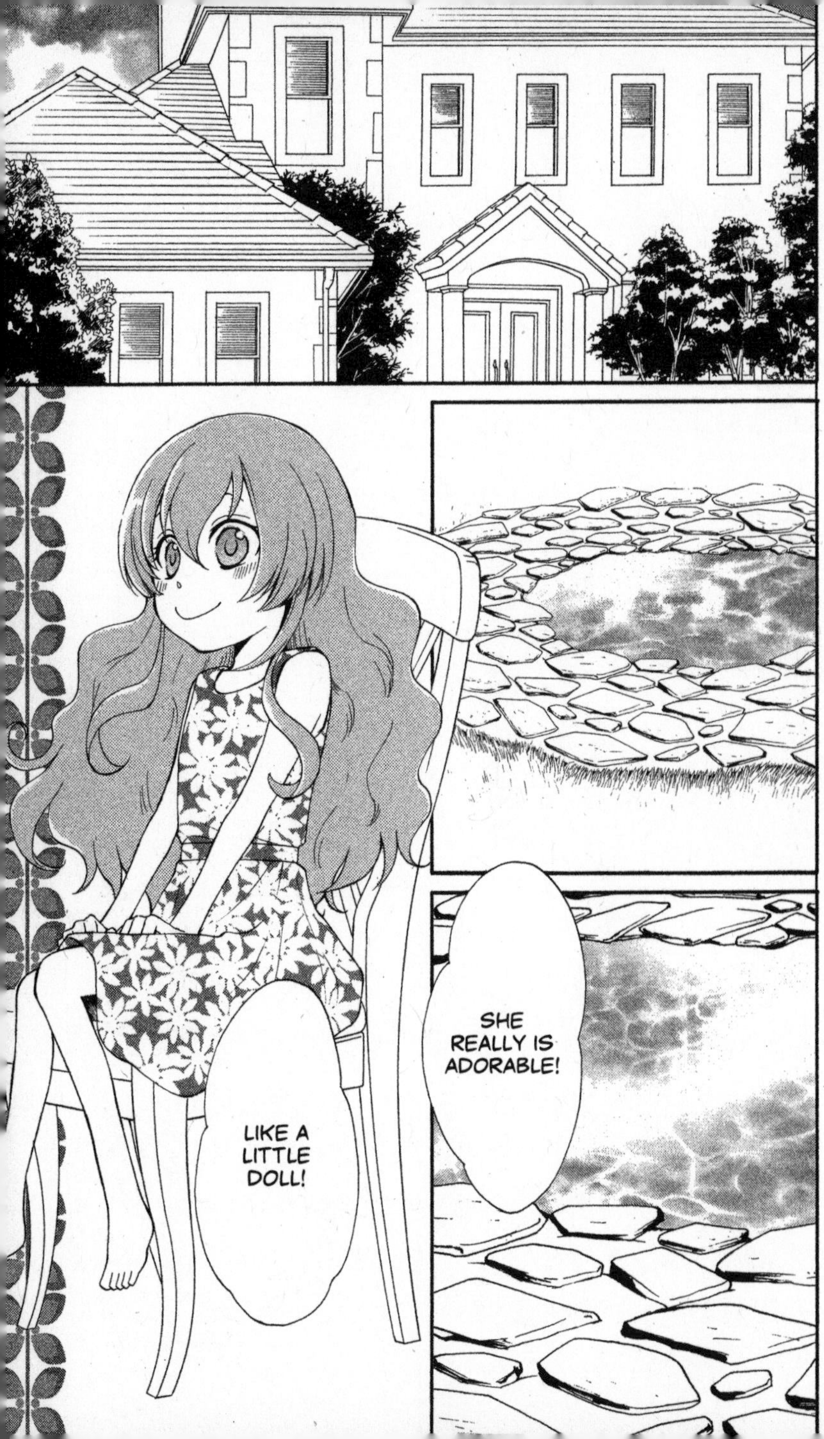
SHE REALLY IS ADORABLE!
LIKE A LITTLE DOLL!

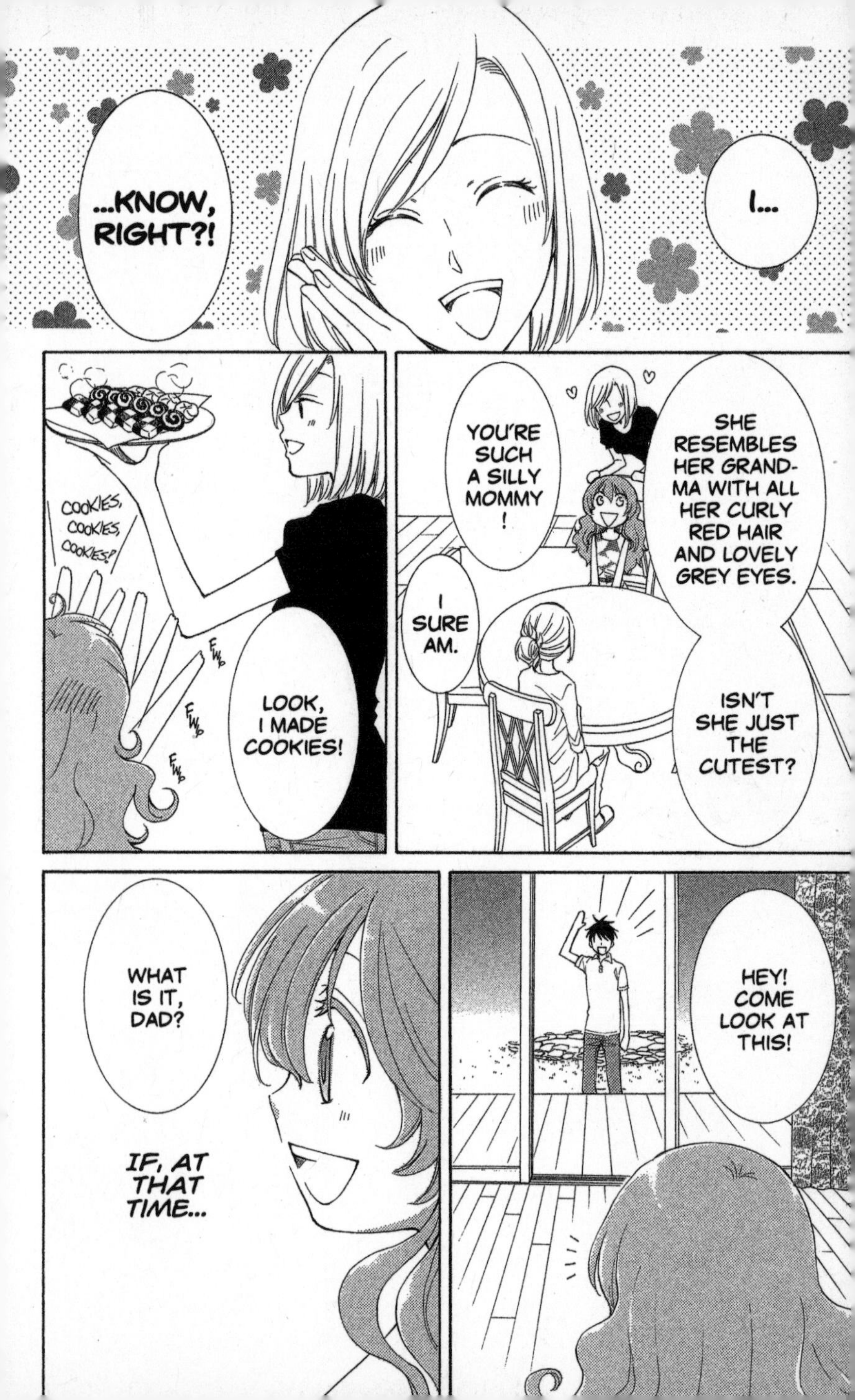
I...
...KNOW, RIGHT?!
SHE RESEMBLES HER GRAND-MA WITH ALL HER CURLY RED HAIR AND LOVELY GREY EYES.
ISN'T SHE JUST THE CUTEST?
YOU'RE SUCH A SILLY MOMMY!
I SURE AM.
LOOK, I MADE COOKIES!
COOKIES, COOKIES, COOKIES!
FWP
FWP
FWP
HEY! COME LOOK AT THIS!
WHAT IS IT, DAD?
IF, AT THAT TIME...

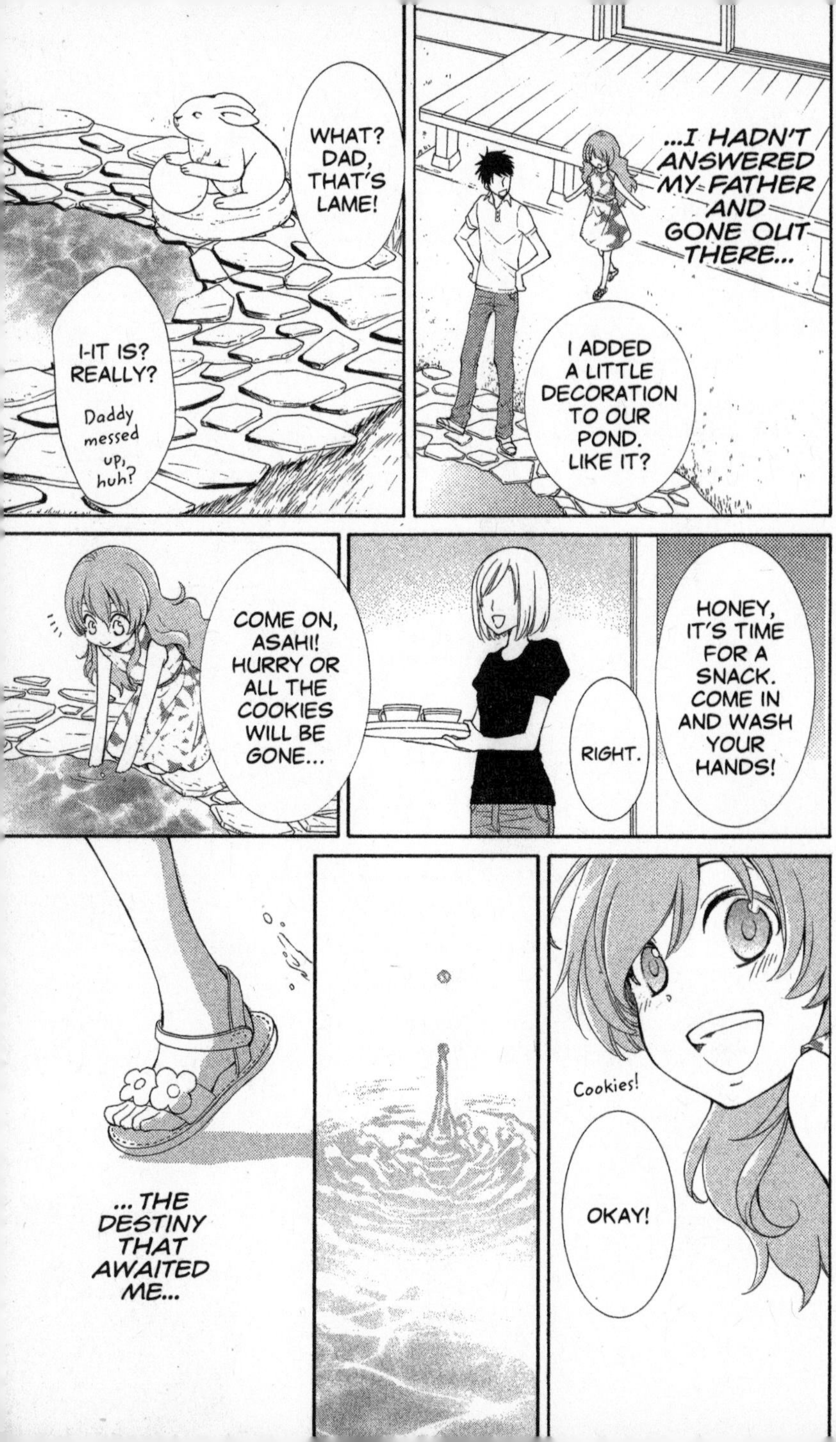
...I HADN'T ANSWERED MY FATHER AND GONE OUT THERE...
I ADDED A LITTLE DECORATION TO OUR POND. LIKE IT?
WHAT? DAD, THAT'S LAME!
I-IT IS? REALLY?
Daddy messed up, huh?
HONEY, IT'S TIME FOR A SNACK. COME IN AND WASH YOUR HANDS!
RIGHT.
COME ON, ASAHI! HURRY OR ALL THE COOKIES WILL BE GONE...
Cookies!
OKAY!
...THE DESTINY THAT AWAITED ME...

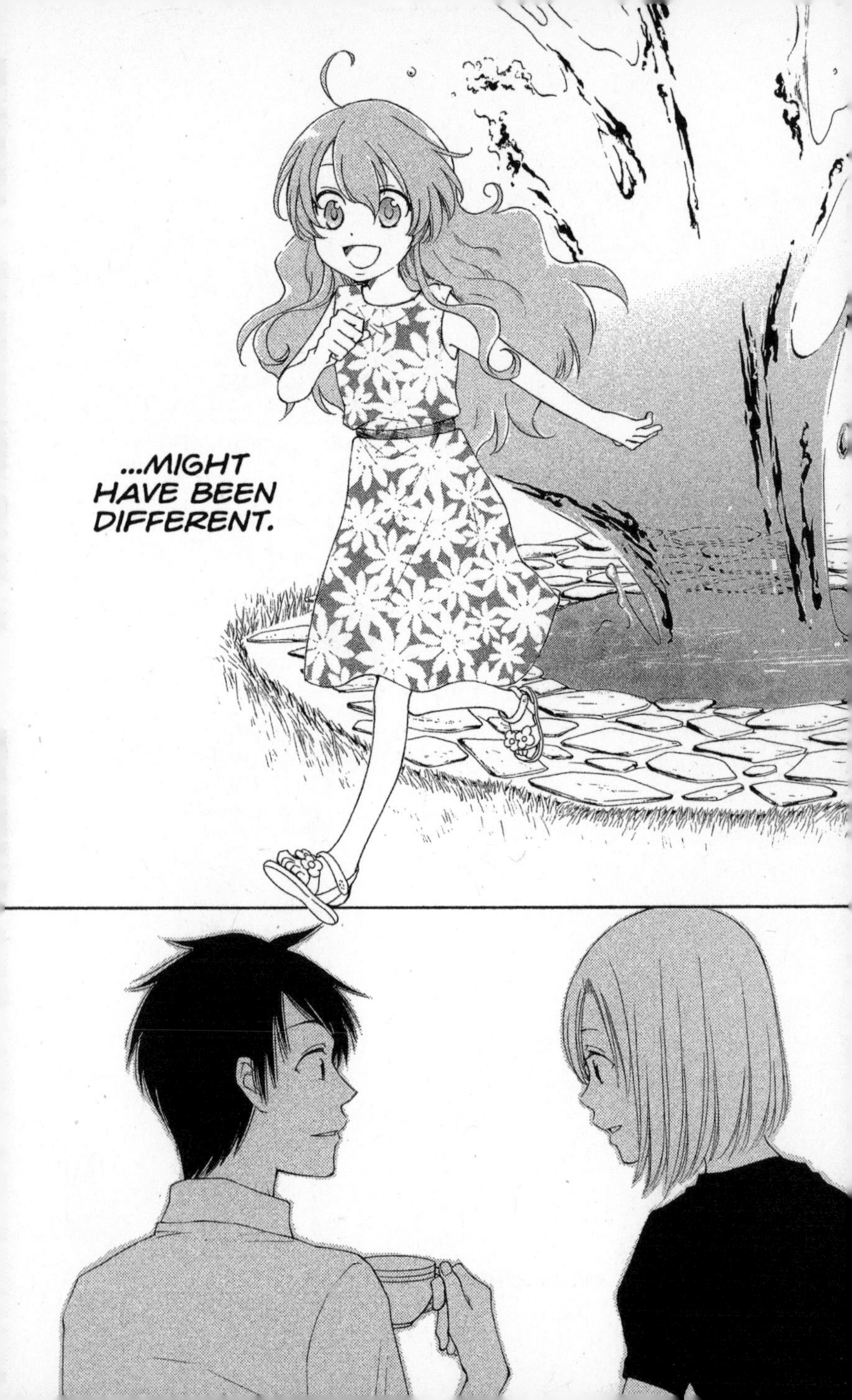
...MIGHT HAVE BEEN DIFFERENT.

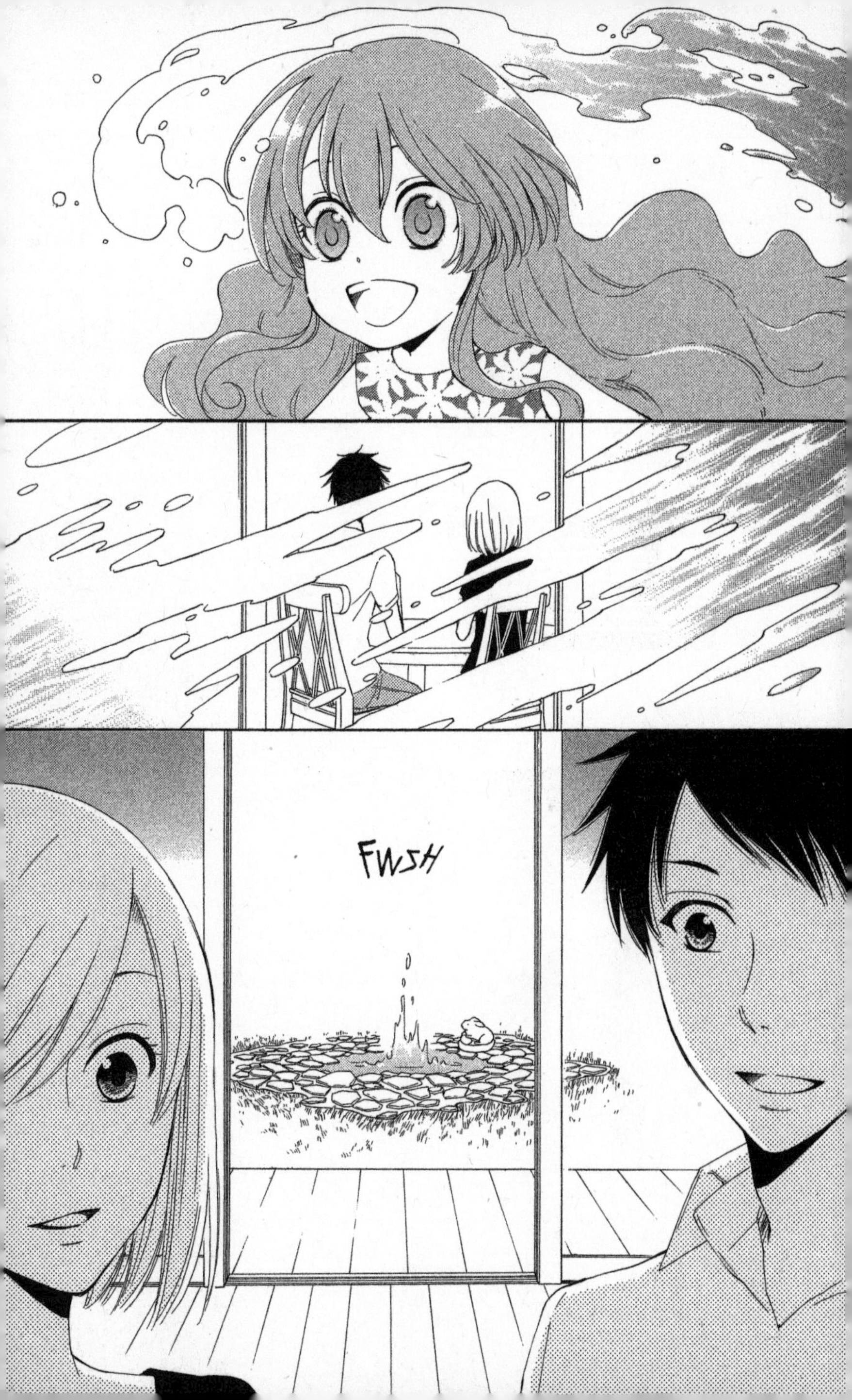
FWSH

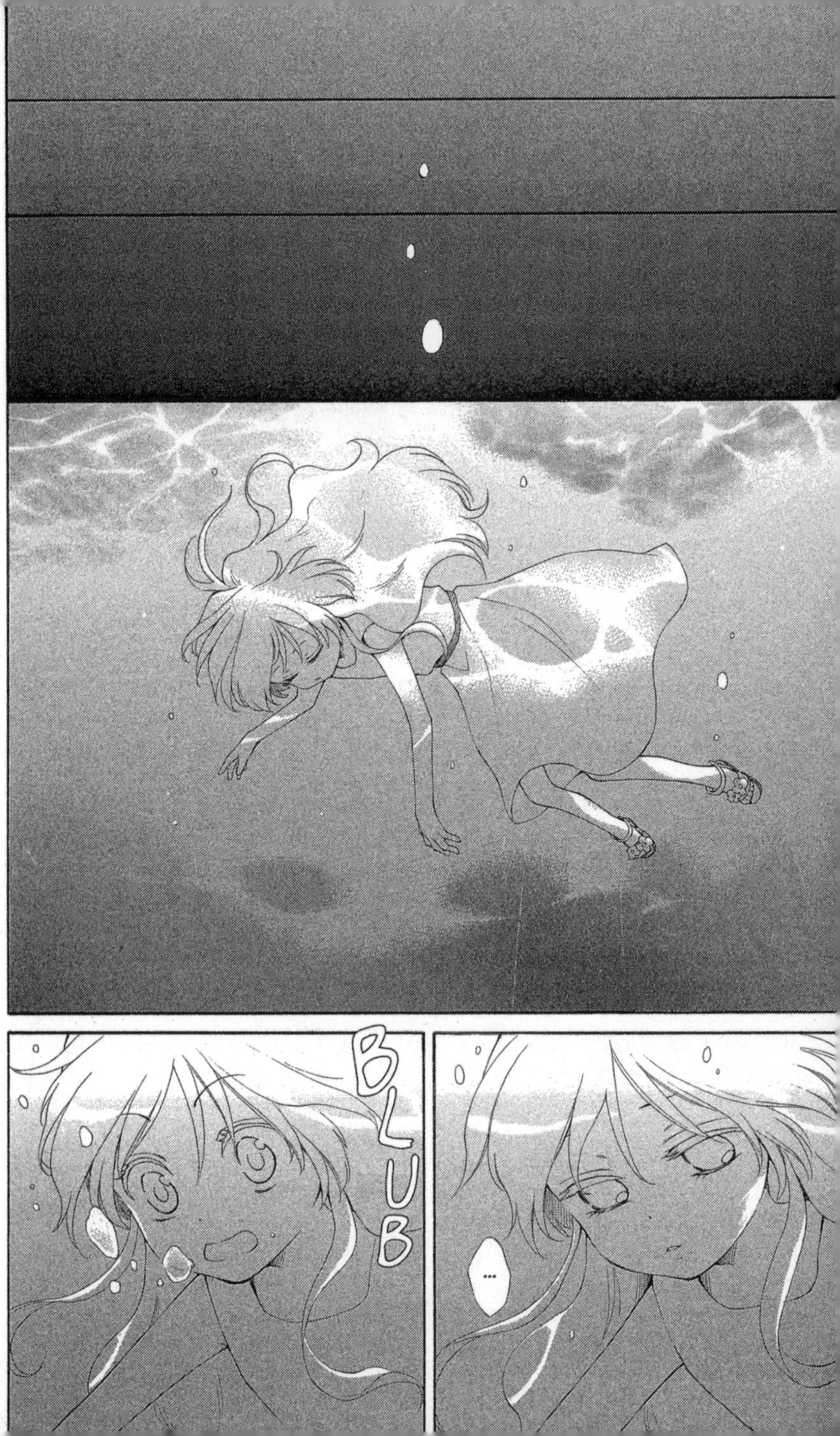
BLUB
...

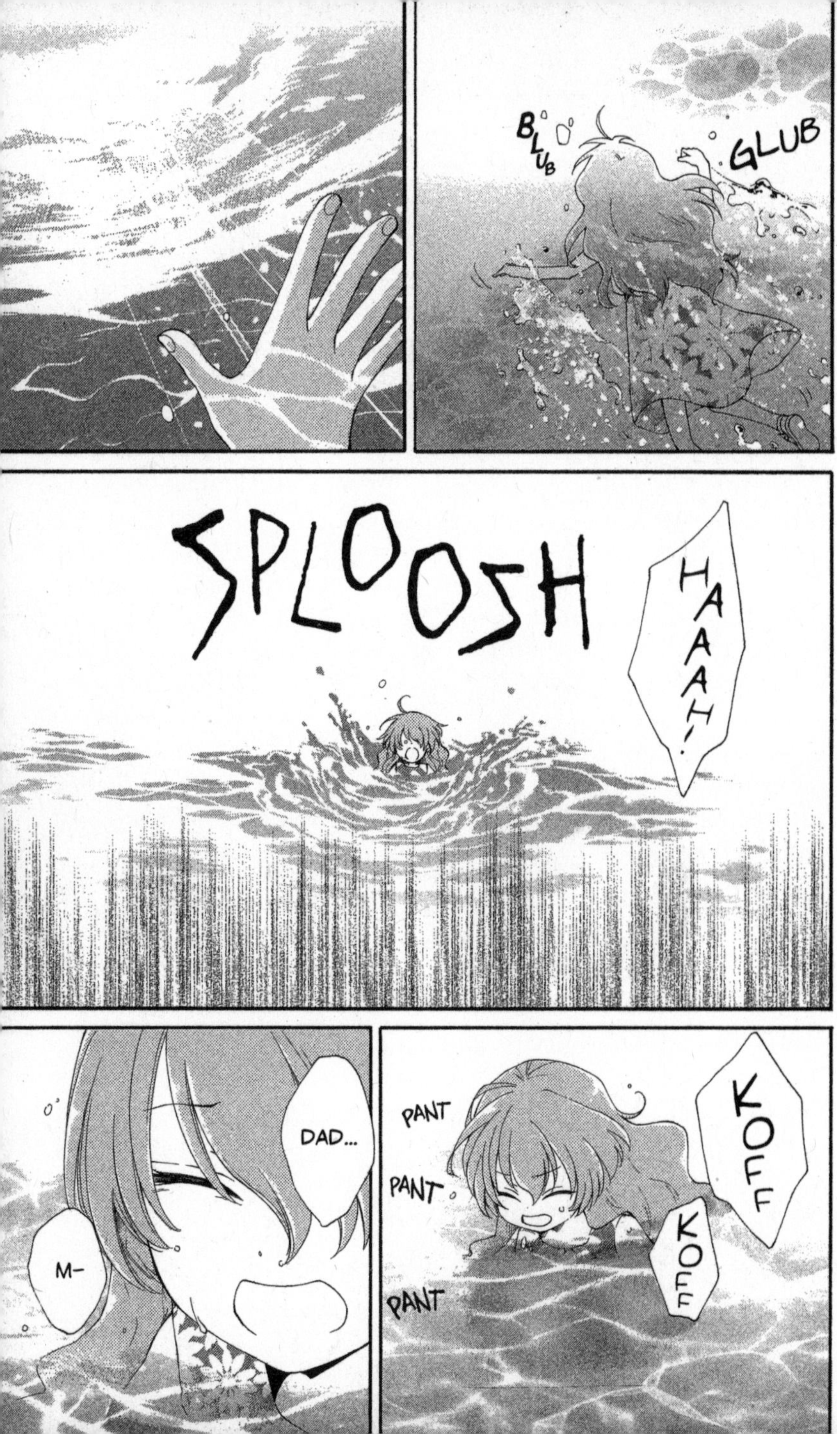
GLUB
BLUB
HAAAAH!
SPLOOSH
KOFF
KOFF
PANT
PANT
PANT
DAD...
M-

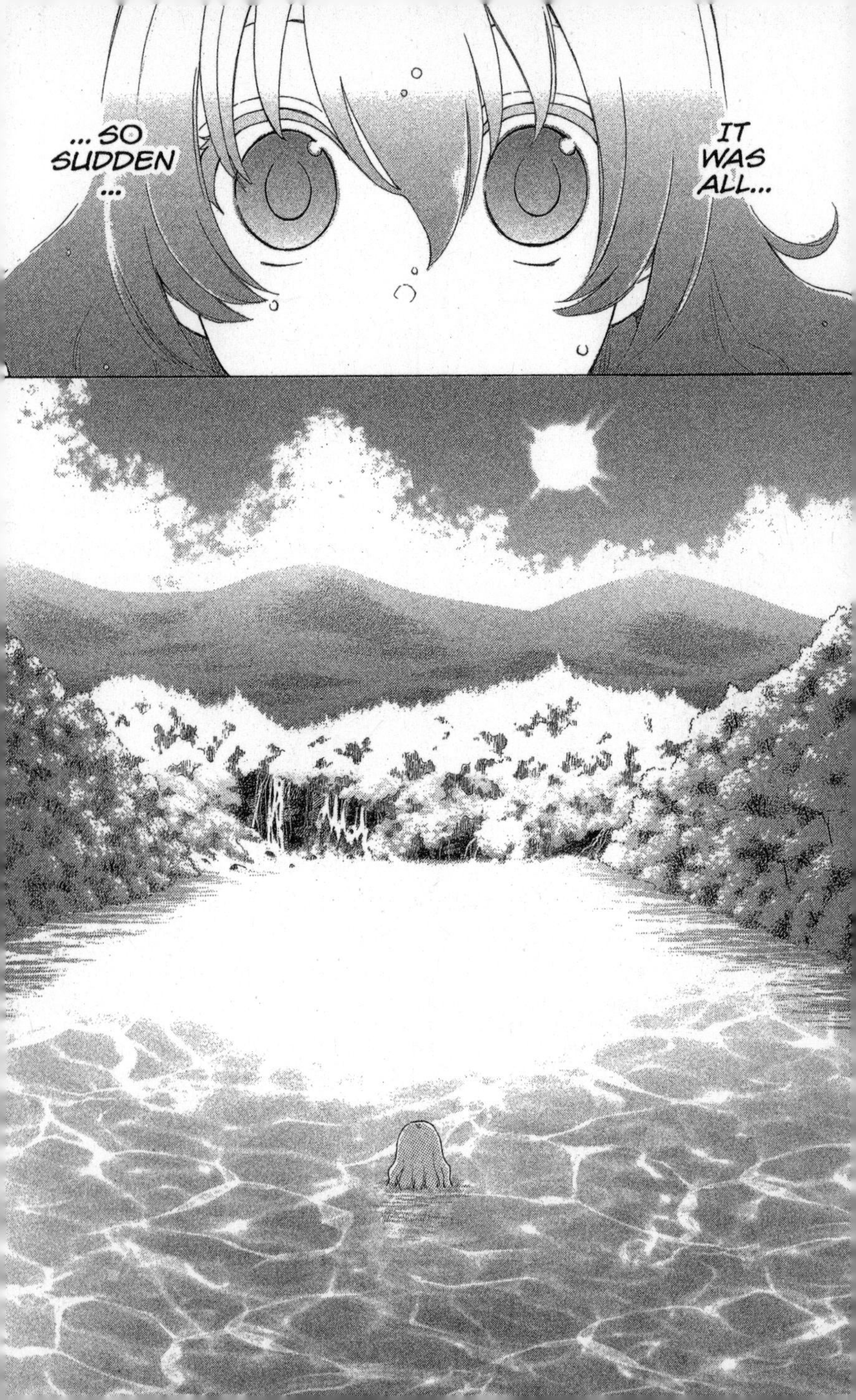
IT WAS ALL...
...SO SUDDEN...

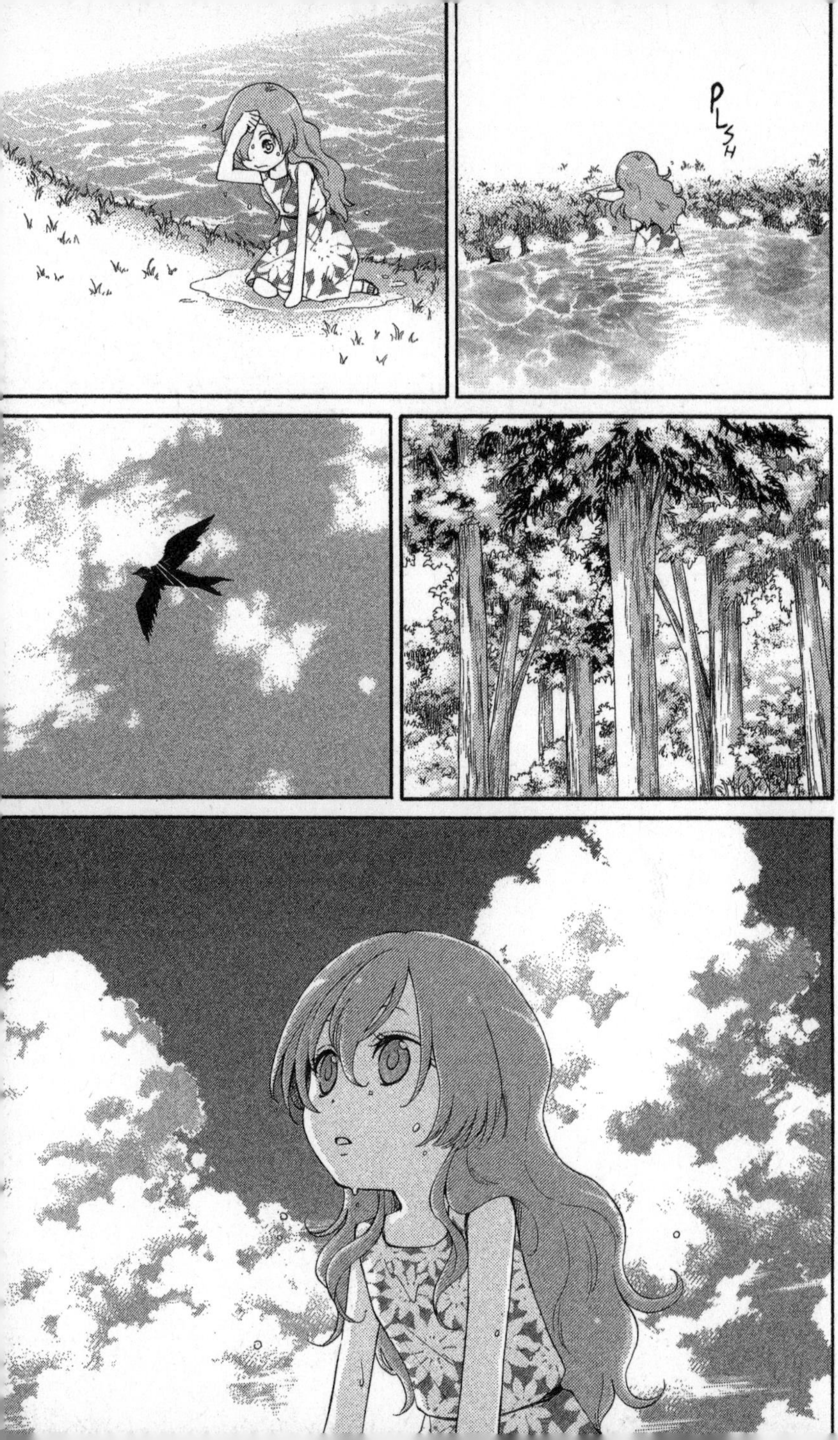
PLSH

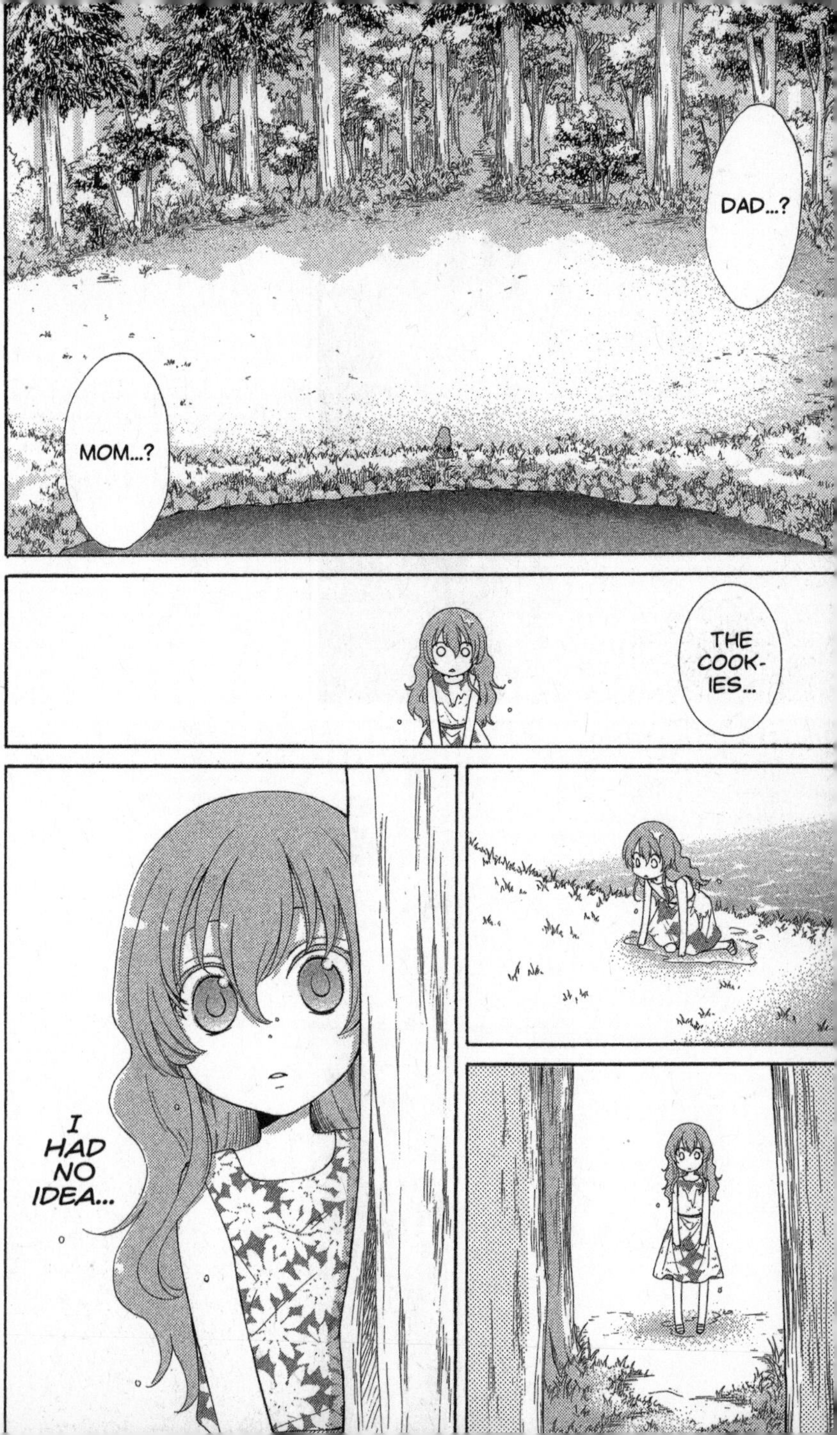
DAD...?
MOM...?
THE COOK-IES...
I HAD NO IDEA...

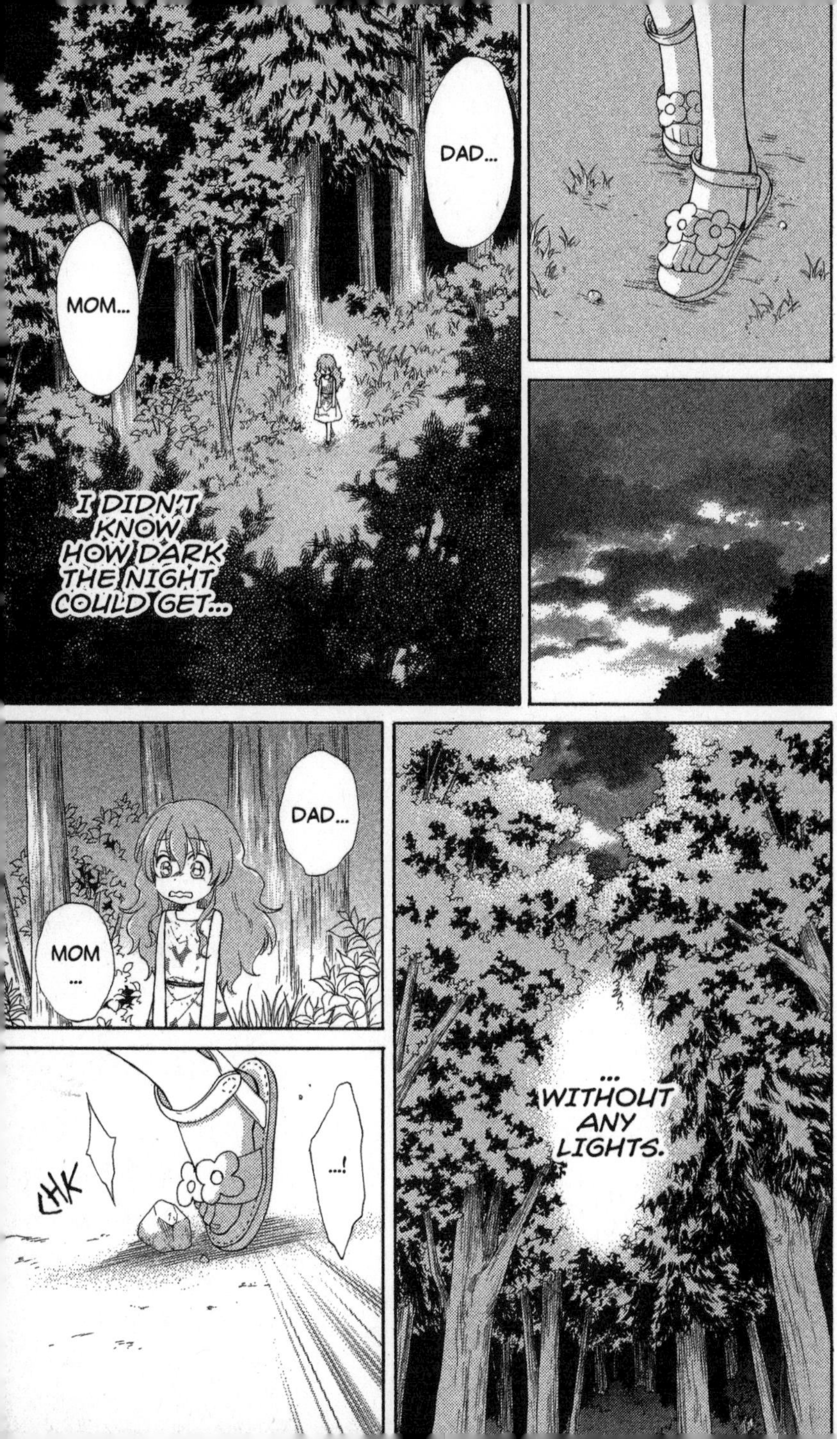
DAD...
MOM...
I DIDN'T KNOW HOW DARK THE NIGHT COULD GET...
...WITHOUT ANY LIGHTS.
DAD...
MOM ...
...!
CHK

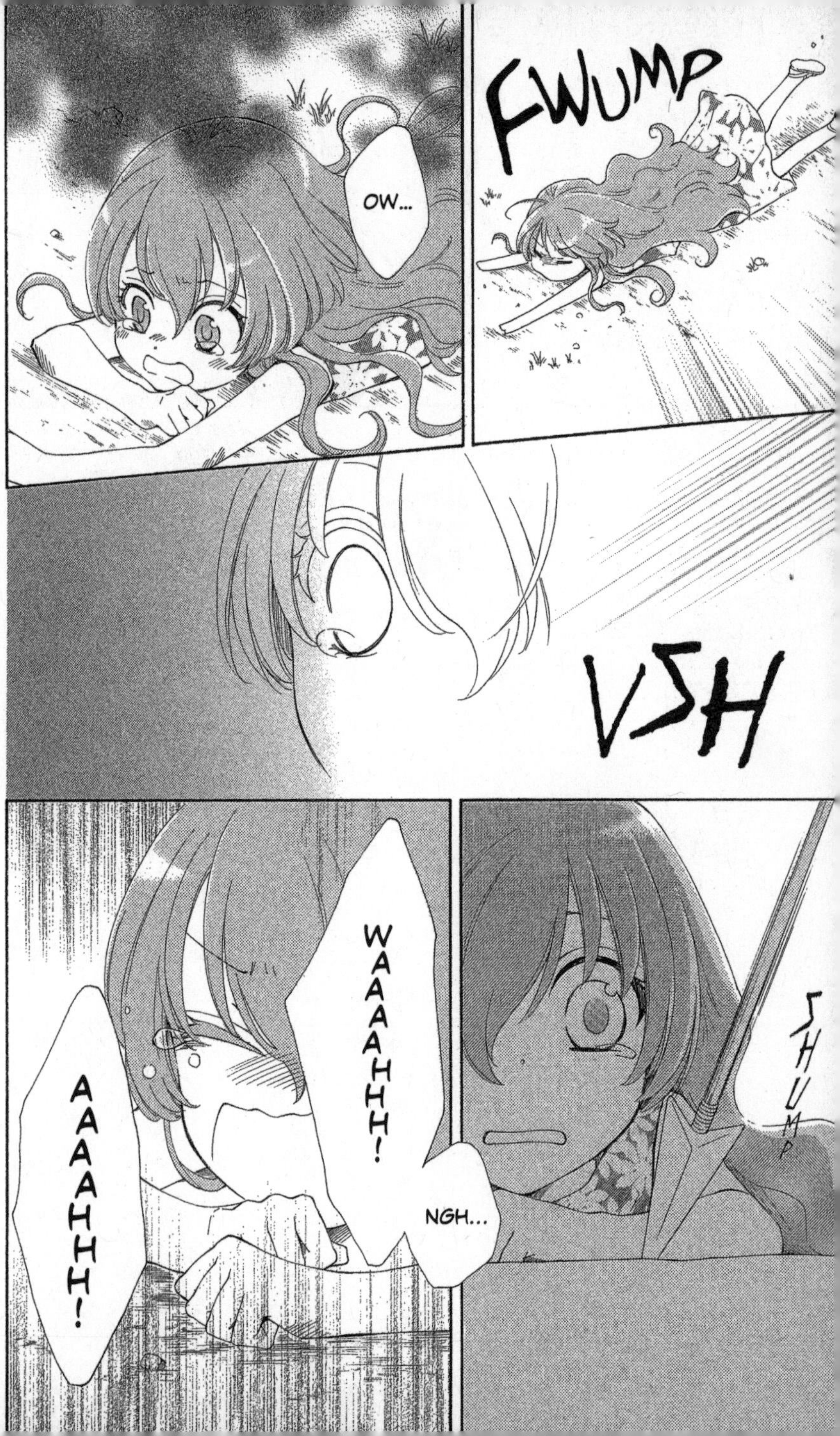
FWUMP
OW...
VSH
SHUMP
NGH...
WAAAAHHH!
AAAAAHHH!

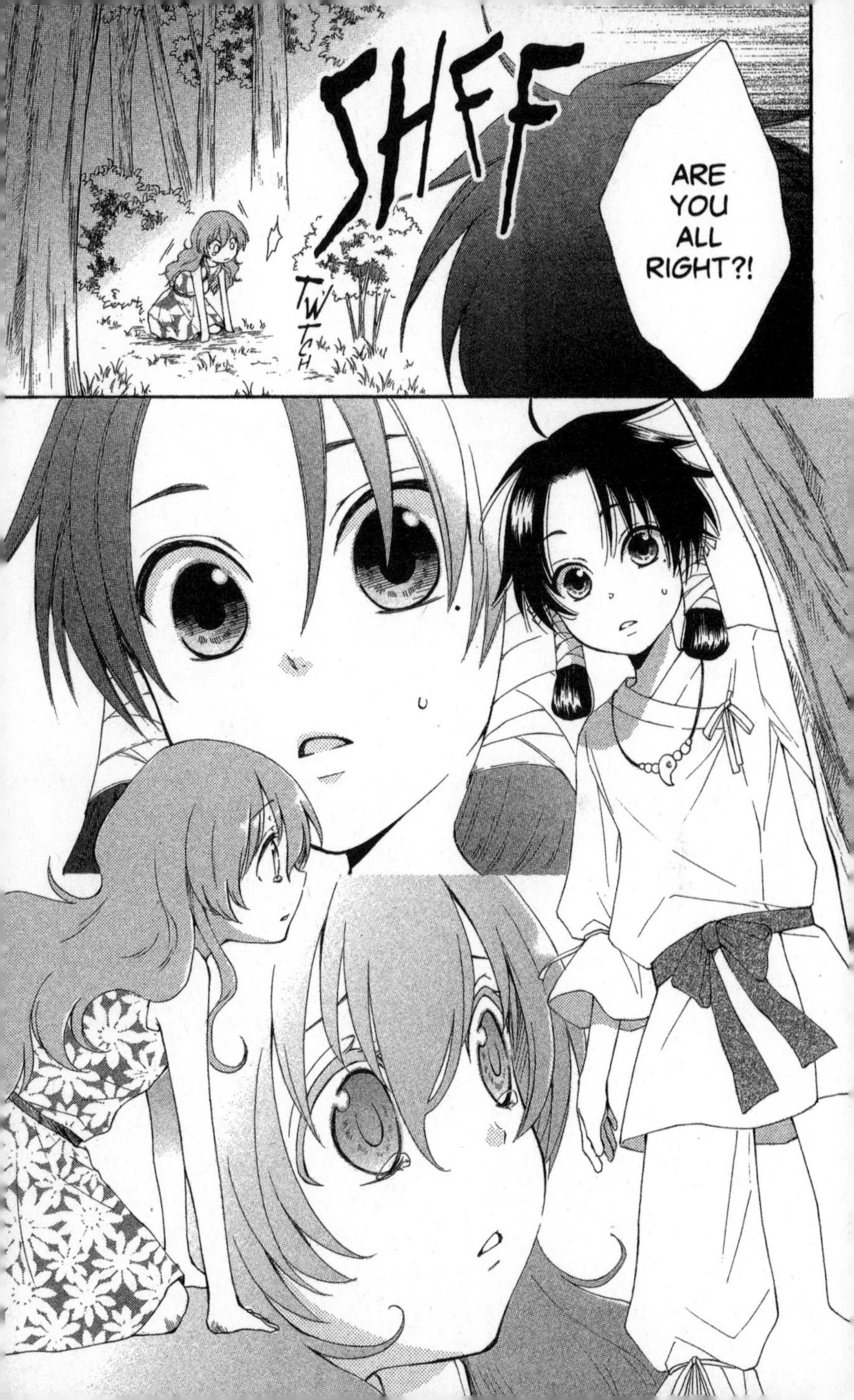
ARE YOU ALL RIGHT?!
SHFF
TWITCH

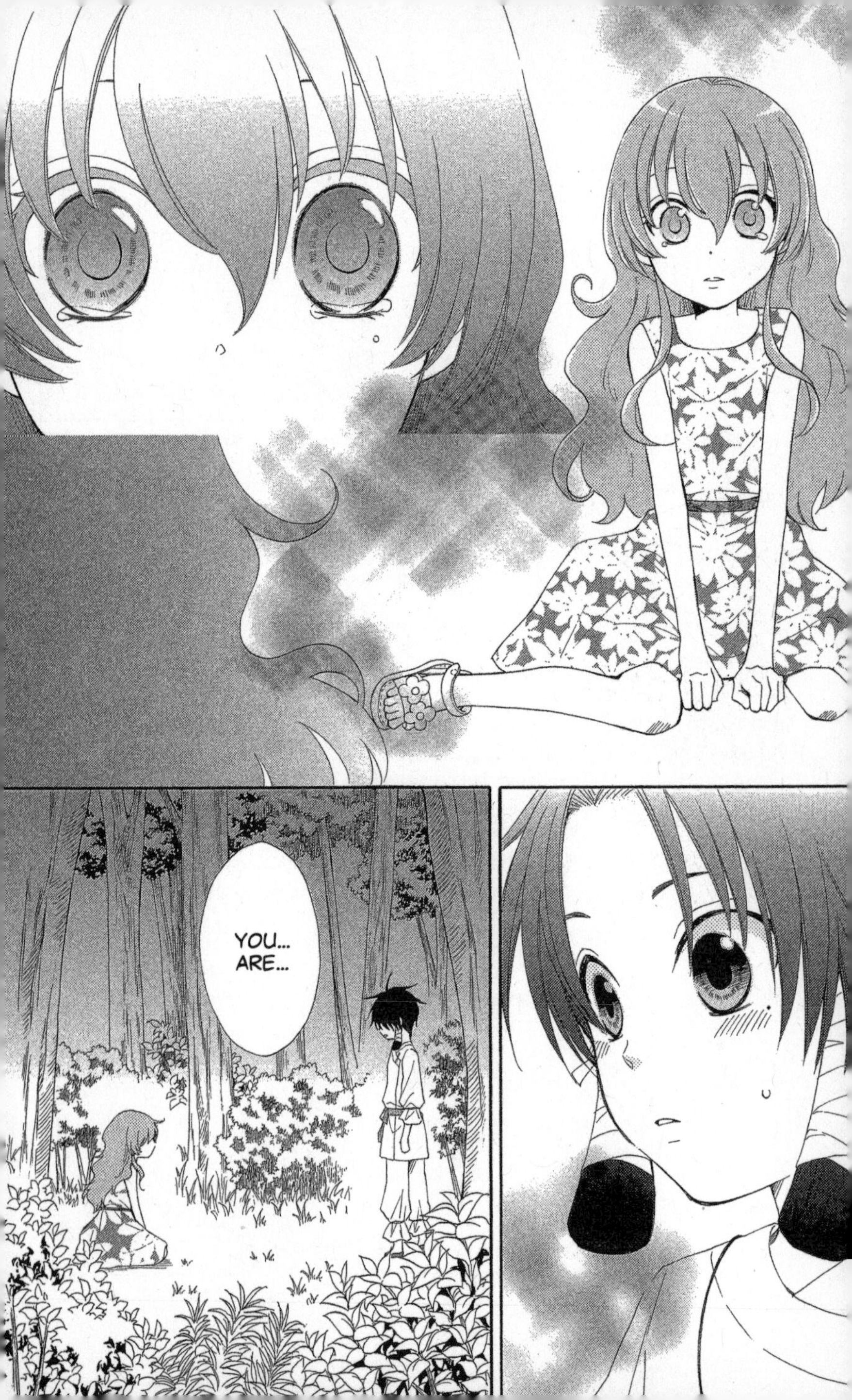
YOU... ARE...

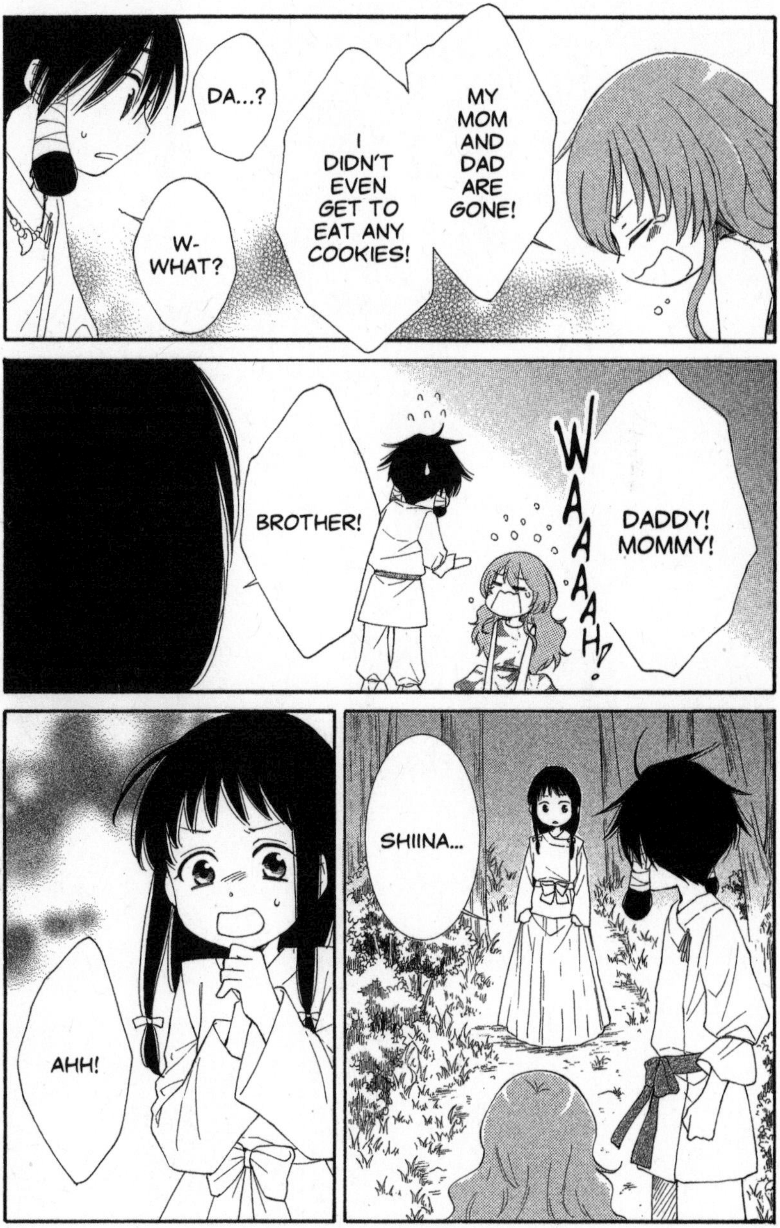
MY MOM AND DAD ARE GONE!
I DIDN'T EVEN GET TO EAT ANY COOKIES!
DA...?
W-WHAT?
DADDY! MOMMY!
WAAAAH!
BROTHER!
SHIINA...
AHH!

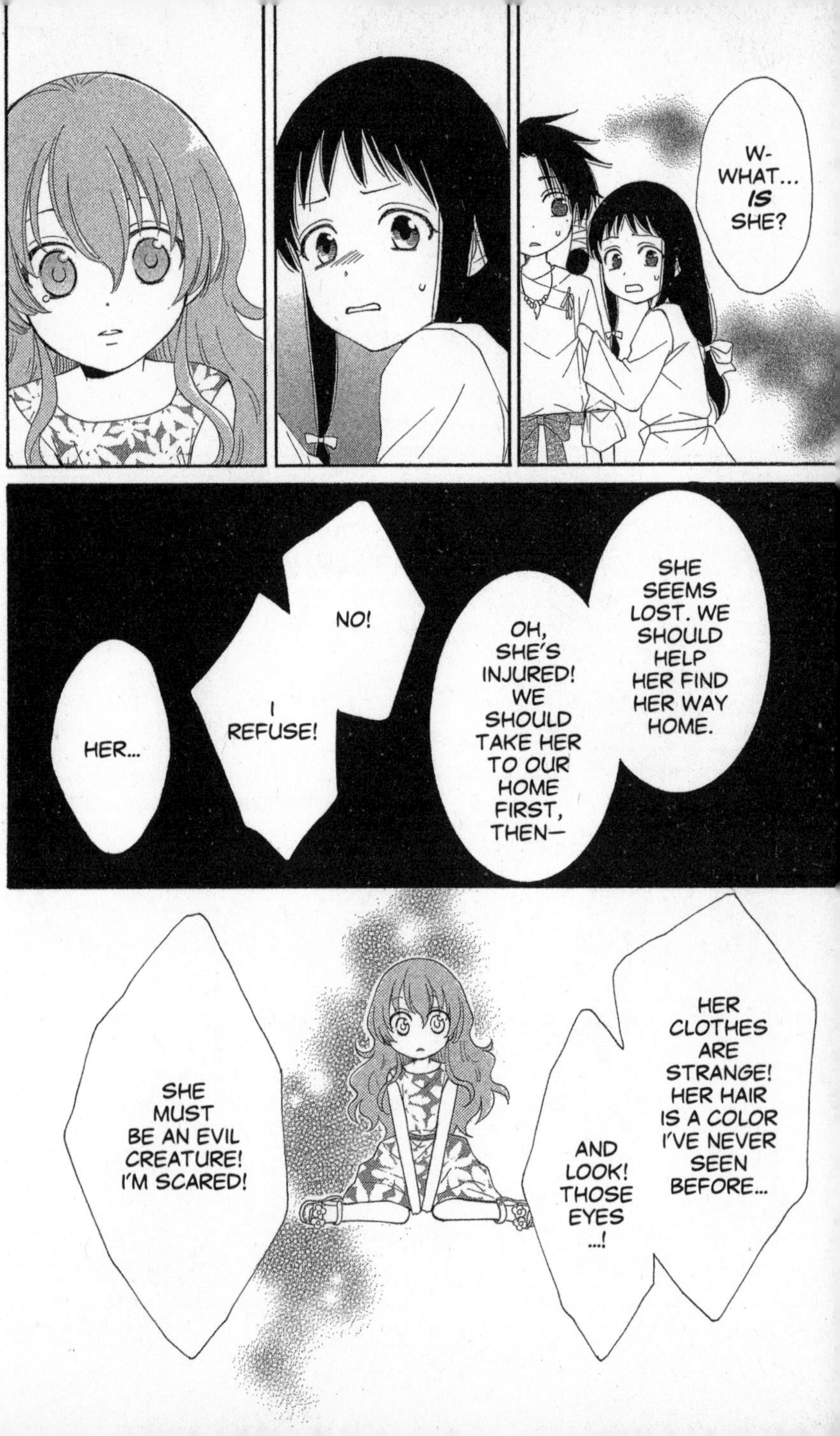
W-WHAT... *IS* SHE?
SHE SEEMS LOST. WE SHOULD HELP HER FIND HER WAY HOME.
OH, SHE'S INJURED! WE SHOULD TAKE HER TO OUR HOME FIRST, THEN—
NO! I REFUSE!
HER...
HER CLOTHES ARE STRANGE! HER HAIR IS A COLOR I'VE NEVER SEEN BEFORE...
AND LOOK! THOSE EYES ...!
SHE MUST BE AN EVIL CREATURE! I'M SCARED!

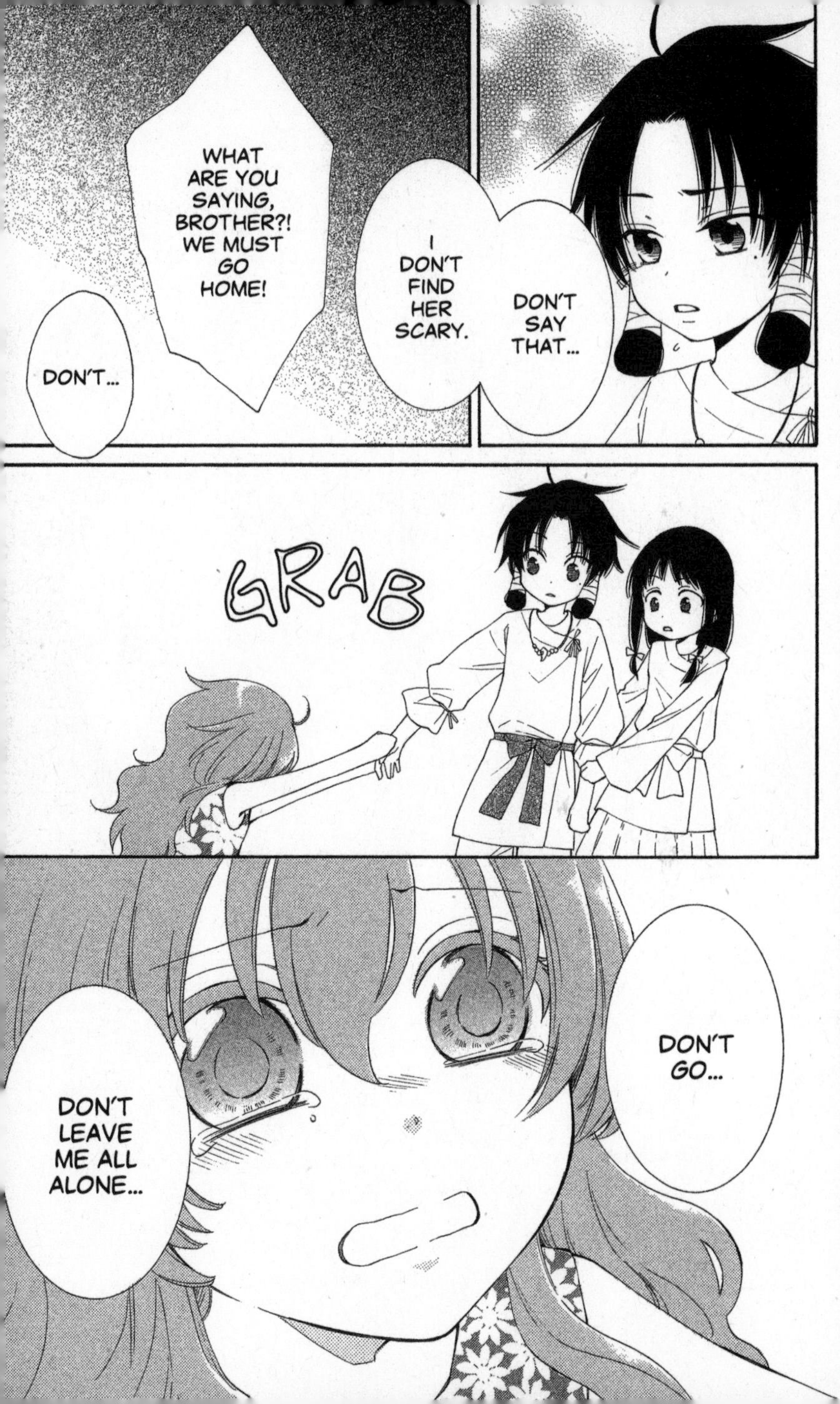
DON'T SAY THAT...
I DON'T FIND HER SCARY.
WHAT ARE YOU SAYING, BROTHER?! WE MUST GO HOME!
DON'T...
GRAB
DON'T GO...
DON'T LEAVE ME ALL ALONE...

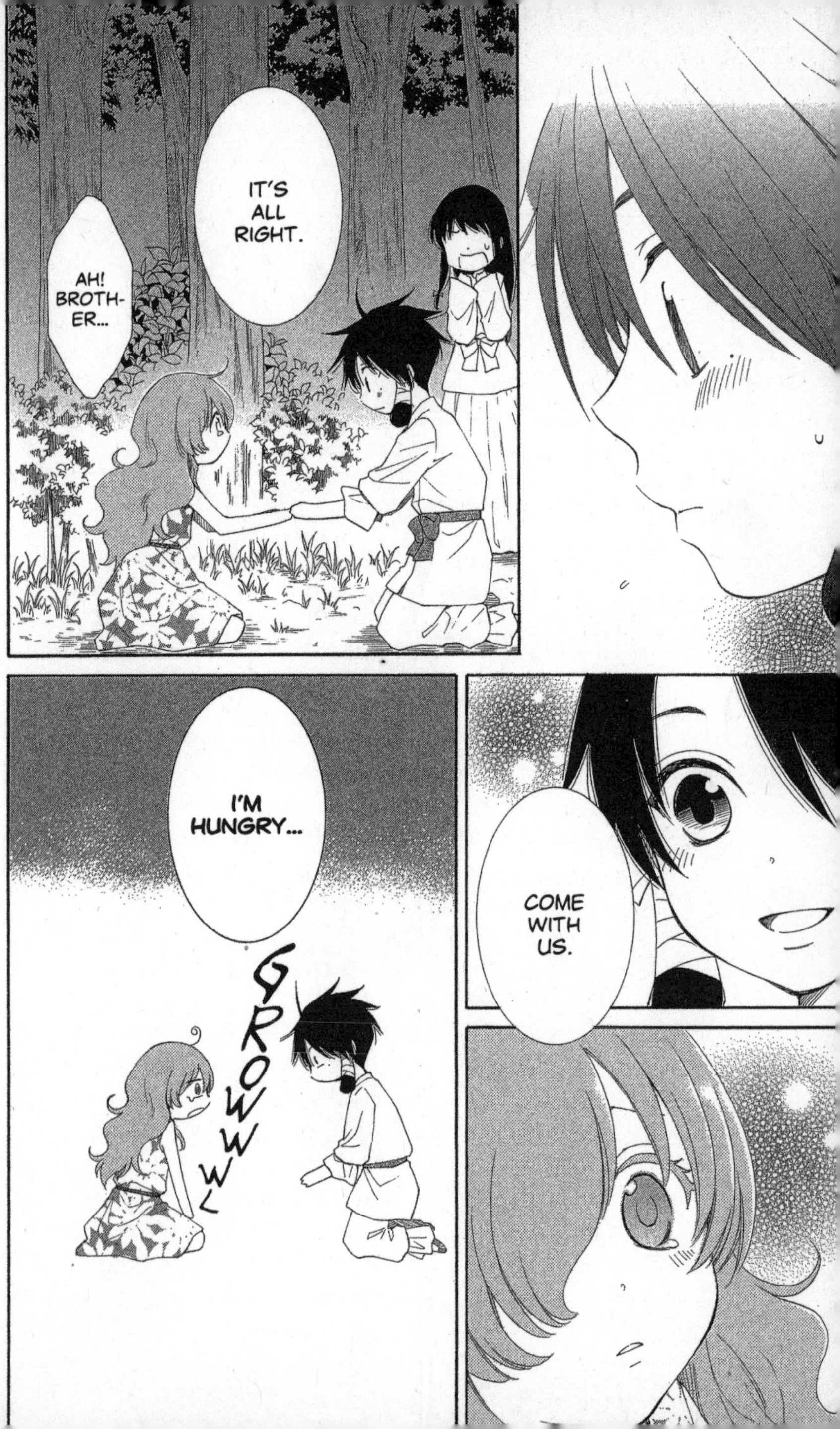
IT'S ALL RIGHT.
AH! BROTHER-ER...
COME WITH US.
I'M HUNGRY...
GROWWWL

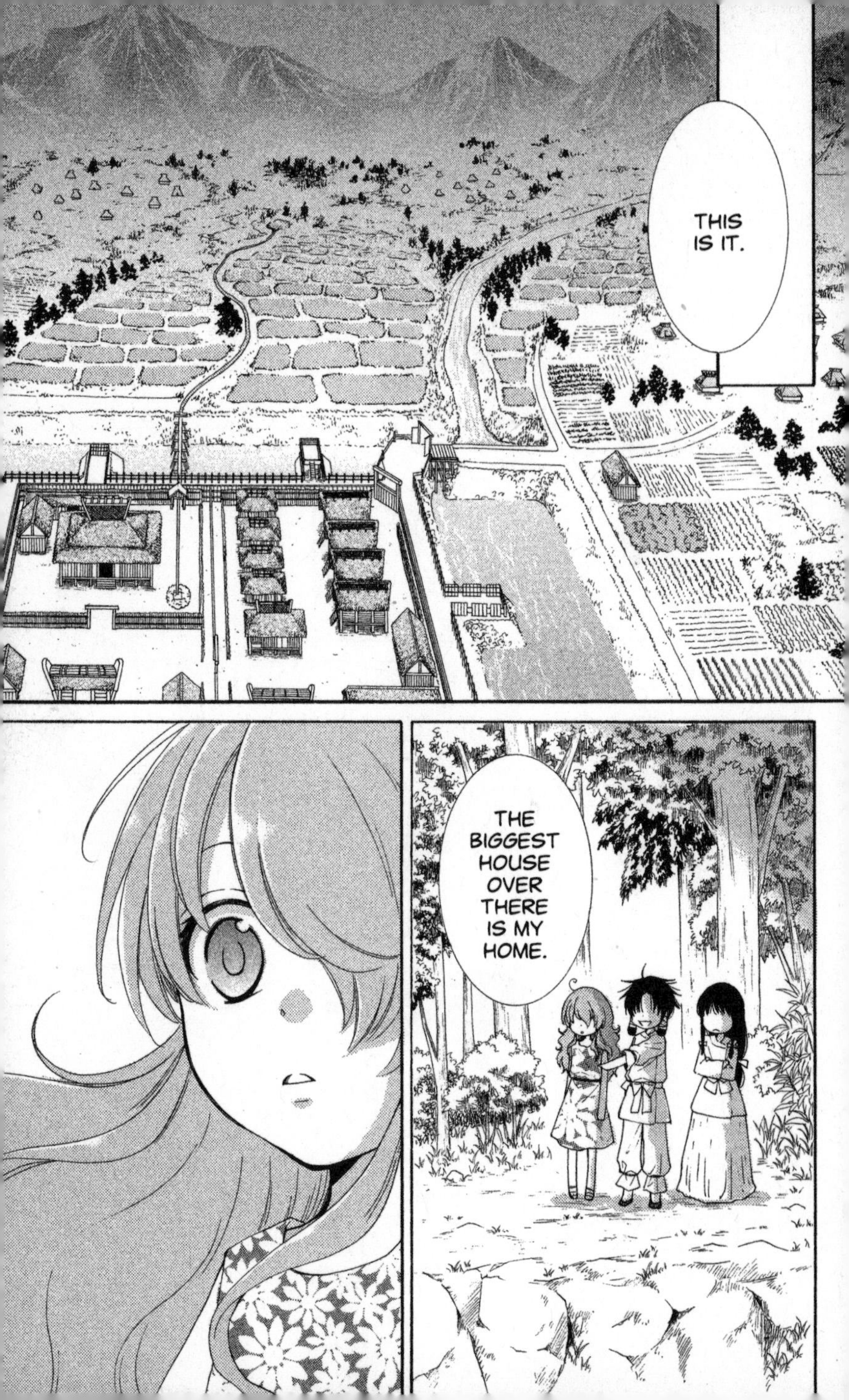
THIS IS IT.
THE BIGGEST HOUSE OVER THERE IS MY HOME.

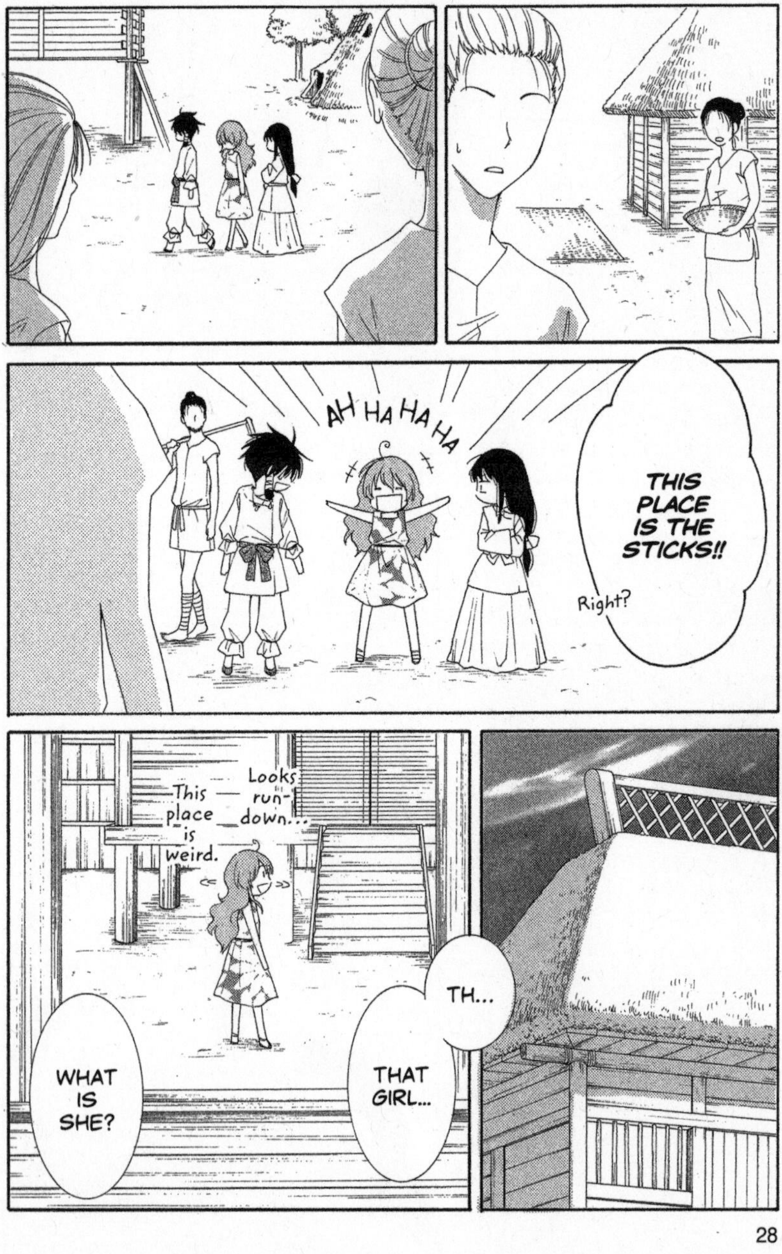
THIS PLACE IS THE STICKS!!
Right?
AH HA HA HA
Looks run-down...
This place is weird.
TH...
THAT GIRL...
WHAT IS SHE?

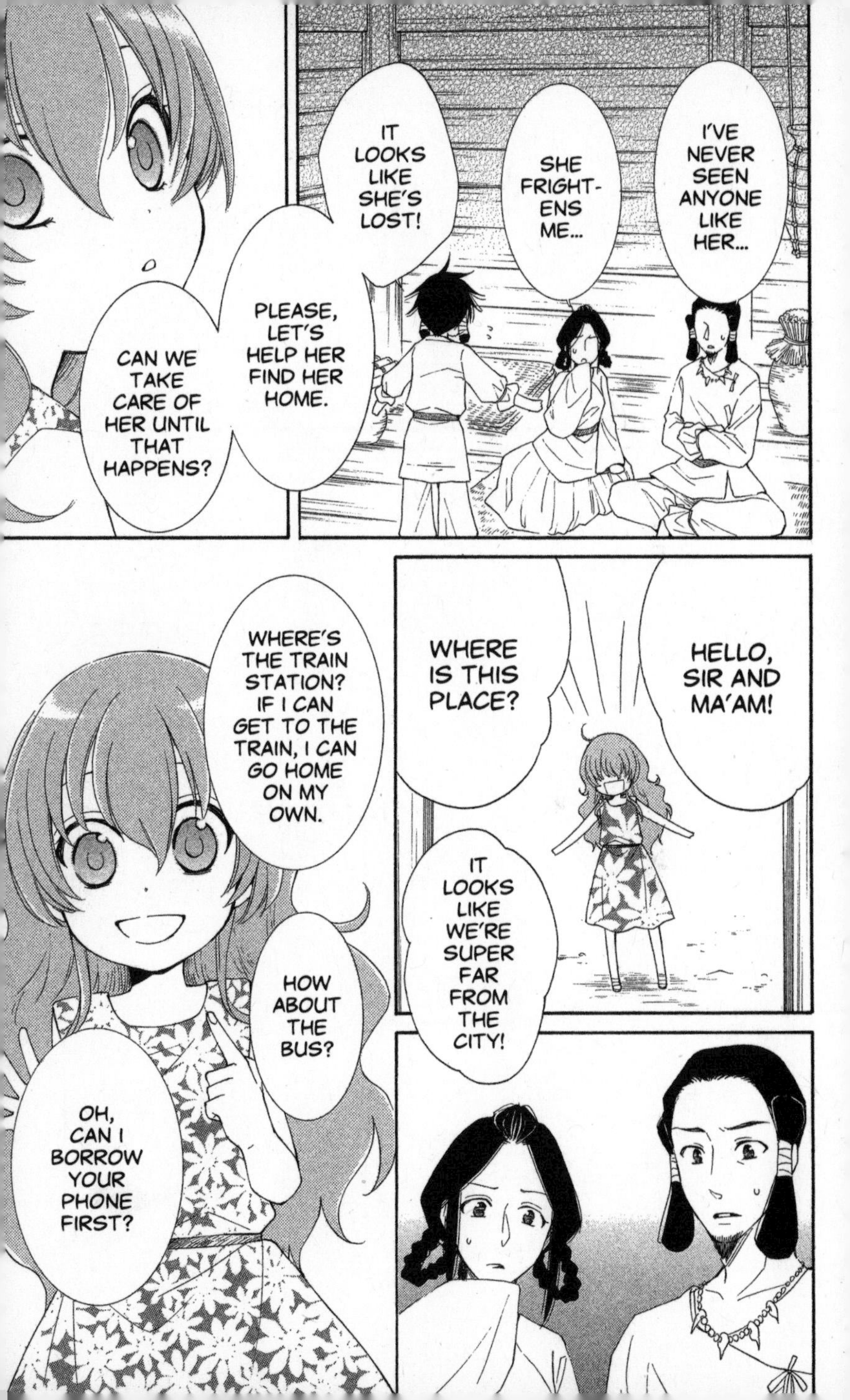
I'VE NEVER SEEN ANYONE LIKE HER...
SHE FRIGHT-ENS ME...
IT LOOKS LIKE SHE'S LOST!
PLEASE, LET'S HELP HER FIND HER HOME.
CAN WE TAKE CARE OF HER UNTIL THAT HAPPENS?
HELLO, SIR AND MA'AM!
WHERE IS THIS PLACE?
IT LOOKS LIKE WE'RE SUPER FAR FROM THE CITY!
WHERE'S THE TRAIN STATION? IF I CAN GET TO THE TRAIN, I CAN GO HOME ON MY OWN.
HOW ABOUT THE BUS?
OH, CAN I BORROW YOUR PHONE FIRST?

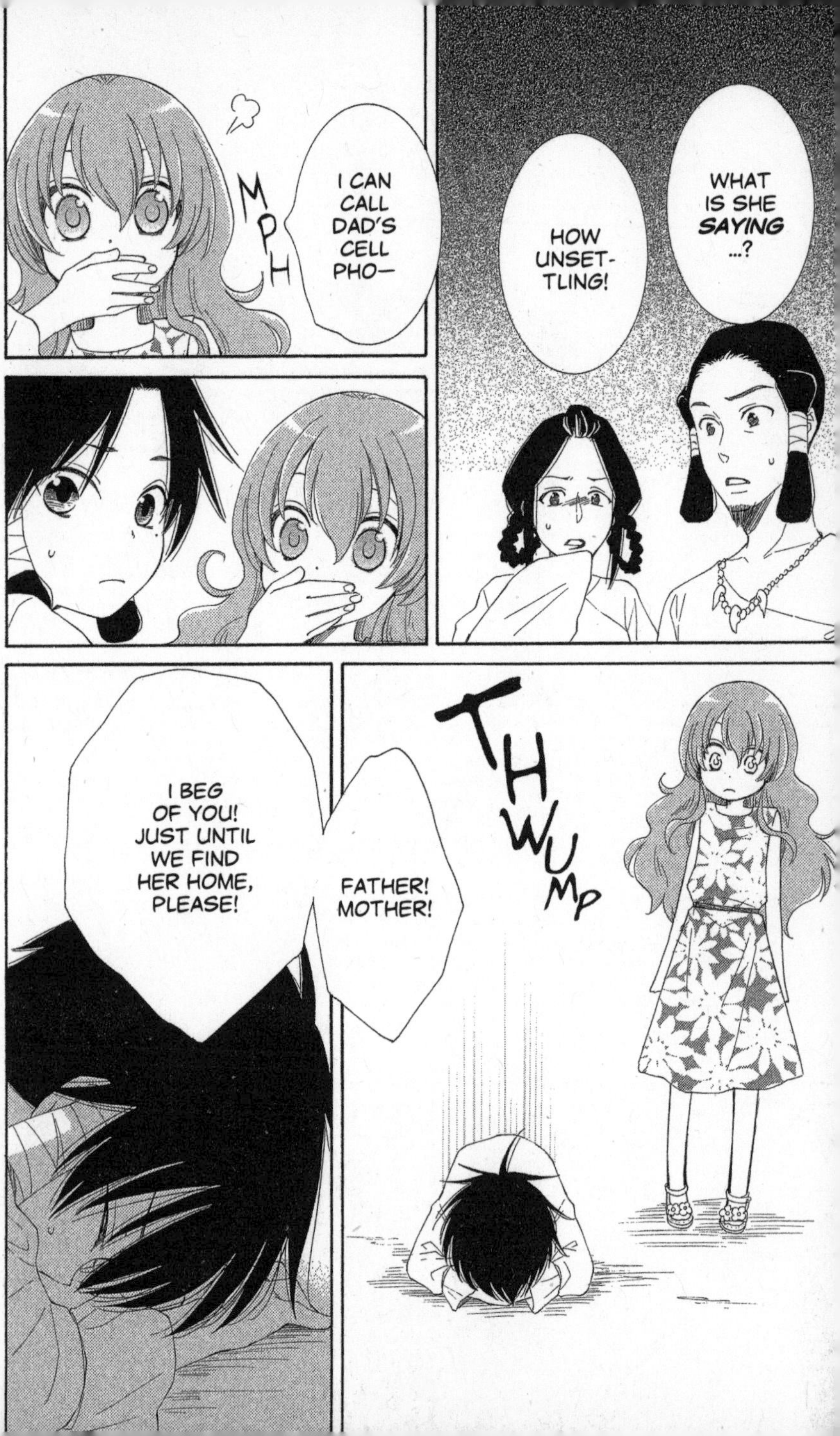
WHAT IS SHE SAYING ...?
HOW UNSET-TLING!
I CAN CALL DAD'S CELL PHO—
MPH
THWUMP
FATHER! MOTHER!
I BEG OF YOU! JUST UNTIL WE FIND HER HOME, PLEASE!

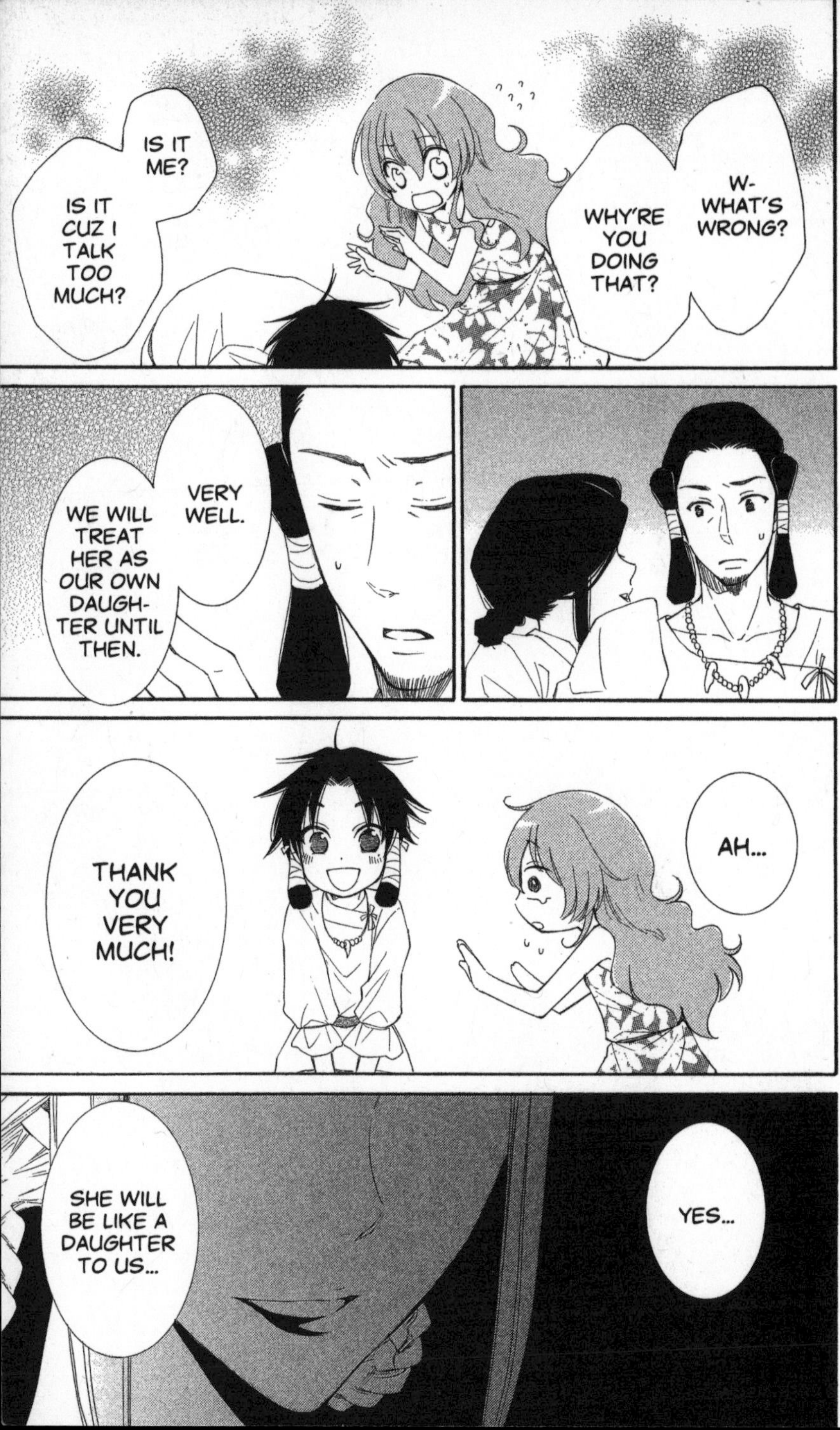
W- WHAT'S WRONG?
WHY'RE YOU DOING THAT?
IS IT ME?
IS IT CUZ I TALK TOO MUCH?
VERY WELL.
WE WILL TREAT HER AS OUR OWN DAUGH-TER UNTIL THEN.
AH...
THANK YOU VERY MUCH!
YES...
SHE WILL BE LIKE A DAUGHTER TO US...

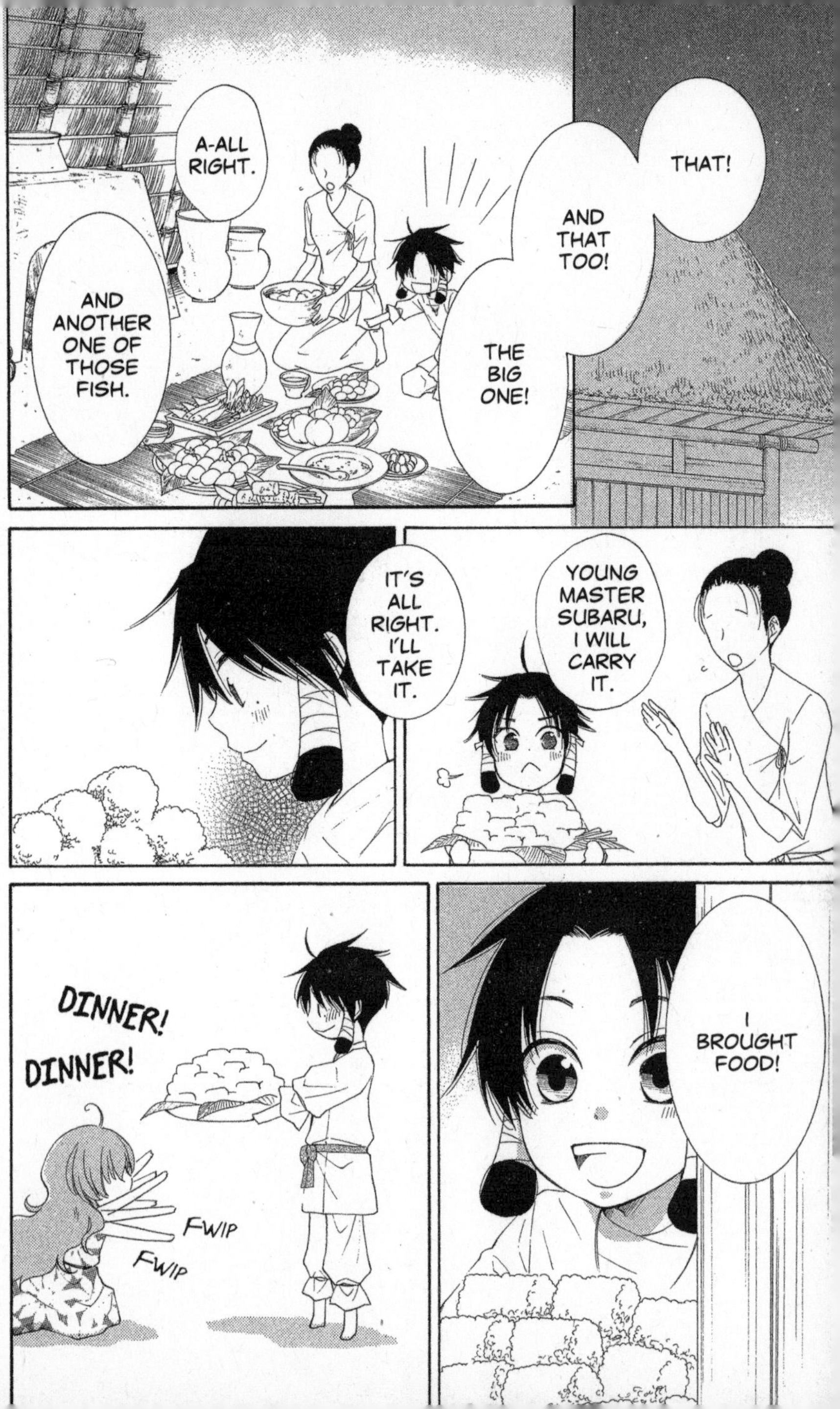
THAT!
AND THAT TOO!
THE BIG ONE!
A-ALL RIGHT.
AND ANOTHER ONE OF THOSE FISH.
YOUNG MASTER SUBARU, I WILL CARRY IT.
IT'S ALL RIGHT. I'LL TAKE IT.
I BROUGHT FOOD!
DINNER!
DINNER!
FWIP
FWIP

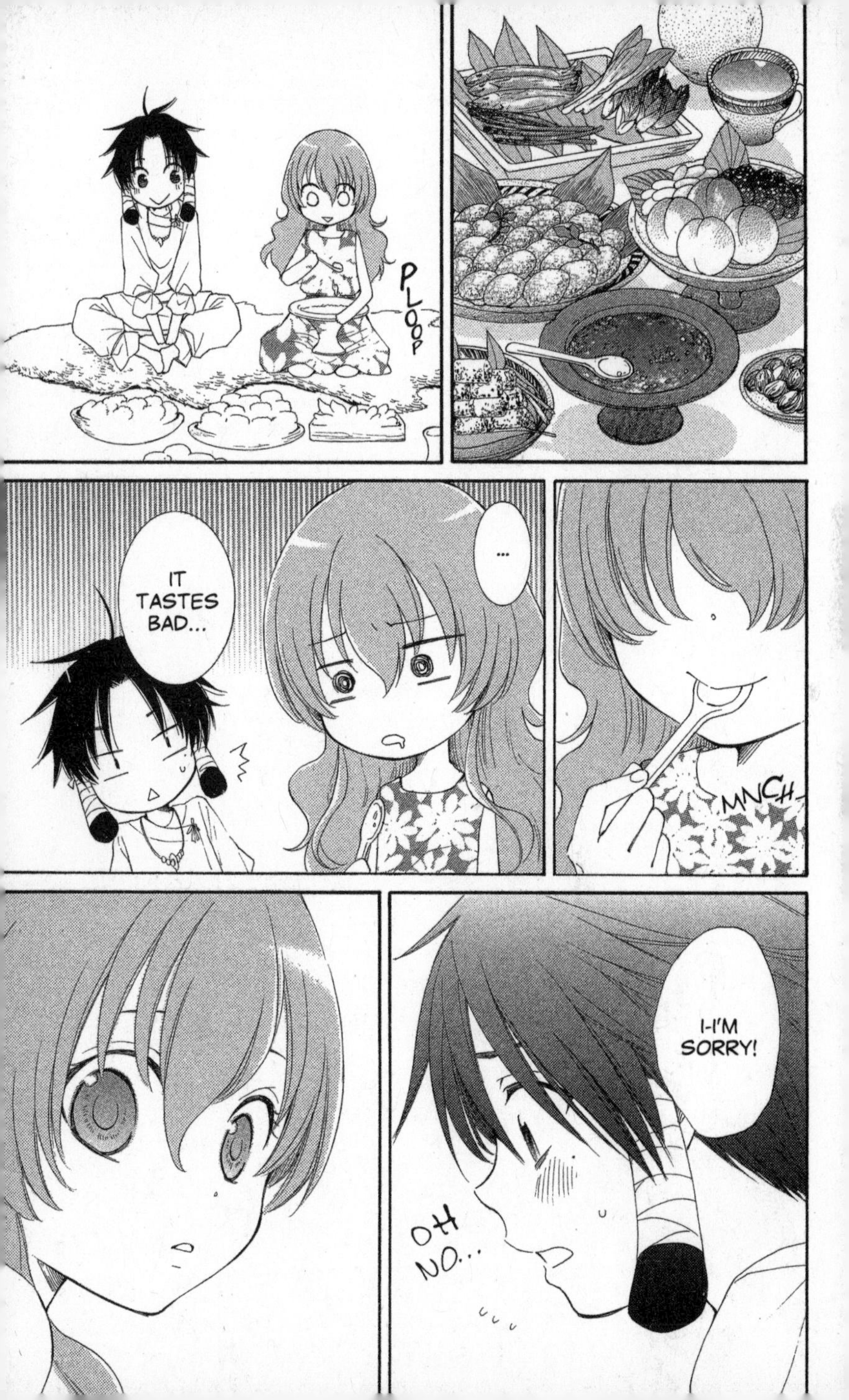
PLOOP
MNCH
...
IT TASTES BAD...
I-I'M SORRY!
OH NO...

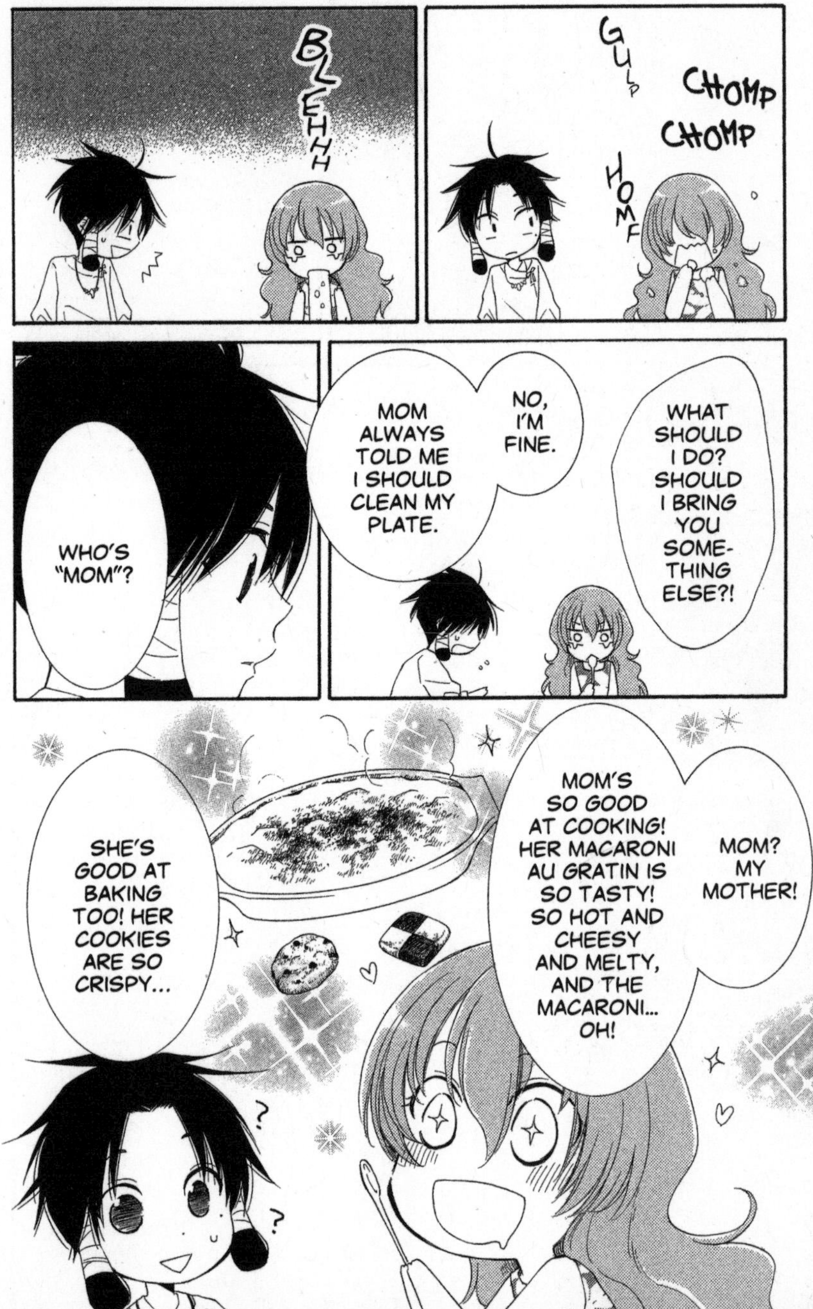
GULP
CHOMP CHOMP
HOMF
BLEHHH
WHAT SHOULD I DO? SHOULD I BRING YOU SOMETHING ELSE?!
NO, I'M FINE.
MOM ALWAYS TOLD ME I SHOULD CLEAN MY PLATE.
WHO'S "MOM"?
MOM? MY MOTHER!
MOM'S SO GOOD AT COOKING! HER MACARONI AU GRATIN IS SO TASTY! SO HOT AND CHEESY AND MELTY, AND THE MACARONI... OH!
SHE'S GOOD AT BAKING TOO! HER COOKIES ARE SO CRISPY...

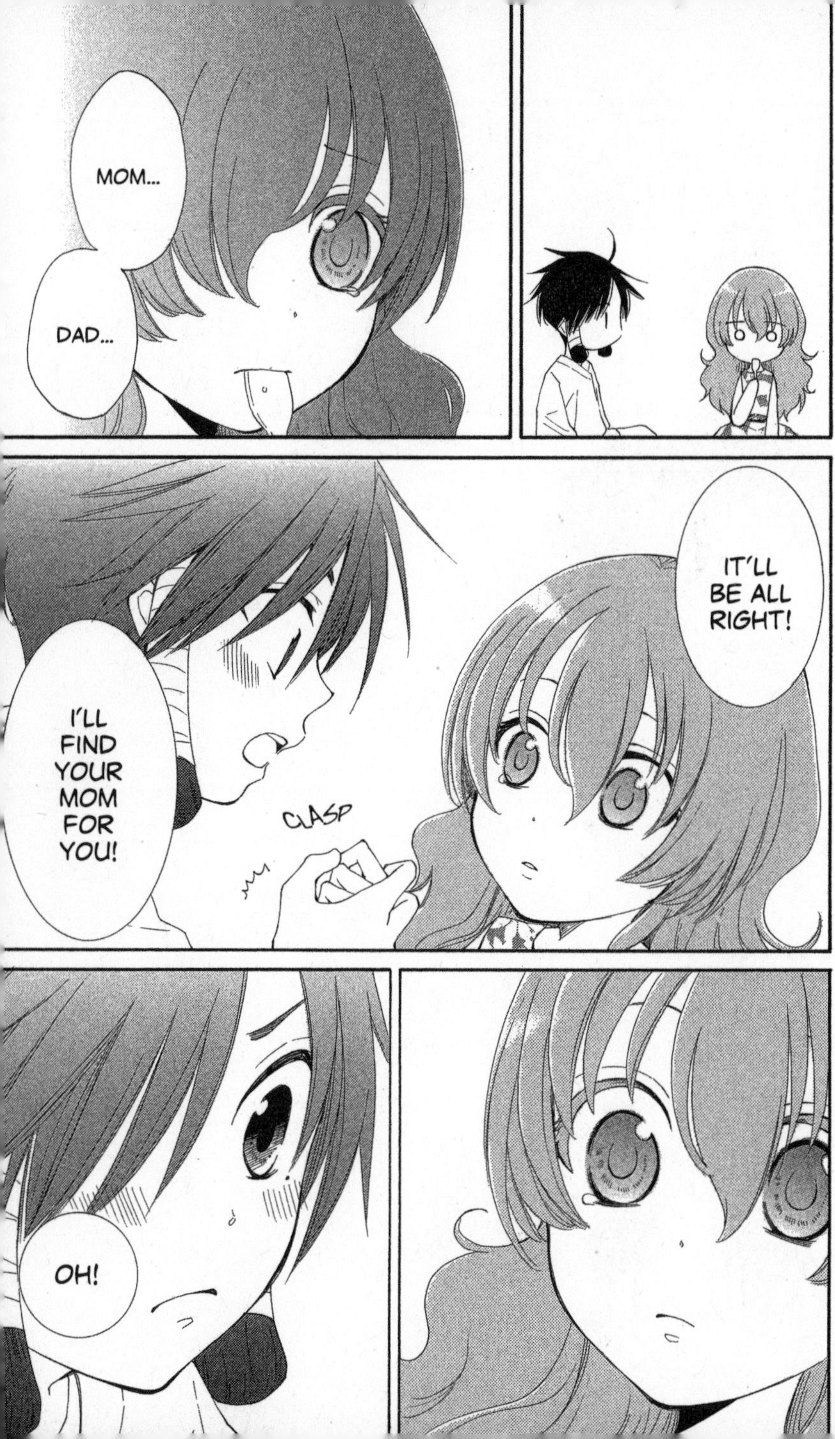
MOM...
DAD...
IT'LL BE ALL RIGHT!
I'LL FIND YOUR MOM FOR YOU!
CLASP
OH!

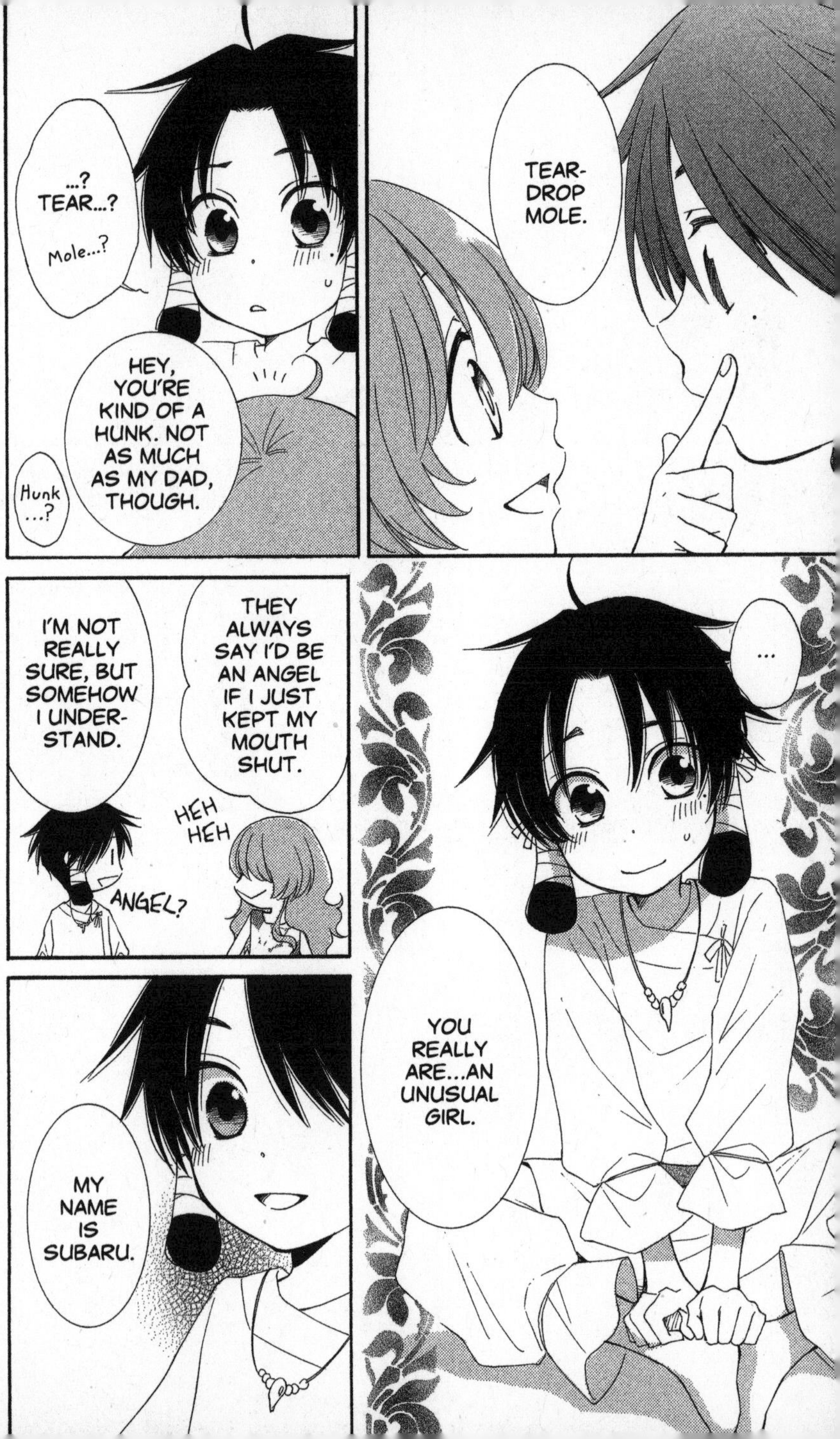
TEAR-DROP MOLE.
...? TEAR...?
Mole...?
HEY, YOU'RE KIND OF A HUNK. NOT AS MUCH AS MY DAD, THOUGH.
Hunk ...?
...
YOU REALLY ARE...AN UNUSUAL GIRL.
THEY ALWAYS SAY I'D BE AN ANGEL IF I JUST KEPT MY MOUTH SHUT.
I'M NOT REALLY SURE, BUT SOMEHOW I UNDER-STAND.
HEH HEH
ANGEL?
MY NAME IS SUBARU.

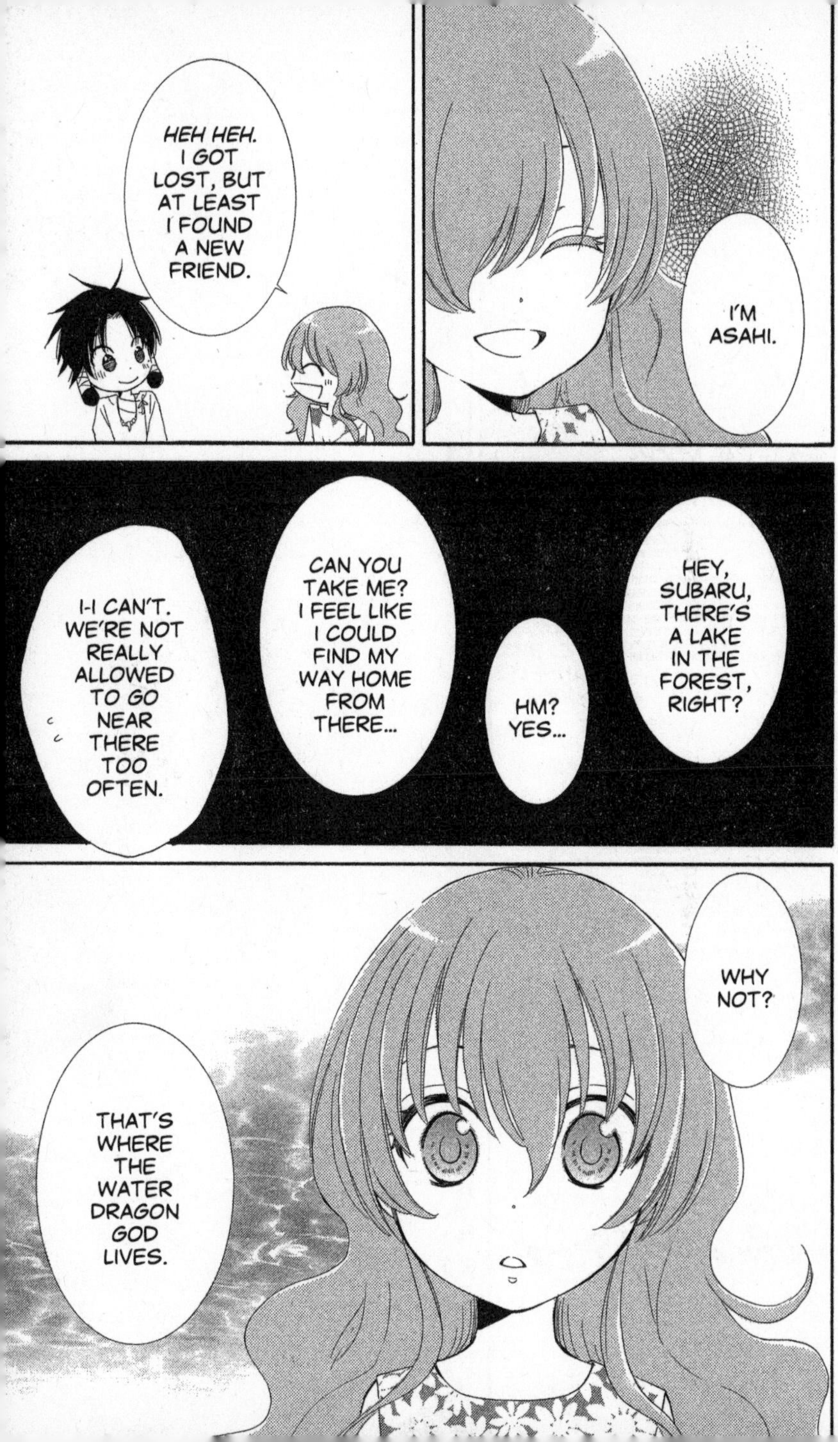
I'M ASAHI.
HEH HEH. I GOT LOST, BUT AT LEAST I FOUND A NEW FRIEND.
HEY, SUBARU, THERE'S A LAKE IN THE FOREST, RIGHT?
HM? YES...
CAN YOU TAKE ME? I FEEL LIKE I COULD FIND MY WAY HOME FROM THERE...
I-I CAN'T. WE'RE NOT REALLY ALLOWED TO GO NEAR THERE TOO OFTEN.
WHY NOT?
THAT'S WHERE THE WATER DRAGON GOD LIVES.

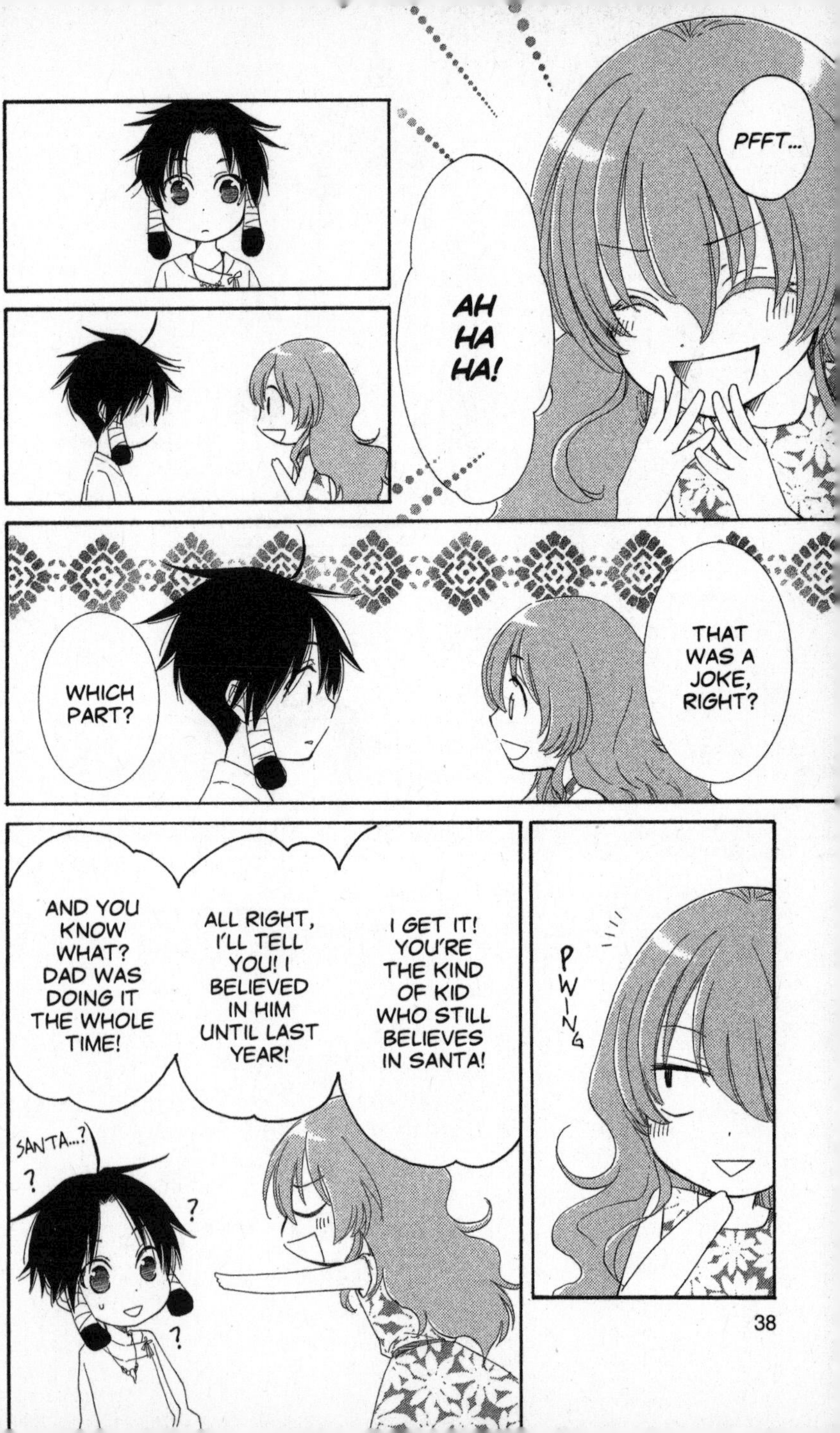
PFFT...
AH HA HA!
THAT WAS A JOKE, RIGHT?
WHICH PART?
PWING
I GET IT! YOU'RE THE KIND OF KID WHO STILL BELIEVES IN SANTA!
ALL RIGHT, I'LL TELL YOU! I BELIEVED IN HIM UNTIL LAST YEAR!
AND YOU KNOW WHAT? DAD WAS DOING IT THE WHOLE TIME!
SANTA...?

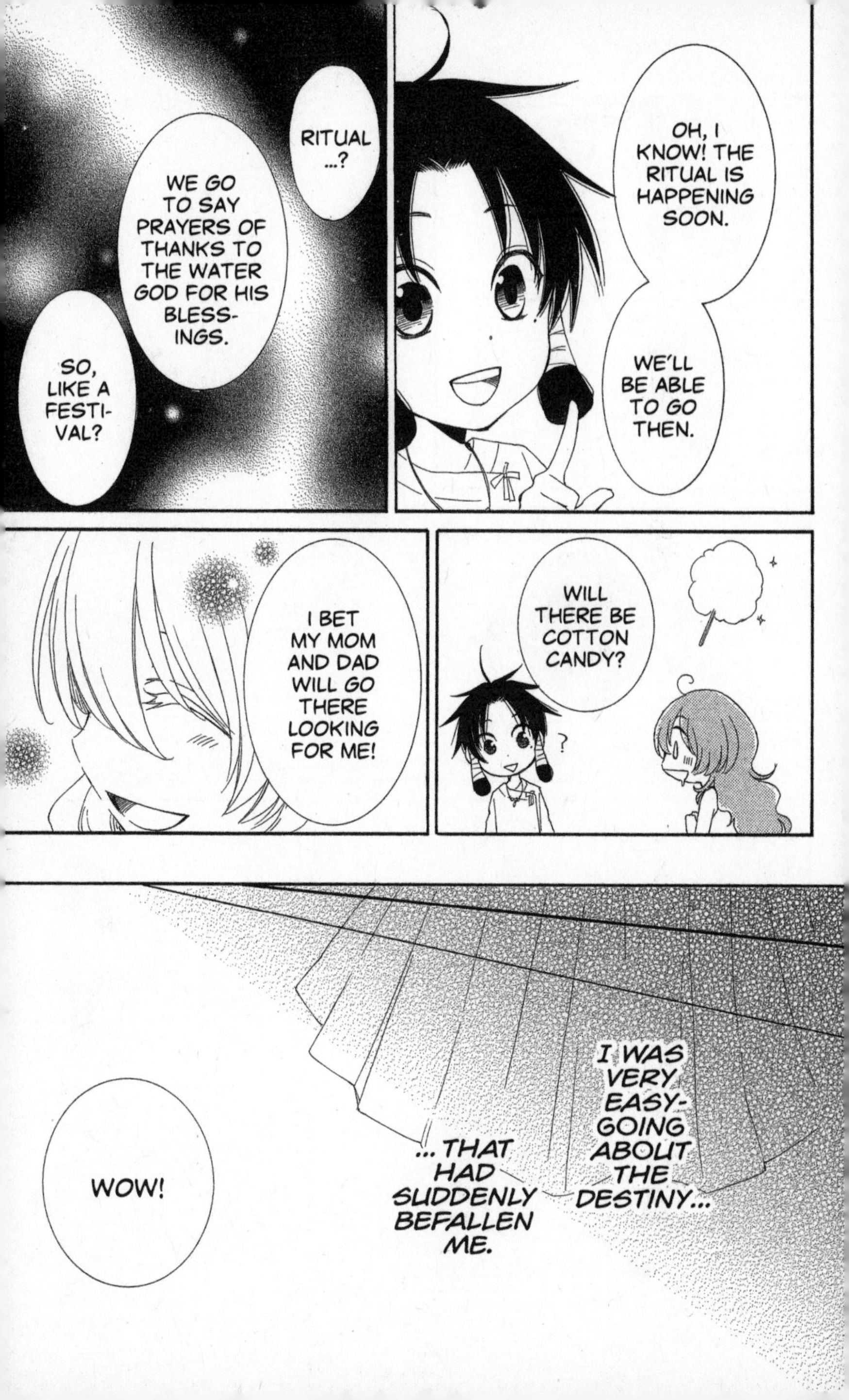
OH, I KNOW! THE RITUAL IS HAPPENING SOON.
WE'LL BE ABLE TO GO THEN.
RITUAL ...?
WE GO TO SAY PRAYERS OF THANKS TO THE WATER GOD FOR HIS BLESS-INGS.
SO, LIKE A FESTI-VAL?
WILL THERE BE COTTON CANDY?
?
I BET MY MOM AND DAD WILL GO THERE LOOKING FOR ME!
I WAS VERY EASY-GOING ABOUT THE DESTINY...
...THAT HAD SUDDENLY BEFALLEN ME.
WOW!

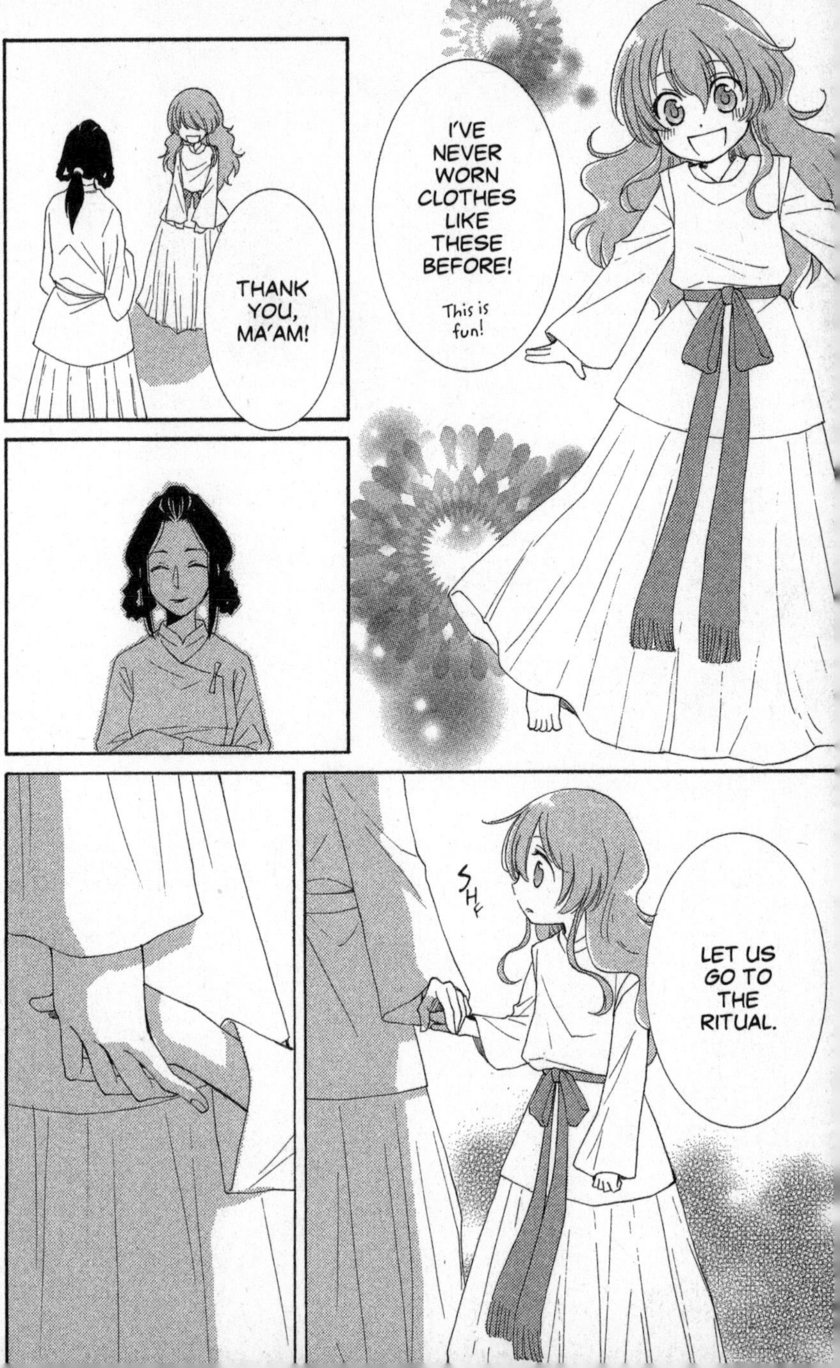
I'VE NEVER WORN CLOTHES LIKE THESE BEFORE!
This is fun!
THANK YOU, MA'AM!
SHF
LET US GO TO THE RITUAL.

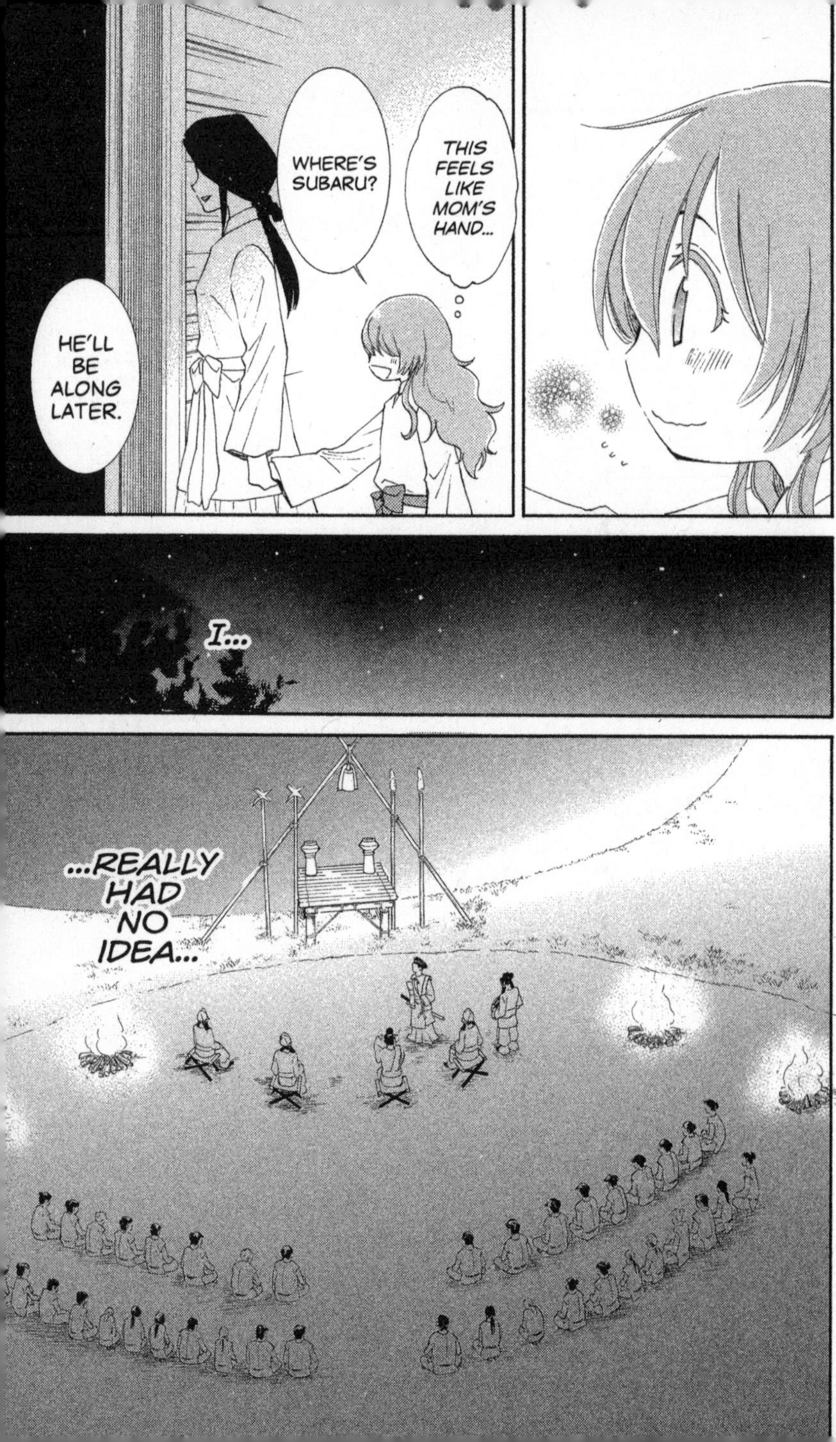
THIS FEELS LIKE MOM'S HAND...
WHERE'S SUBARU?
HE'LL BE ALONG LATER.
I...
...REALLY HAD NO IDEA...

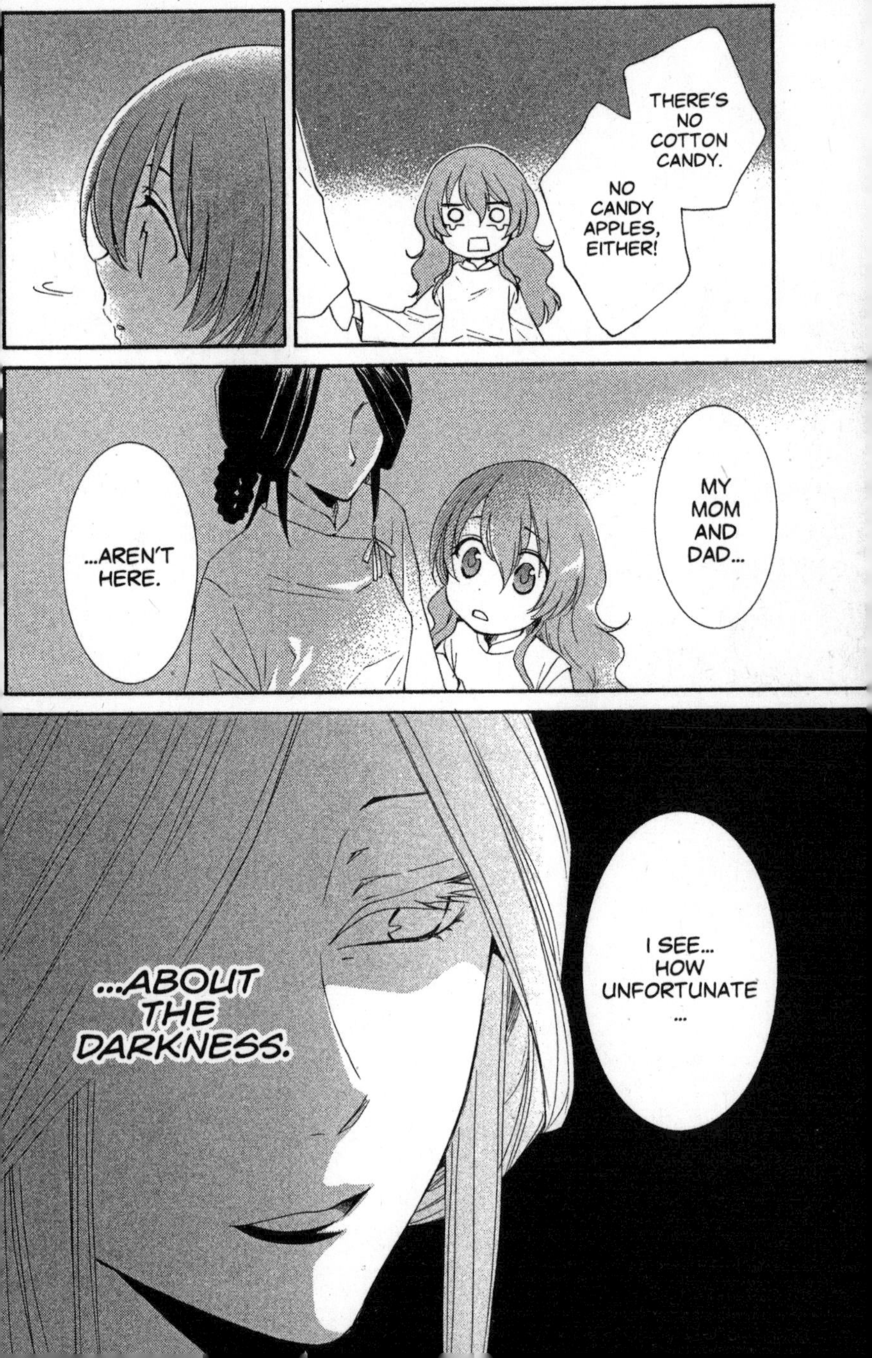
THERE'S NO COTTON CANDY.
NO CANDY APPLES, EITHER!
MY MOM AND DAD...
...AREN'T HERE.
I SEE... HOW UNFORTUNATE...
...ABOUT THE DARKNESS.

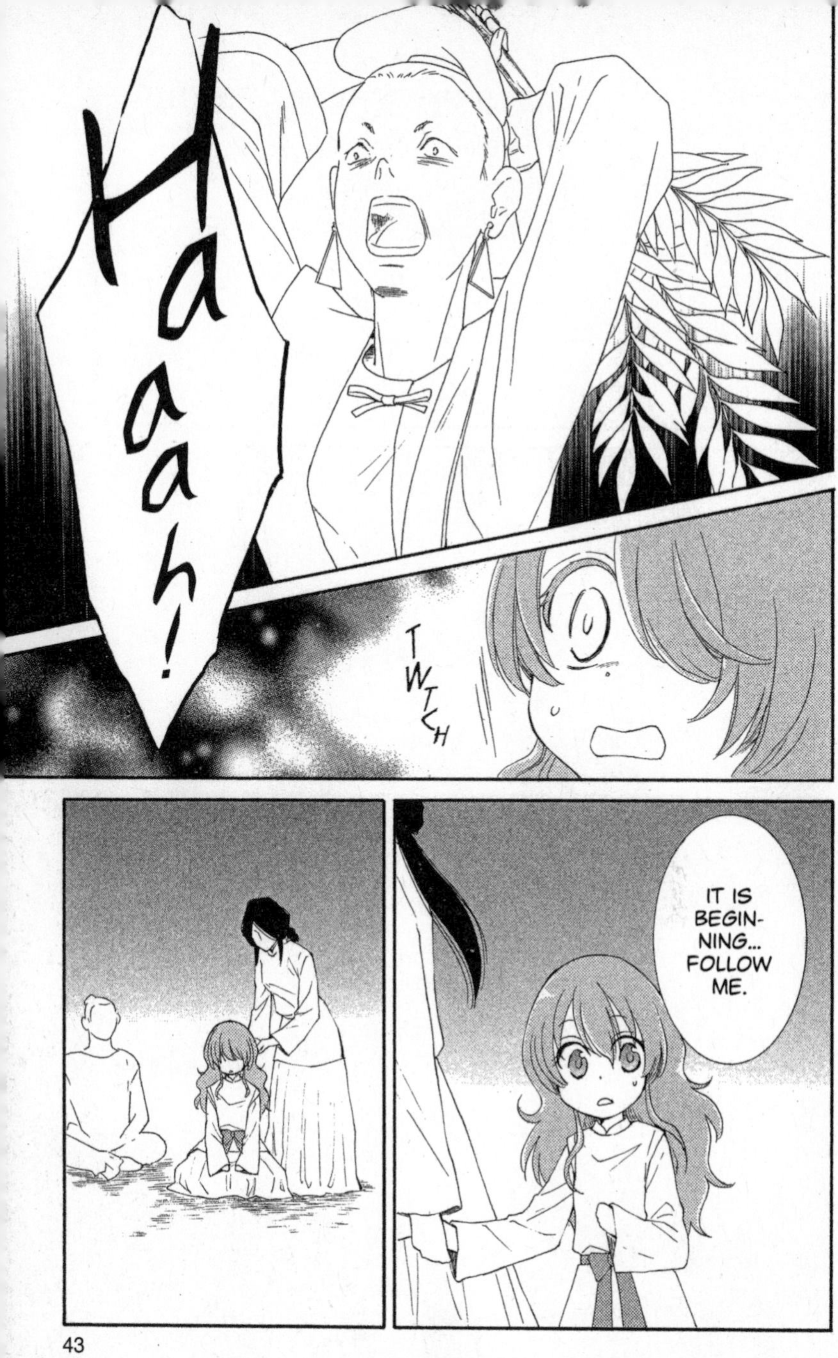
Haaah!
TWITCH
IT IS BEGIN-NING... FOLLOW ME.

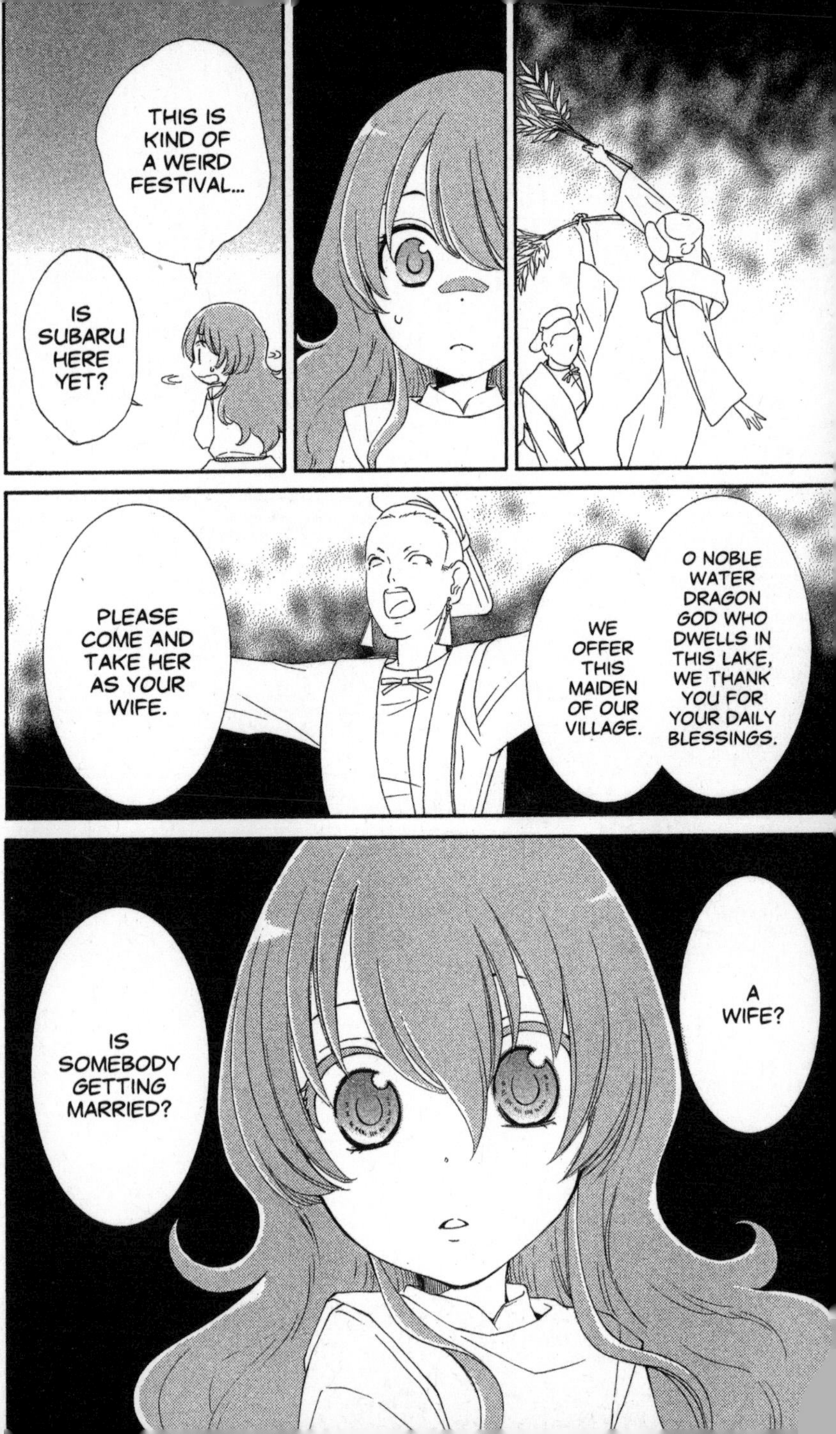
THIS IS KIND OF A WEIRD FESTIVAL...
IS SUBARU HERE YET?
O NOBLE WATER DRAGON GOD WHO DWELLS IN THIS LAKE, WE THANK YOU FOR YOUR DAILY BLESSINGS.
WE OFFER THIS MAIDEN OF OUR VILLAGE.
PLEASE COME AND TAKE HER AS YOUR WIFE.
A WIFE?
IS SOMEBODY GETTING MARRIED?

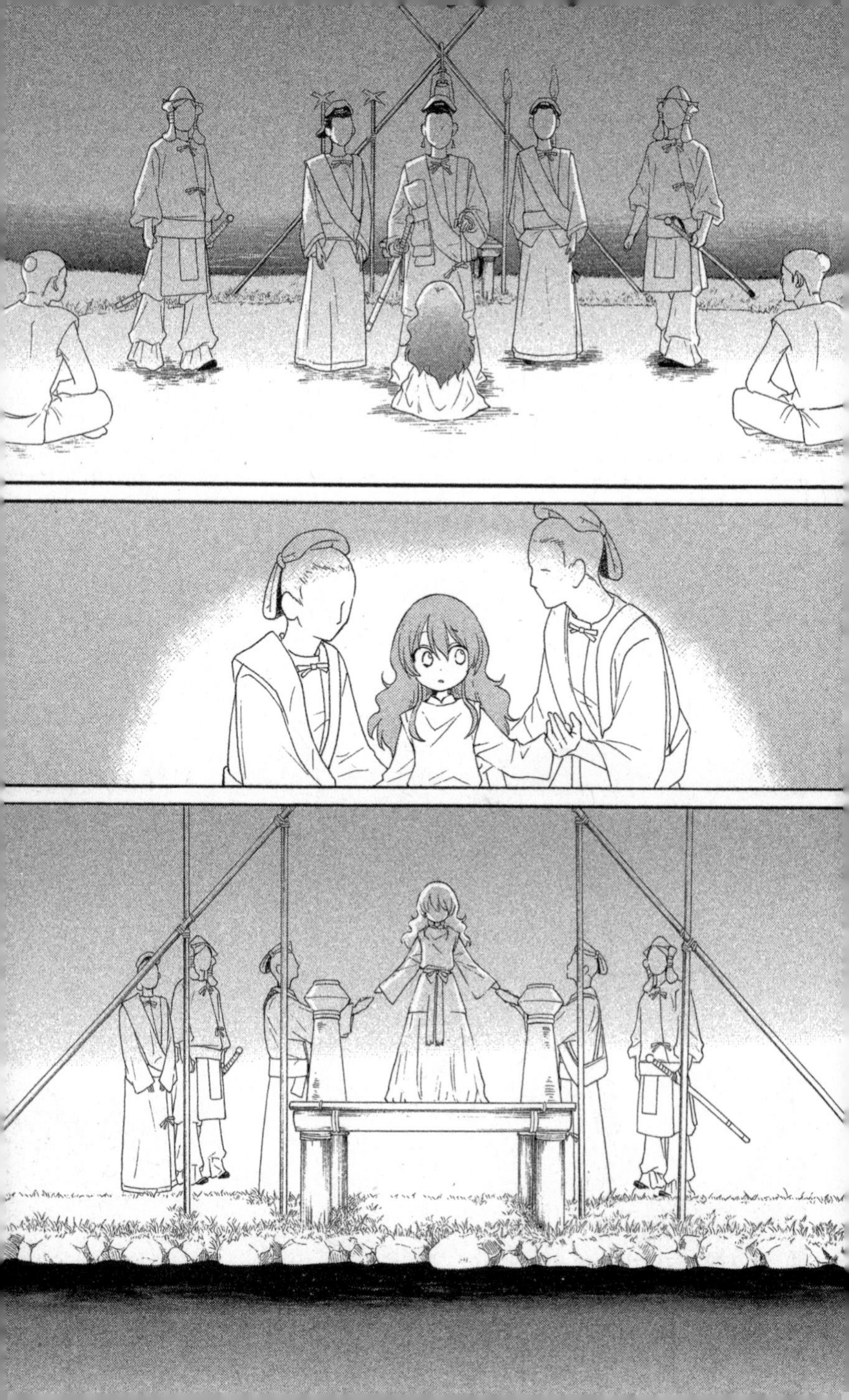

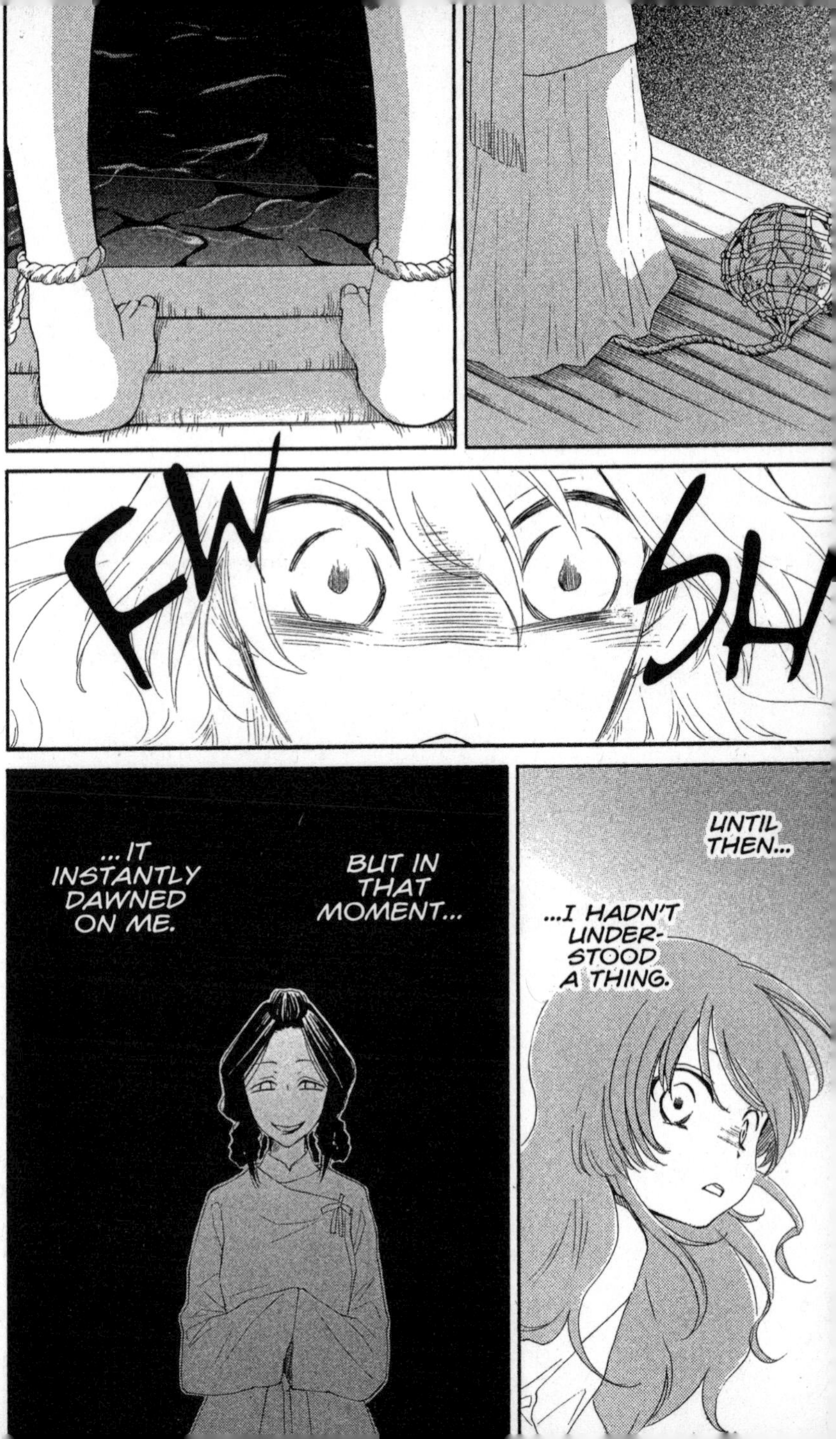
FW
SH
UNTIL THEN...
...I HADN'T UNDER-STOOD A THING.
BUT IN THAT MOMENT...
...IT INSTANTLY DAWNED ON ME.

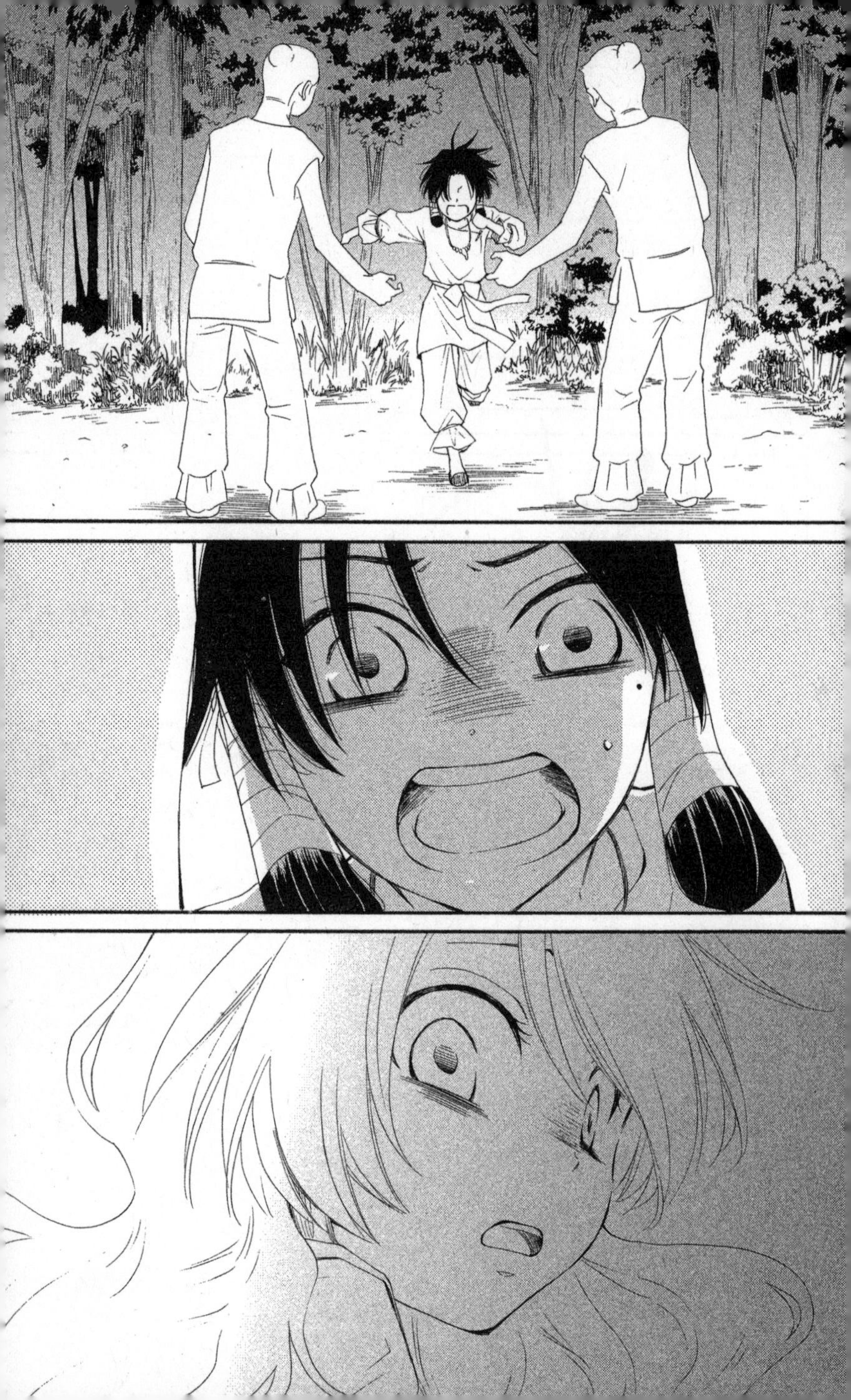

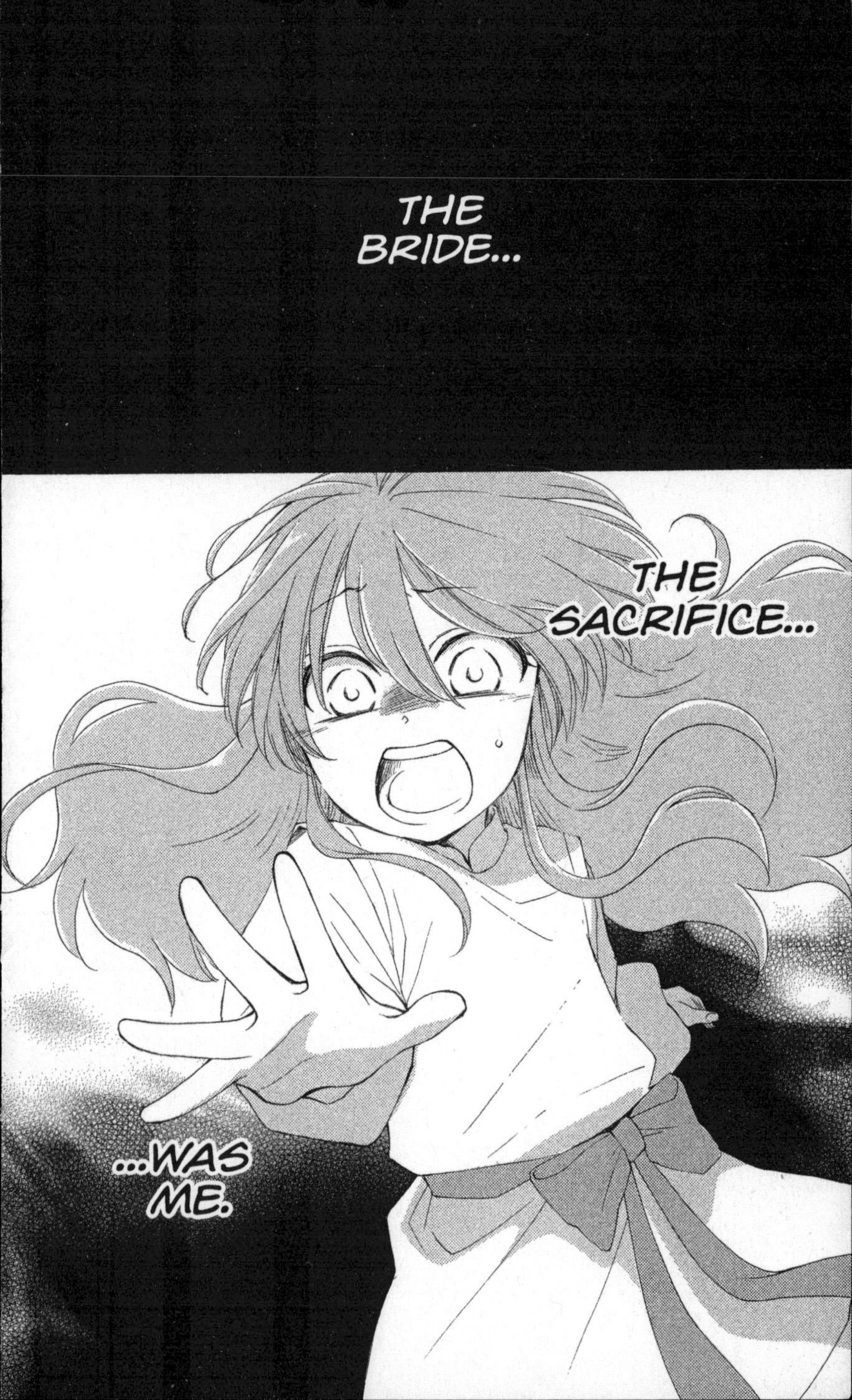
THE BRIDE...
THE SACRIFICE...
...WAS ME.

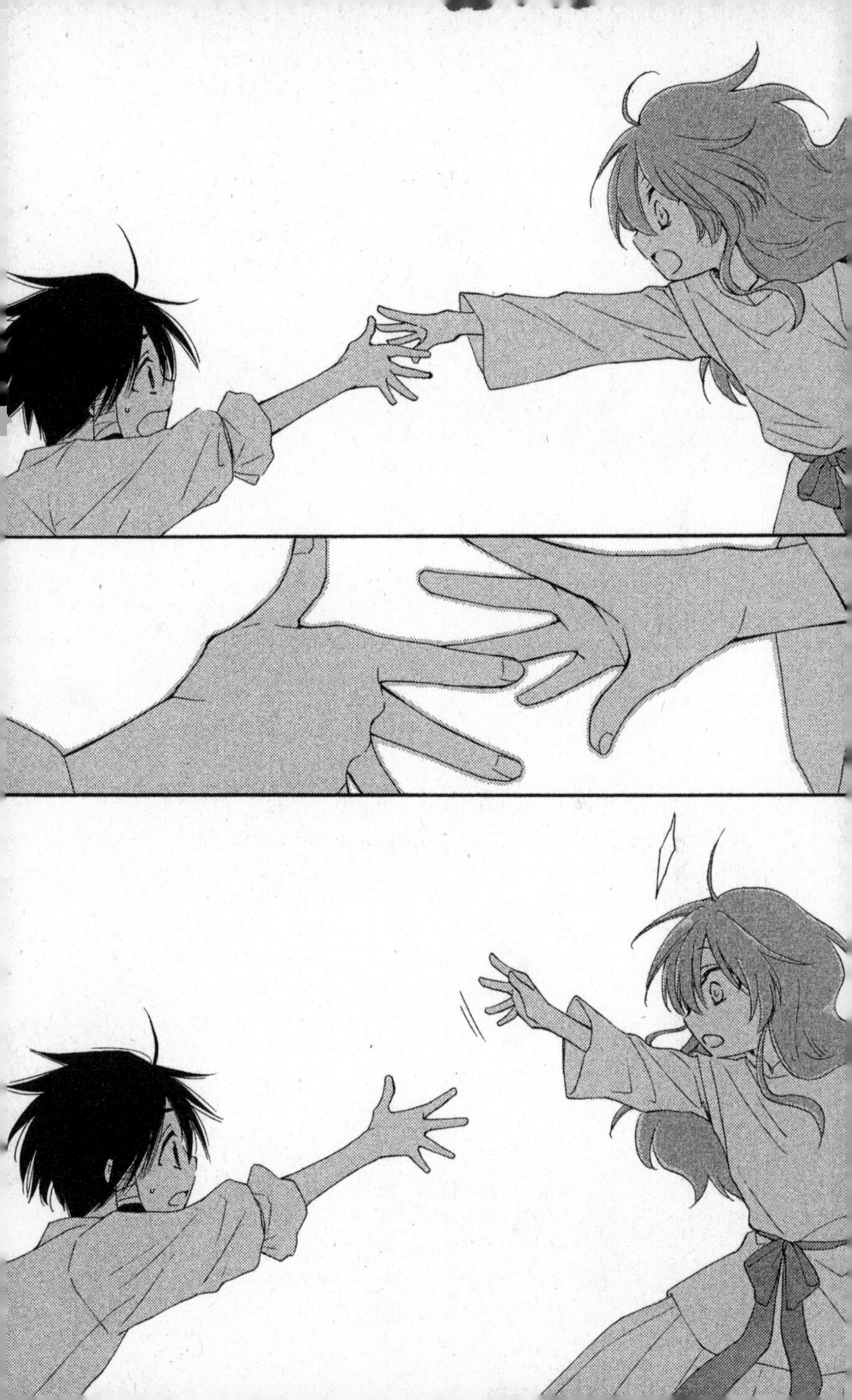

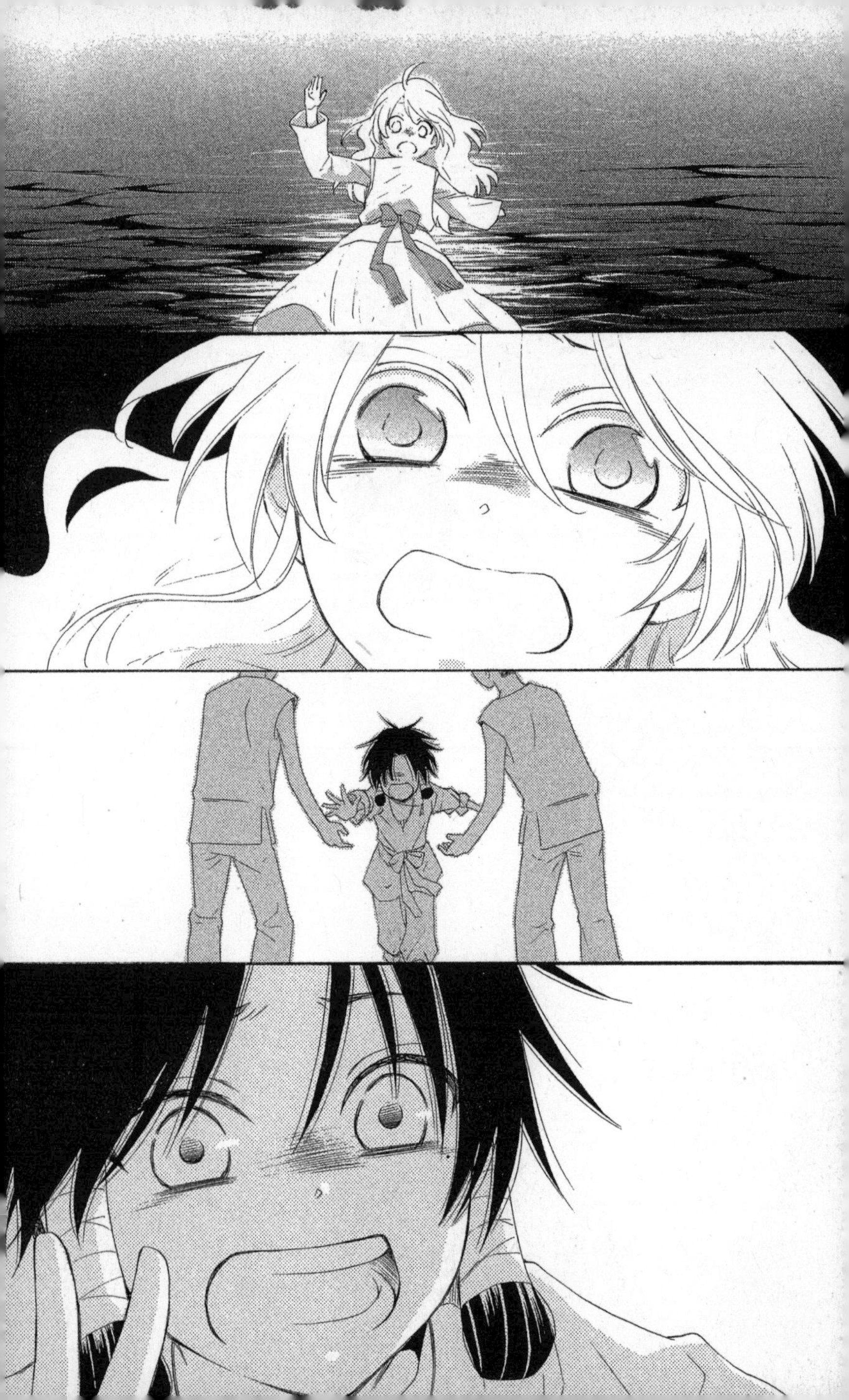

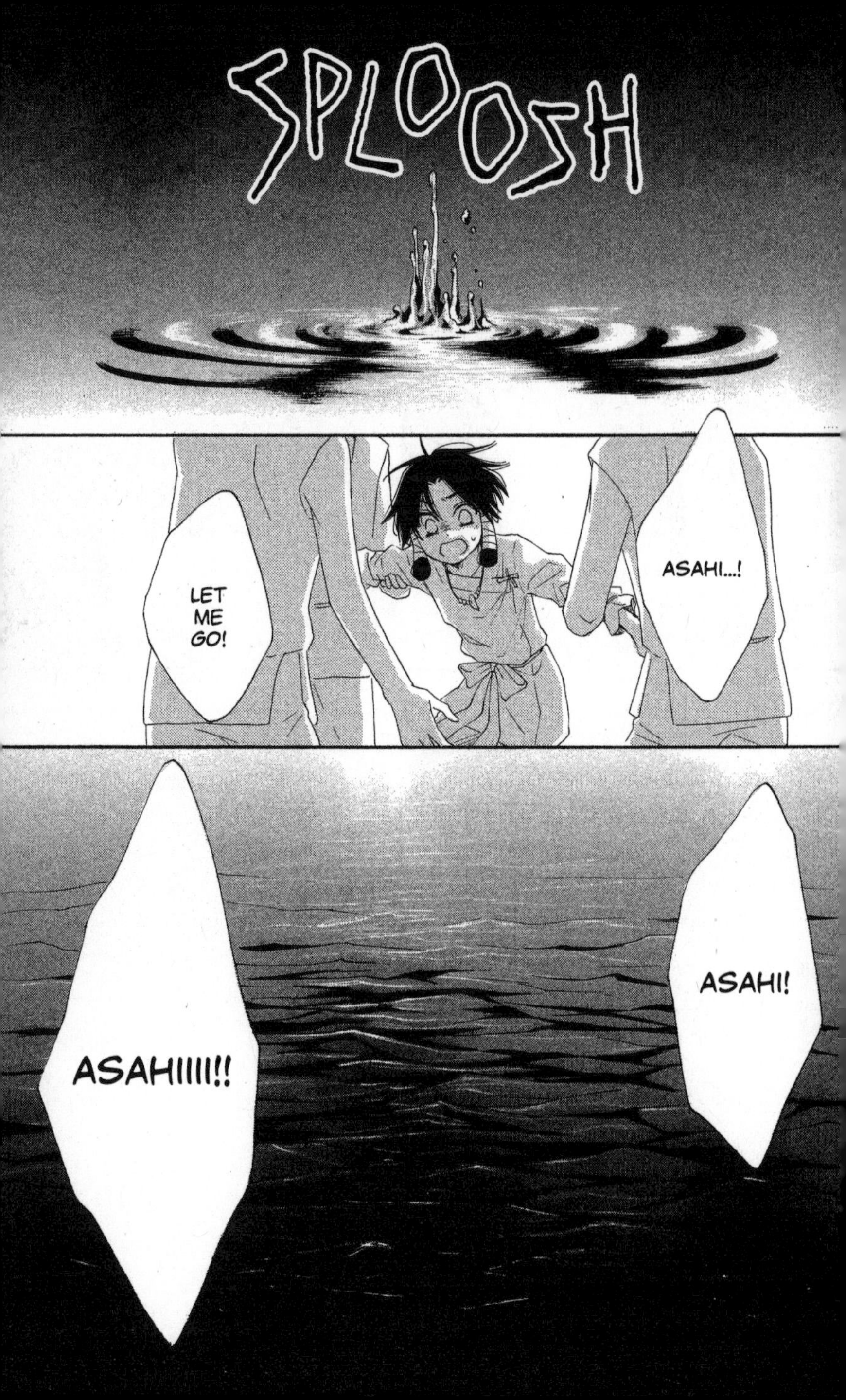
SPLOOSH
ASAHI...!
LET ME GO!
ASAHI!
ASAHIIIII!!

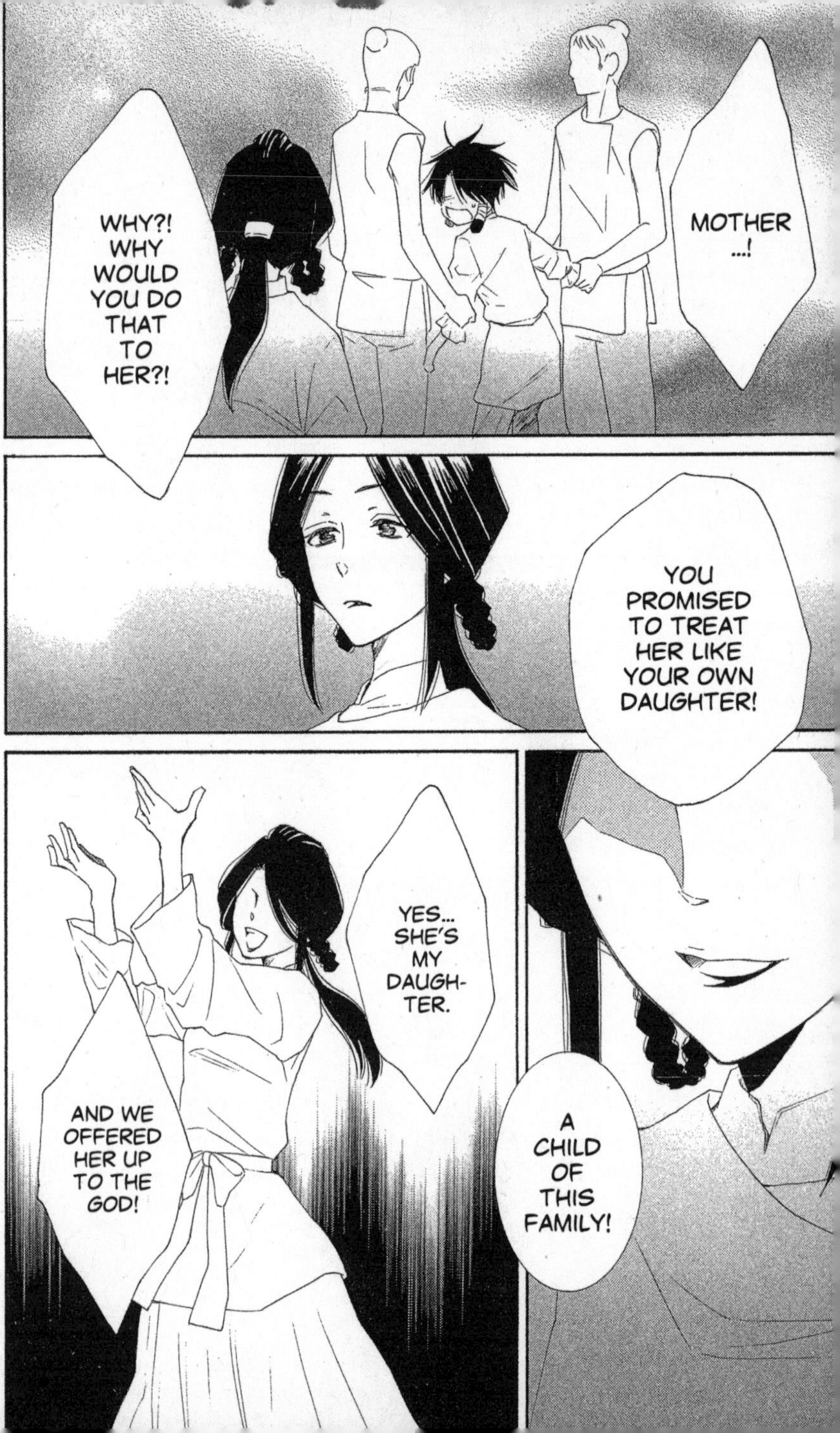
MOTHER ...!
WHY?! WHY WOULD YOU DO THAT TO HER?!
YOU PROMISED TO TREAT HER LIKE YOUR OWN DAUGHTER!
A CHILD OF THIS FAMILY!
YES... SHE'S MY DAUGH- TER.
AND WE OFFERED HER UP TO THE GOD!

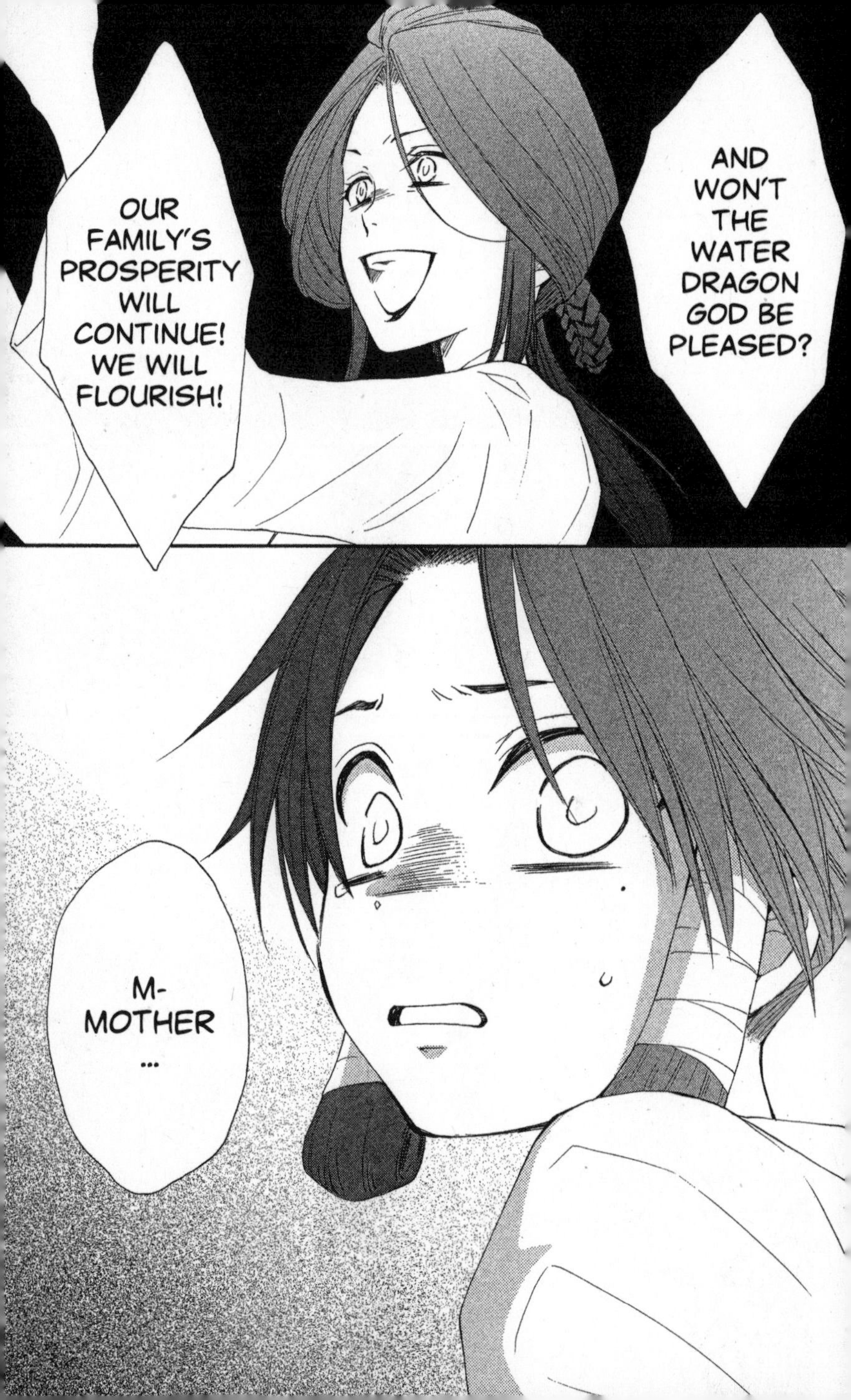
AND WON'T THE WATER DRAGON GOD BE PLEASED?
OUR FAMILY'S PROSPERITY WILL CONTINUE! WE WILL FLOURISH!
M-MOTHER...

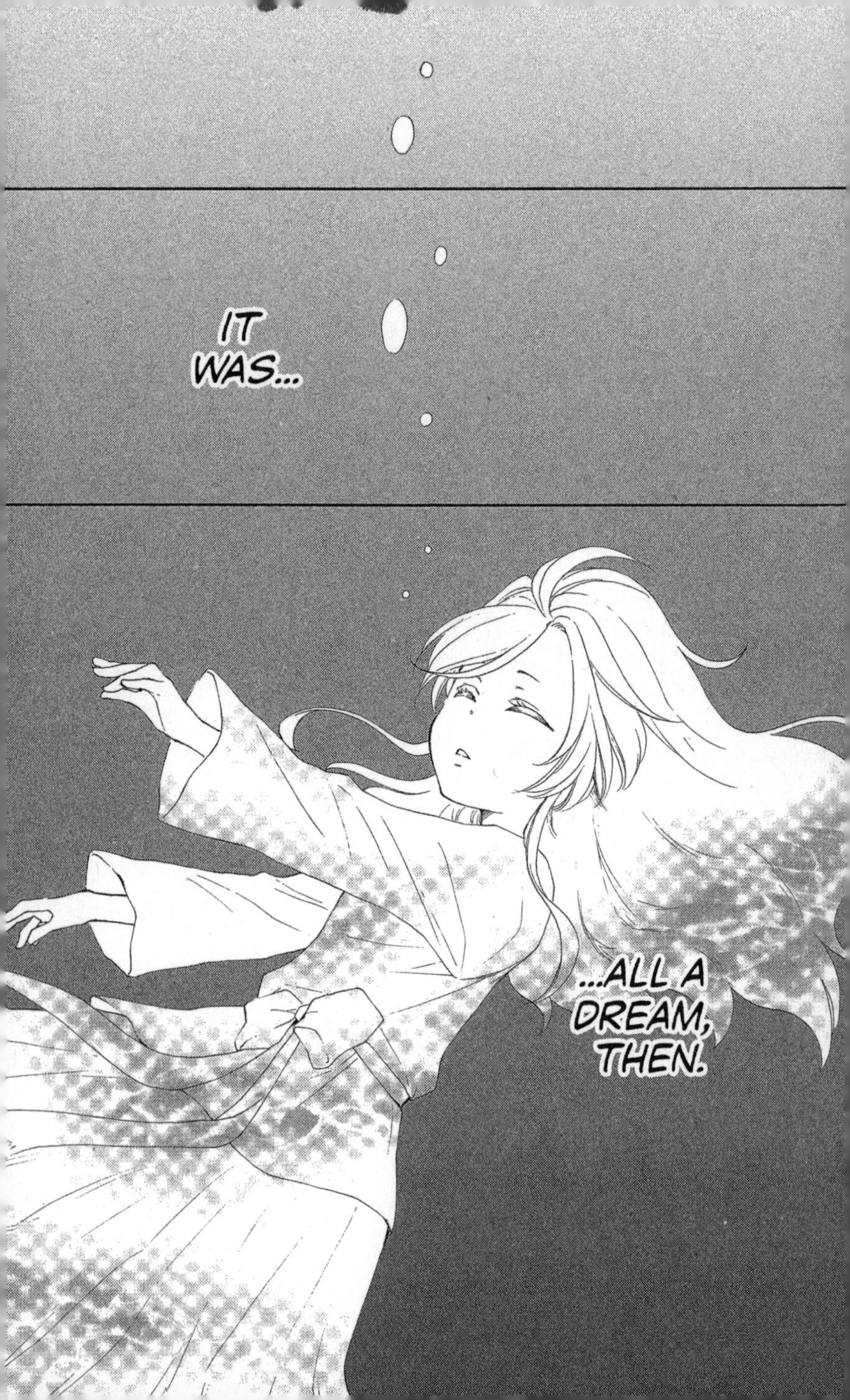
IT WAS...
...ALL A DREAM, THEN.

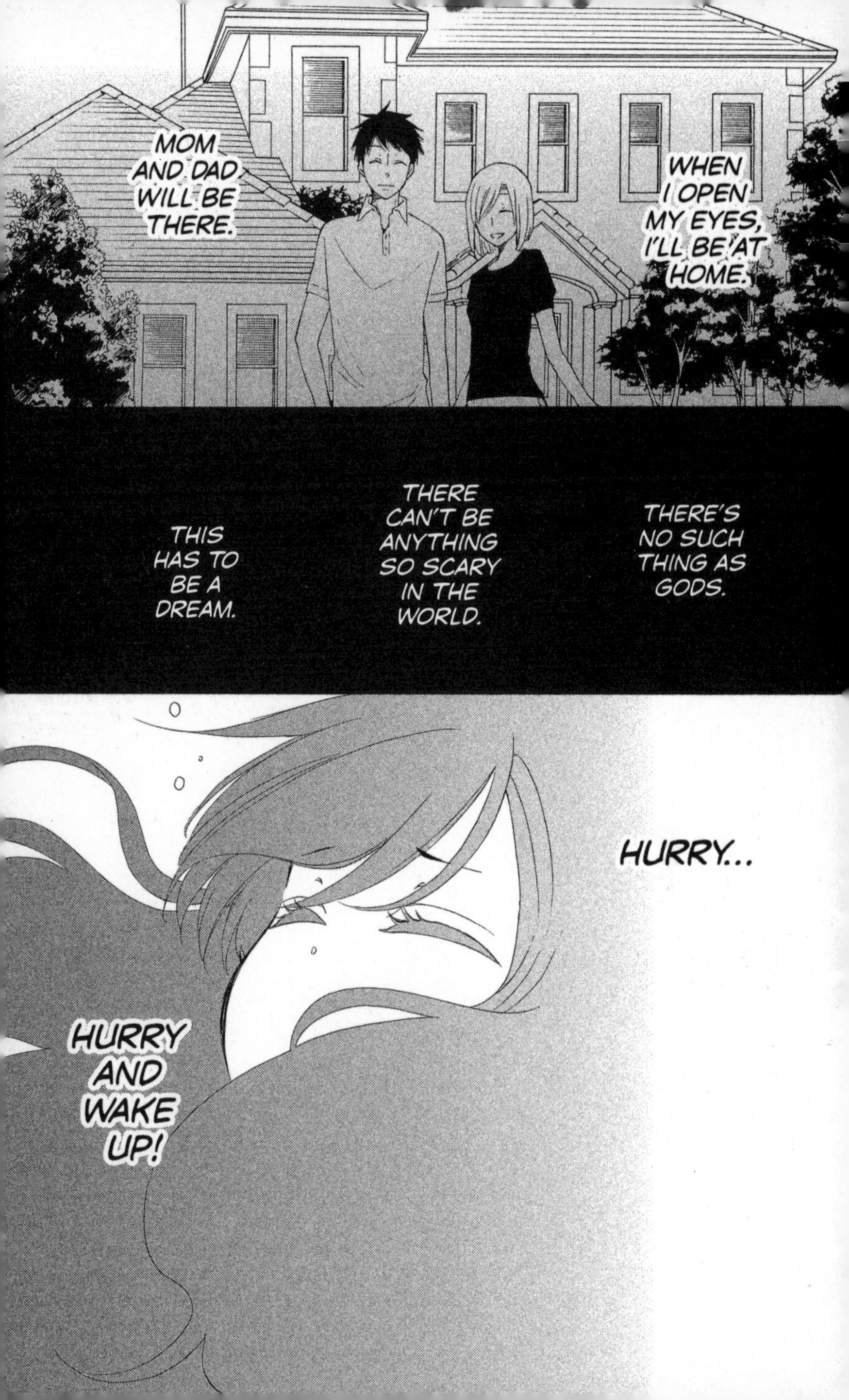
WHEN I OPEN MY EYES, I'LL BE AT HOME.
MOM AND DAD WILL BE THERE.
THERE'S NO SUCH THING AS GODS.
THERE CAN'T BE ANYTHING SO SCARY IN THE WORLD.
THIS HAS TO BE A DREAM.
HURRY...
HURRY AND WAKE UP!

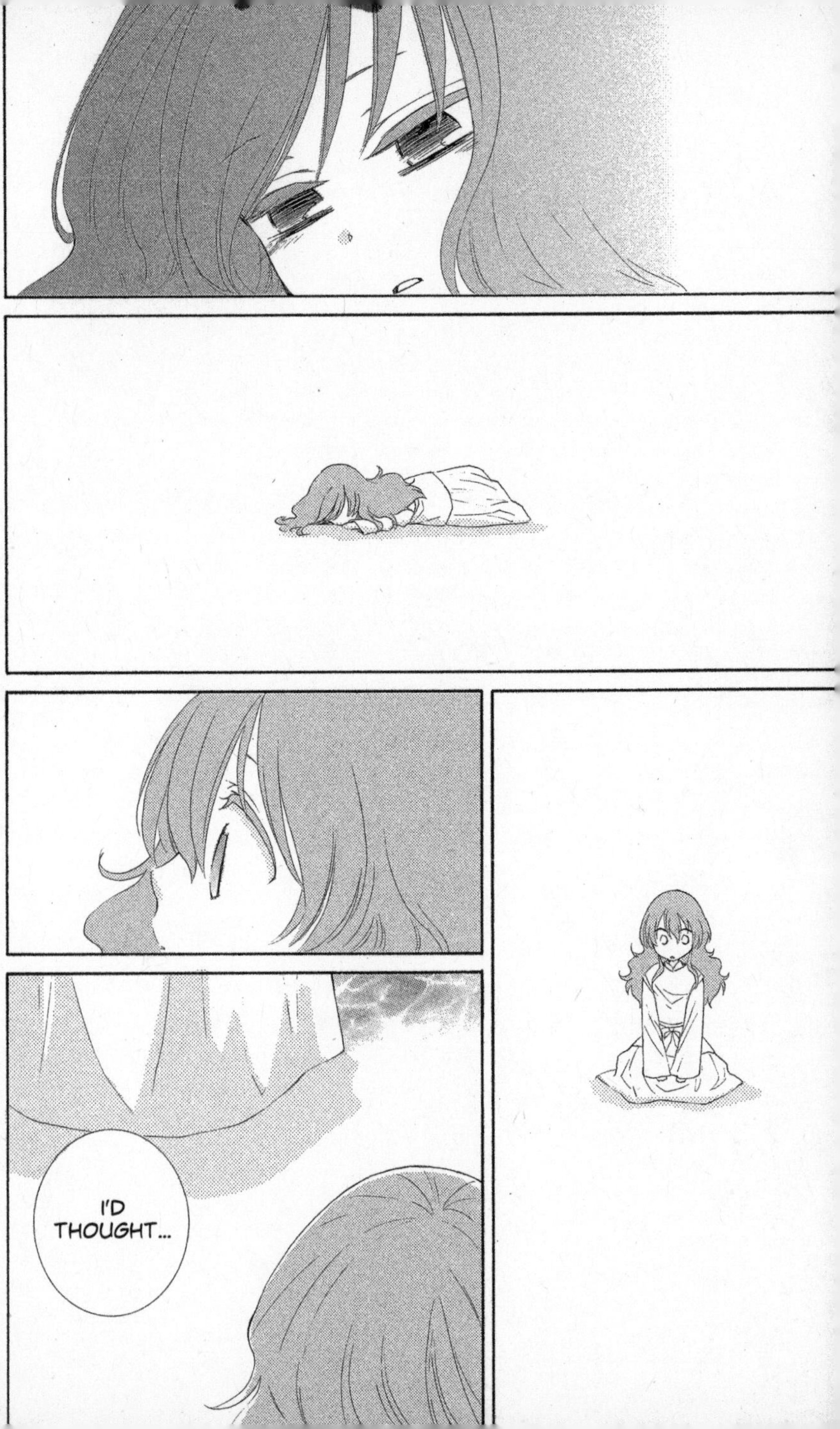

I'D THOUGHT...

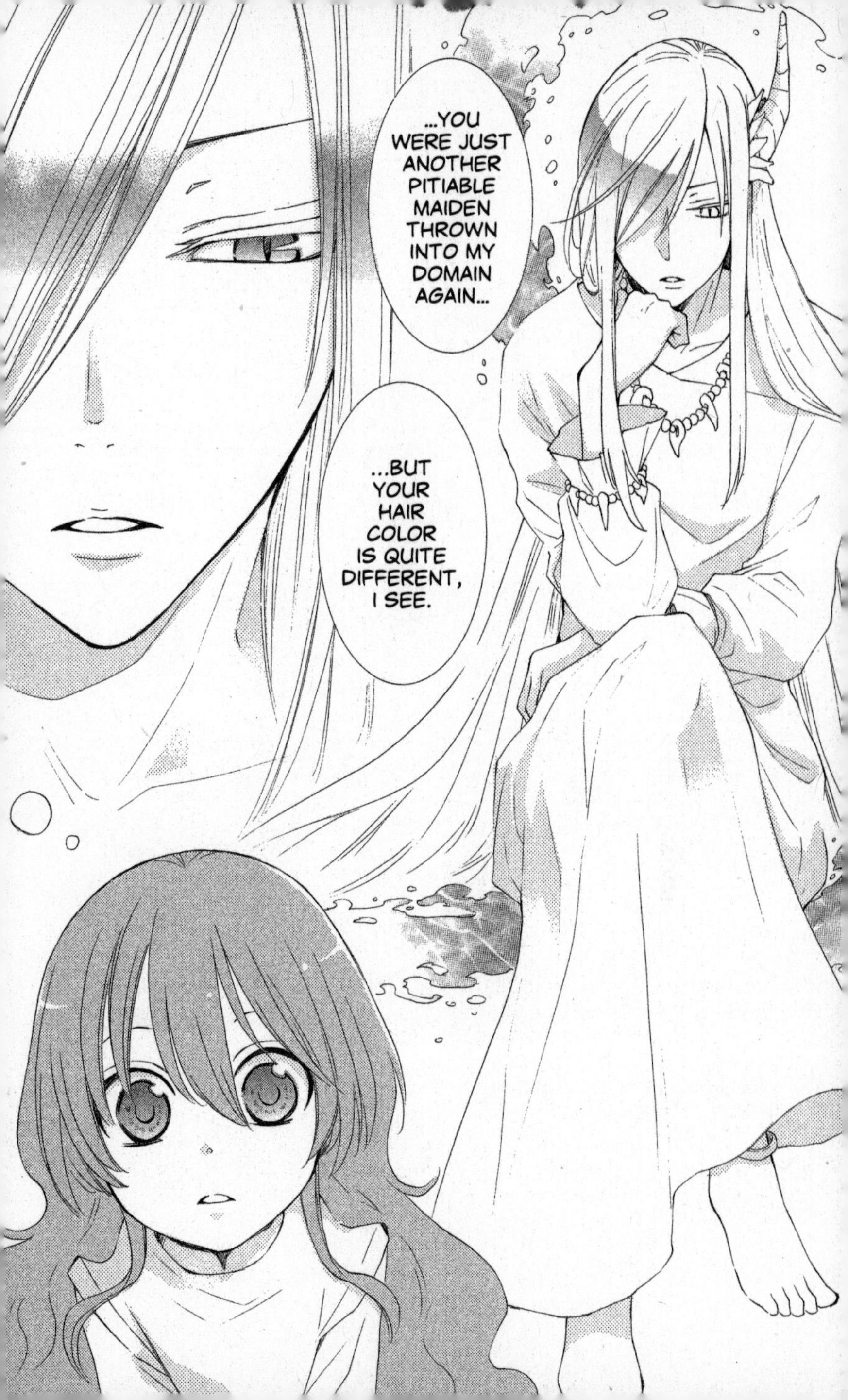
...YOU WERE JUST ANOTHER PITIABLE MAIDEN THROWN INTO MY DOMAIN AGAIN...
...BUT YOUR HAIR COLOR IS QUITE DIFFERENT, I SEE.

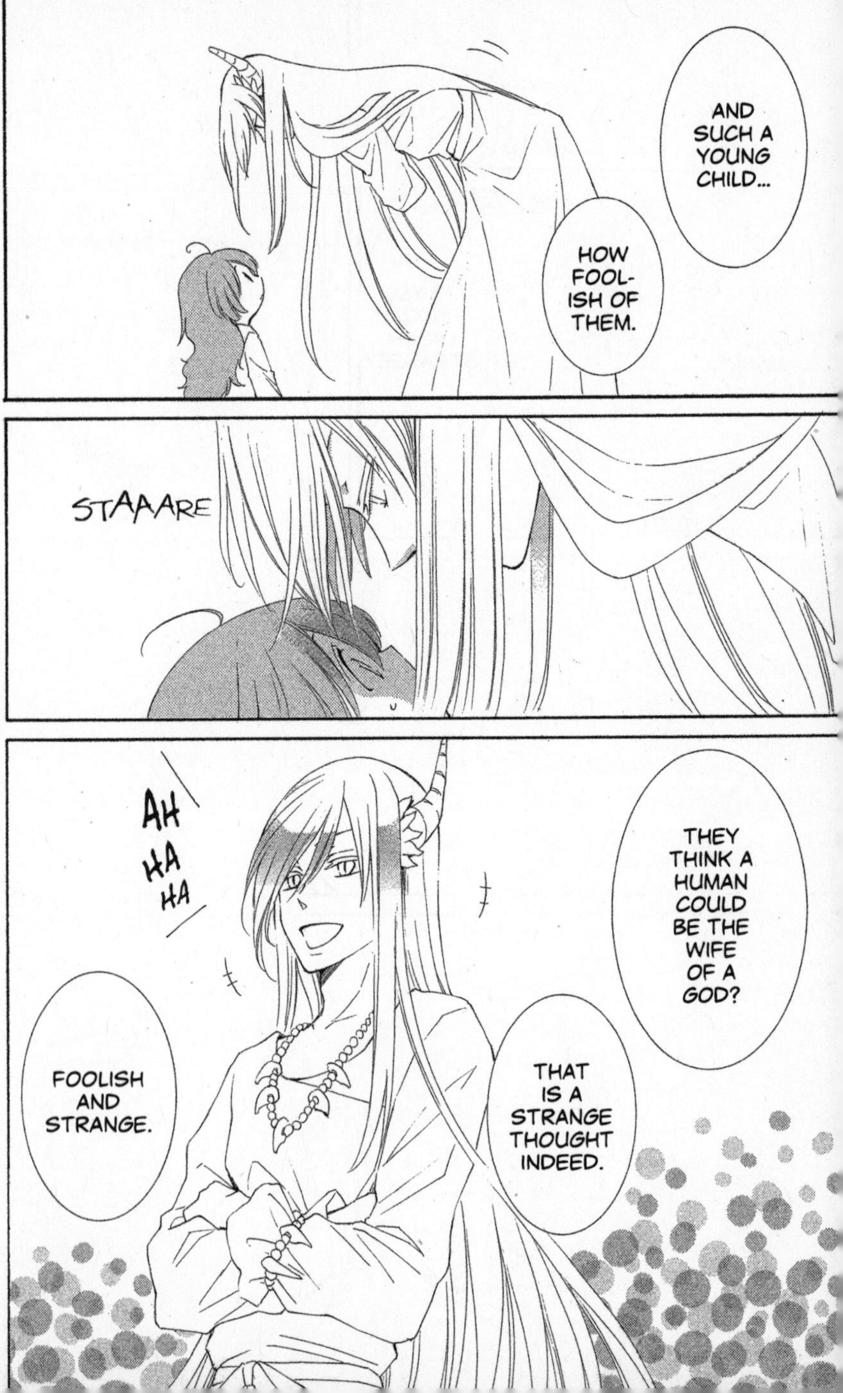
AND SUCH A YOUNG CHILD...
HOW FOOL-ISH OF THEM.
STAAARE
THEY THINK A HUMAN COULD BE THE WIFE OF A GOD?
AH HA HA
THAT IS A STRANGE THOUGHT INDEED.
FOOLISH AND STRANGE.

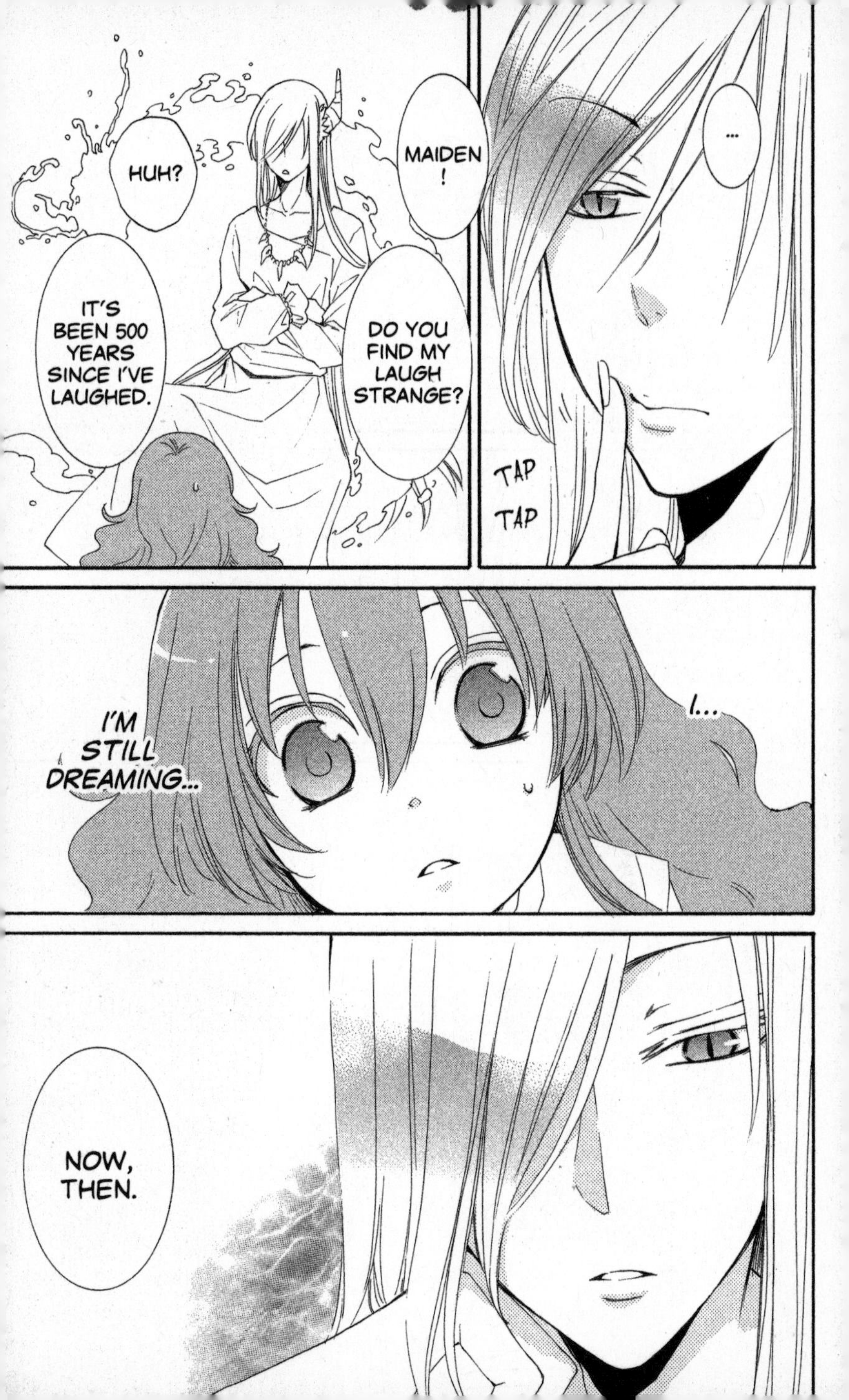
...
TAP
TAP
MAIDEN!
HUH?
DO YOU FIND MY LAUGH STRANGE?
IT'S BEEN 500 YEARS SINCE I'VE LAUGHED.
I...
I'M STILL DREAMING...
NOW, THEN.

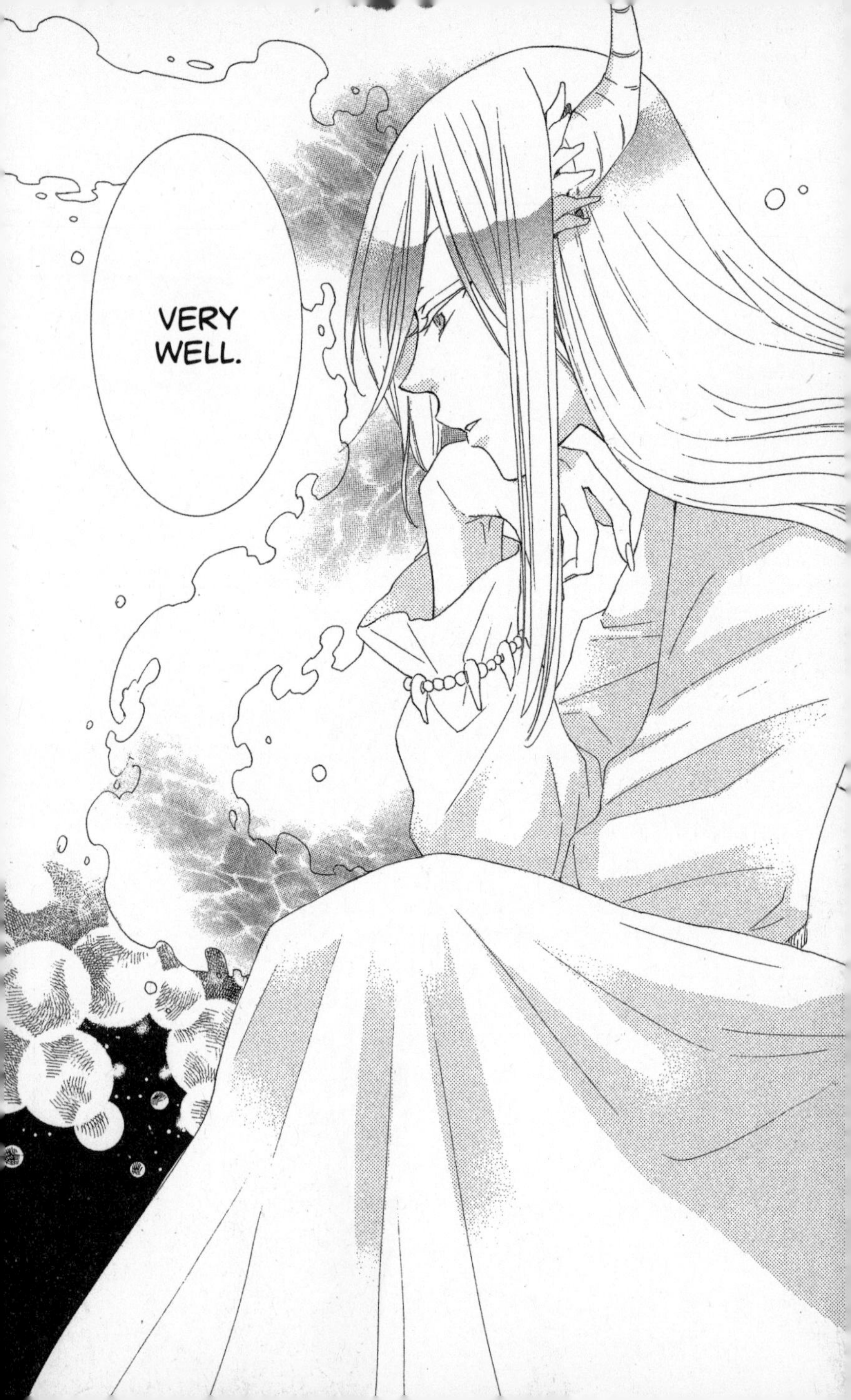
VERY WELL.

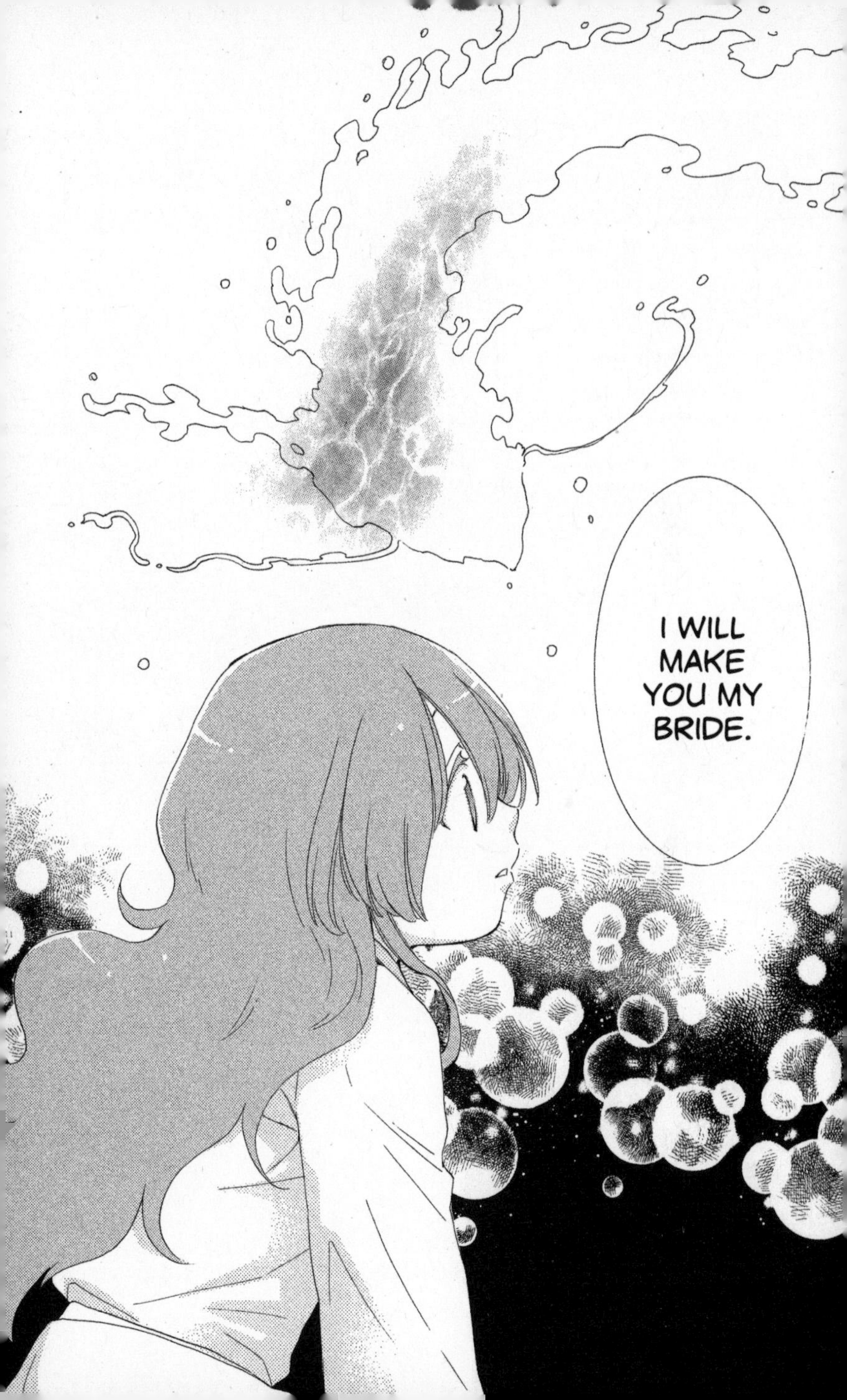
I WILL MAKE YOU MY BRIDE.

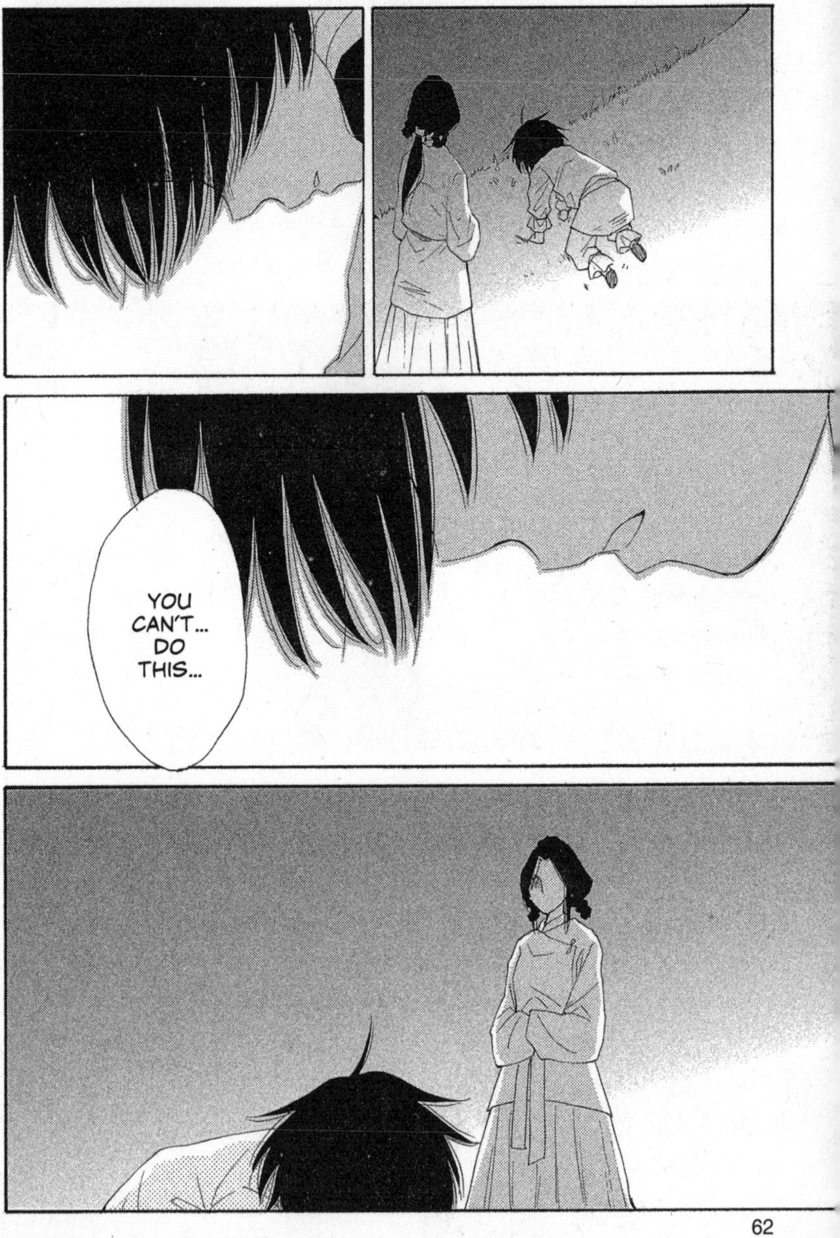
YOU CAN'T... DO THIS...

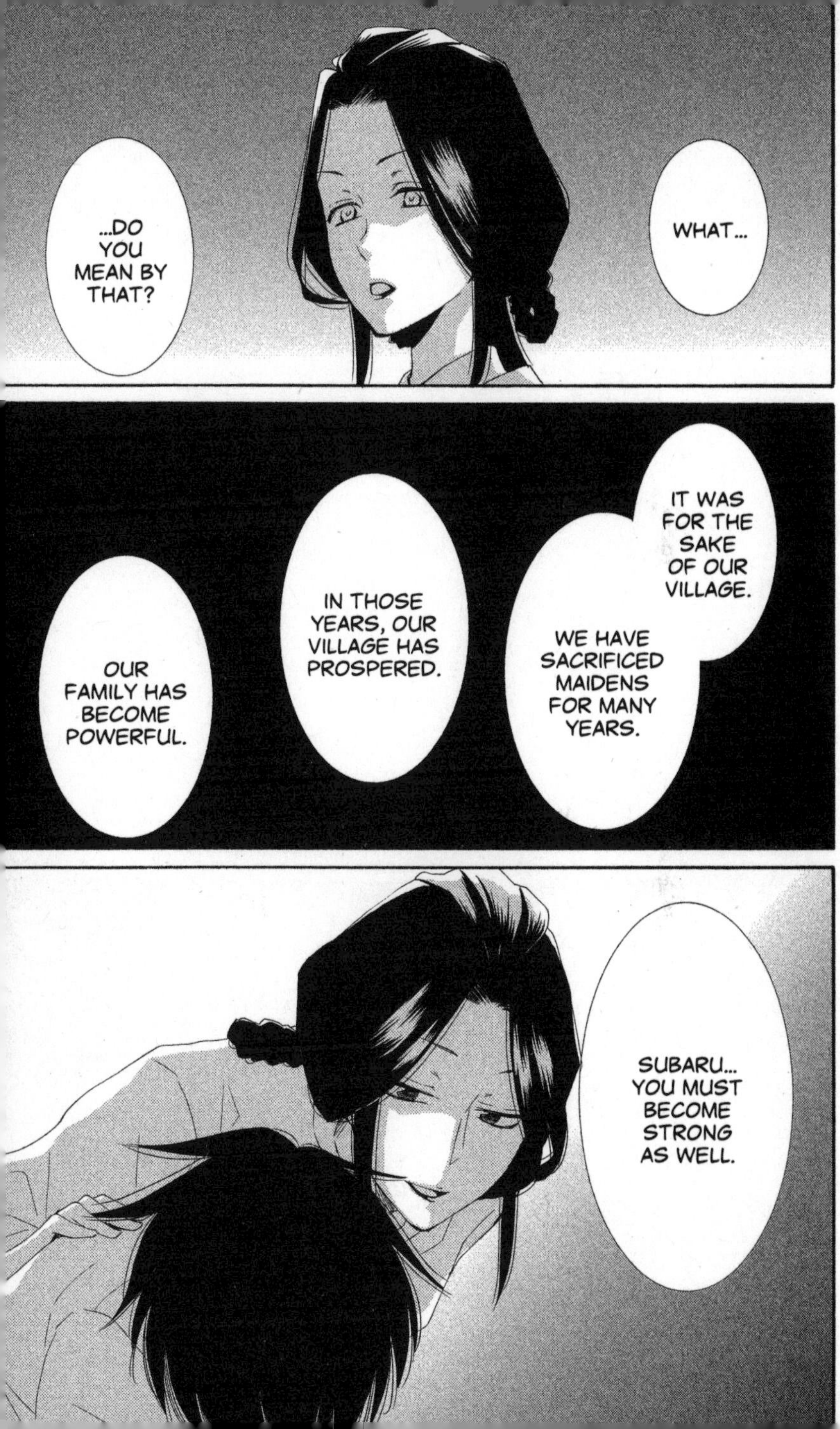
WHAT...
...DO YOU MEAN BY THAT?
IT WAS FOR THE SAKE OF OUR VILLAGE.
WE HAVE SACRIFICED MAIDENS FOR MANY YEARS.
IN THOSE YEARS, OUR VILLAGE HAS PROSPERED.
OUR FAMILY HAS BECOME POWERFUL.
SUBARU... YOU MUST BECOME STRONG AS WELL.

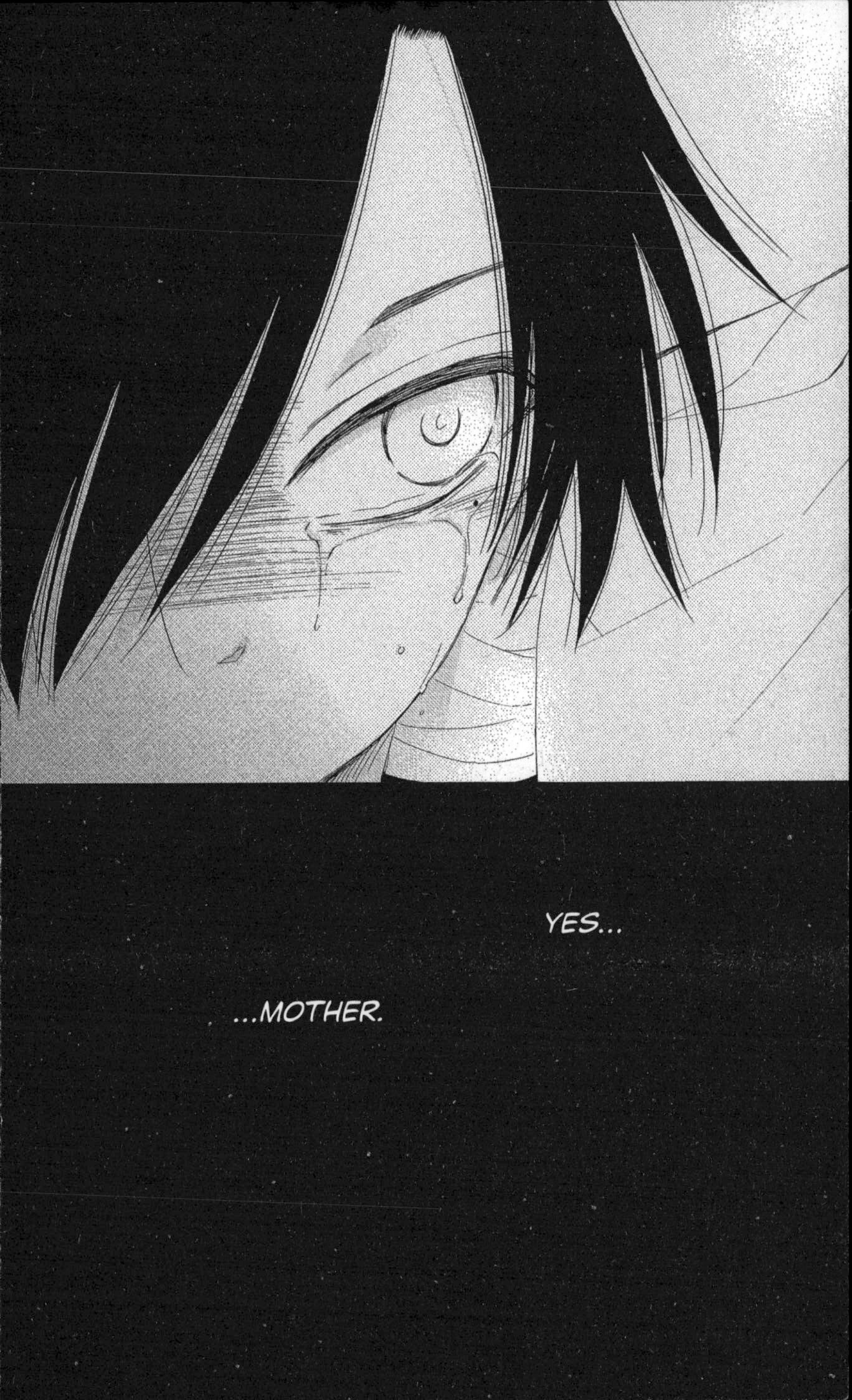
YES...
...MOTHER.

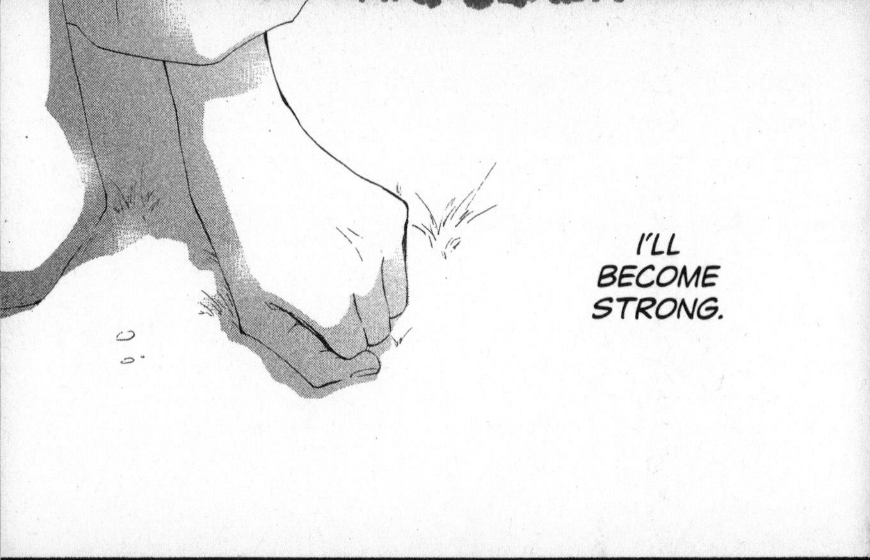
I'LL BECOME STRONG.

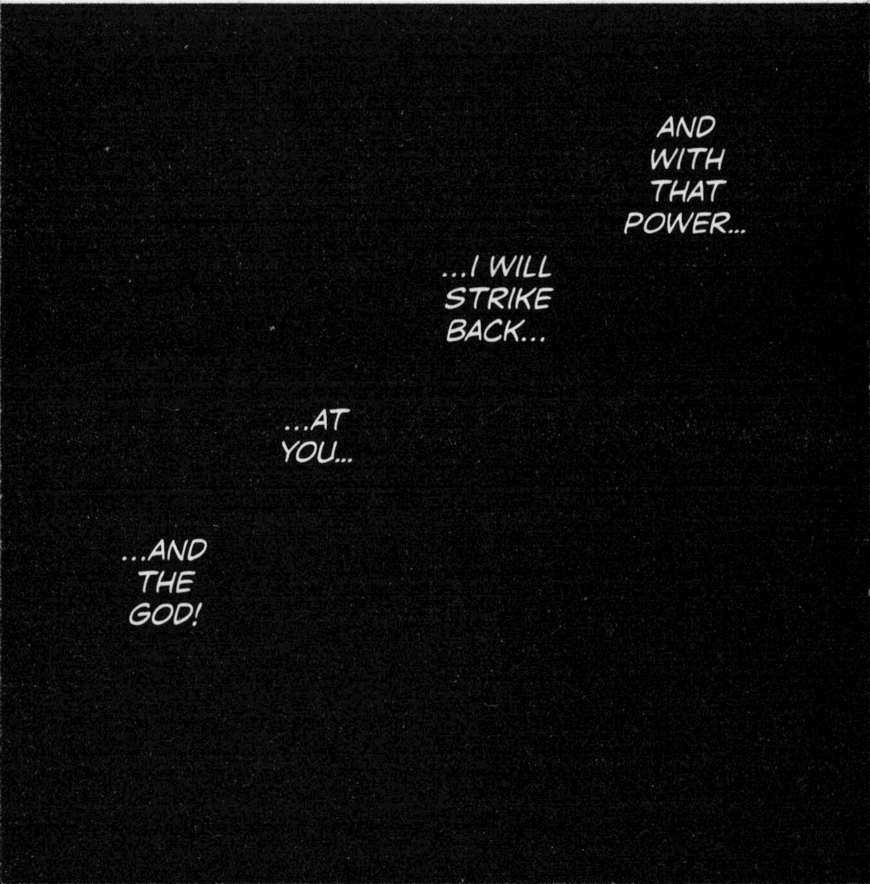
AND WITH THAT POWER...
...I WILL STRIKE BACK...
...AT YOU...
...AND THE GOD!

Hello, I'm Rei Toma, and this is volume 1 of **The Water Dragon's Bride**. It ended up being another fantasy story. I hope you're all excited for it!

The setting is an ancient Japan-style fantasy world.
I was trying for something like the Kofun period. This is an age characterized by haniwa clay figures, magatama beads and the side-knot hairdo. It's a very interesting sort of era! I'm looking forward to getting used to drawing it.

I can't wait until I get to draw all the water god's water scenes in color. There're so many things I want to draw!

CHAPTER 2

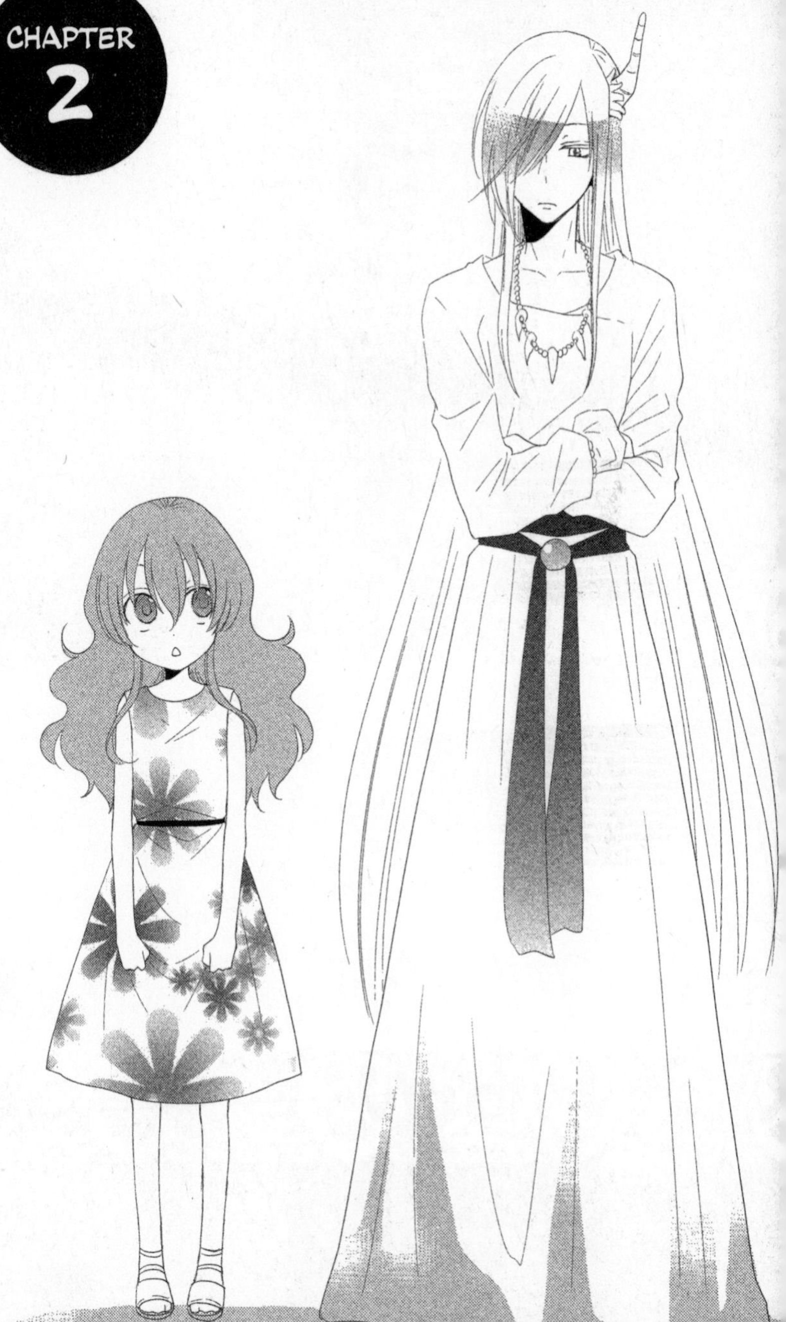

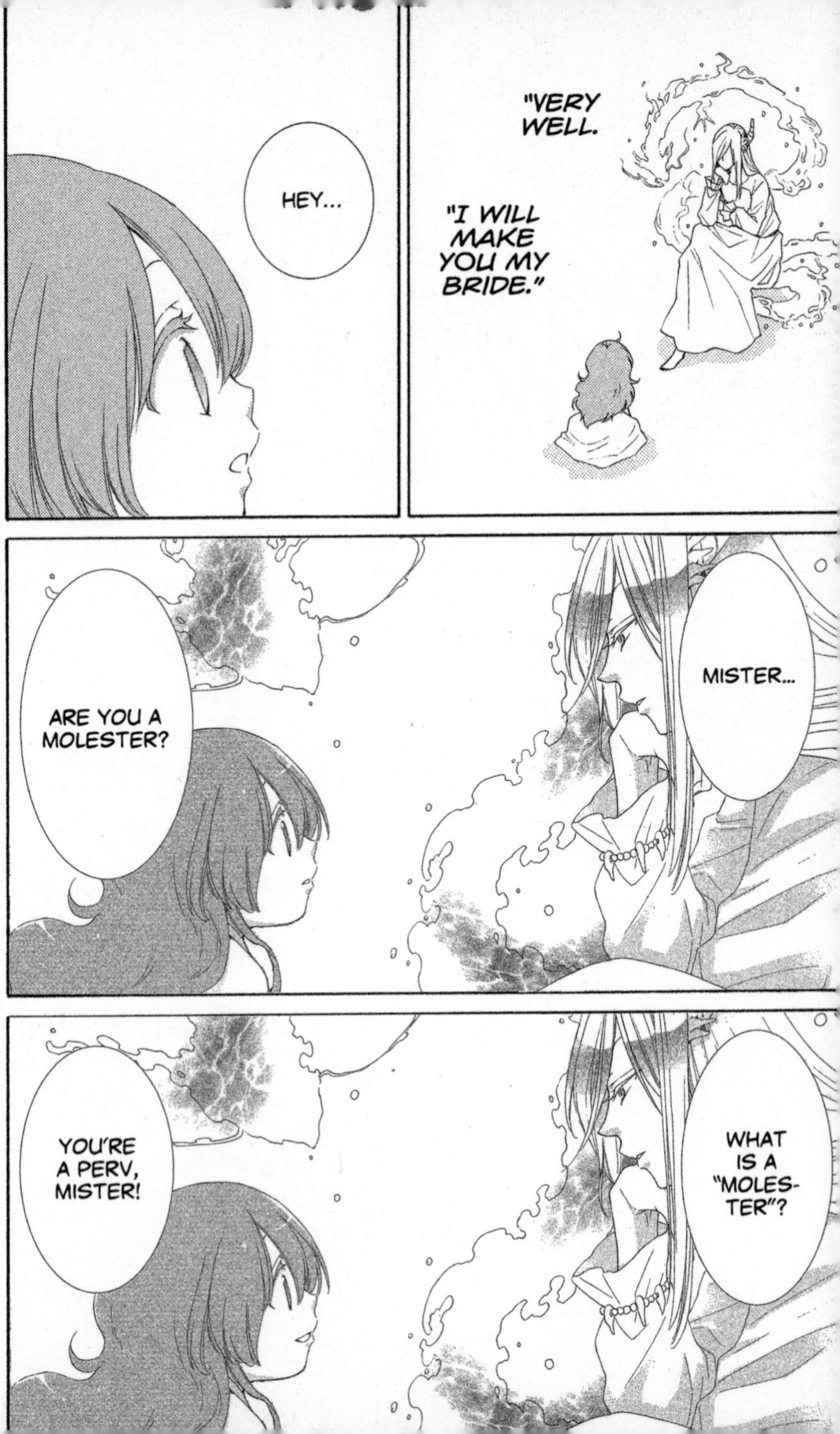
"VERY WELL.
"I WILL MAKE YOU MY BRIDE."
HEY...
MISTER...
ARE YOU A MOLESTER?
WHAT IS A "MOLESTER"?
YOU'RE A PERV, MISTER!

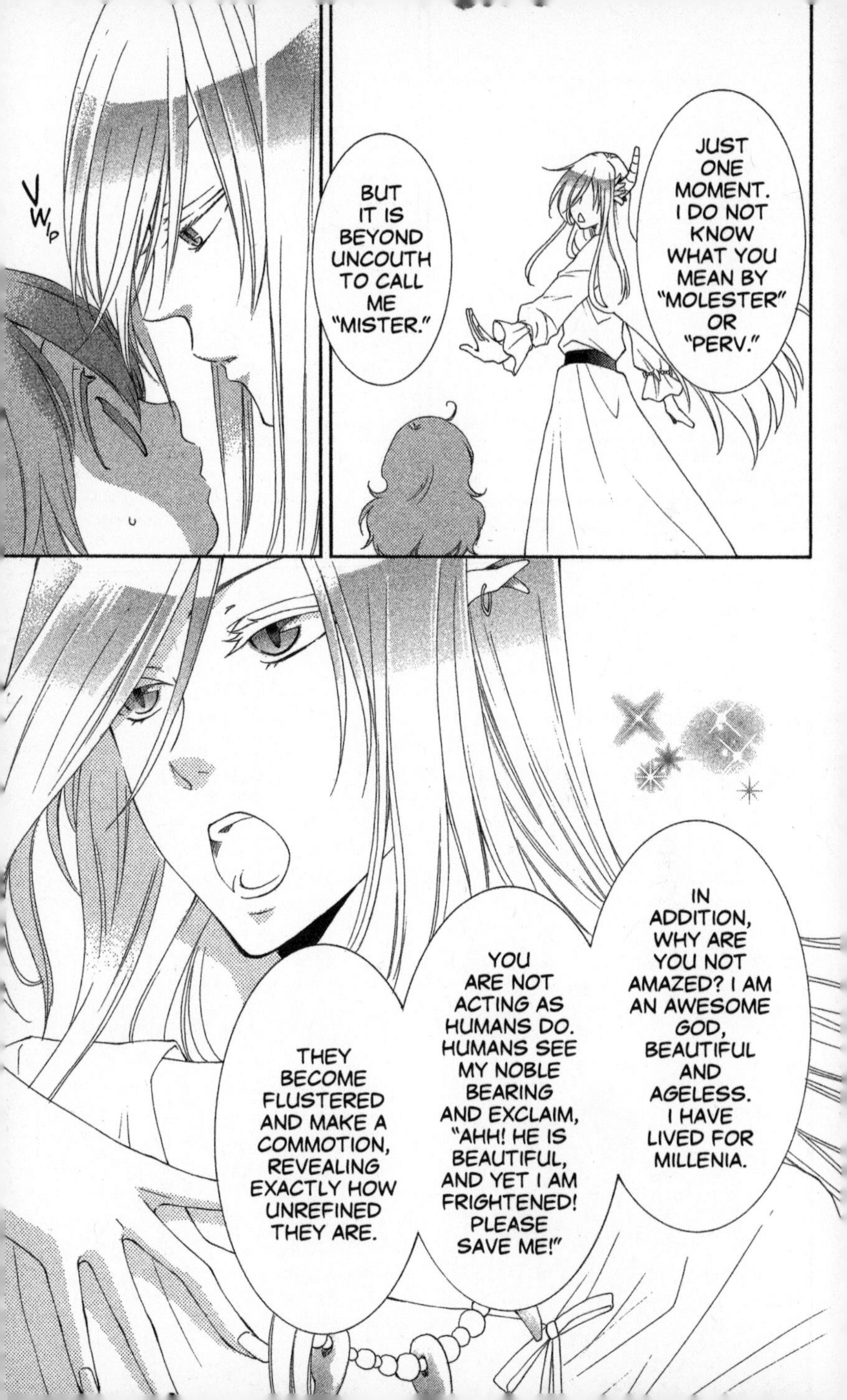
JUST ONE MOMENT. I DO NOT KNOW WHAT YOU MEAN BY "MOLESTER" OR "PERV."
BUT IT IS BEYOND UNCOUTH TO CALL ME "MISTER."
IN ADDITION, WHY ARE YOU NOT AMAZED? I AM AN AWESOME GOD, BEAUTIFUL AND AGELESS. I HAVE LIVED FOR MILLENIA.
YOU ARE NOT ACTING AS HUMANS DO. HUMANS SEE MY NOBLE BEARING AND EXCLAIM, "AHH! HE IS BEAUTIFUL, AND YET I AM FRIGHTENED! PLEASE SAVE ME!"
THEY BECOME FLUSTERED AND MAKE A COMMOTION, REVEALING EXACTLY HOW UNREFINED THEY ARE.

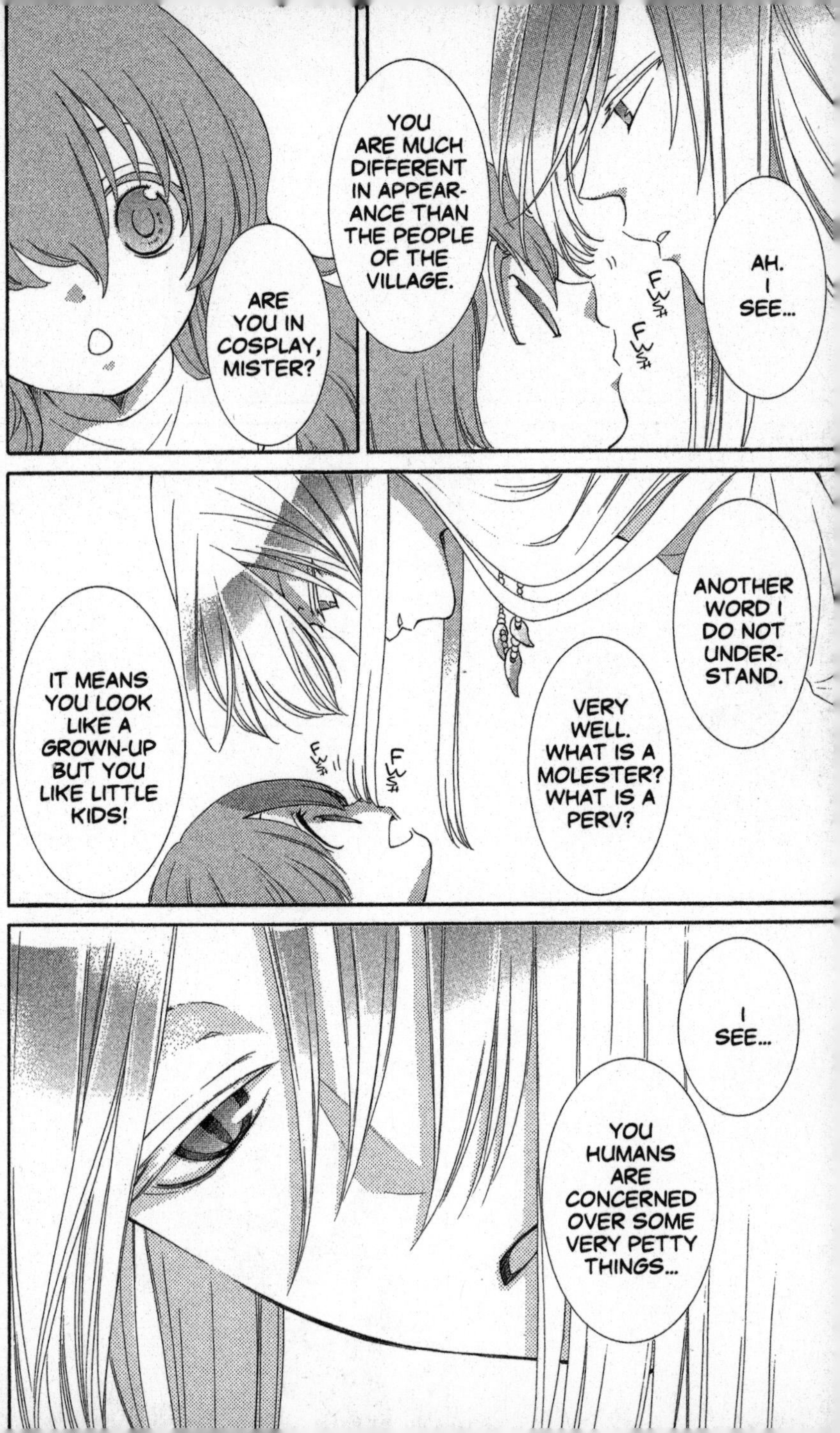
AH. I SEE...
YOU ARE MUCH DIFFERENT IN APPEARANCE THAN THE PEOPLE OF THE VILLAGE.
ARE YOU IN COSPLAY, MISTER?
ANOTHER WORD I DO NOT UNDERSTAND.
VERY WELL. WHAT IS A MOLESTER? WHAT IS A PERV?
IT MEANS YOU LOOK LIKE A GROWN-UP BUT YOU LIKE LITTLE KIDS!
I SEE...
YOU HUMANS ARE CONCERNED OVER SOME VERY PETTY THINGS...

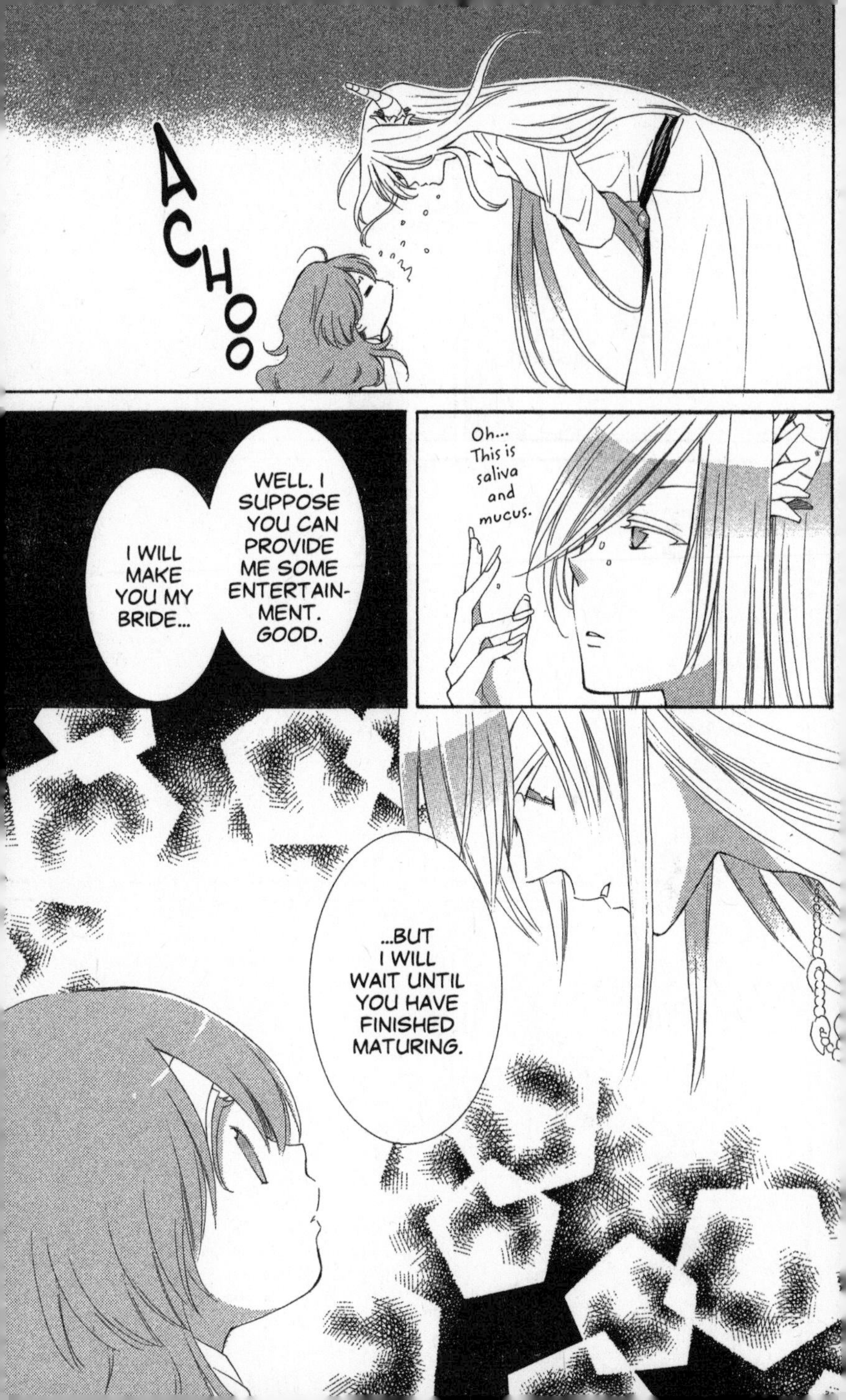
ACHOO
Oh... This is saliva and mucus.
WELL. I SUPPOSE YOU CAN PROVIDE ME SOME ENTERTAIN-MENT. GOOD.
I WILL MAKE YOU MY BRIDE...
...BUT I WILL WAIT UNTIL YOU HAVE FINISHED MATURING.

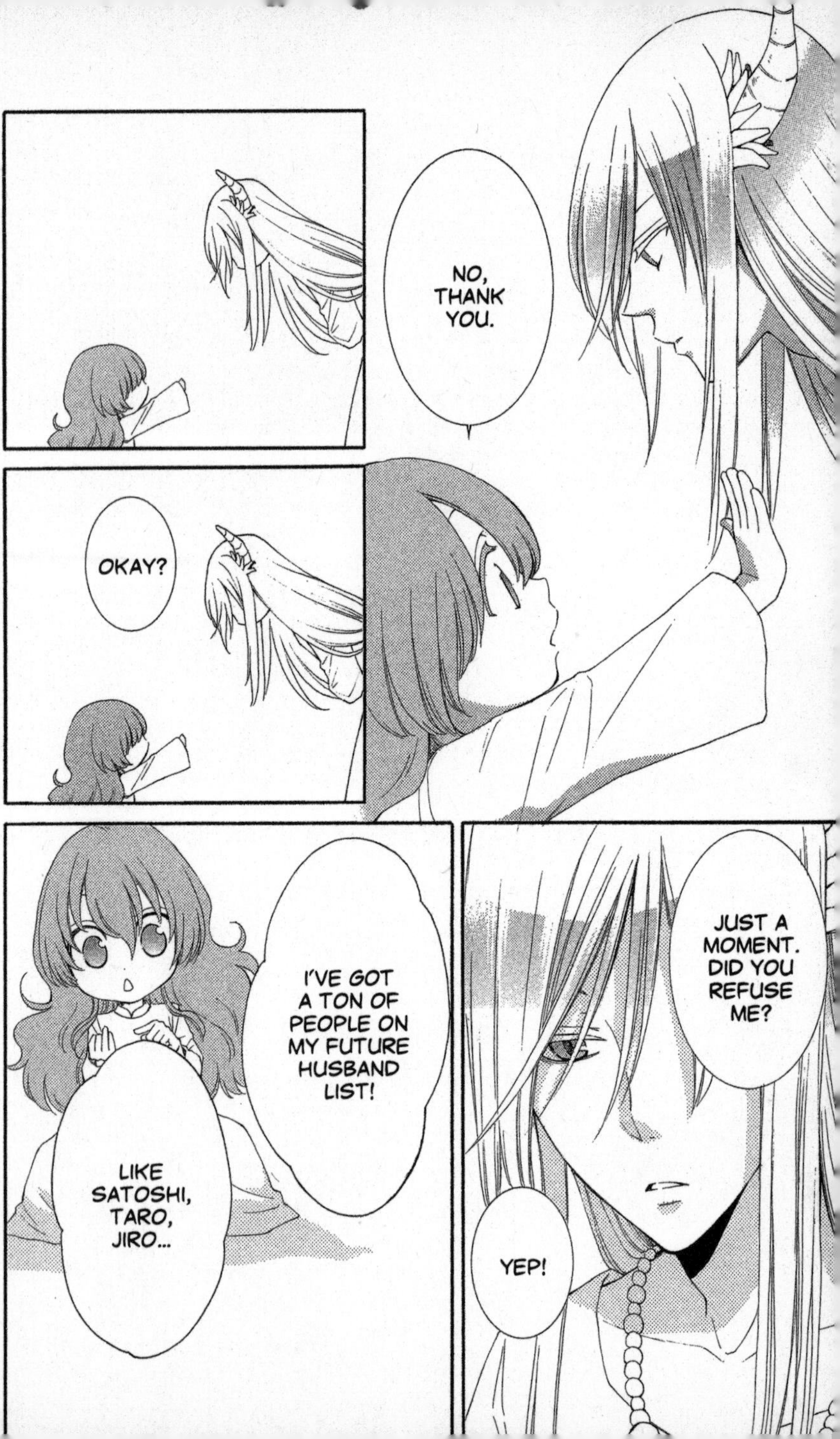
NO, THANK YOU.
OKAY?
JUST A MOMENT. DID YOU REFUSE ME?
YEP!
I'VE GOT A TON OF PEOPLE ON MY FUTURE HUSBAND LIST!
LIKE SATOSHI, TARO, JIRO...

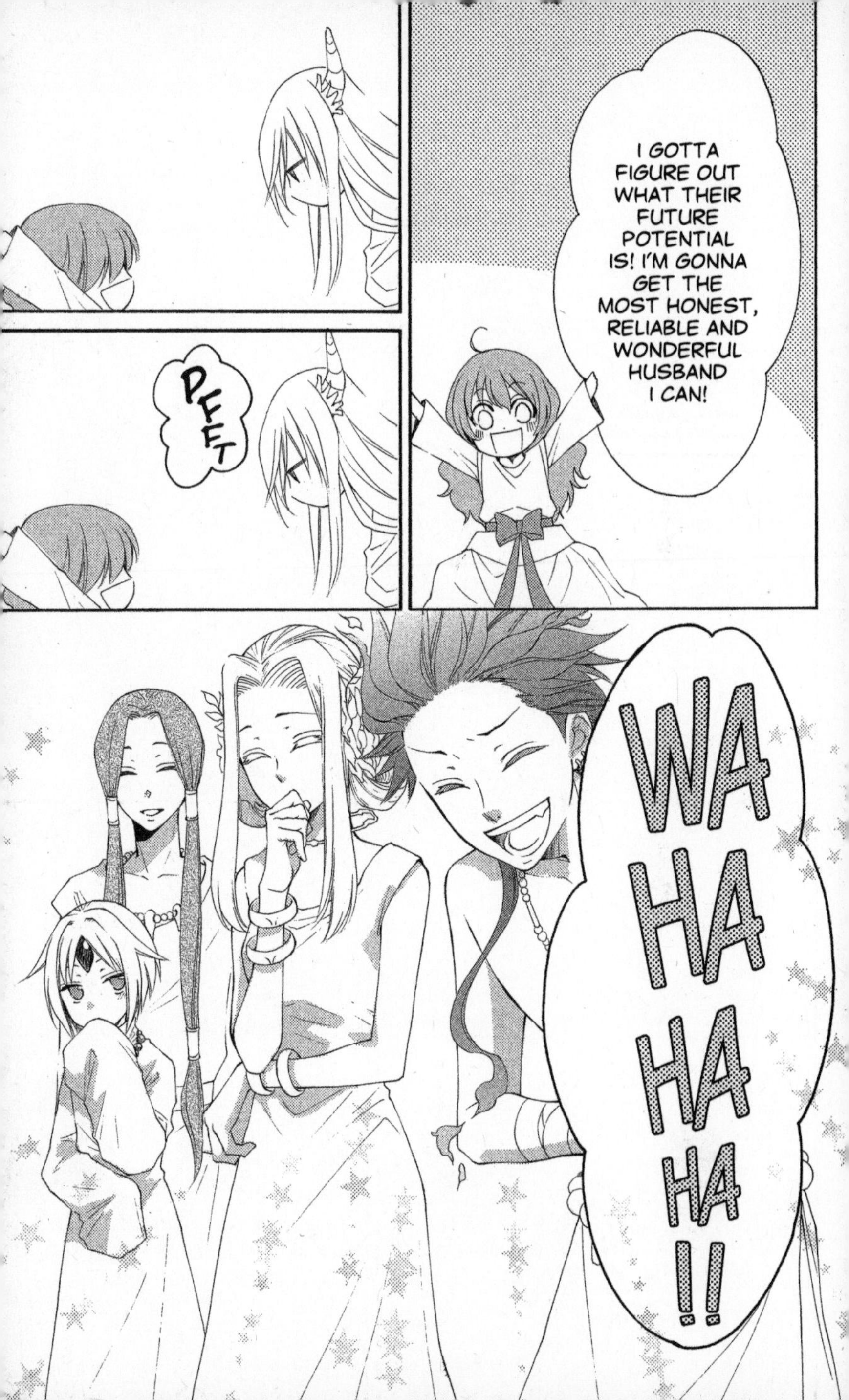
I GOTTA FIGURE OUT WHAT THEIR FUTURE POTENTIAL IS! I'M GONNA GET THE MOST HONEST, RELIABLE AND WONDERFUL HUSBAND I CAN!
PFFT
WA HA HA HA HA!!

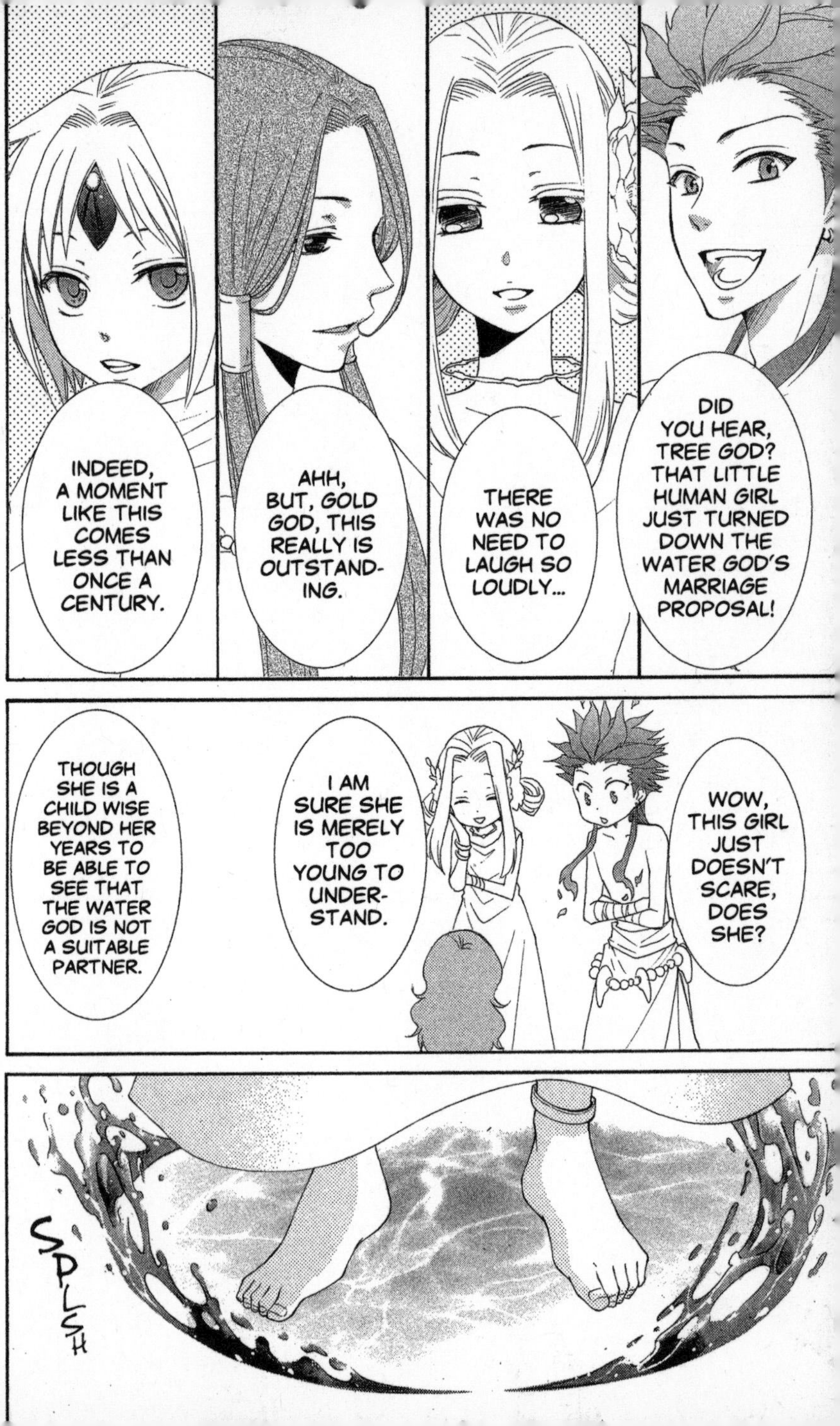
DID YOU HEAR, TREE GOD? THAT LITTLE HUMAN GIRL JUST TURNED DOWN THE WATER GOD'S MARRIAGE PROPOSAL!
THERE WAS NO NEED TO LAUGH SO LOUDLY...
AHH, BUT, GOLD GOD, THIS REALLY IS OUTSTAND-ING.
INDEED, A MOMENT LIKE THIS COMES LESS THAN ONCE A CENTURY.
WOW, THIS GIRL JUST DOESN'T SCARE, DOES SHE?
I AM SURE SHE IS MERELY TOO YOUNG TO UNDER-STAND.
THOUGH SHE IS A CHILD WISE BEYOND HER YEARS TO BE ABLE TO SEE THAT THE WATER GOD IS NOT A SUITABLE PARTNER.
SPLSH

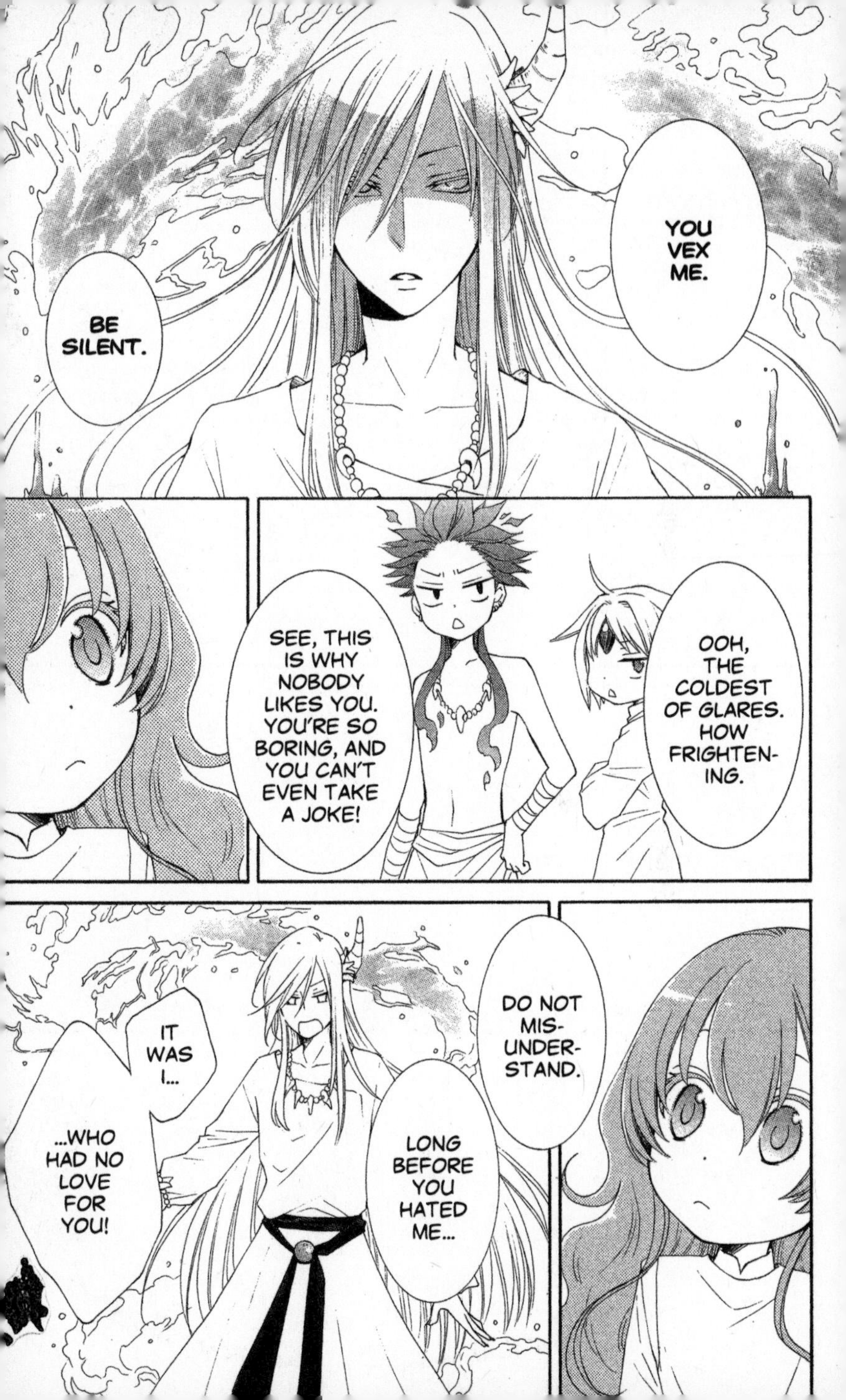
YOU VEX ME.
BE SILENT.
OOH, THE COLDEST OF GLARES. HOW FRIGHTEN-ING.
SEE, THIS IS WHY NOBODY LIKES YOU. YOU'RE SO BORING, AND YOU CAN'T EVEN TAKE A JOKE!
DO NOT MIS-UNDER-STAND.
LONG BEFORE YOU HATED ME...
IT WAS I...
...WHO HAD NO LOVE FOR YOU!

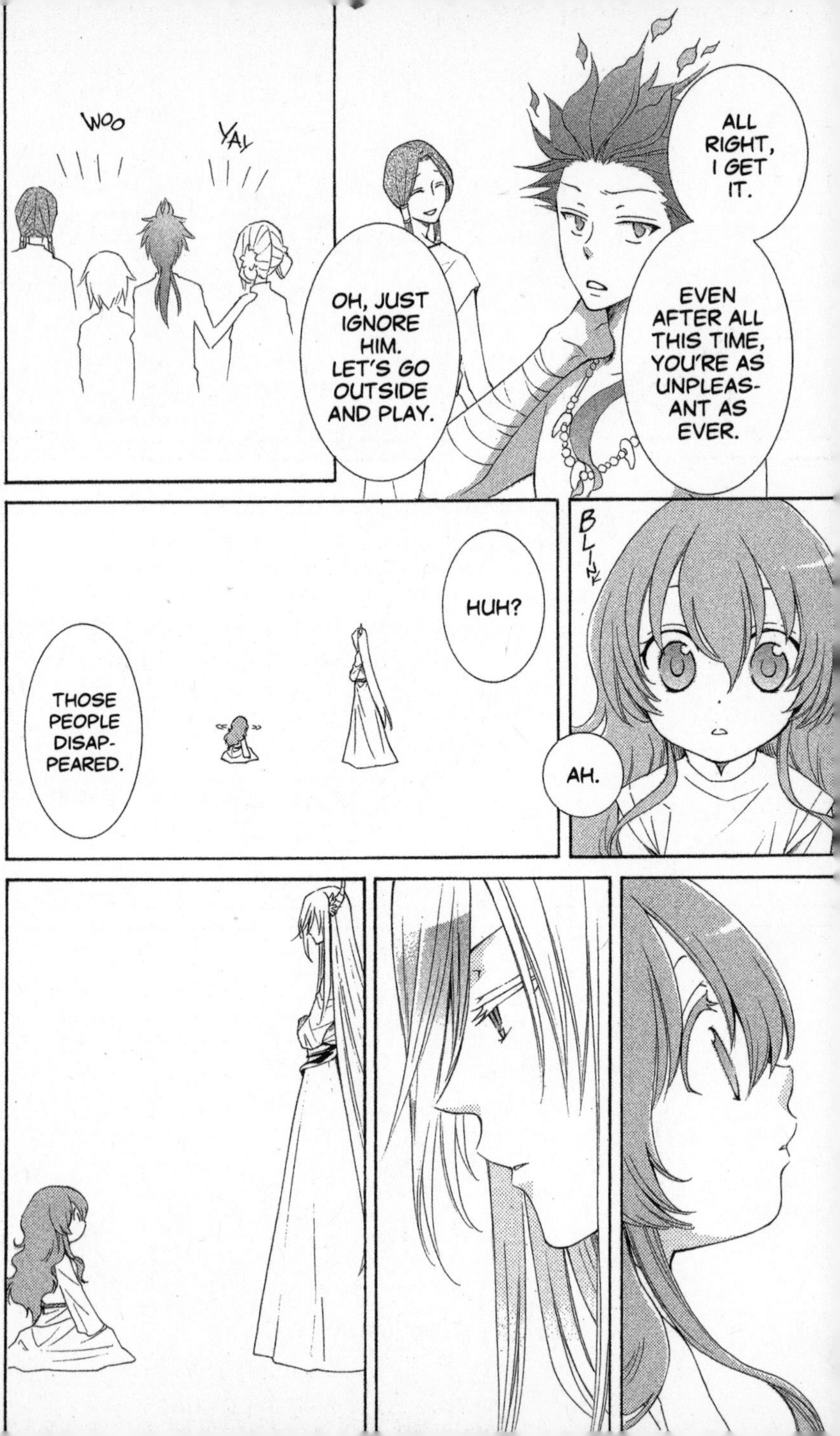
ALL RIGHT, I GET IT.
EVEN AFTER ALL THIS TIME, YOU'RE AS UNPLEAS-ANT AS EVER.
OH, JUST IGNORE HIM. LET'S GO OUTSIDE AND PLAY.
WOO
YAY
BLINK
AH.
HUH?
THOSE PEOPLE DISAP-PEARED.

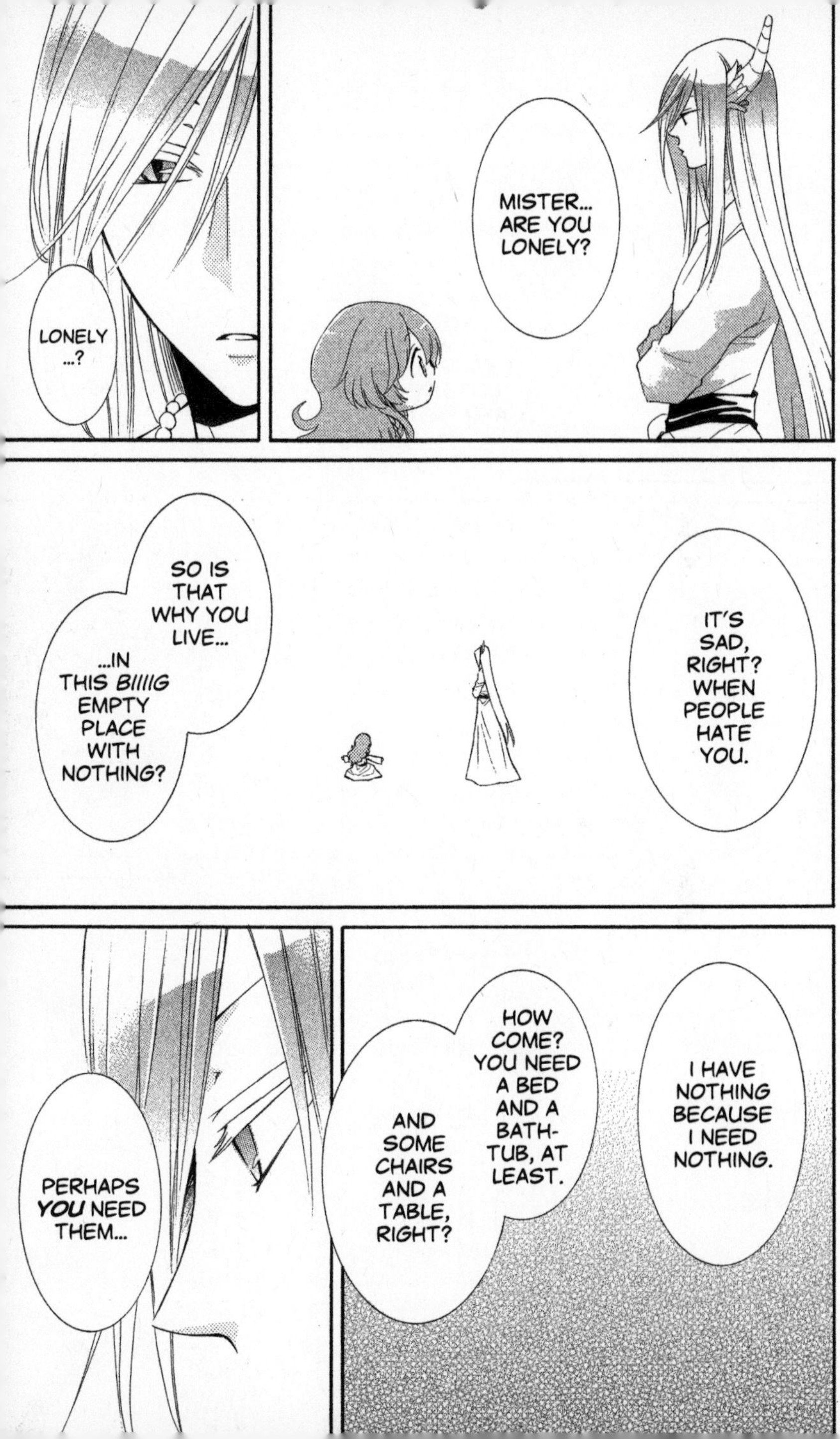
MISTER... ARE YOU LONELY?
LONELY ...?
IT'S SAD, RIGHT? WHEN PEOPLE HATE YOU.
SO IS THAT WHY YOU LIVE...
...IN THIS *BIIIIG* EMPTY PLACE WITH NOTHING?
I HAVE NOTHING BECAUSE I NEED NOTHING.
HOW COME? YOU NEED A BED AND A BATH-TUB, AT LEAST.
AND SOME CHAIRS AND A TABLE, RIGHT?
PERHAPS ***YOU*** NEED THEM...

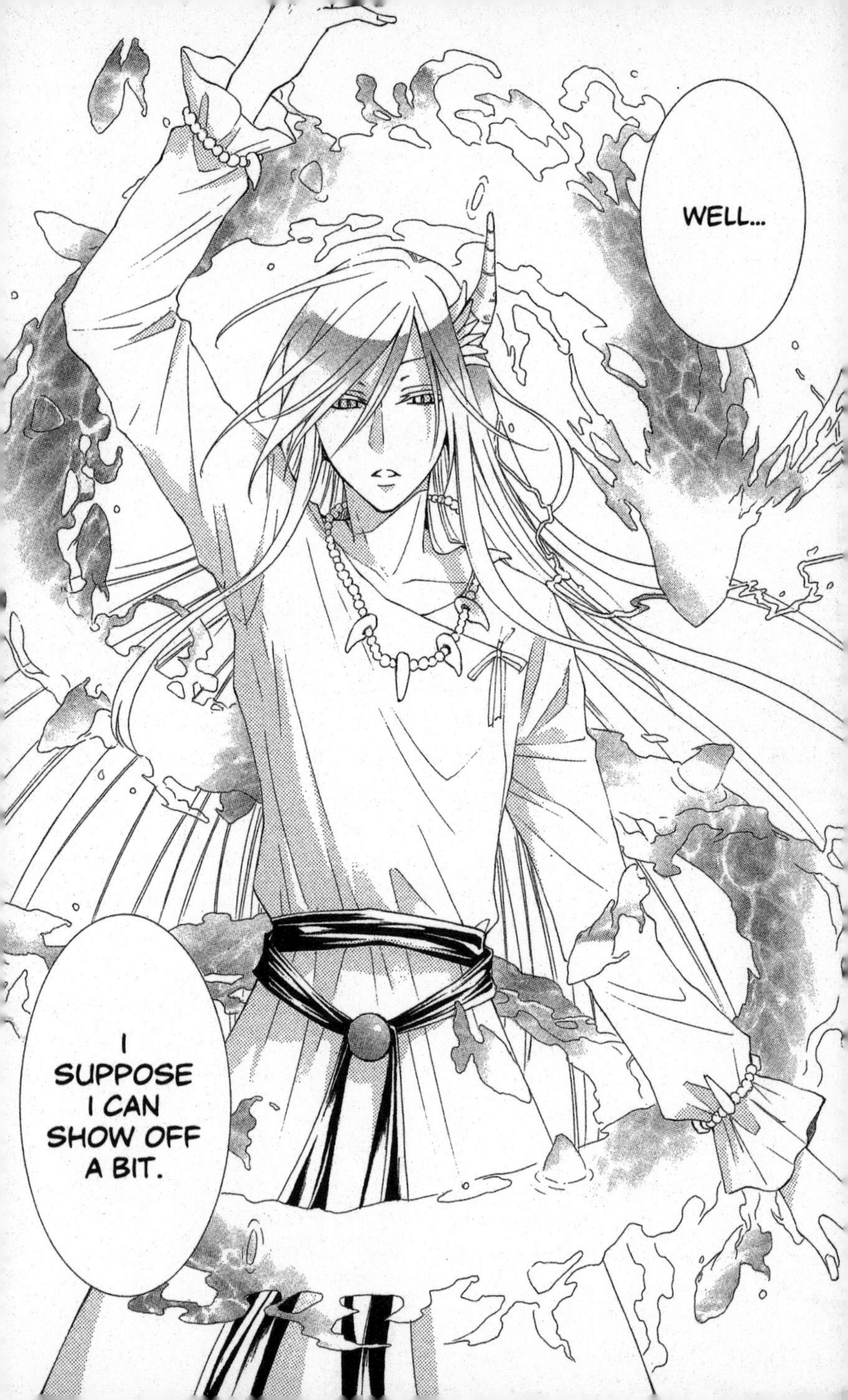
WELL...
I SUPPOSE I CAN SHOW OFF A BIT.

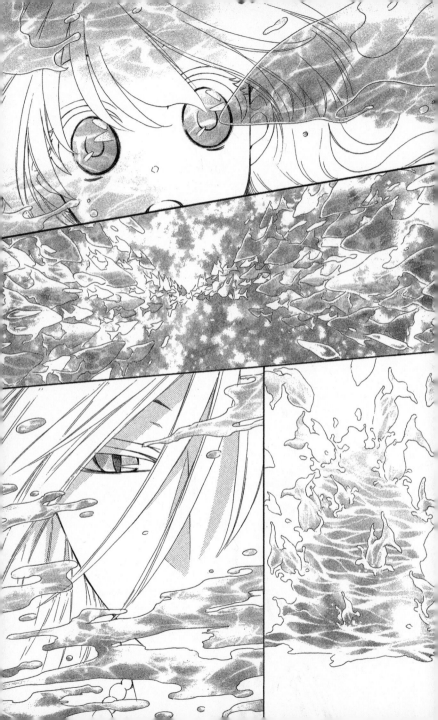

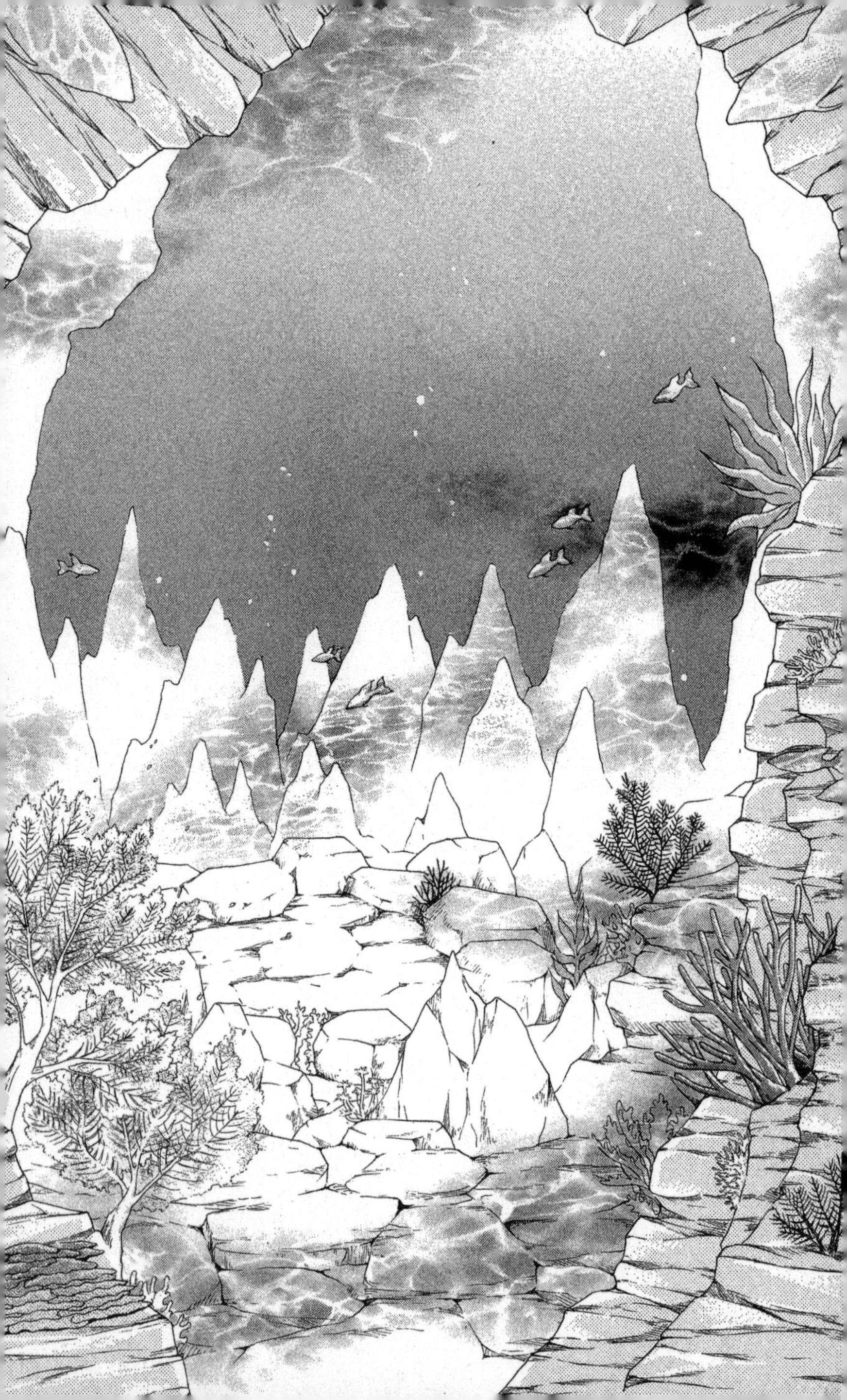

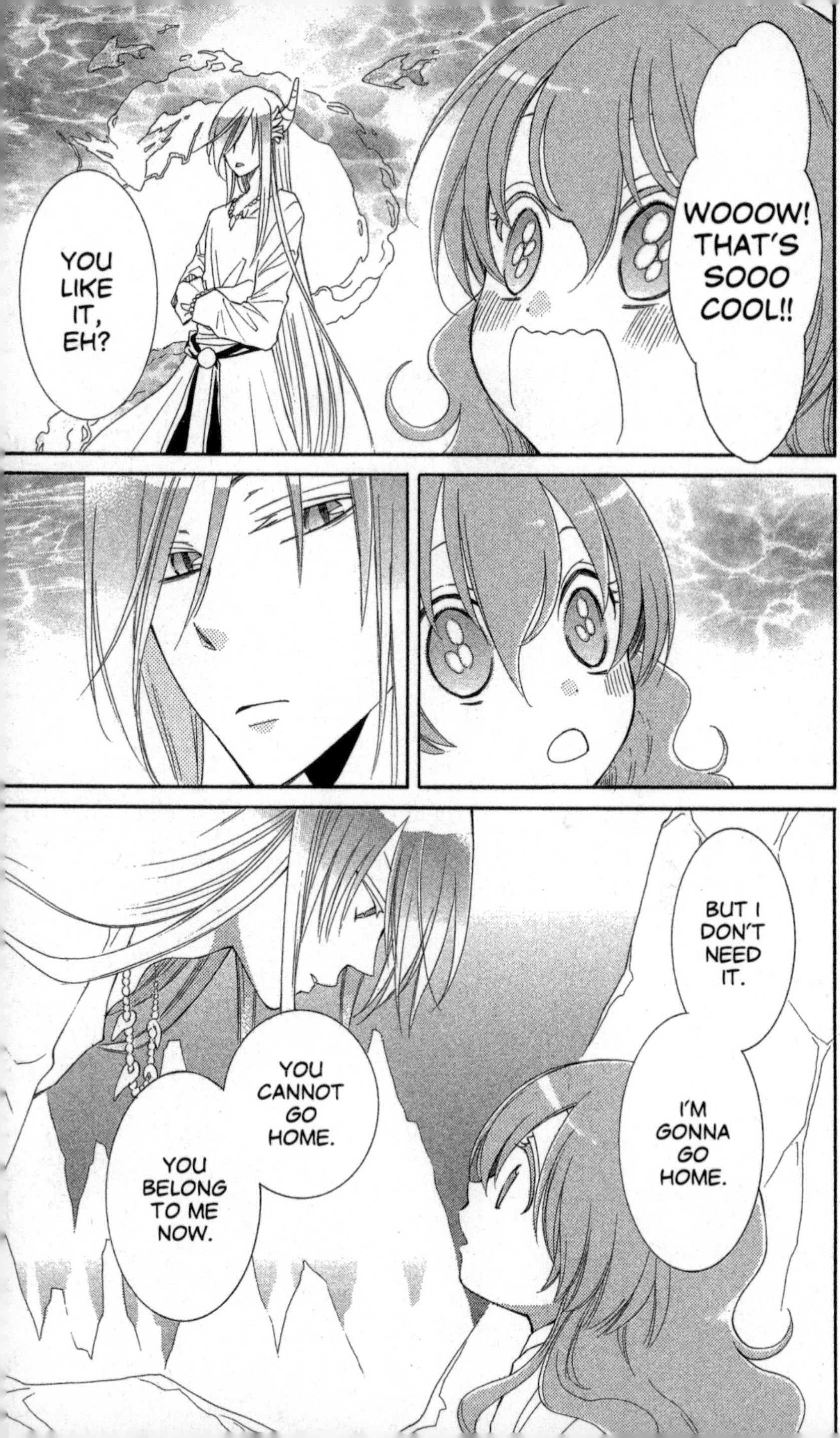
WOOOW! THAT'S SOOO COOL!!
YOU LIKE IT, EH?
BUT I DON'T NEED IT.
I'M GONNA GO HOME.
YOU CANNOT GO HOME.
YOU BELONG TO ME NOW.

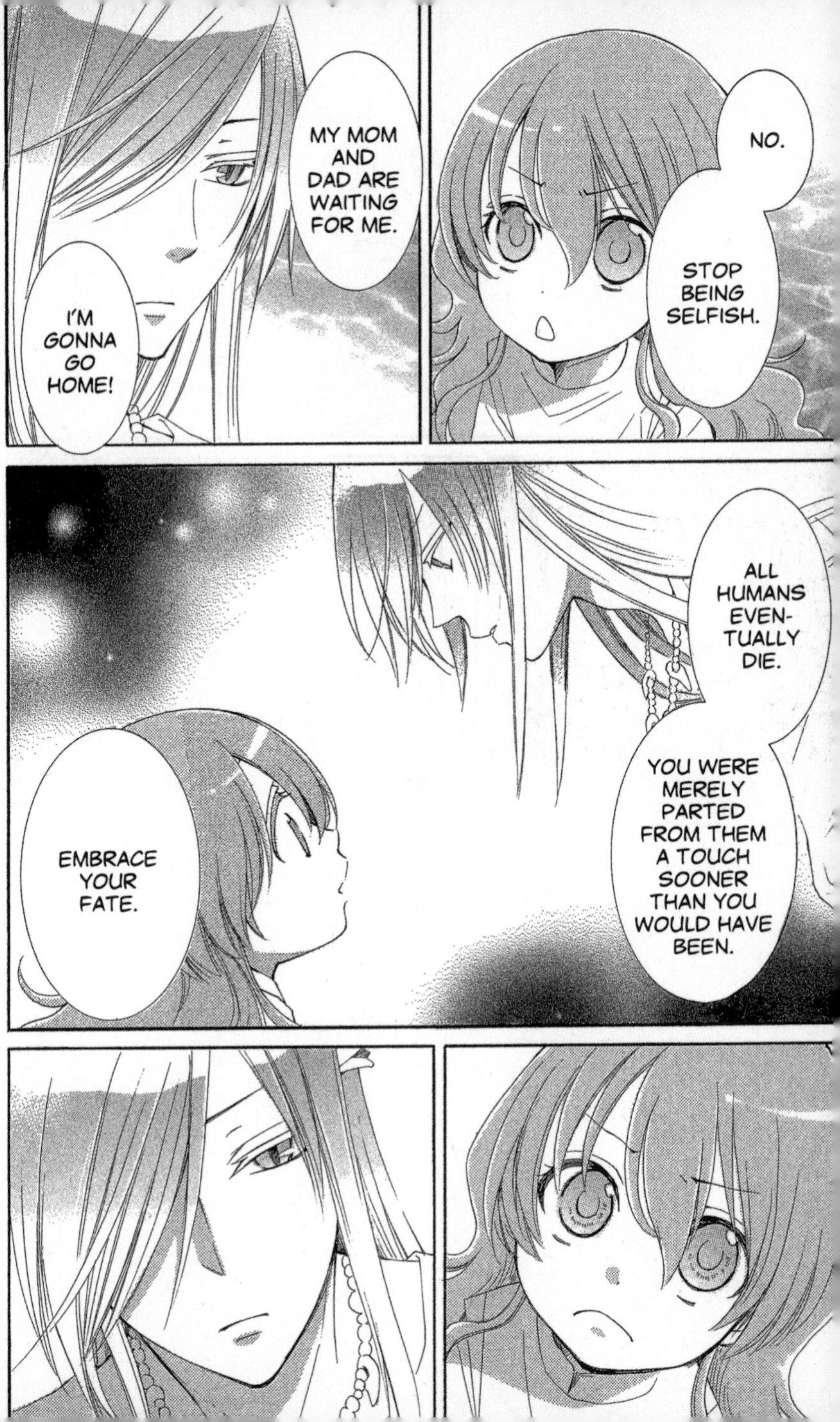
NO.
STOP BEING SELFISH.
MY MOM AND DAD ARE WAITING FOR ME.
I'M GONNA GO HOME!
ALL HUMANS EVEN-TUALLY DIE.
YOU WERE MERELY PARTED FROM THEM A TOUCH SOONER THAN YOU WOULD HAVE BEEN.
EMBRACE YOUR FATE.

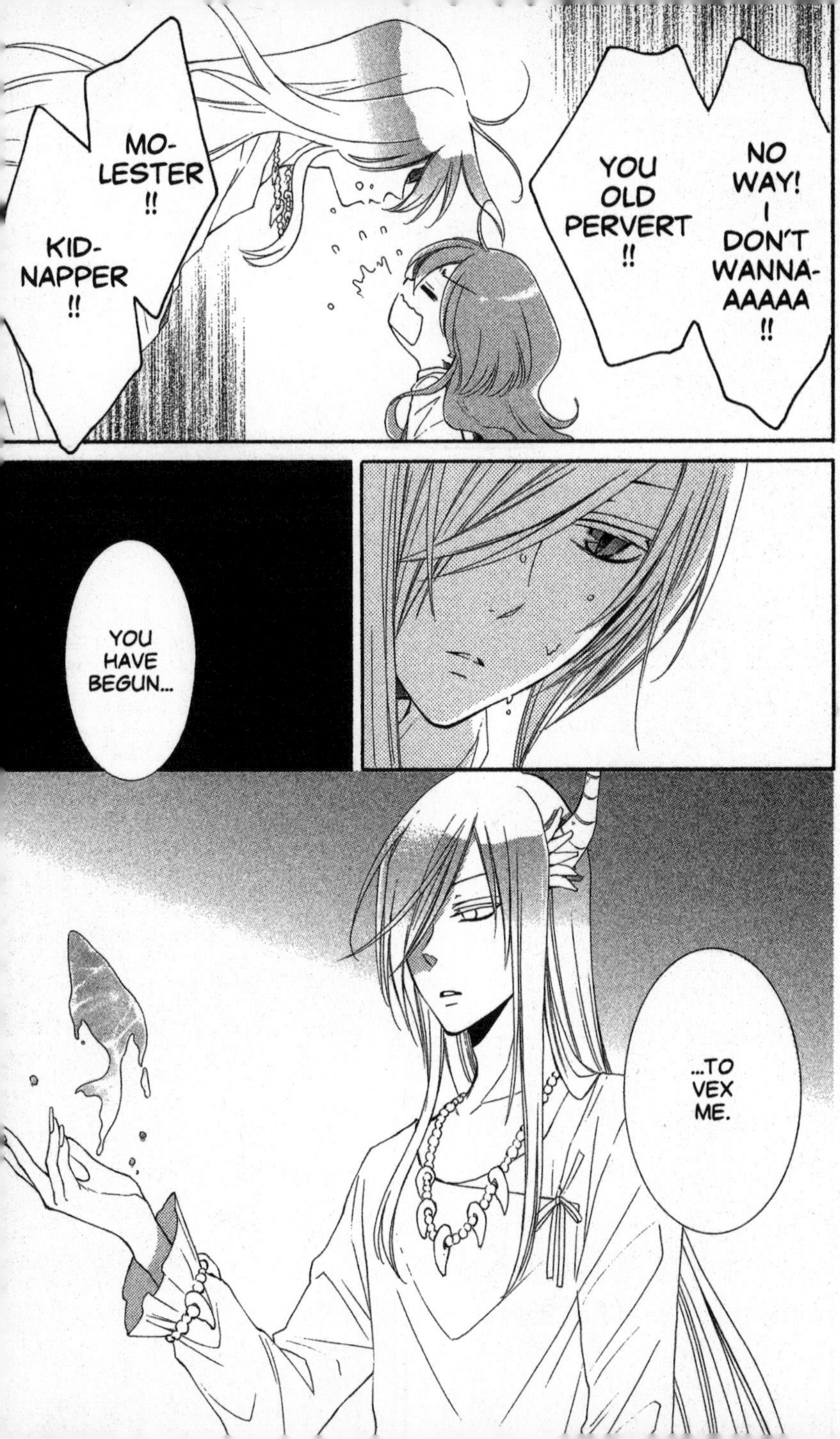
NO WAY! I DON'T WANNA-AAAAA!!
YOU OLD PERVERT!!
MO-LESTER!!
KID-NAPPER!!
YOU HAVE BEGUN...
...TO VEX ME.

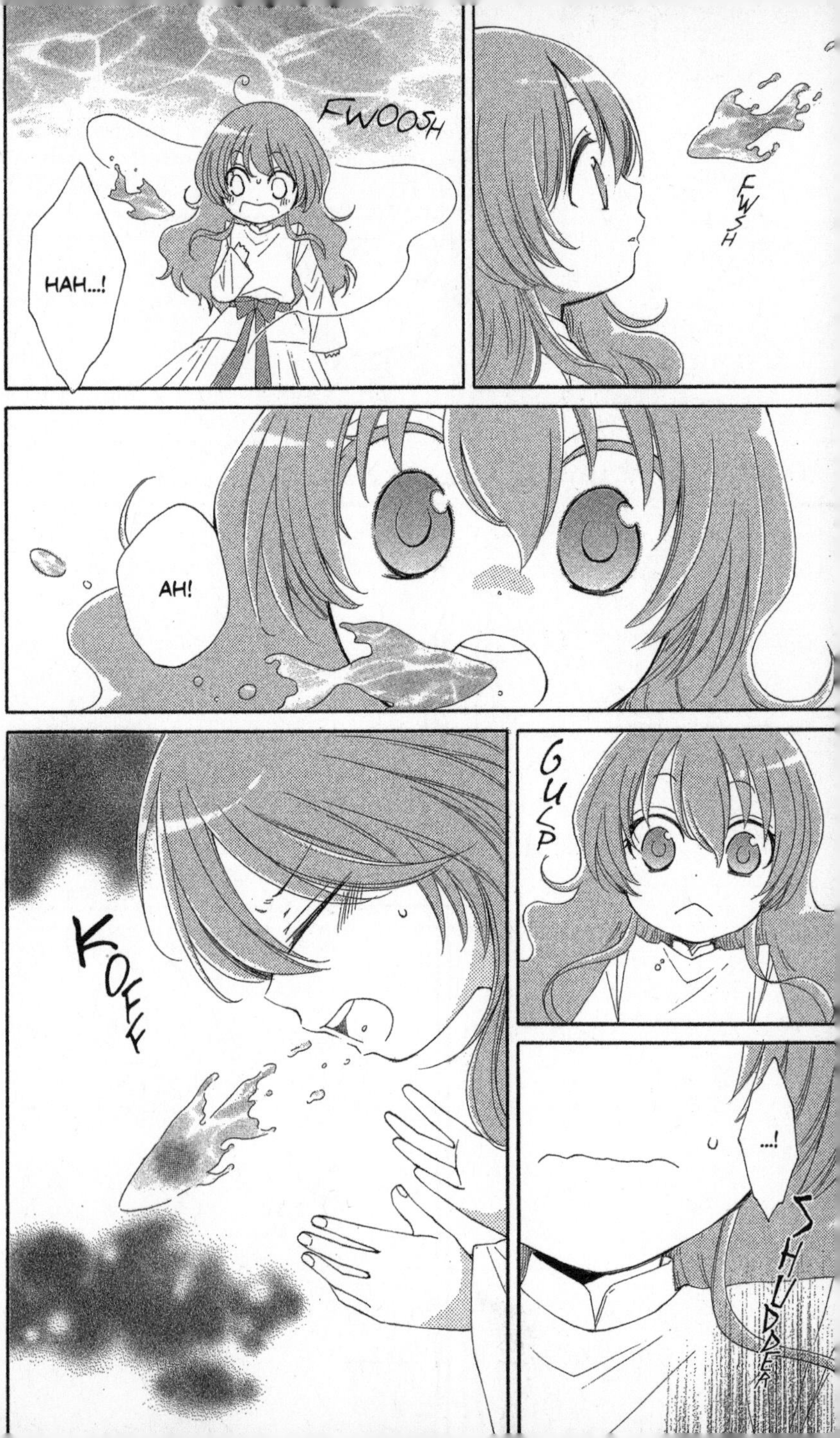
FWSH
FWOOSH
HAH...!
AH!
GULP
...!
SHUDDER
KOFF

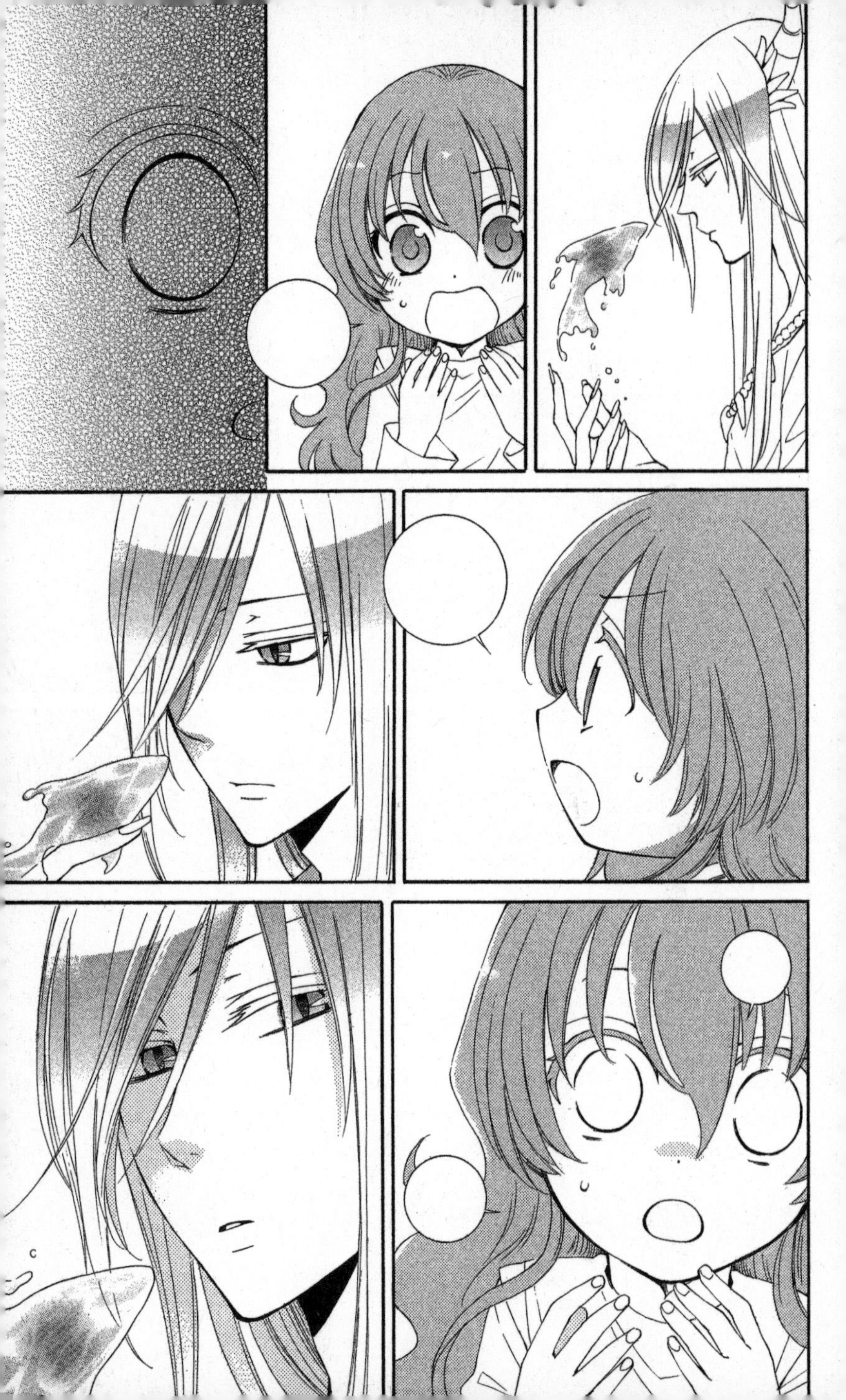

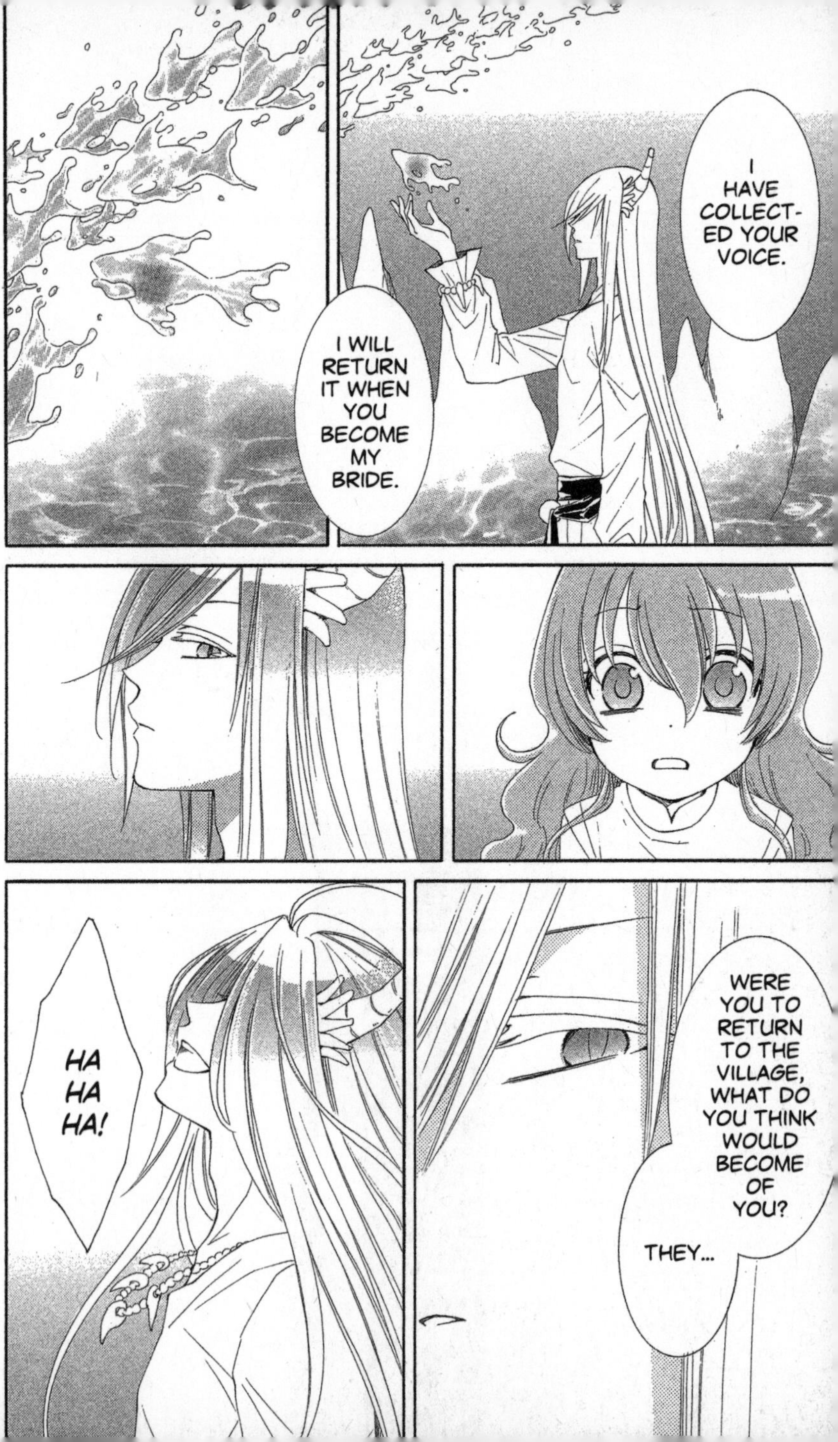
I HAVE COLLECTED YOUR VOICE.
I WILL RETURN IT WHEN YOU BECOME MY BRIDE.
WERE YOU TO RETURN TO THE VILLAGE, WHAT DO YOU THINK WOULD BECOME OF YOU?
THEY...
HA HA HA!

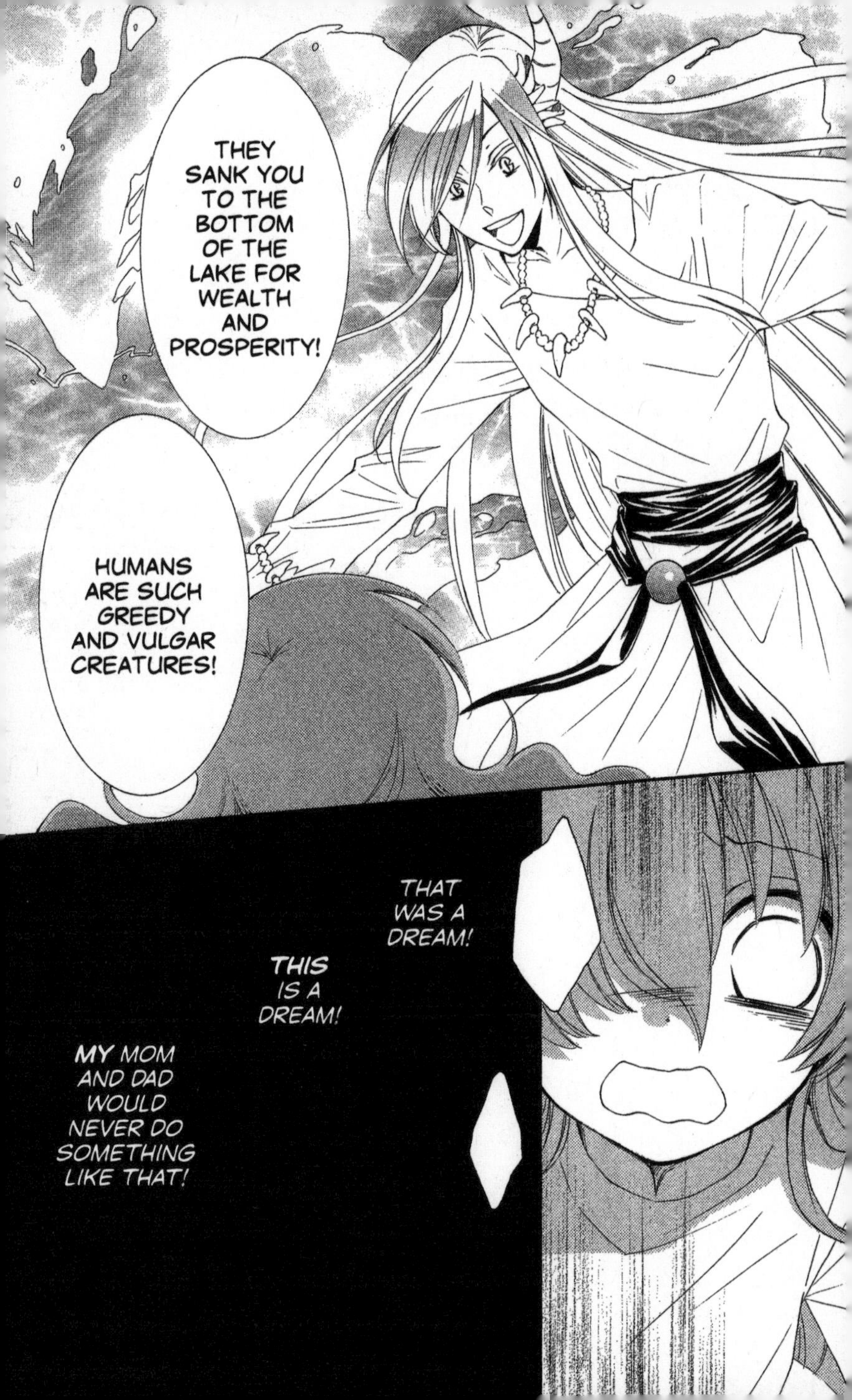
THEY SANK YOU TO THE BOTTOM OF THE LAKE FOR WEALTH AND PROSPERITY!
HUMANS ARE SUCH GREEDY AND VULGAR CREATURES!
THAT WAS A DREAM!
THIS IS A DREAM!
MY MOM AND DAD WOULD NEVER DO SOMETHING LIKE THAT!

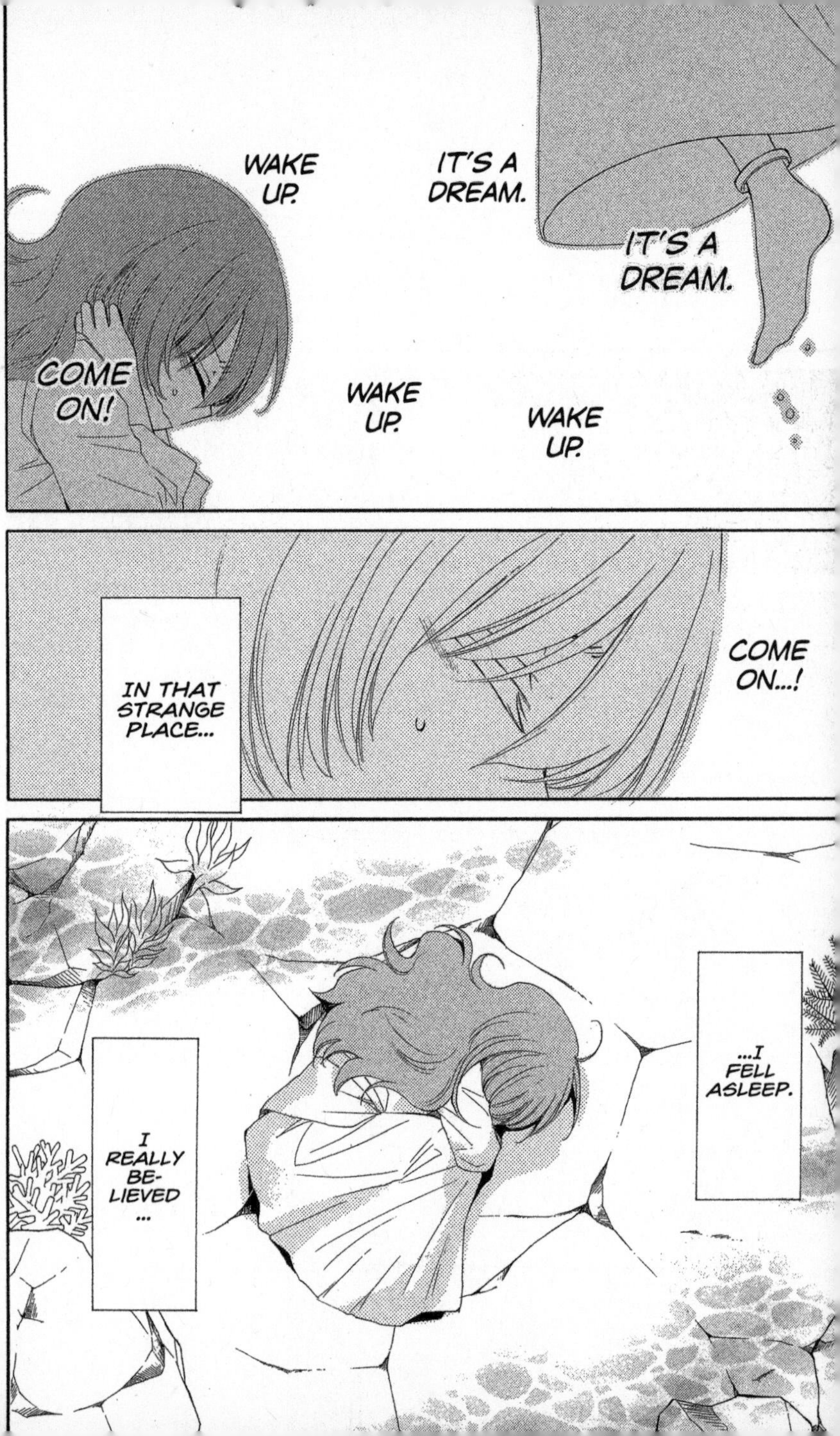
IT'S A DREAM.
IT'S A DREAM.
WAKE UP.
WAKE UP.
WAKE UP.
COME ON!
COME ON...!
IN THAT STRANGE PLACE...
...I FELL ASLEEP.
I REALLY BE- LIEVED ...

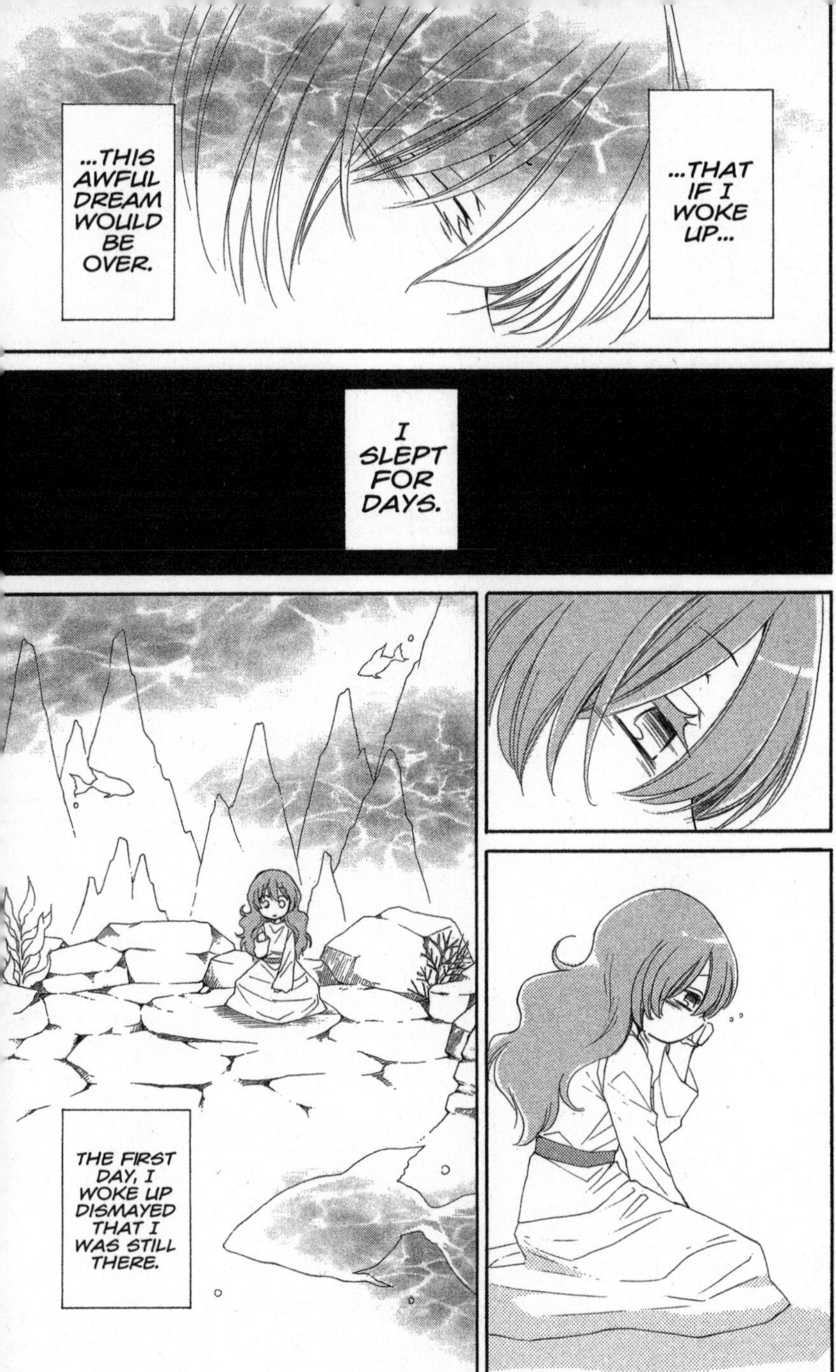
...THAT IF I WOKE UP...
...THIS AWFUL DREAM WOULD BE OVER.
I SLEPT FOR DAYS.
THE FIRST DAY, I WOKE UP DISMAYED THAT I WAS STILL THERE.

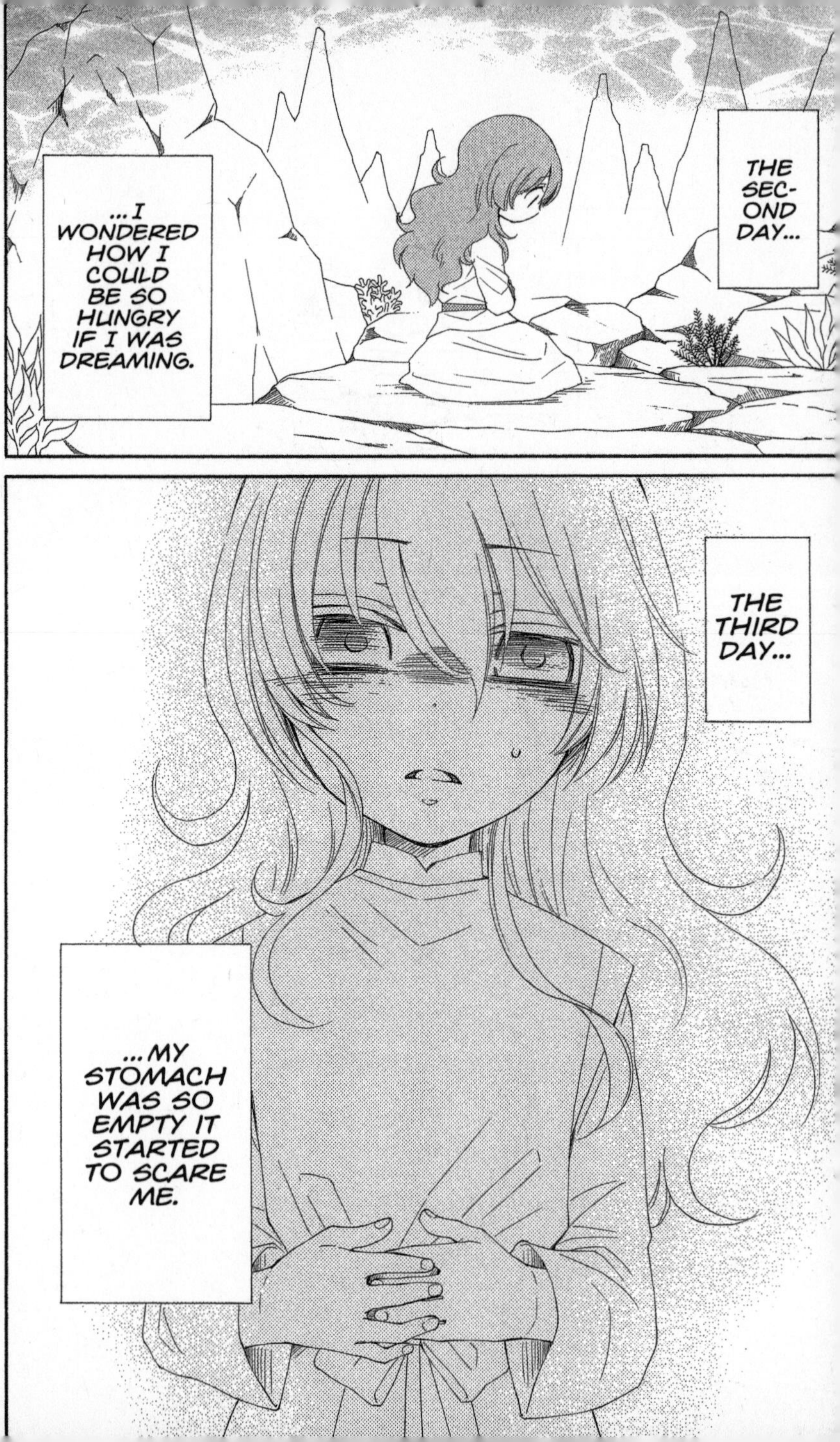
THE SEC-OND DAY...
...I WONDERED HOW I COULD BE SO HUNGRY IF I WAS DREAMING.
THE THIRD DAY...
...MY STOMACH WAS SO EMPTY IT STARTED TO SCARE ME.

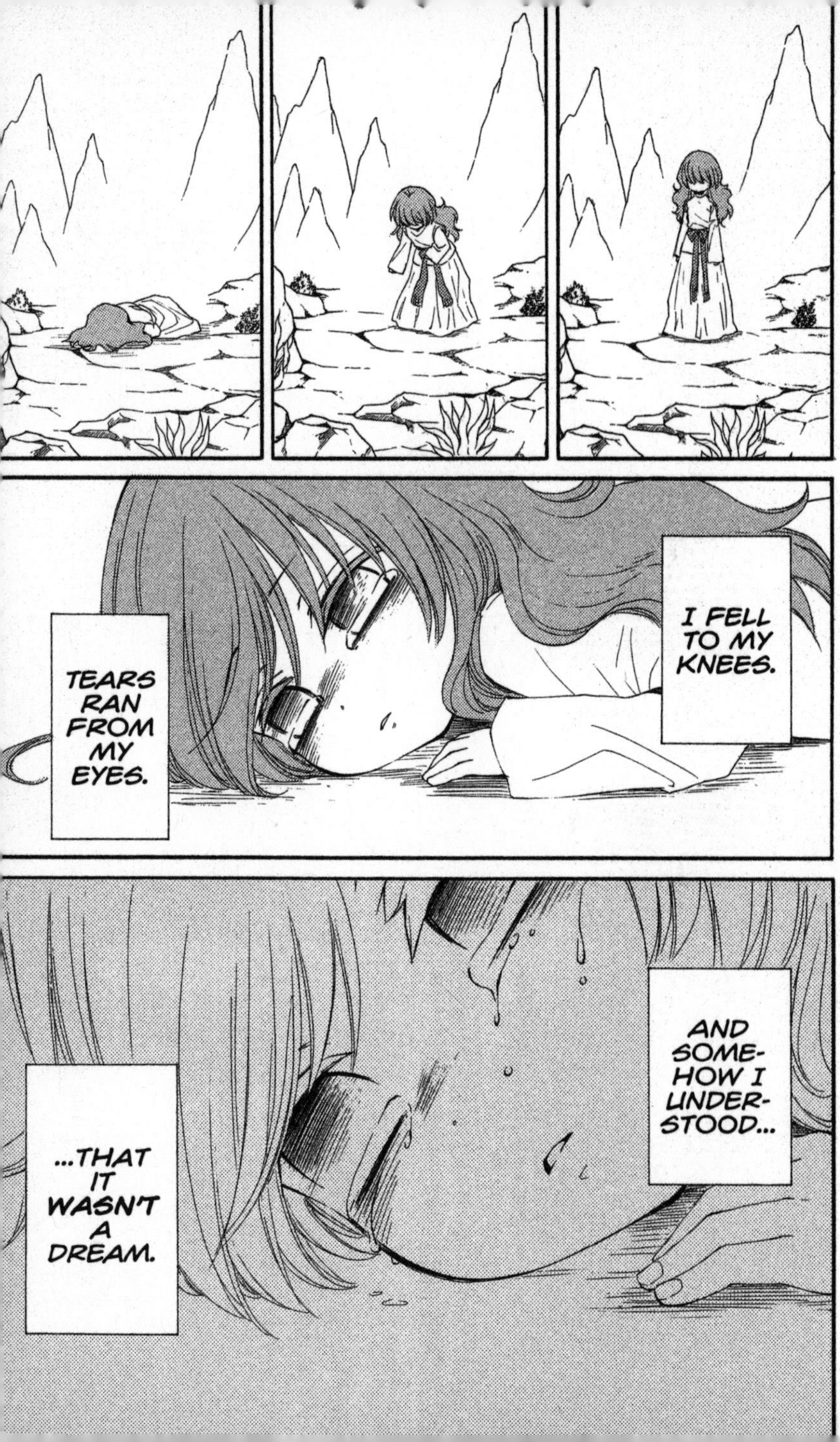
I FELL TO MY KNEES.
TEARS RAN FROM MY EYES.
AND SOME-HOW I UNDER-STOOD...
...THAT IT WASN'T A DREAM.

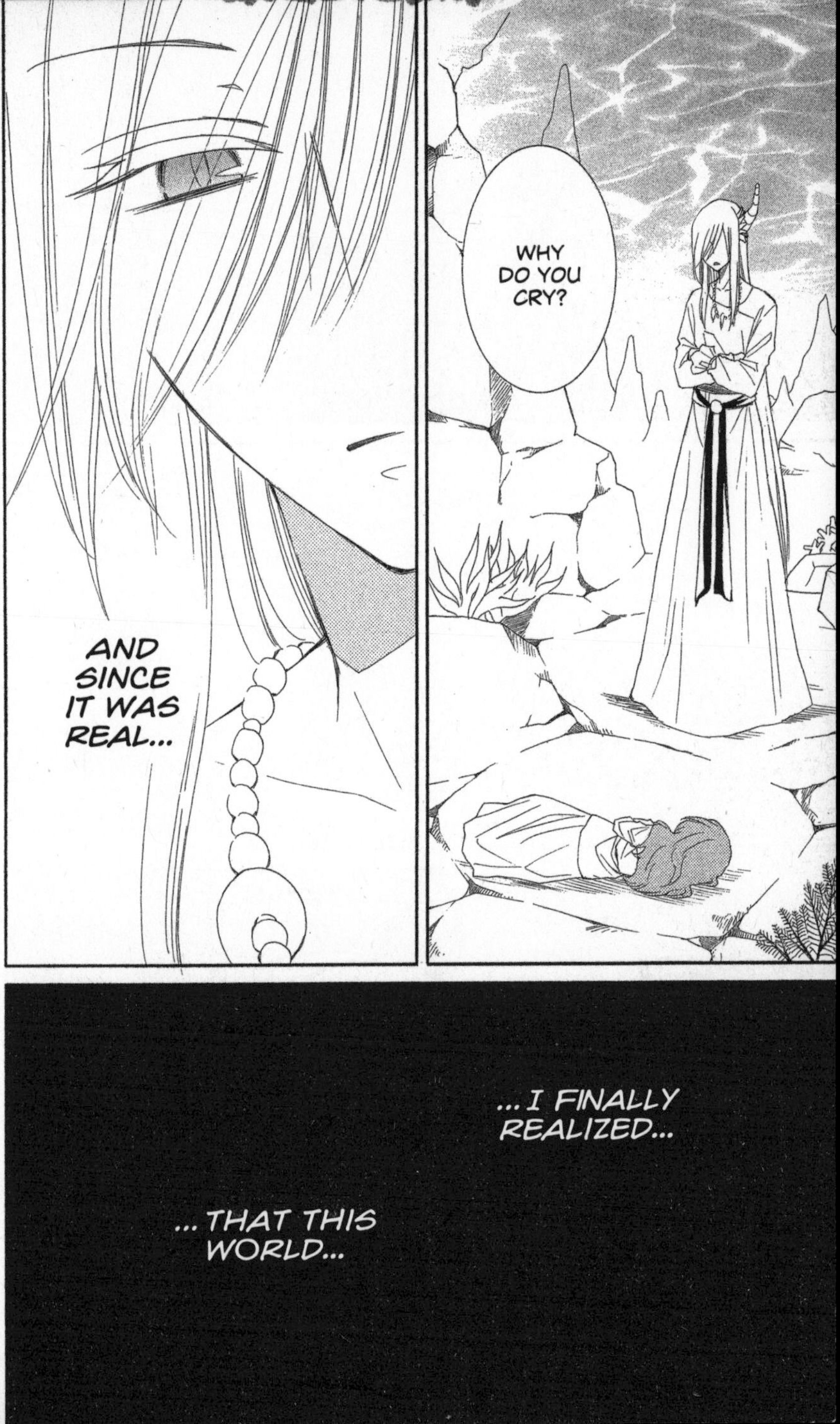
WHY DO YOU CRY?
AND SINCE IT WAS REAL...
...I FINALLY REALIZED...
...THAT THIS WORLD...

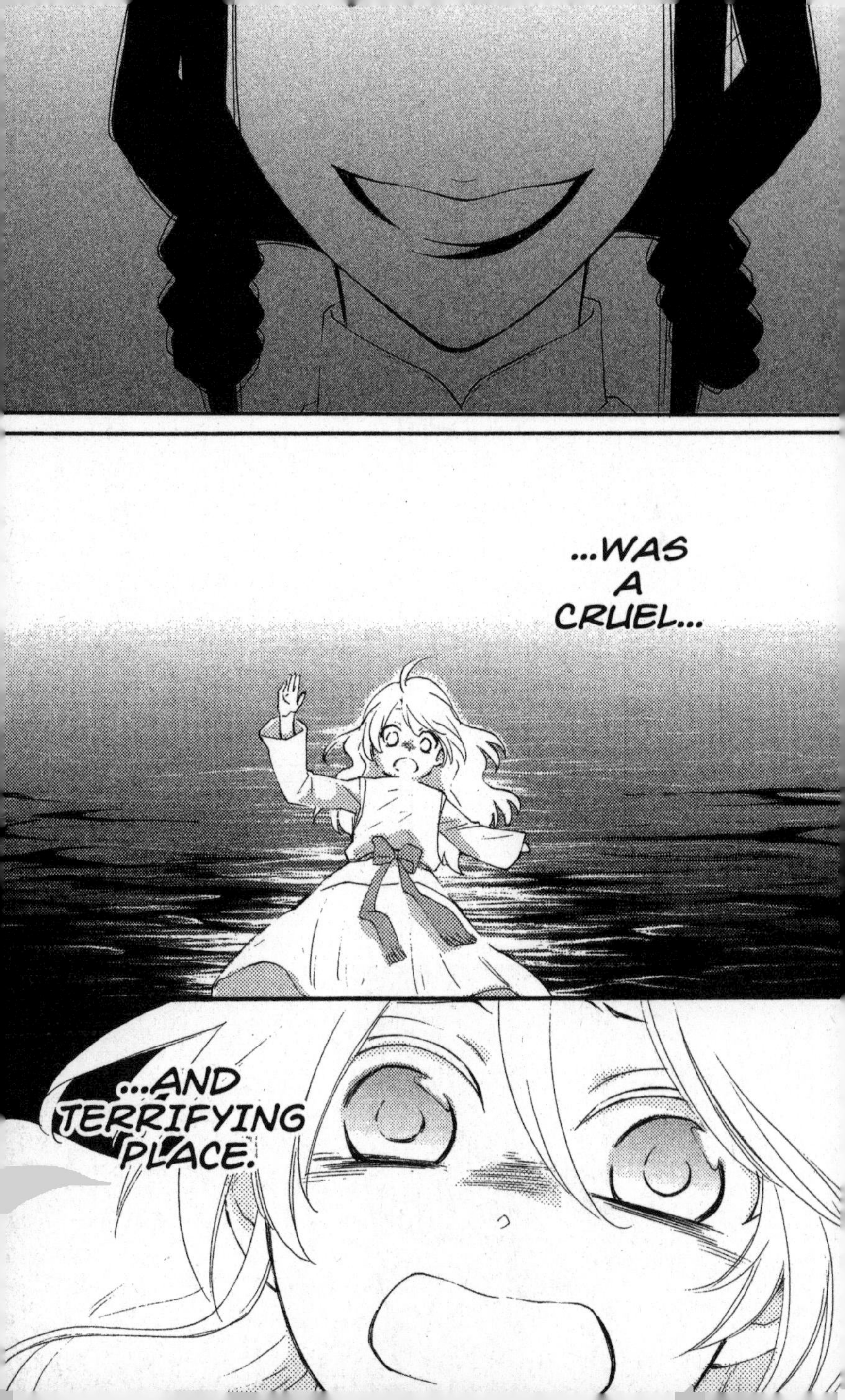
...WAS A CRUEL...
...AND TERRIFYING PLACE.

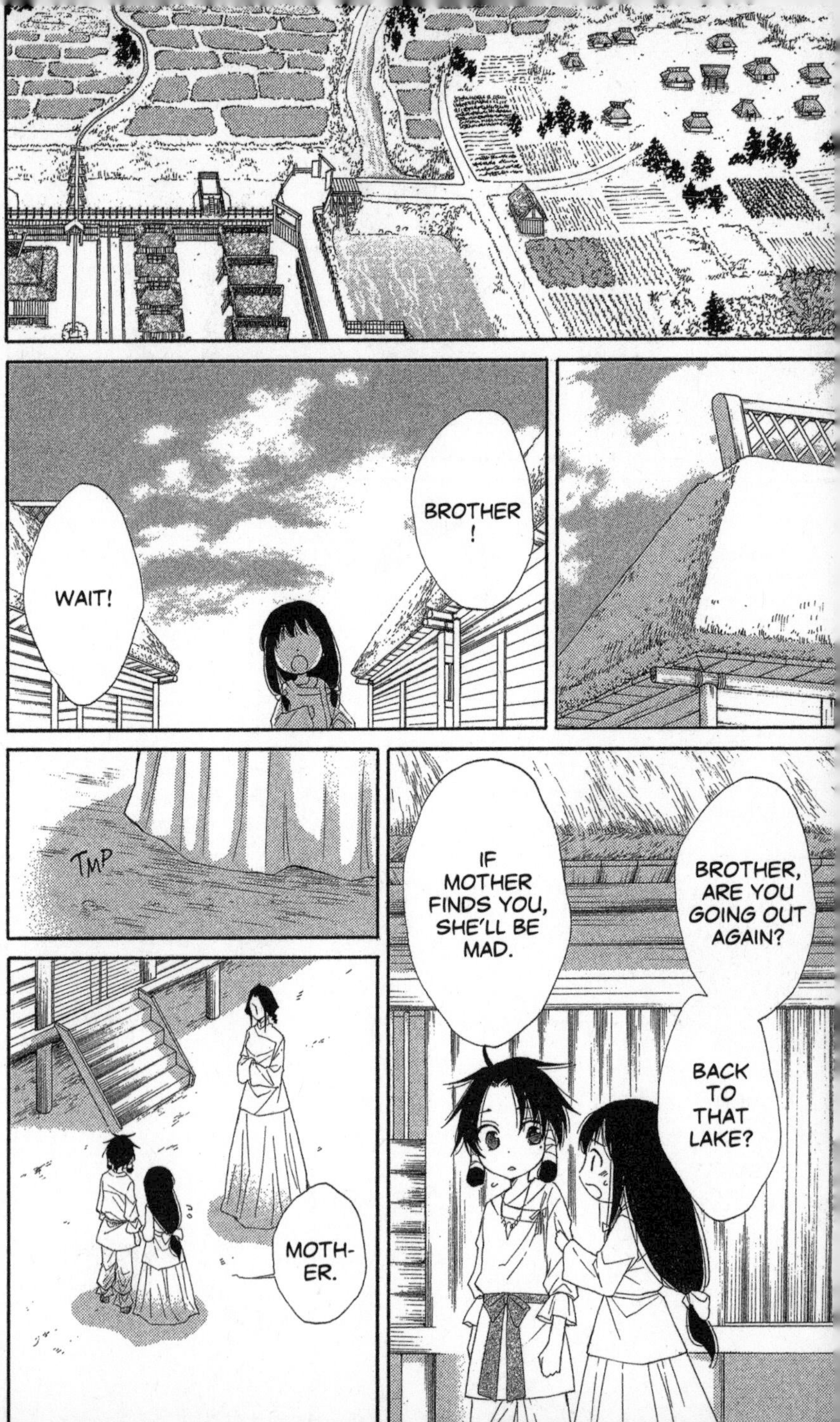
BROTHER!
WAIT!
BROTHER, ARE YOU GOING OUT AGAIN?
BACK TO THAT LAKE?
IF MOTHER FINDS YOU, SHE'LL BE MAD.
TMP
MOTH-ER.

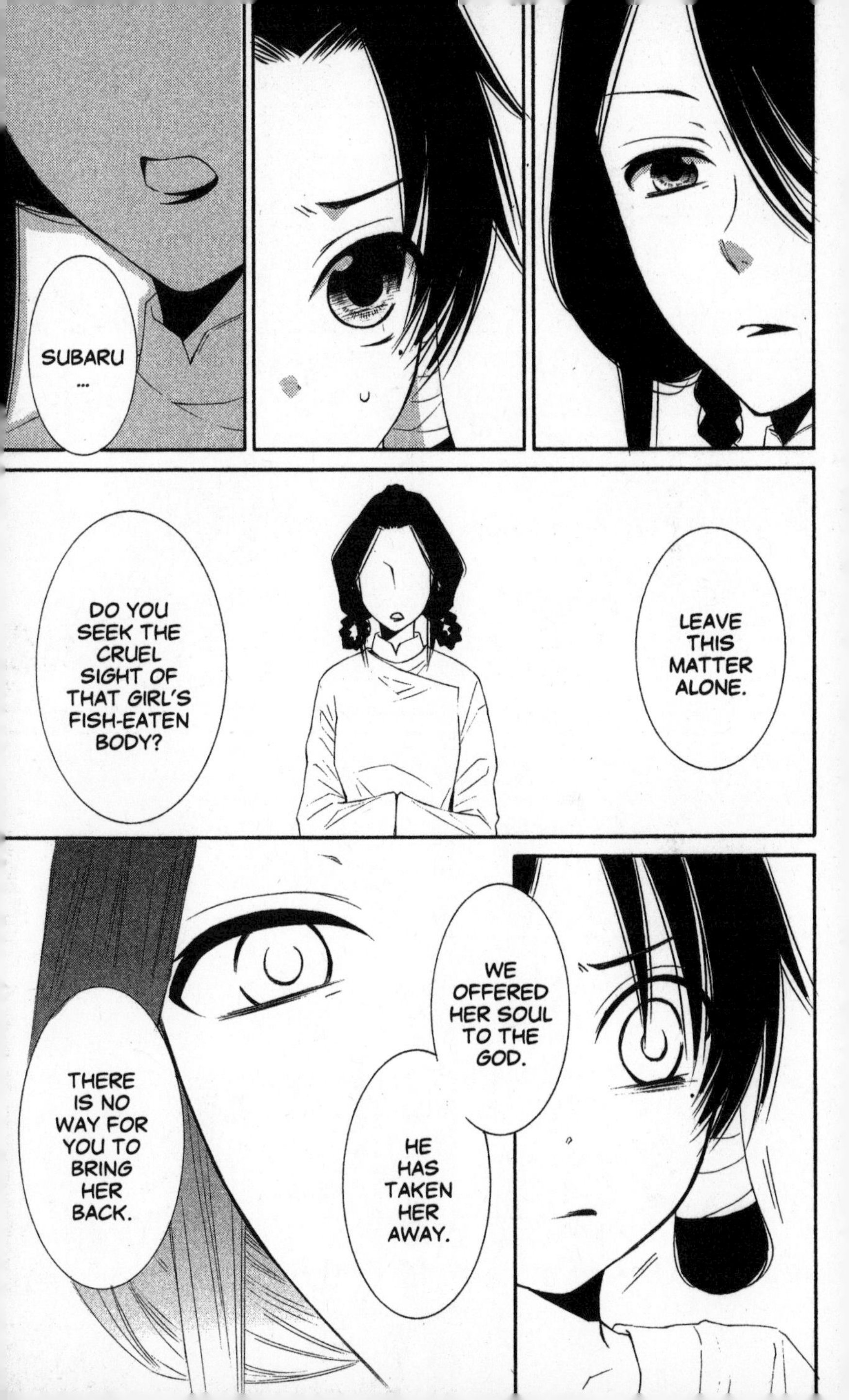
SUBARU ...
LEAVE THIS MATTER ALONE.
DO YOU SEEK THE CRUEL SIGHT OF THAT GIRL'S FISH-EATEN BODY?
WE OFFERED HER SOUL TO THE GOD.
HE HAS TAKEN HER AWAY.
THERE IS NO WAY FOR YOU TO BRING HER BACK.

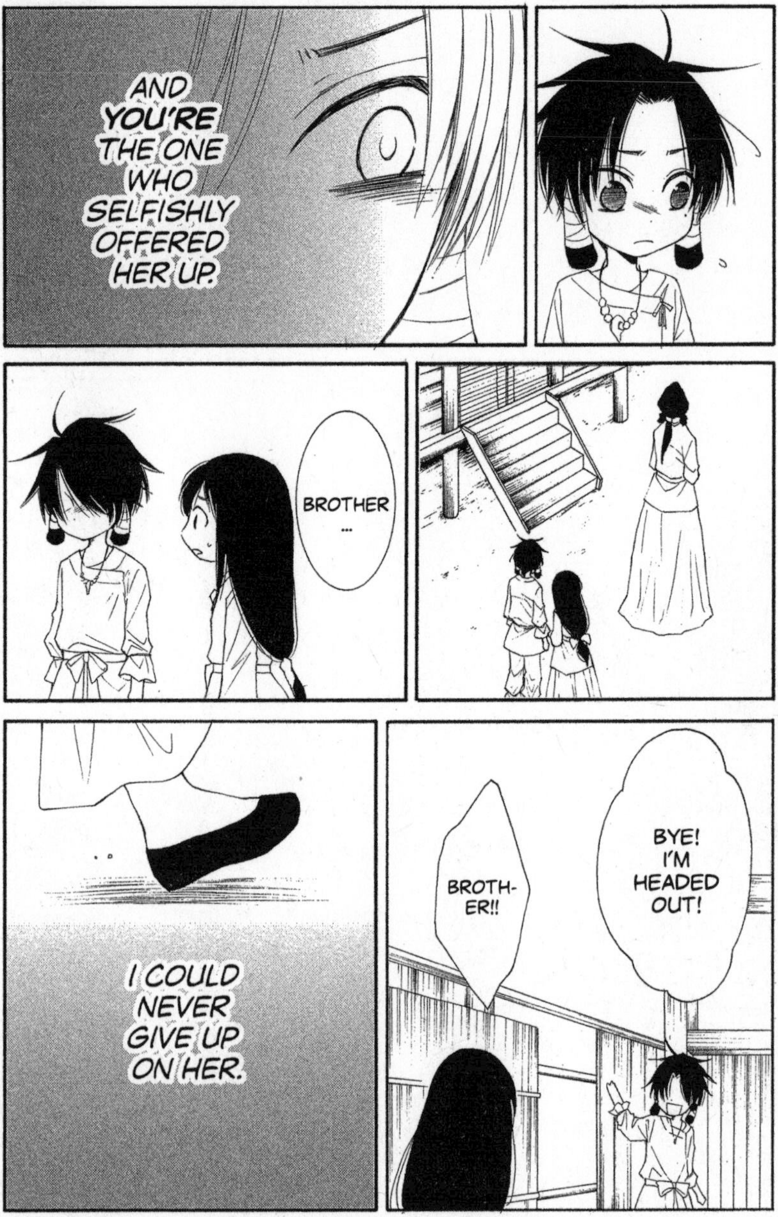
AND YOU'RE THE ONE WHO SELFISHLY OFFERED HER UP.
BROTHER...
BYE! I'M HEADED OUT!
BROTH-ER!!
I COULD NEVER GIVE UP ON HER.

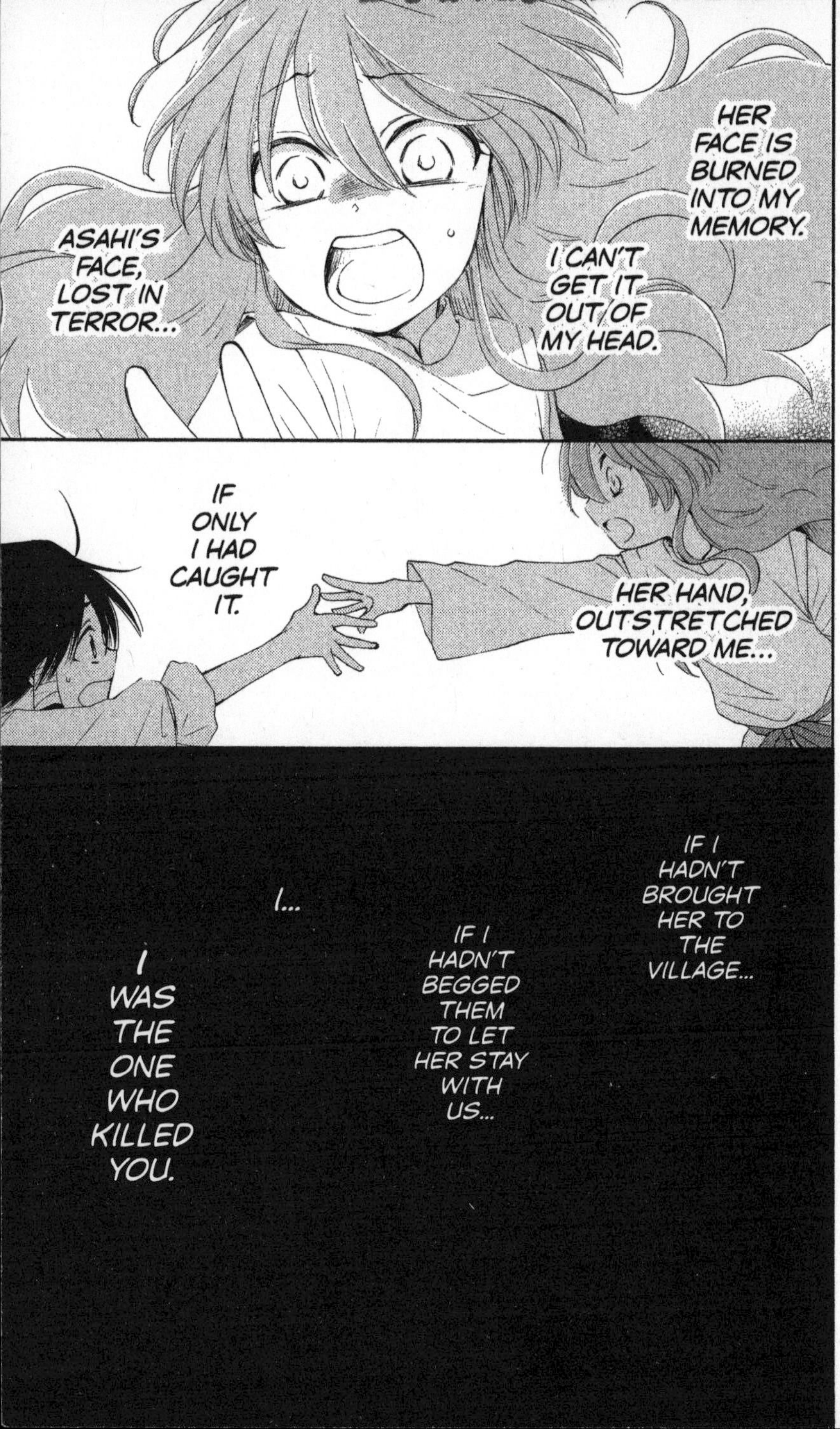
HER FACE IS BURNED INTO MY MEMORY.
I CAN'T GET IT OUT OF MY HEAD.
ASAHI'S FACE, LOST IN TERROR...
HER HAND, OUTSTRETCHED TOWARD ME...
IF ONLY I HAD CAUGHT IT.
IF I HADN'T BROUGHT HER TO THE VILLAGE...
IF I HADN'T BEGGED THEM TO LET HER STAY WITH US...
I...
I WAS THE ONE WHO KILLED YOU.

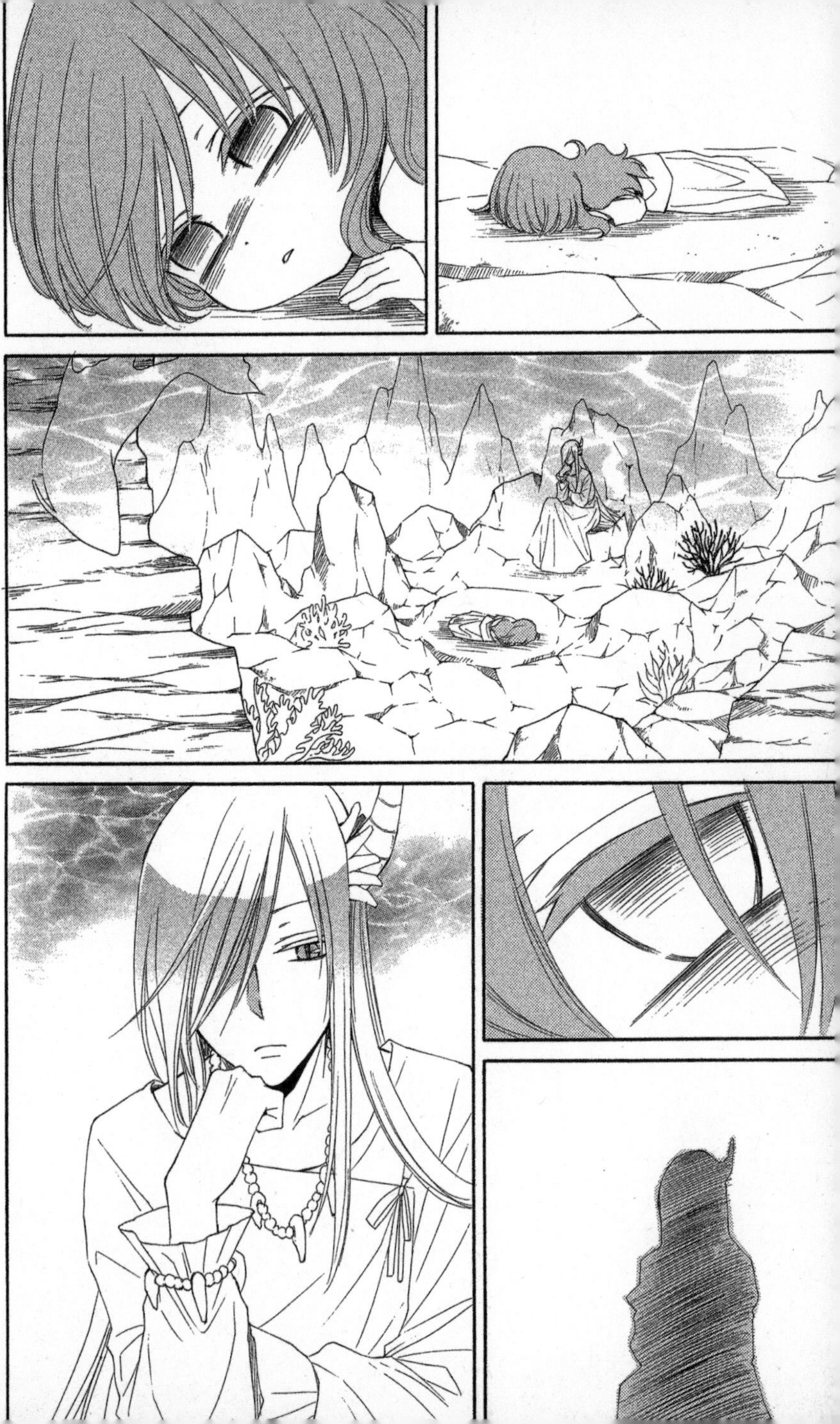

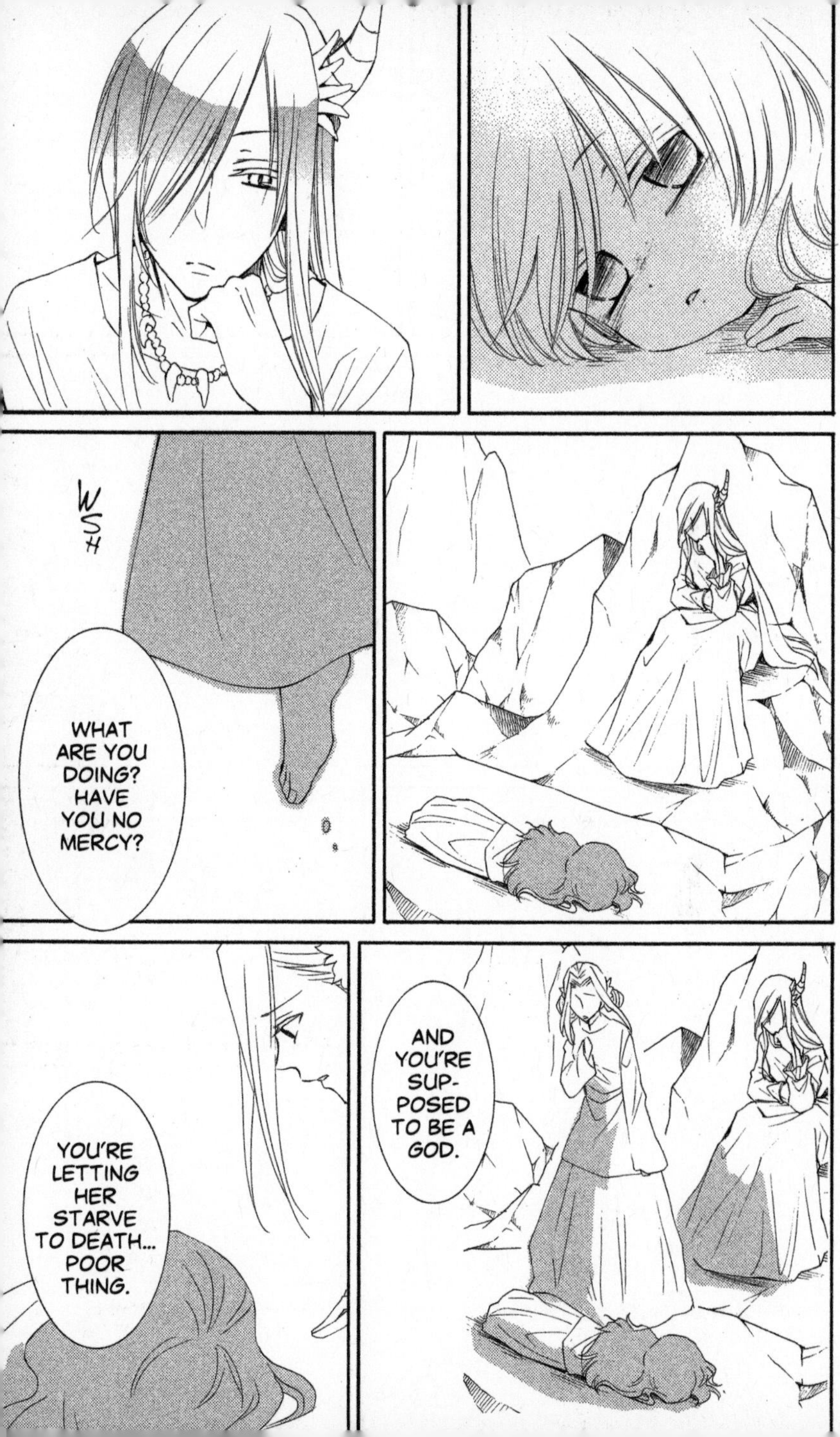
WSH
WHAT ARE YOU DOING? HAVE YOU NO MERCY?
AND YOU'RE SUP-POSED TO BE A GOD.
YOU'RE LETTING HER STARVE TO DEATH... POOR THING.

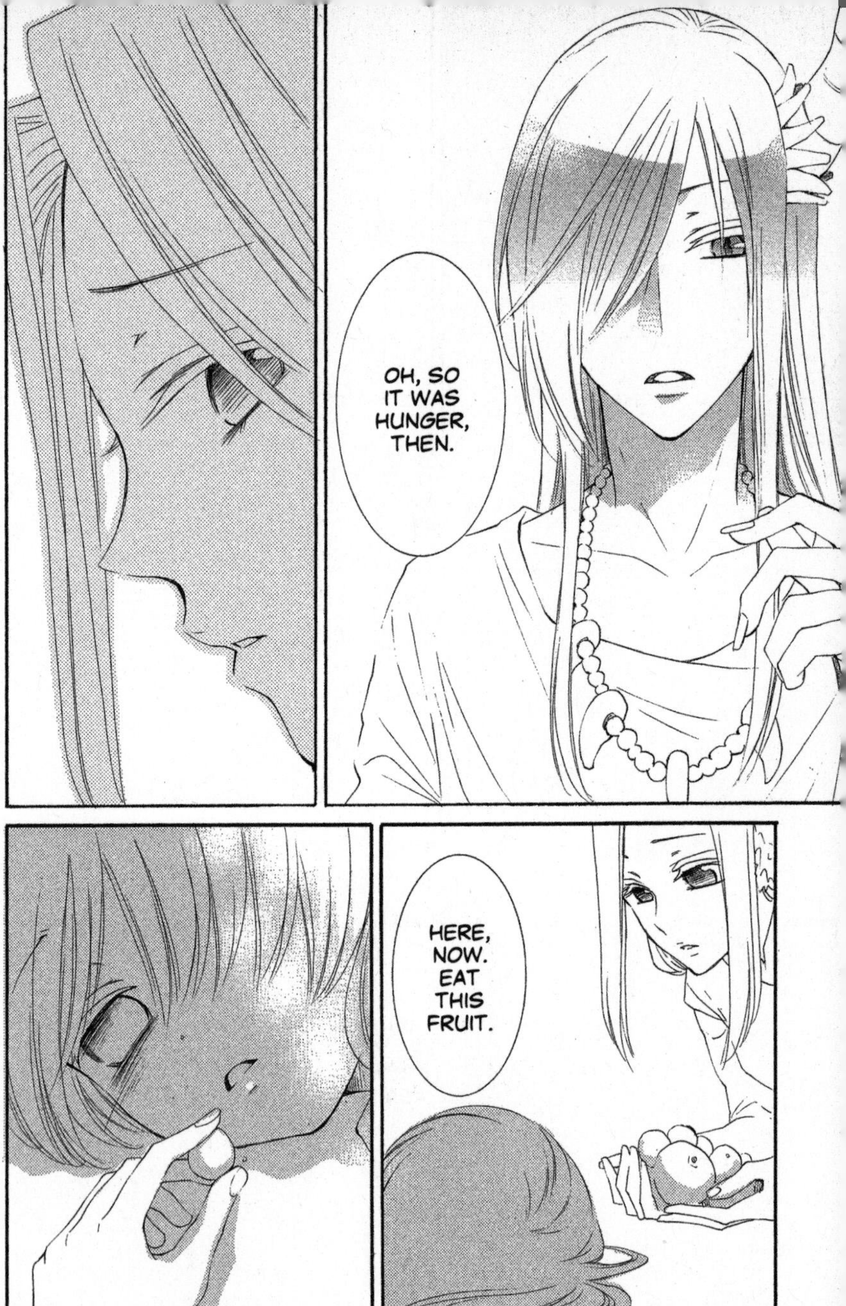
OH, SO IT WAS HUNGER, THEN.
HERE, NOW. EAT THIS FRUIT.

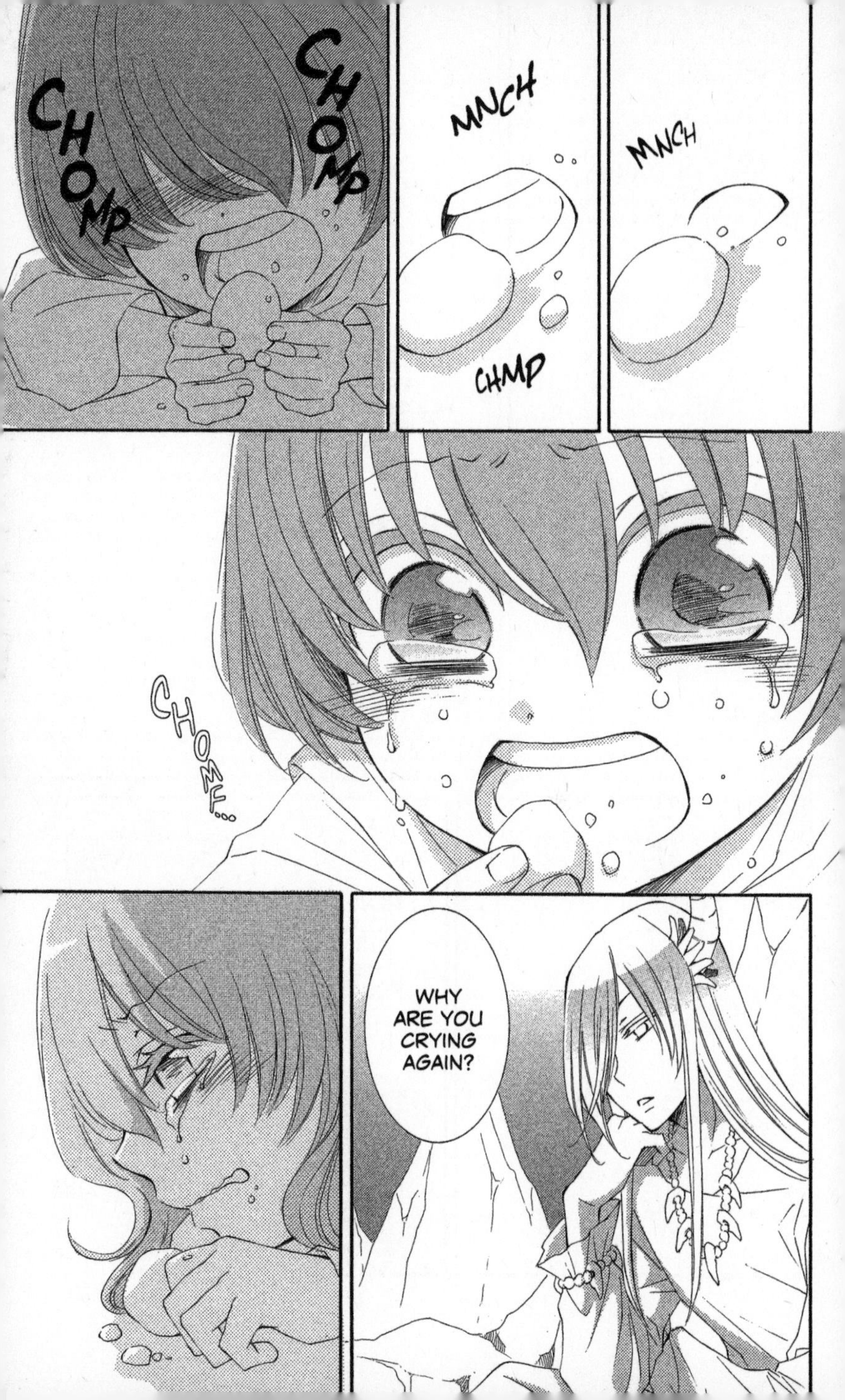
MNCH
MNCH
CHMP
CHOMP
CHOMP
CHOMF...
WHY ARE YOU CRYING AGAIN?

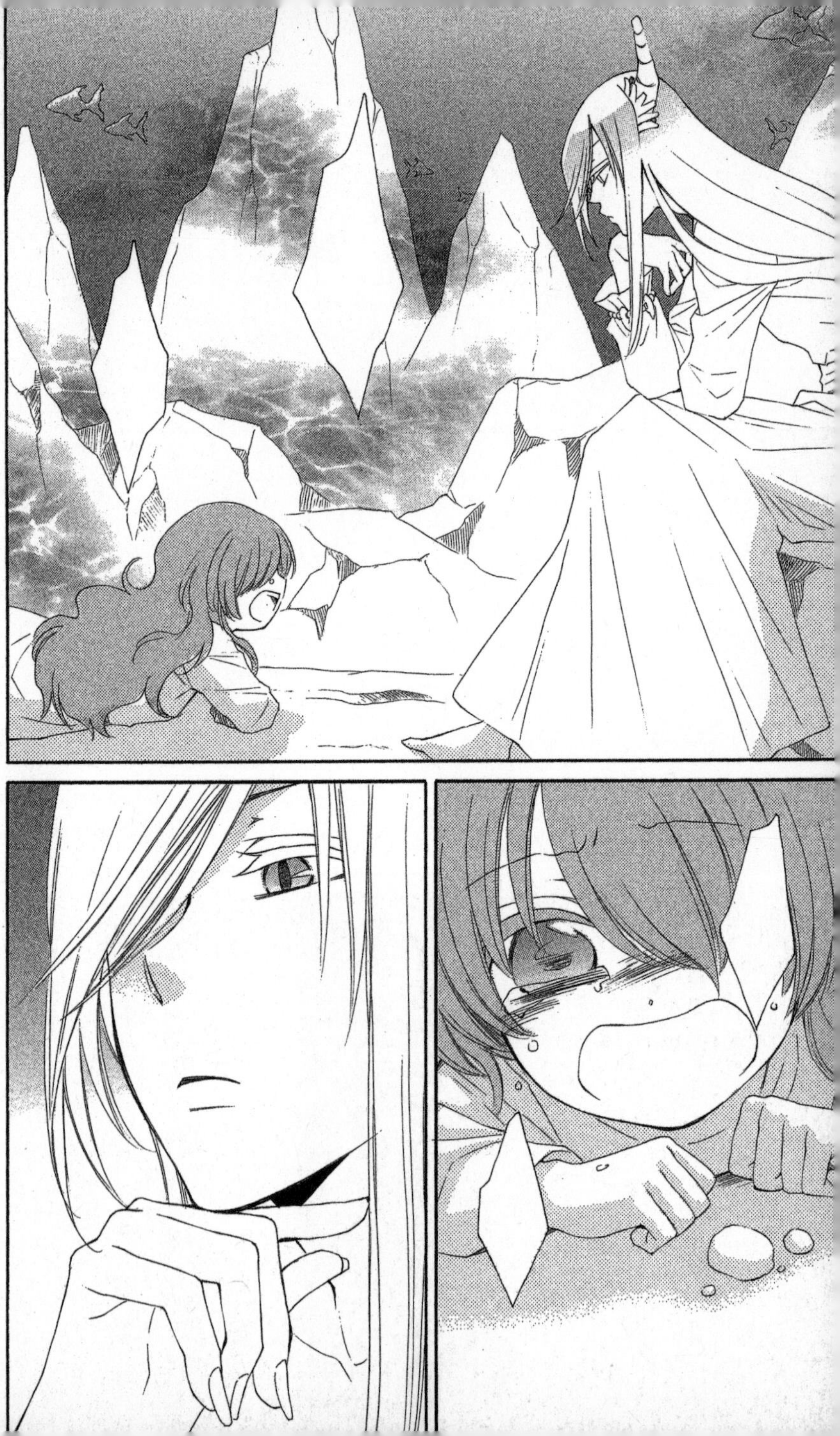

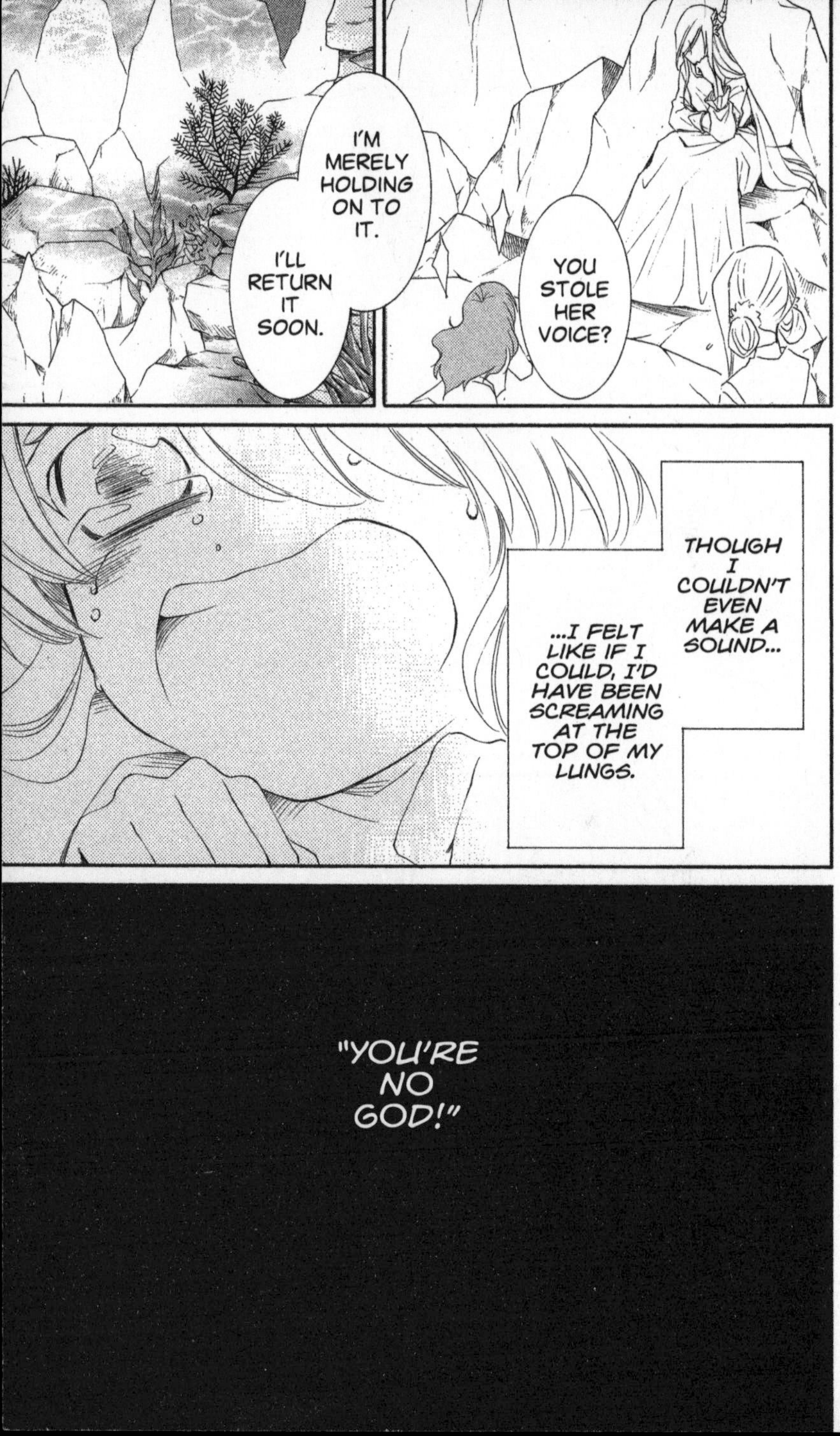
YOU STOLE HER VOICE?
I'M MERELY HOLDING ON TO IT.
I'LL RETURN IT SOON.
THOUGH I COULDN'T EVEN MAKE A SOUND...
...I FELT LIKE IF I COULD, I'D HAVE BEEN SCREAMING AT THE TOP OF MY LUNGS.
"YOU'RE NO GOD!"

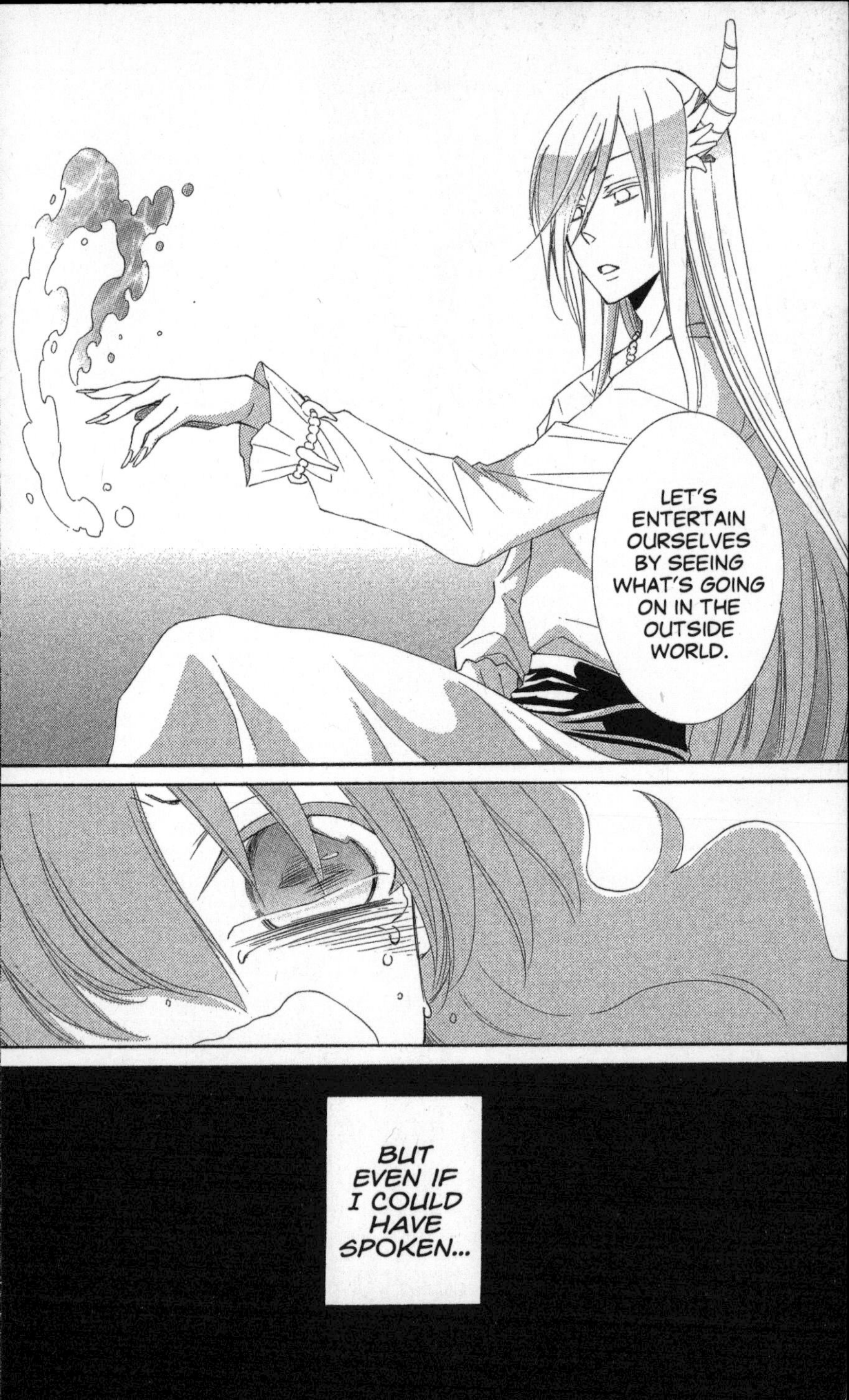
LET'S ENTERTAIN OURSELVES BY SEEING WHAT'S GOING ON IN THE OUTSIDE WORLD.
BUT EVEN IF I COULD HAVE SPOKEN...

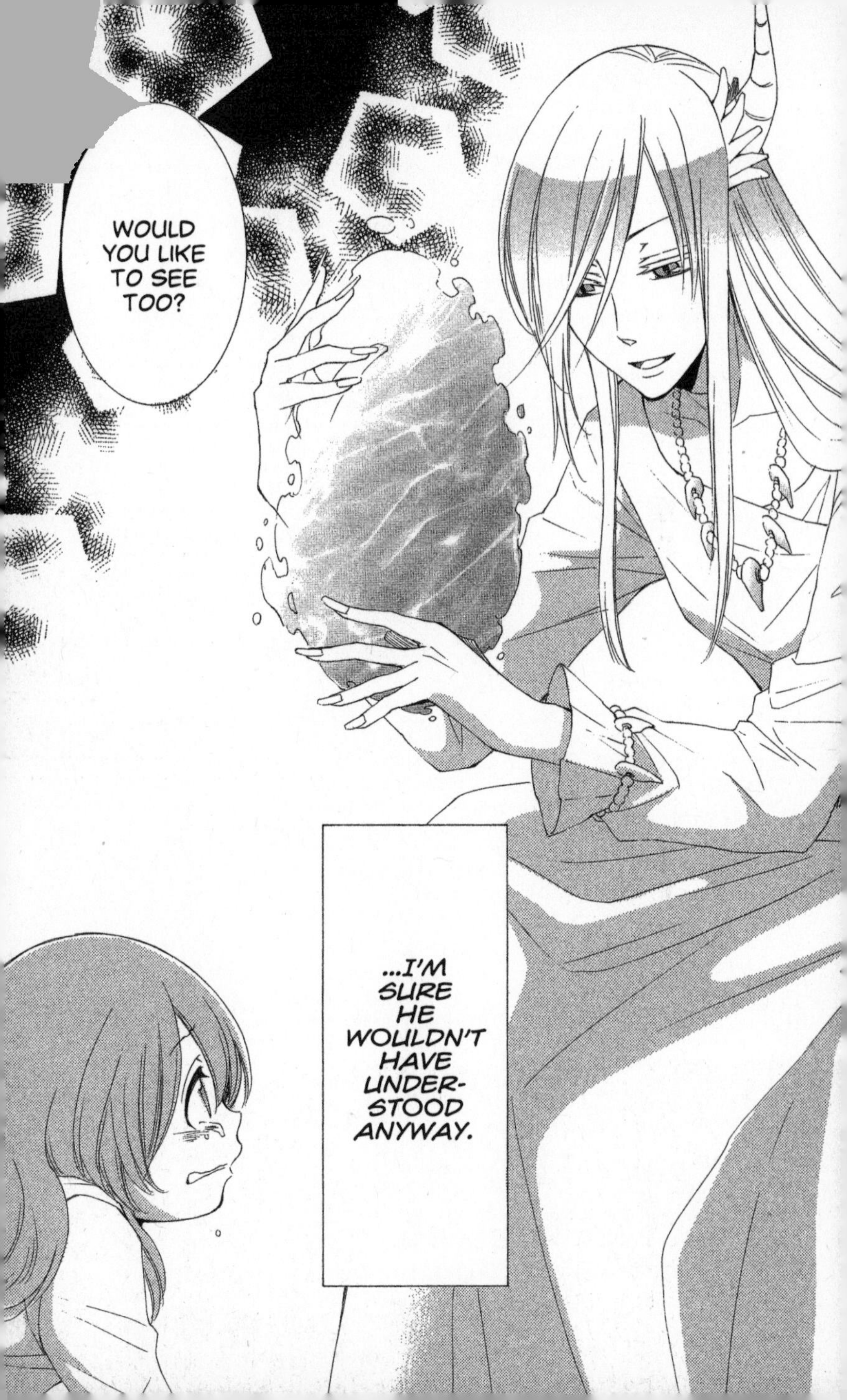
WOULD YOU LIKE TO SEE TOO?
...I'M SURE HE WOULDN'T HAVE UNDER-STOOD ANYWAY.

When I'm coming up with a character, I always think about them in color, so my concept has a color attached in my head. Asahi's color is pink, or maybe a light scarlet. I conceived of her having red hair, but Nakaba, the main character from my last comic, *Dawn of the Arcana*, was a redhead too! This time I wanted it to be a little more natural-looking. I pictured a more orangey red this time, but when I went to color it, it just ended up being pink. It's a faint scarlet or a sort of dawn-like color, so I named her Asahi, after the rising sun. Subaru's name also came from his theme color. I envisioned him as green, so the first character in his name is a word for green. Of course, the water god is pale blue. The other gods have pretty simple theme colors too. Red for fire, etc. I'm really excited to draw all the gods in color.

Send your thoughts here! ↓
Rei Toma
c/o The Water Dragon's Bride Editor
VIZ Media
P.O. Box 77010
San Francisco,
CA 94107

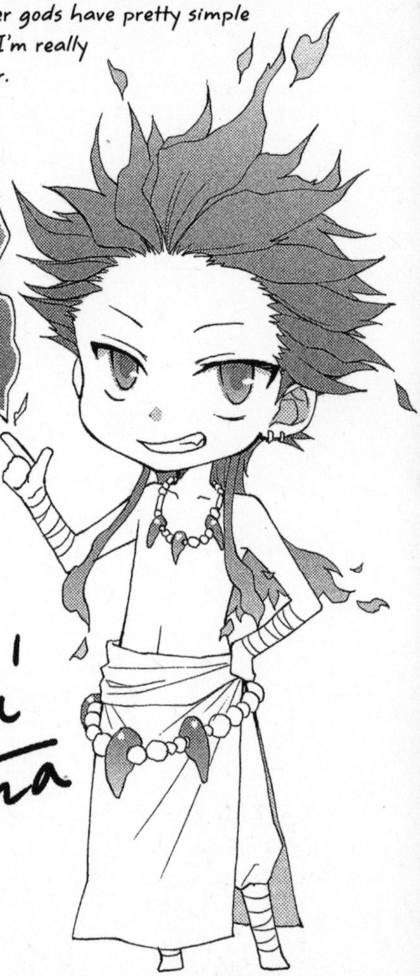

Volume 2 is all ready to go! Hope you like it! (End of commercial.) See you again in volume 2!

Rei Toma

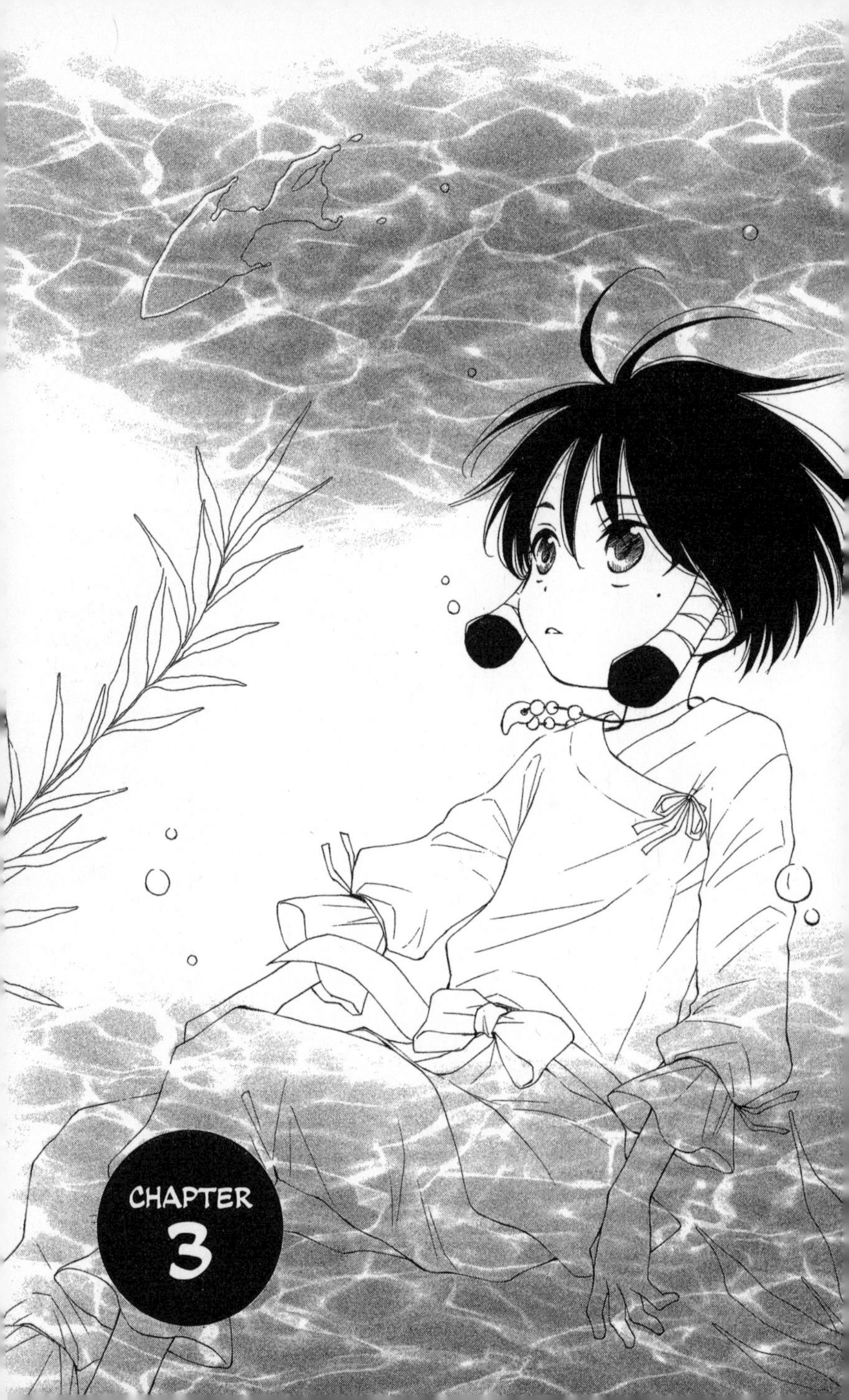
CHAPTER
3

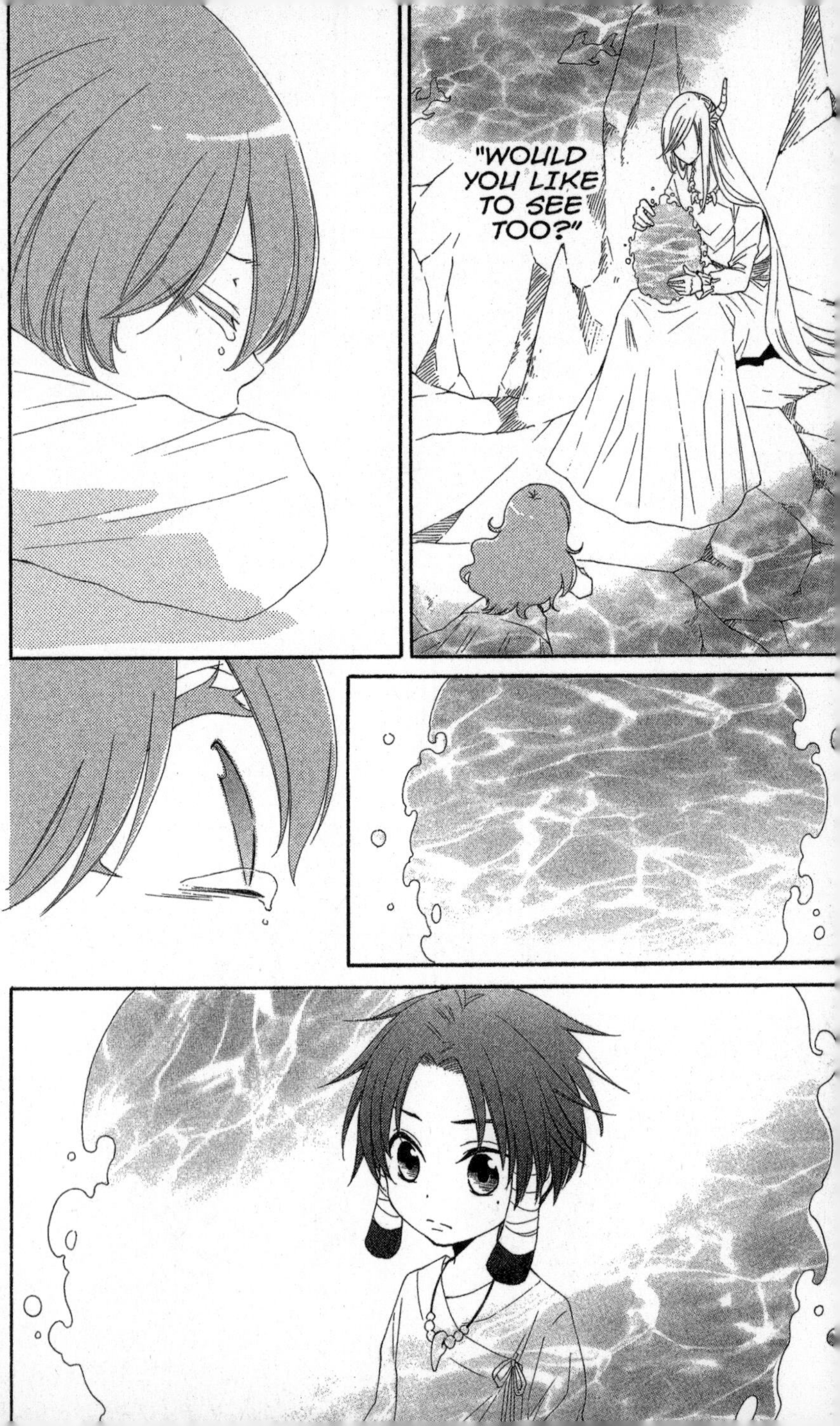
"WOULD YOU LIKE TO SEE TOO?"

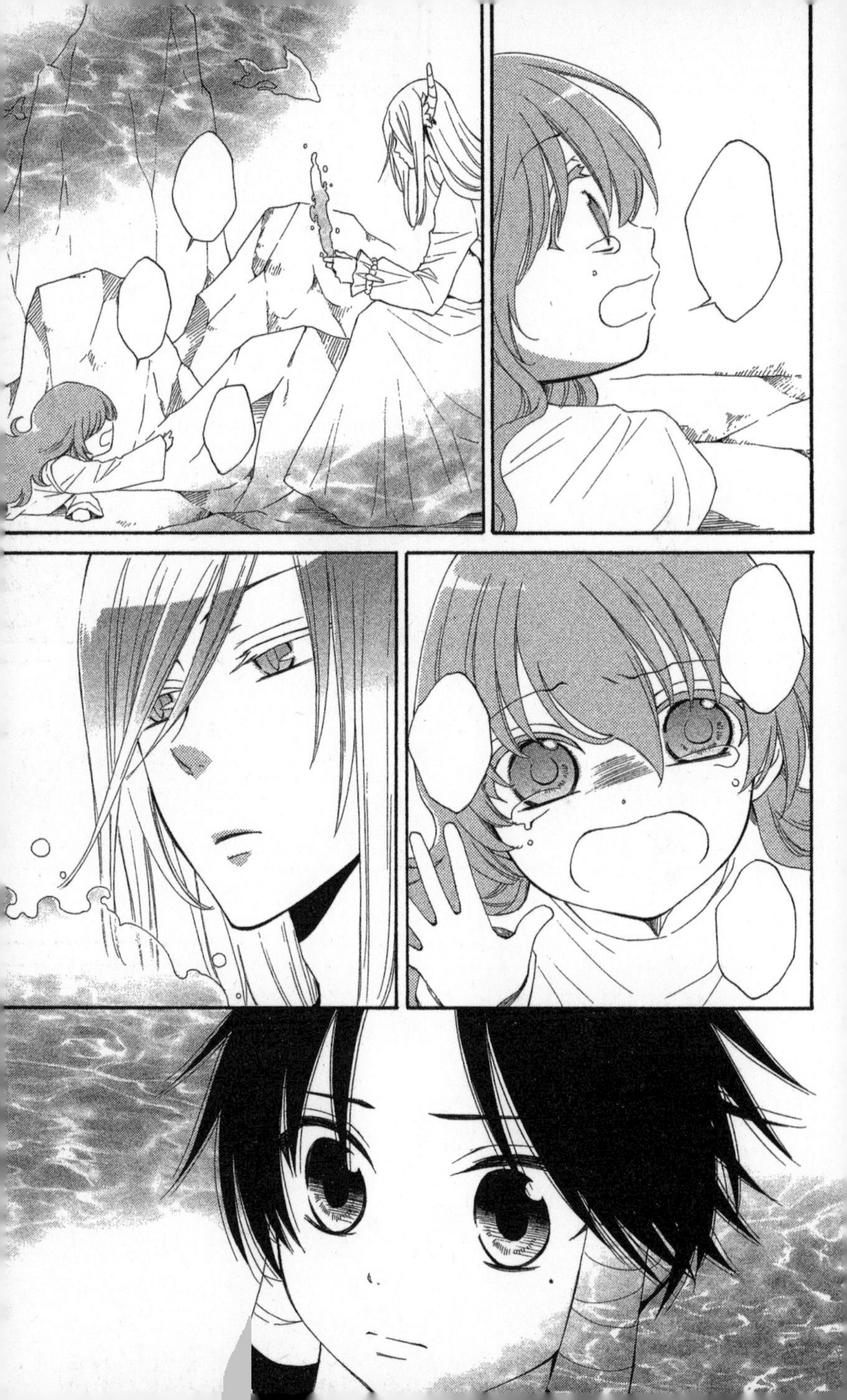

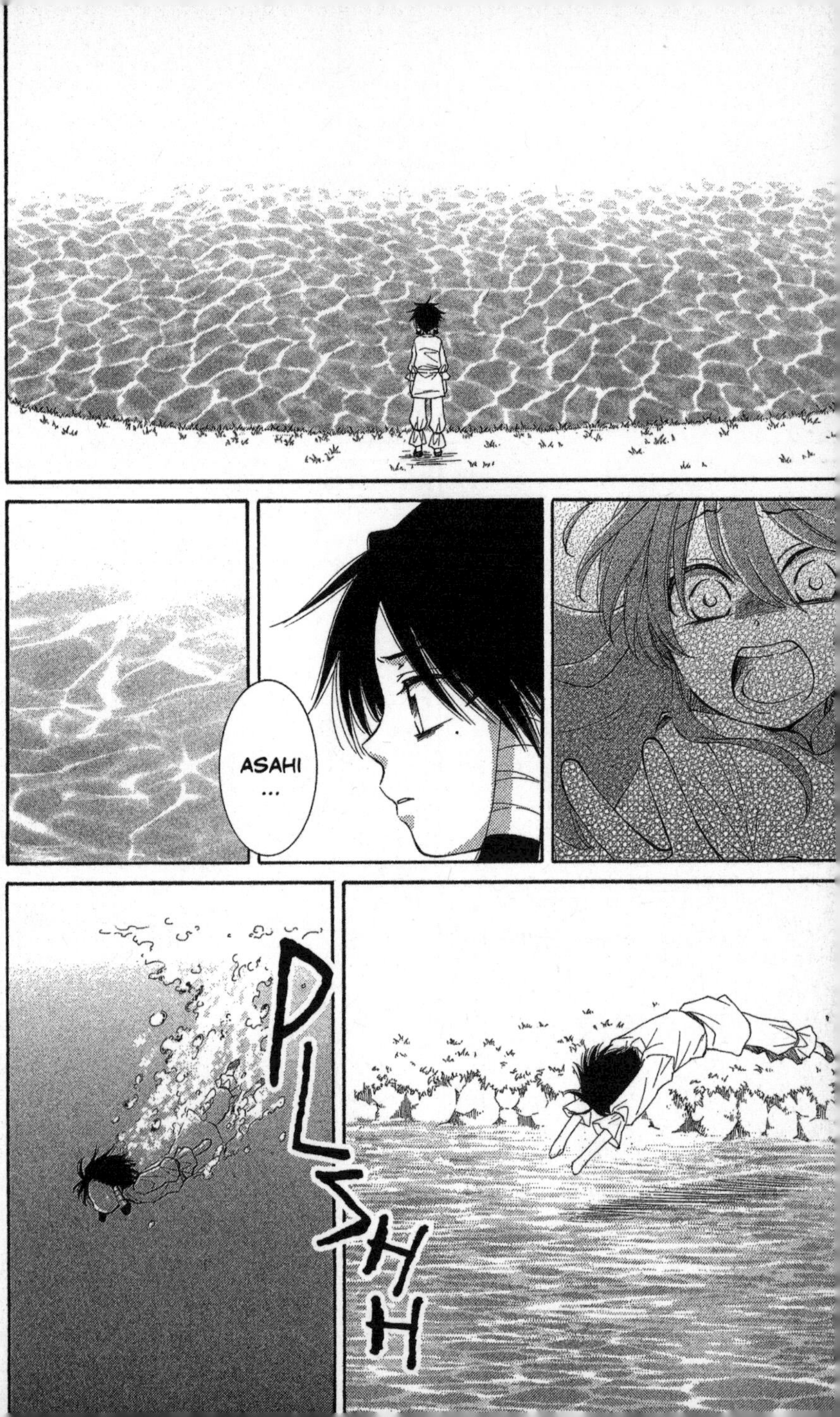
ASAHI
...
PLSHH

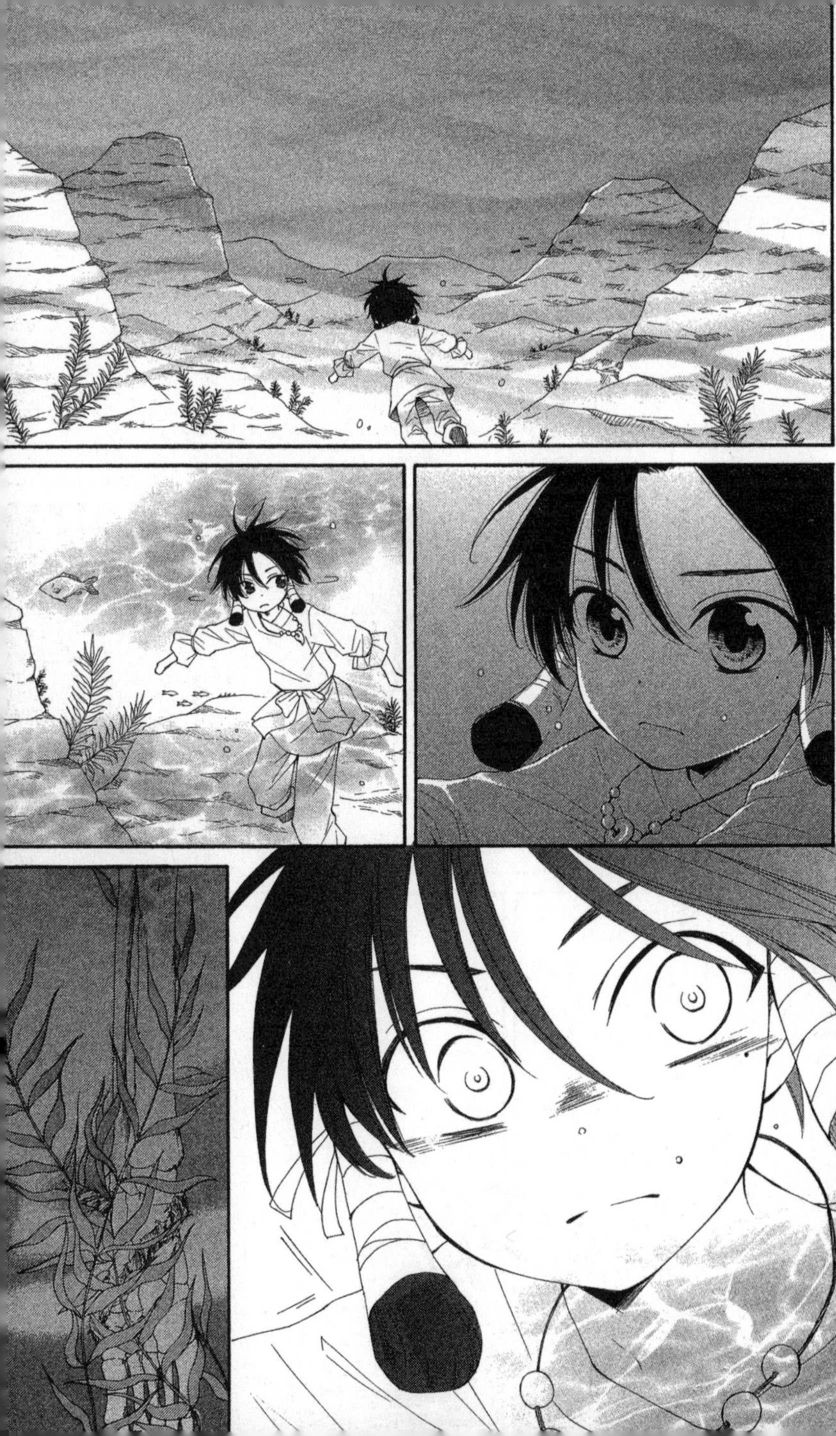

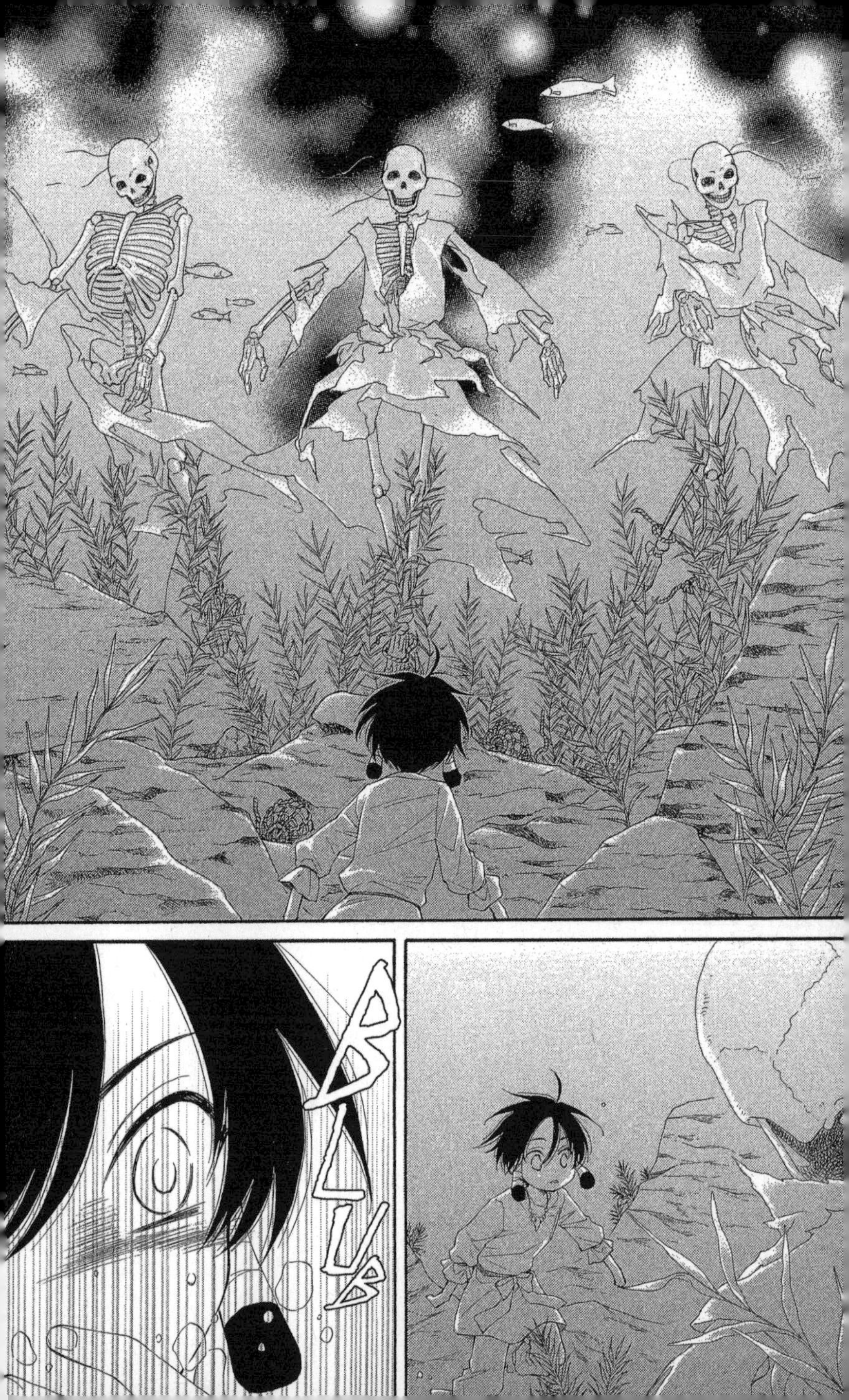
BLUB

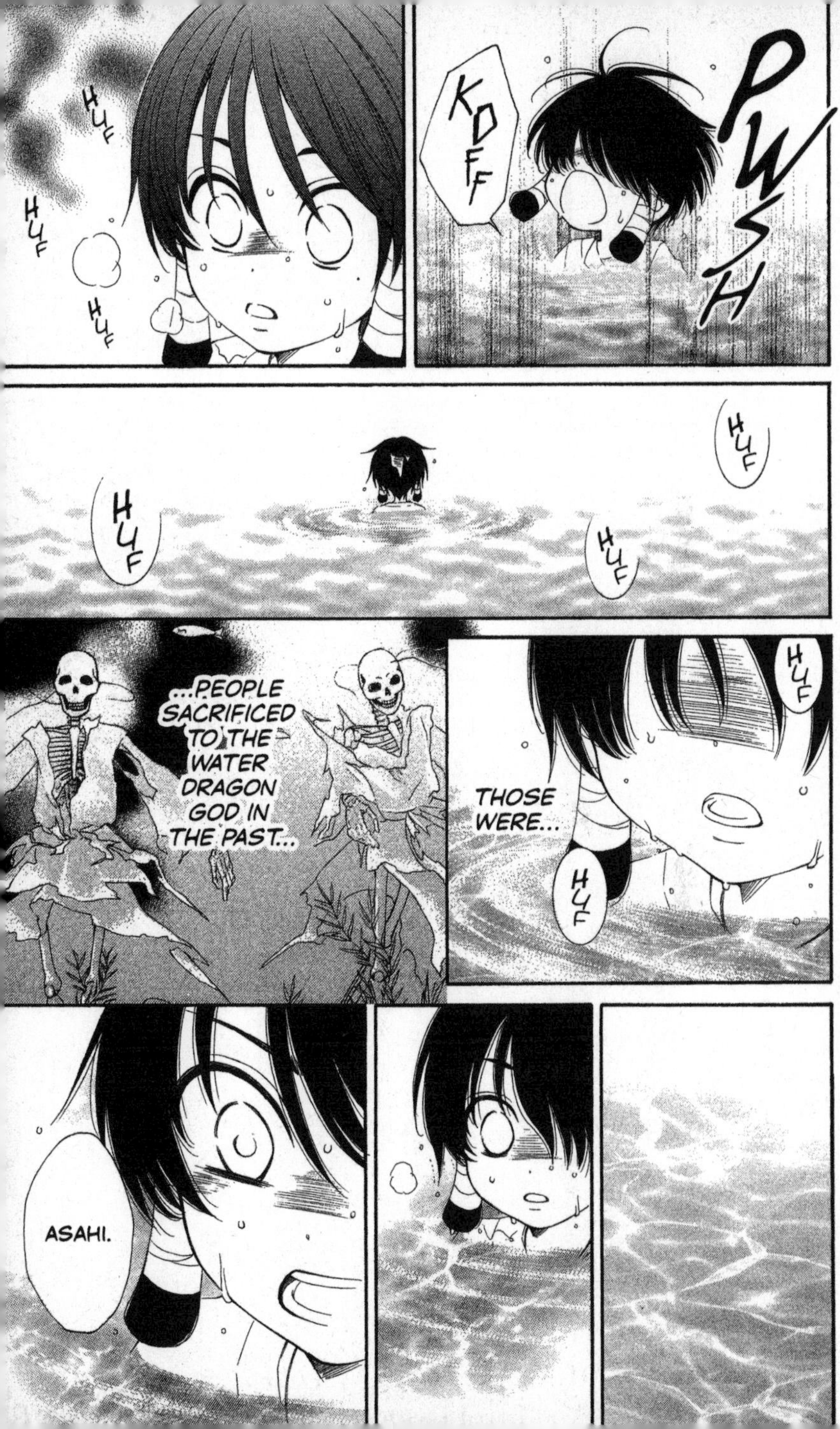
PWSH
KOFF
HUF
HUF
HUF
HUF
HUF
HUF
HUF
THOSE WERE...
HUF
...PEOPLE SACRIFICED TO THE WATER DRAGON GOD IN THE PAST...
ASAHI.

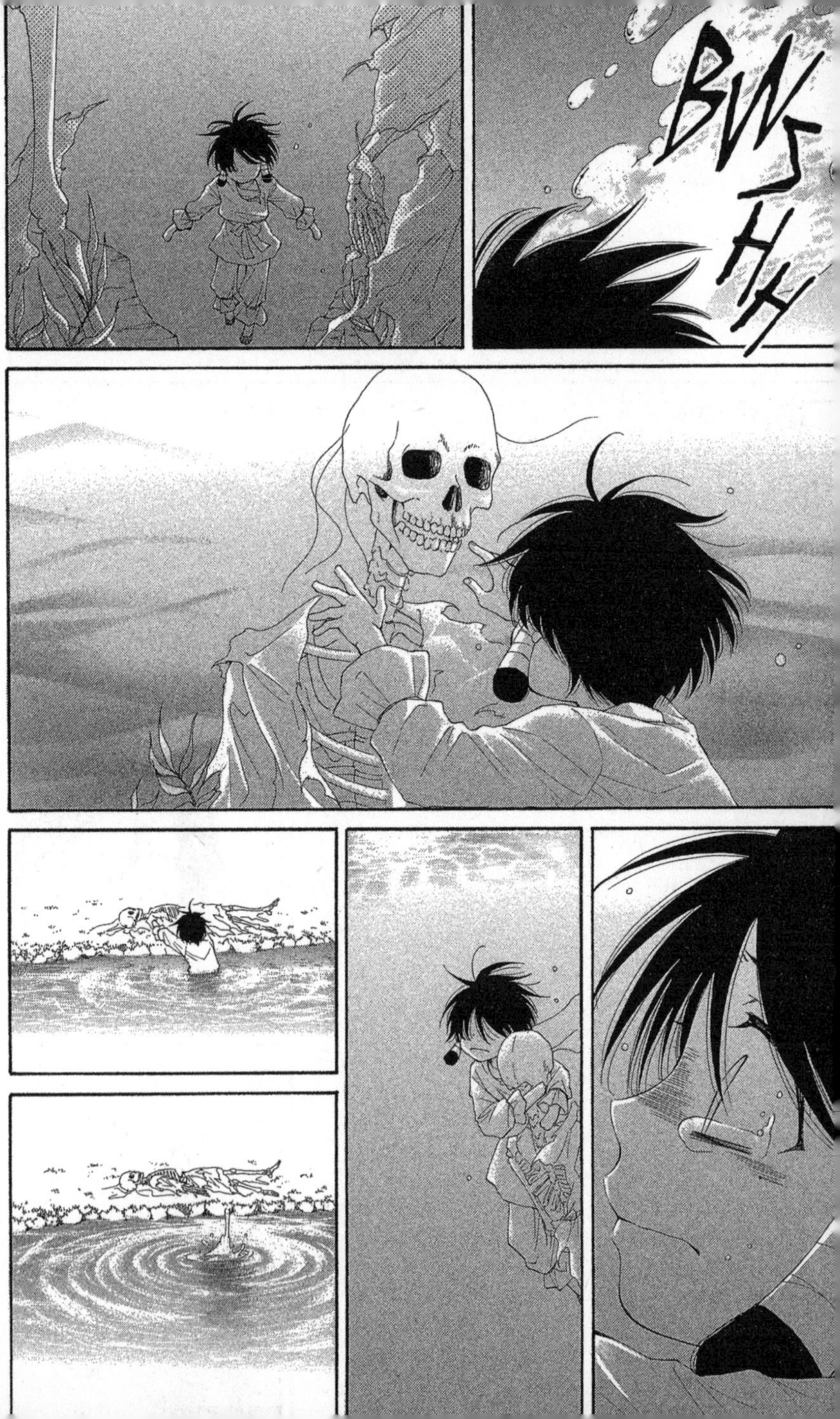
BWSHHH

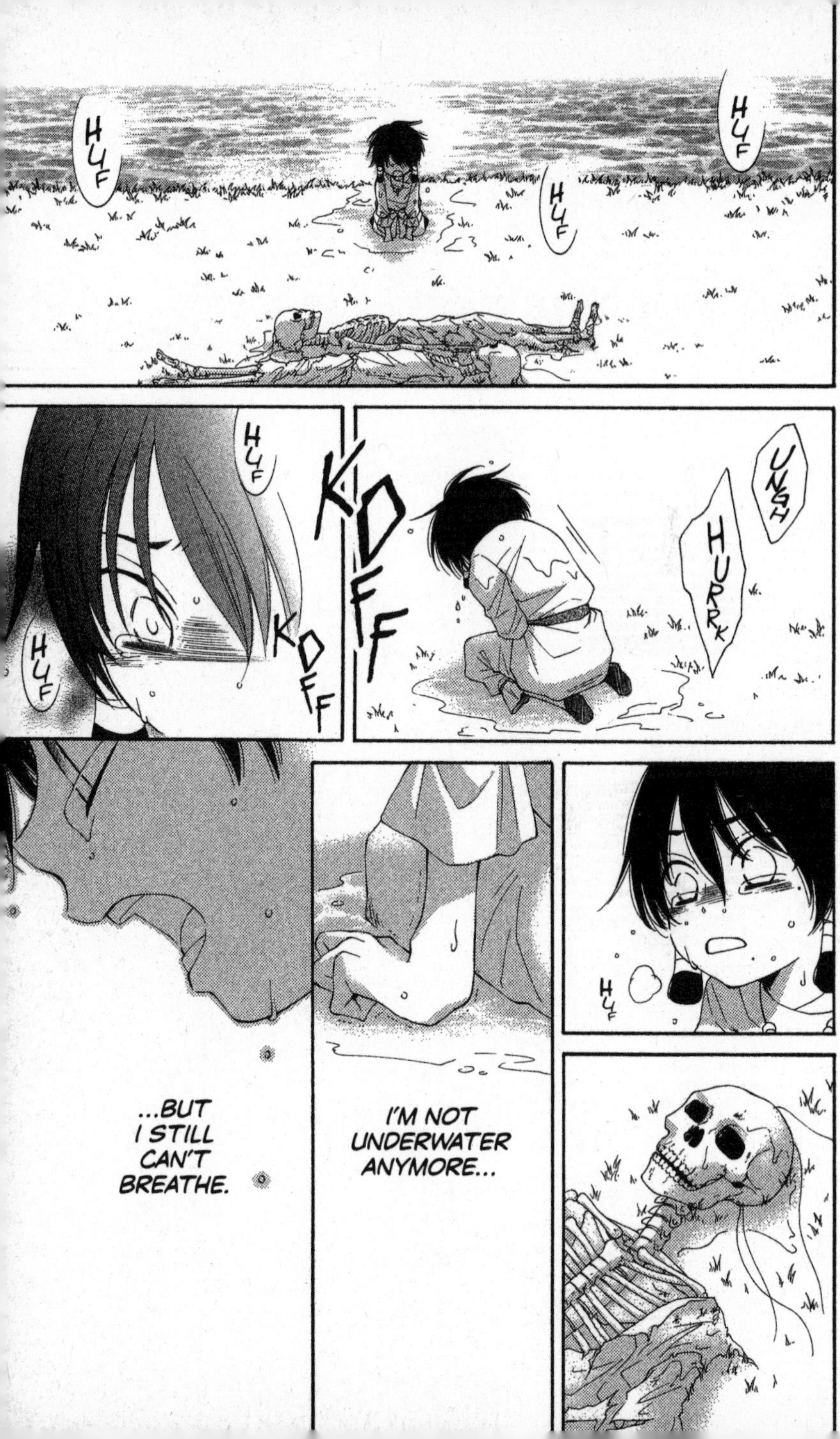
HUF
HUF
HUF
UNGH
HURRK
KOFF
HUF
KOFF
HUF
HUF
I'M NOT UNDERWATER ANYMORE...
...BUT I STILL CAN'T BREATHE.

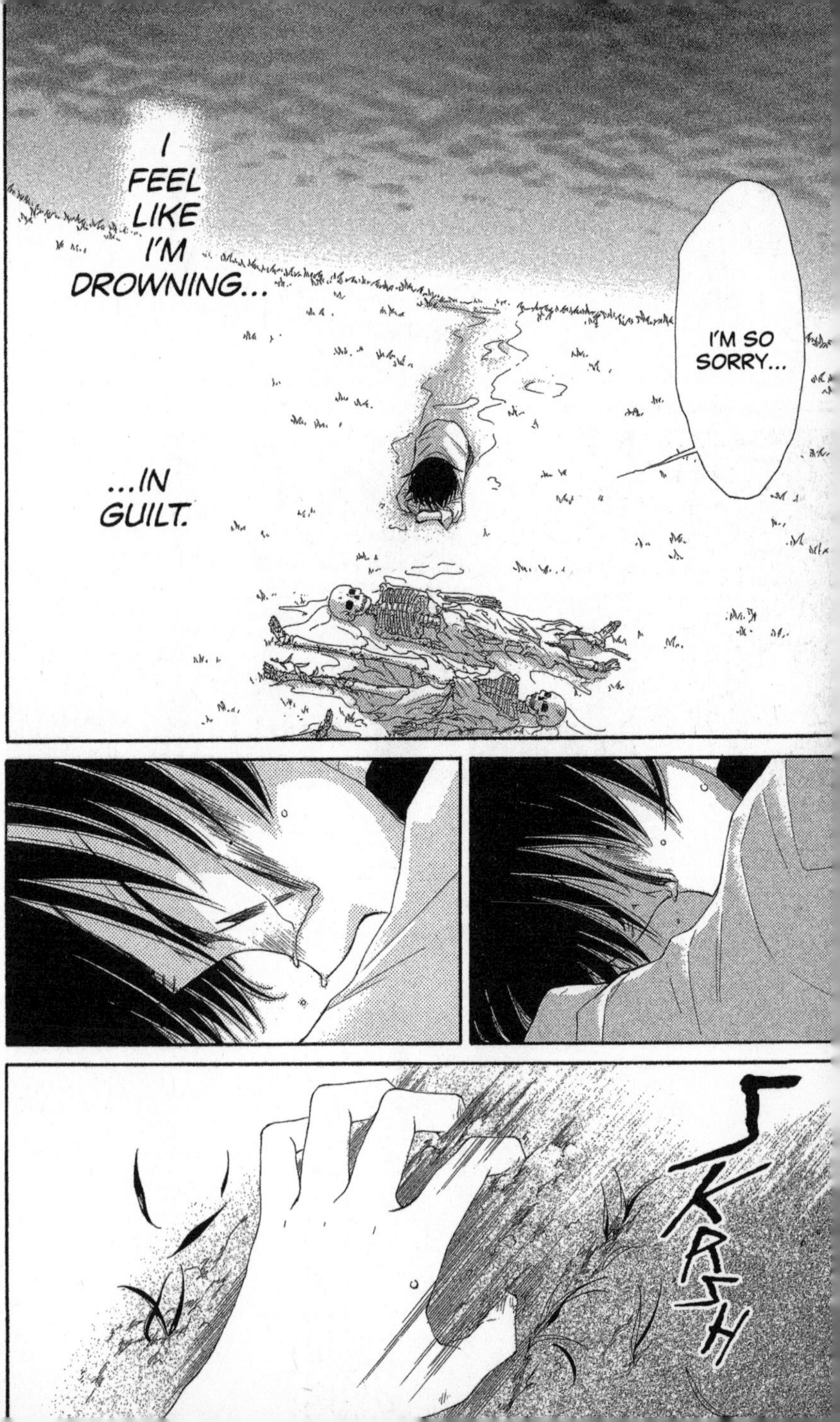
I'M SO SORRY...
I FEEL LIKE I'M DROWNING...
...IN GUILT.
KRSH

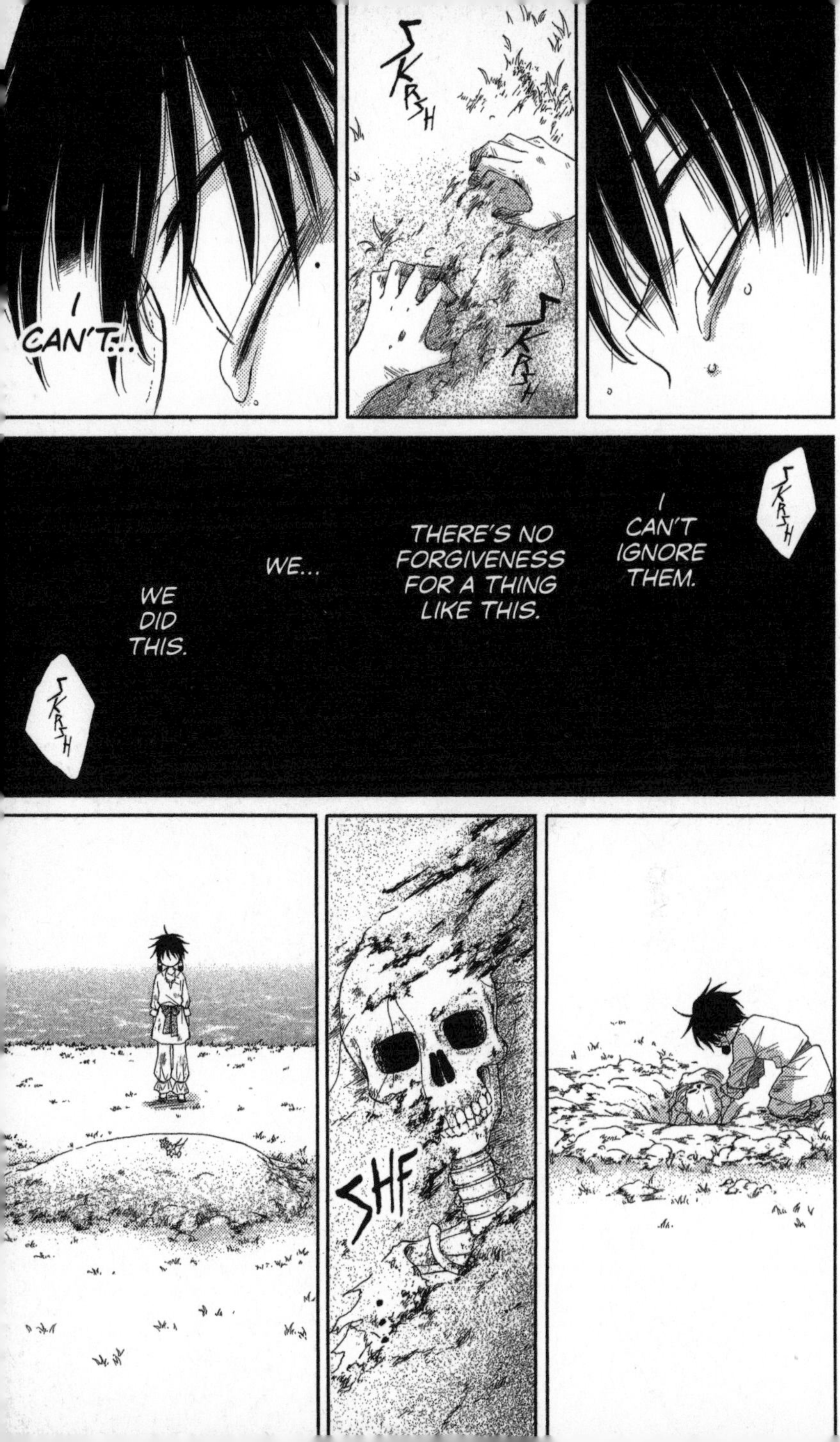
SKRSH
SKRSH
I CAN'T...
SKRSH
I CAN'T IGNORE THEM.
THERE'S NO FORGIVENESS FOR A THING LIKE THIS.
WE...
WE DID THIS.
SKRSH
SHF

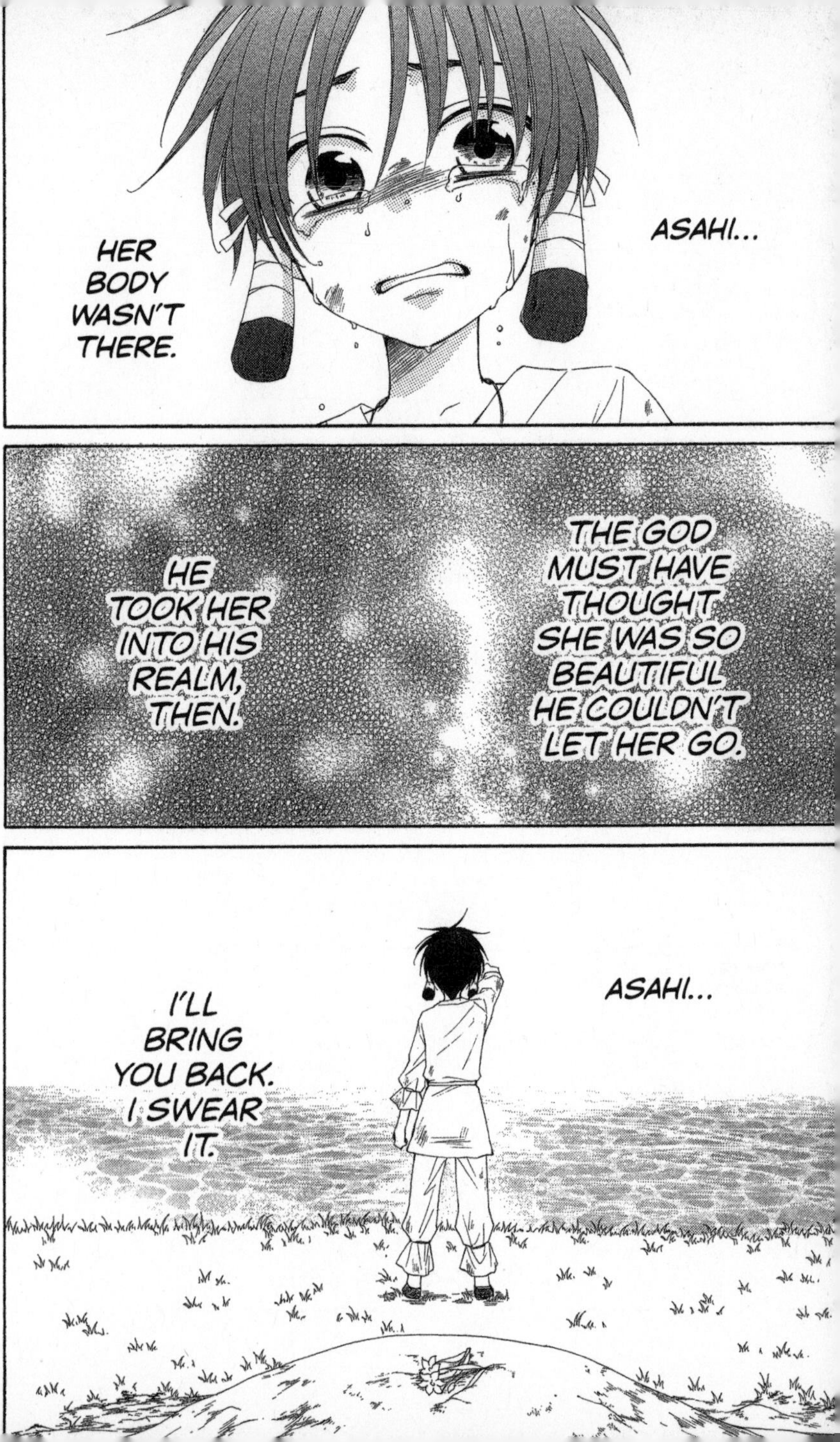
ASAHI...
HER BODY WASN'T THERE.
THE GOD MUST HAVE THOUGHT SHE WAS SO BEAUTIFUL HE COULDN'T LET HER GO.
HE TOOK HER INTO HIS REALM, THEN.
ASAHI...
I'LL BRING YOU BACK. I SWEAR IT.

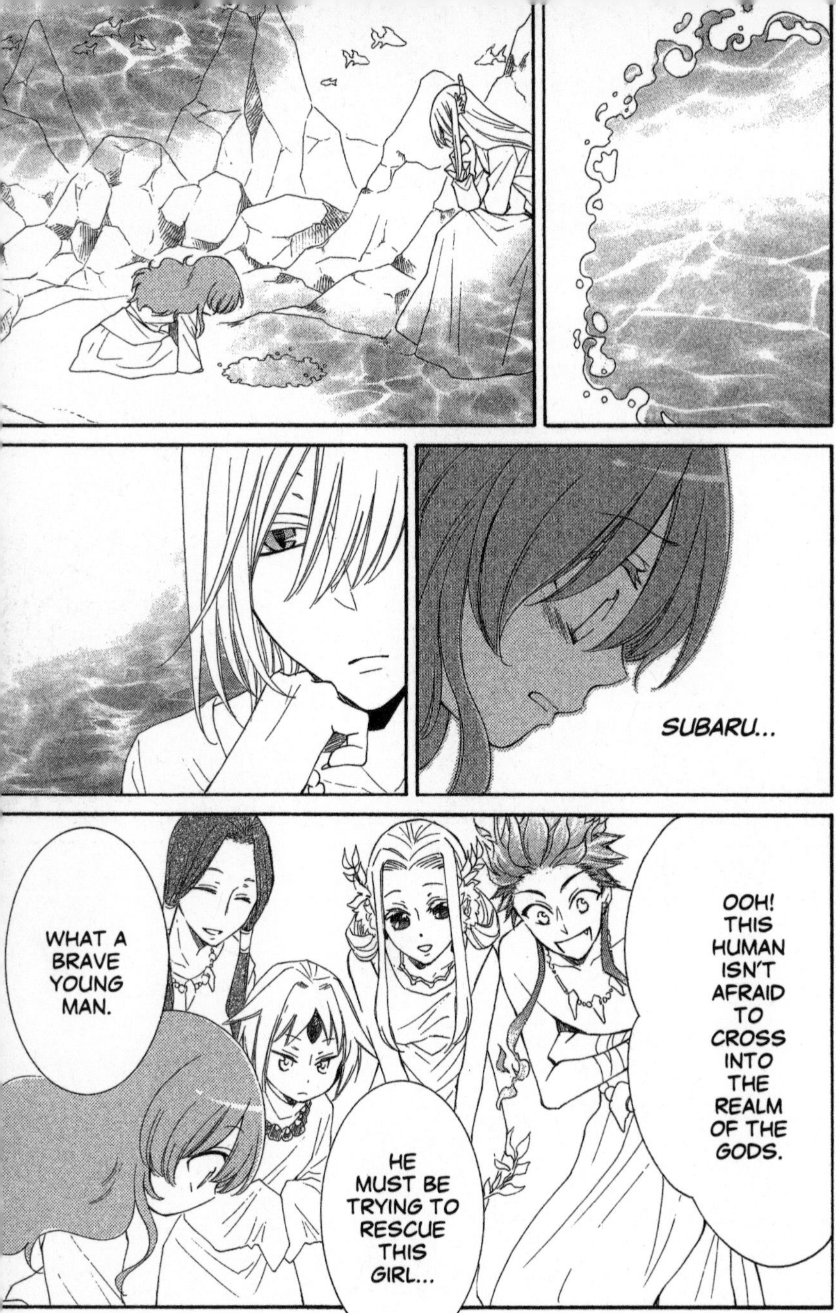
SUBARU...
OOH! THIS HUMAN ISN'T AFRAID TO CROSS INTO THE REALM OF THE GODS.
WHAT A BRAVE YOUNG MAN.
HE MUST BE TRYING TO RESCUE THIS GIRL...

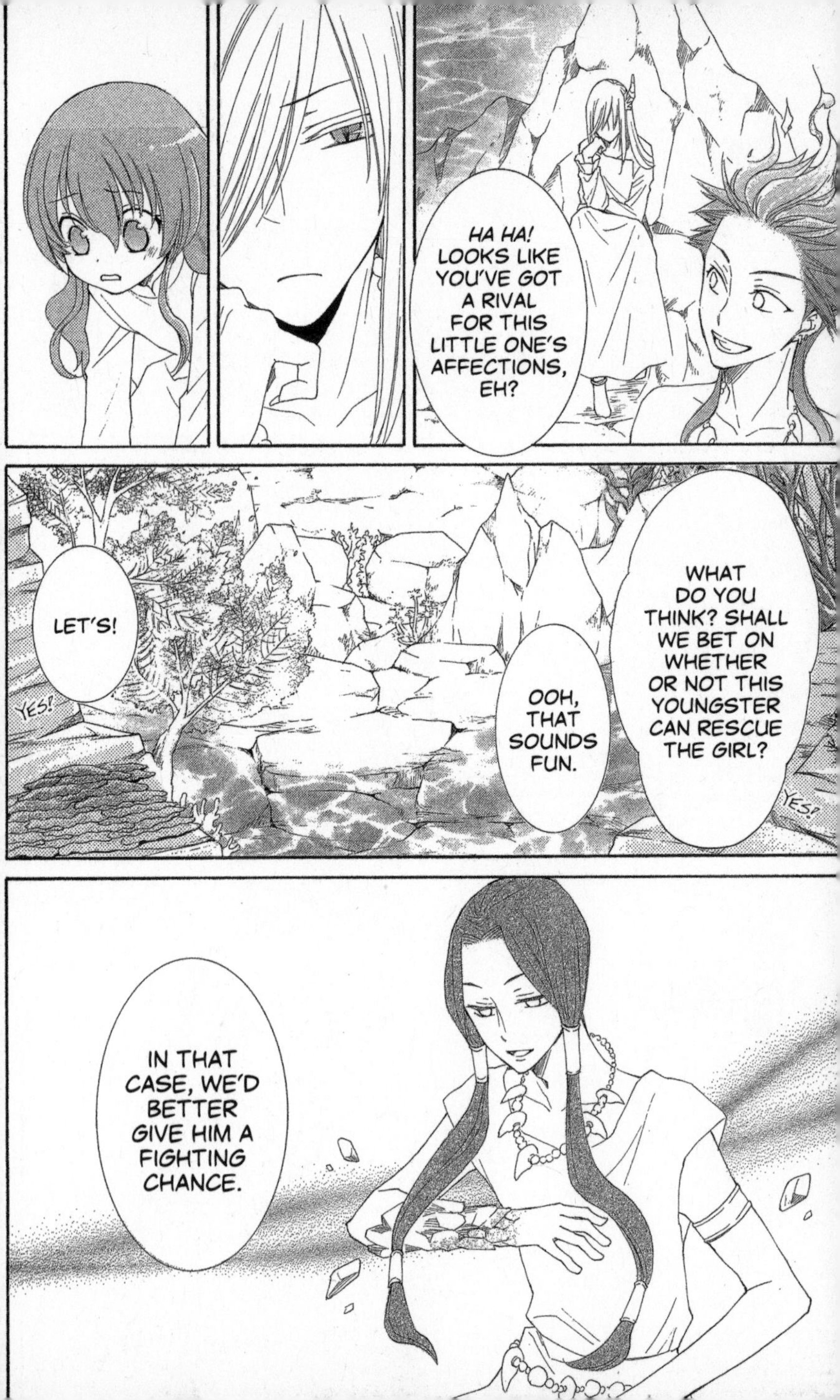
HA HA! LOOKS LIKE YOU'VE GOT A RIVAL FOR THIS LITTLE ONE'S AFFECTIONS, EH?
WHAT DO YOU THINK? SHALL WE BET ON WHETHER OR NOT THIS YOUNGSTER CAN RESCUE THE GIRL?
YES!
OOH, THAT SOUNDS FUN.
LET'S!
YES!
IN THAT CASE, WE'D BETTER GIVE HIM A FIGHTING CHANCE.

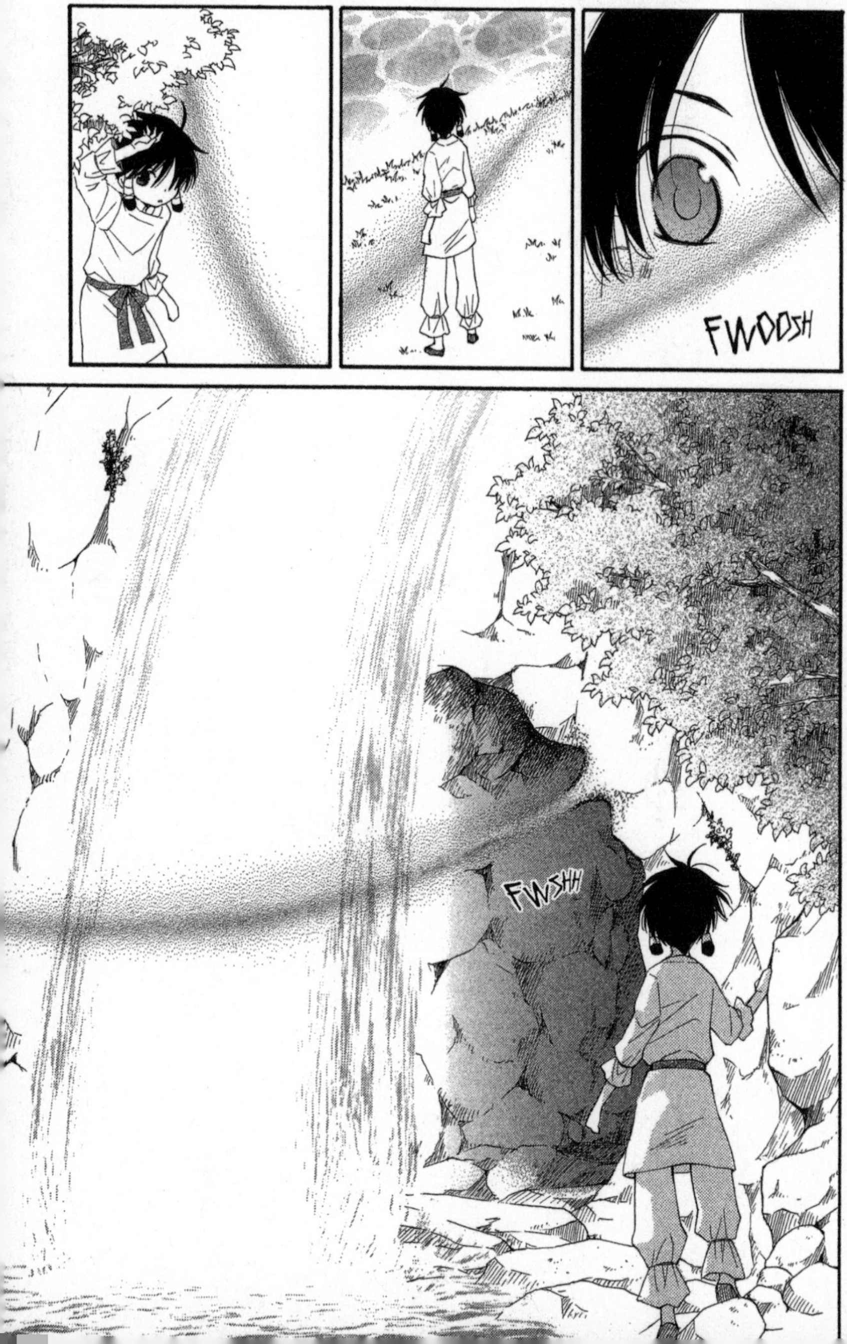
FWOOSH
FWSHH

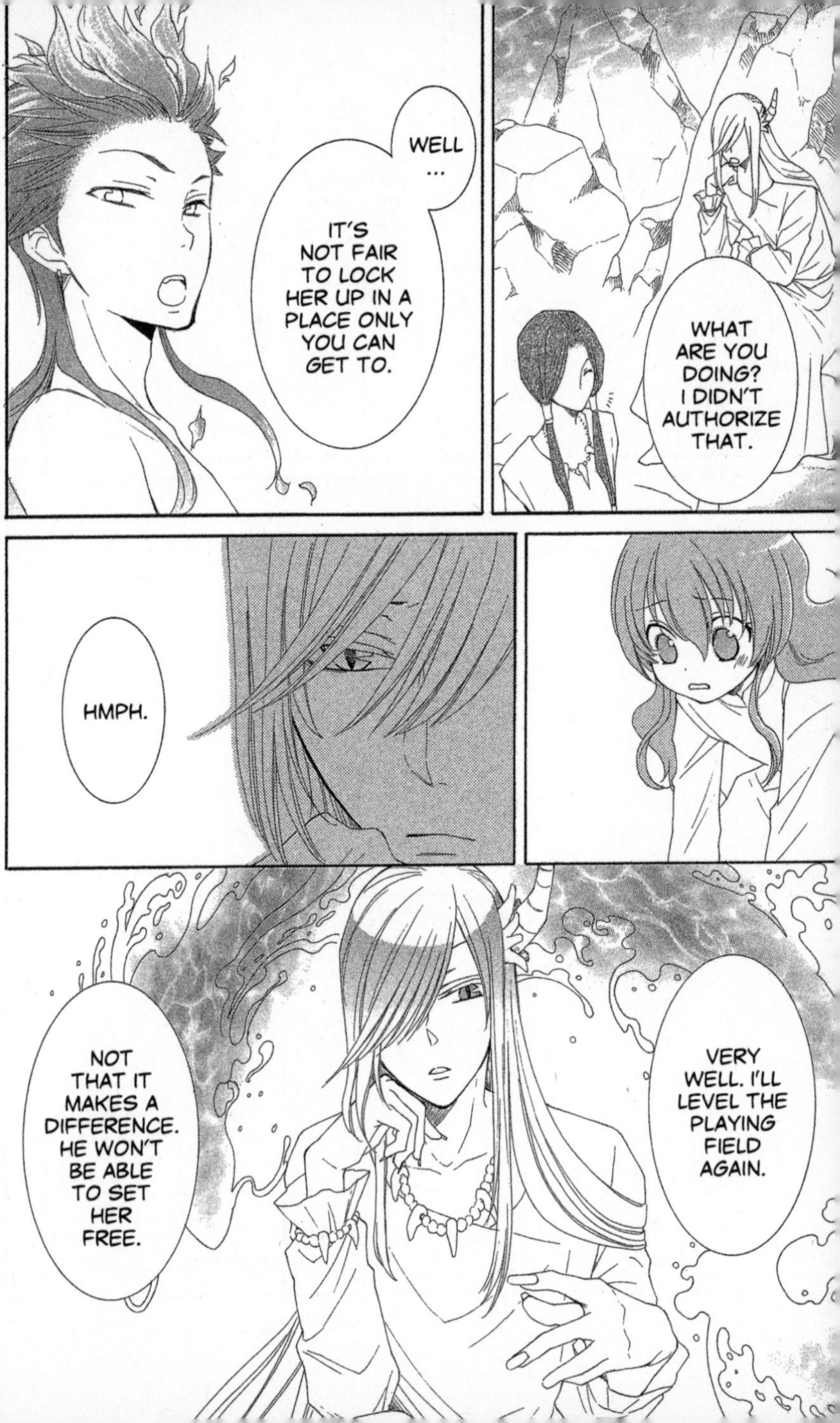
WHAT ARE YOU DOING? I DIDN'T AUTHORIZE THAT.
WELL ...
IT'S NOT FAIR TO LOCK HER UP IN A PLACE ONLY YOU CAN GET TO.
HMPH.
VERY WELL. I'LL LEVEL THE PLAYING FIELD AGAIN.
NOT THAT IT MAKES A DIFFERENCE. HE WON'T BE ABLE TO SET HER FREE.

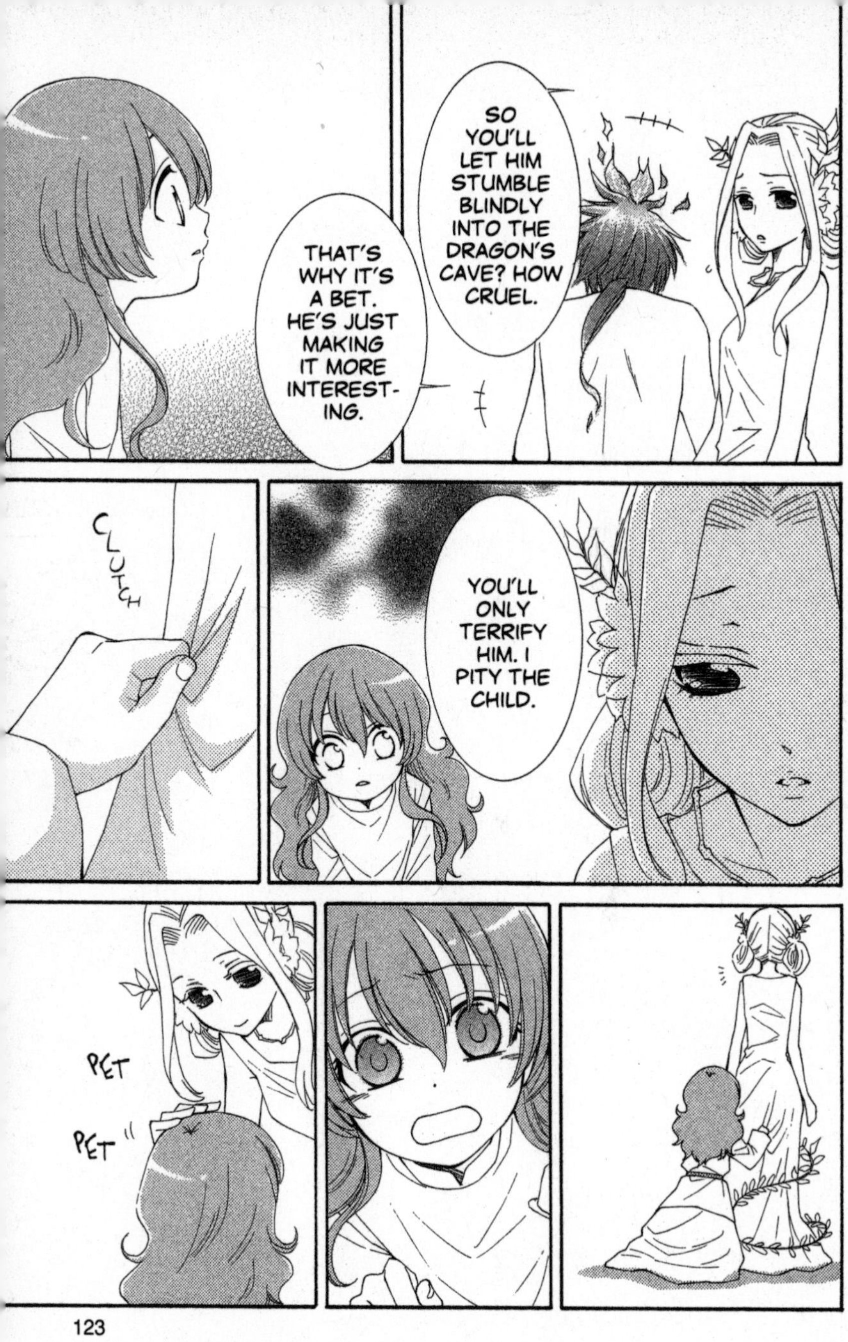
SO YOU'LL LET HIM STUMBLE BLINDLY INTO THE DRAGON'S CAVE? HOW CRUEL.
THAT'S WHY IT'S A BET. HE'S JUST MAKING IT MORE INTEREST-ING.
YOU'LL ONLY TERRIFY HIM. I PITY THE CHILD.
CLUTCH
PET
PET

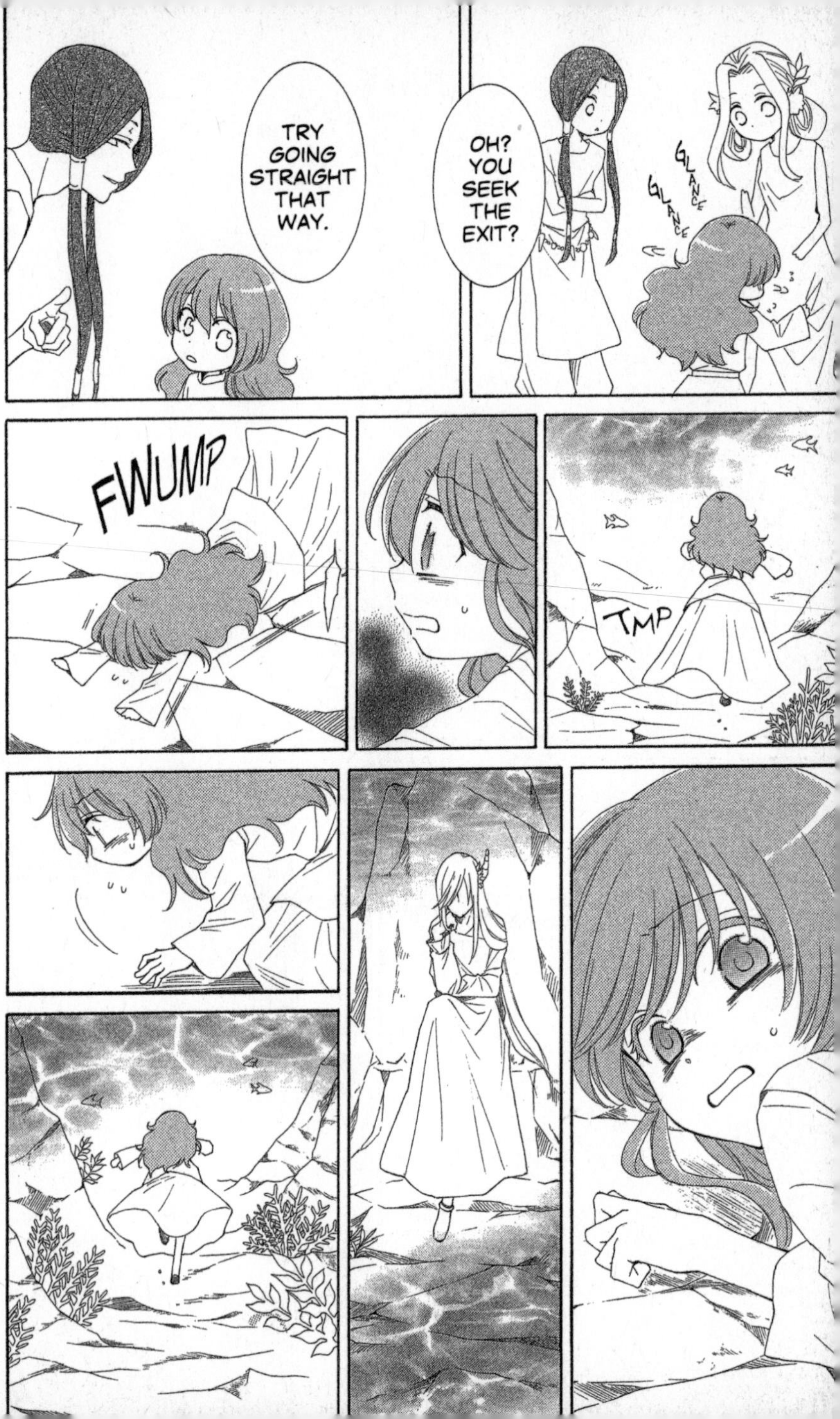
GLANCE
GLANCE
OH? YOU SEEK THE EXIT?
TRY GOING STRAIGHT THAT WAY.
TMP
FWUMP

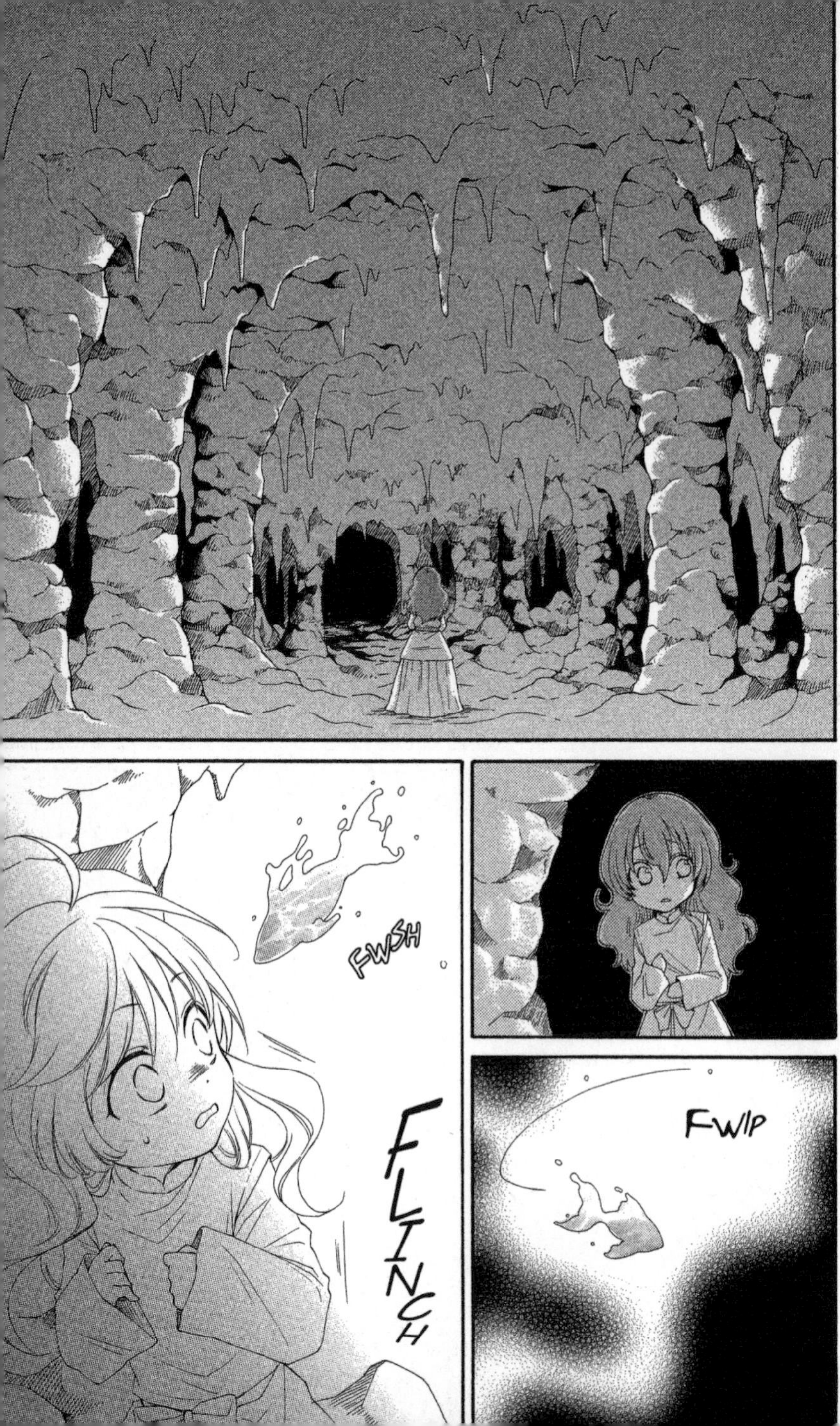
FWIP
FWSH
FLINCH

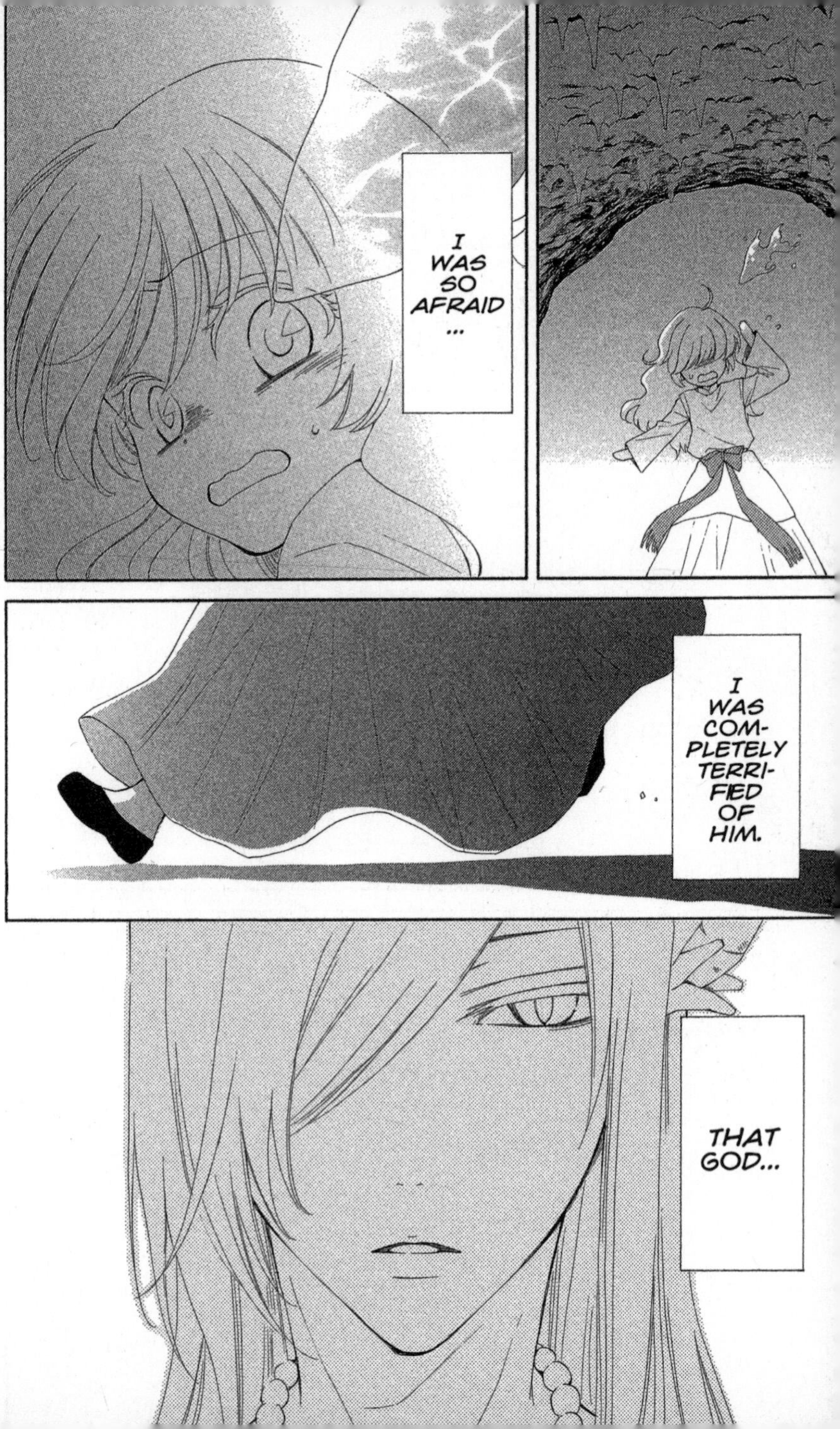
I WAS SO AFRAID...
I WAS COMPLETELY TERRIFIED OF HIM.
THAT GOD...

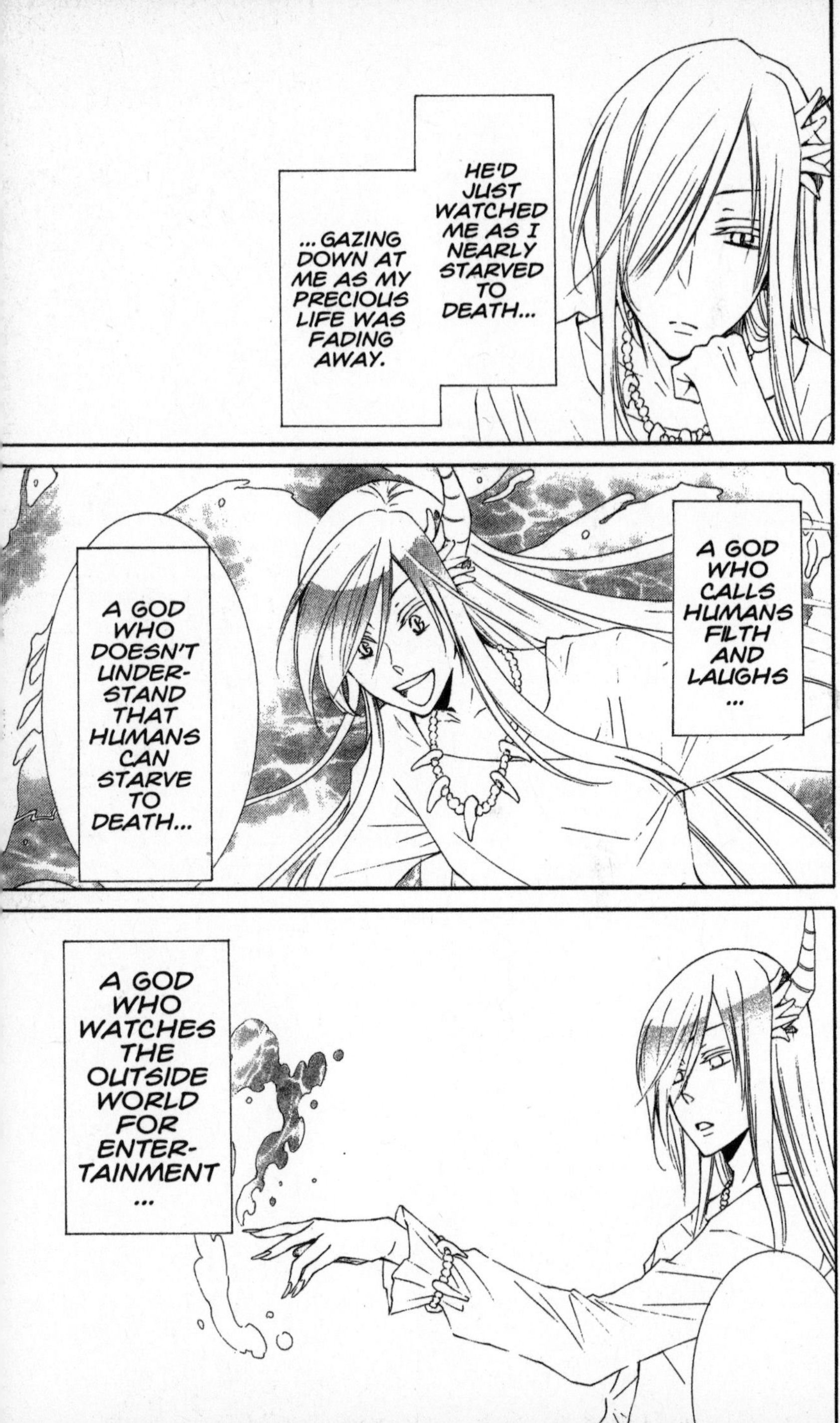
HE'D JUST WATCHED ME AS I NEARLY STARVED TO DEATH...
...GAZING DOWN AT ME AS MY PRECIOUS LIFE WAS FADING AWAY.
A GOD WHO CALLS HUMANS FILTH AND LAUGHS...
A GOD WHO DOESN'T UNDER-STAND THAT HUMANS CAN STARVE TO DEATH...
A GOD WHO WATCHES THE OUTSIDE WORLD FOR ENTER-TAINMENT...

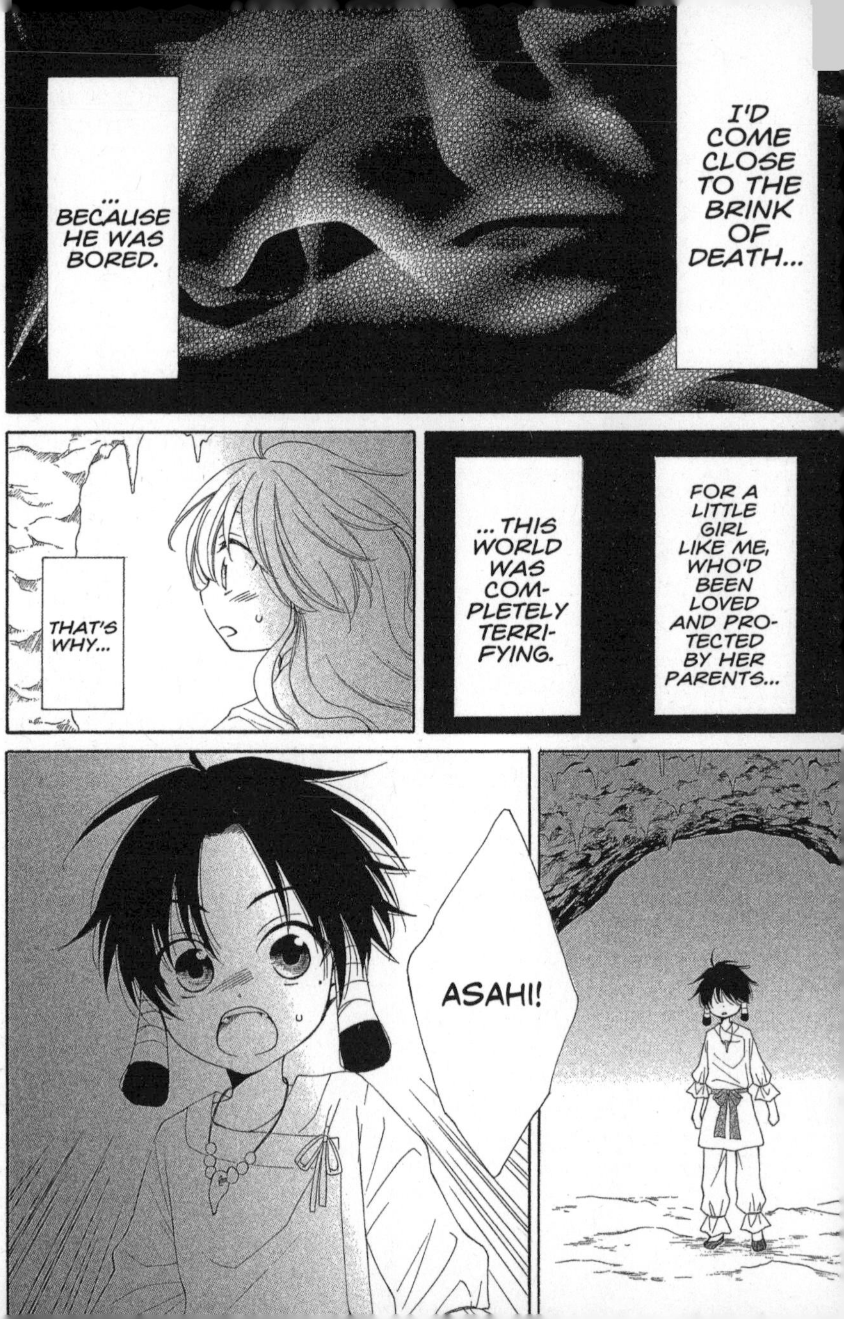
I'D COME CLOSE TO THE BRINK OF DEATH...
... BECAUSE HE WAS BORED.
FOR A LITTLE GIRL LIKE ME, WHO'D BEEN LOVED AND PROTECTED BY HER PARENTS...
... THIS WORLD WAS COMPLETELY TERRIFYING.
THAT'S WHY...
ASAHI!

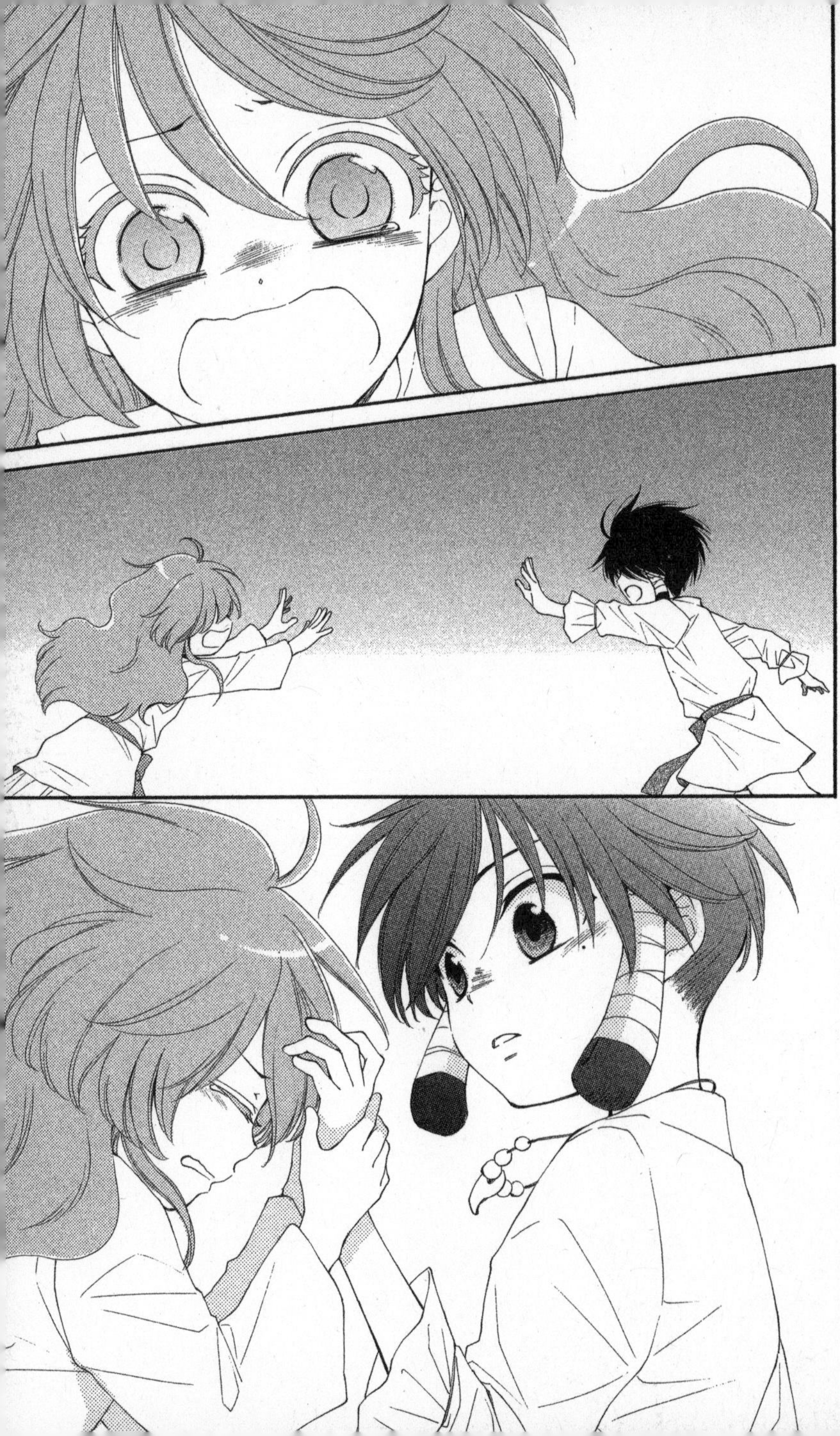

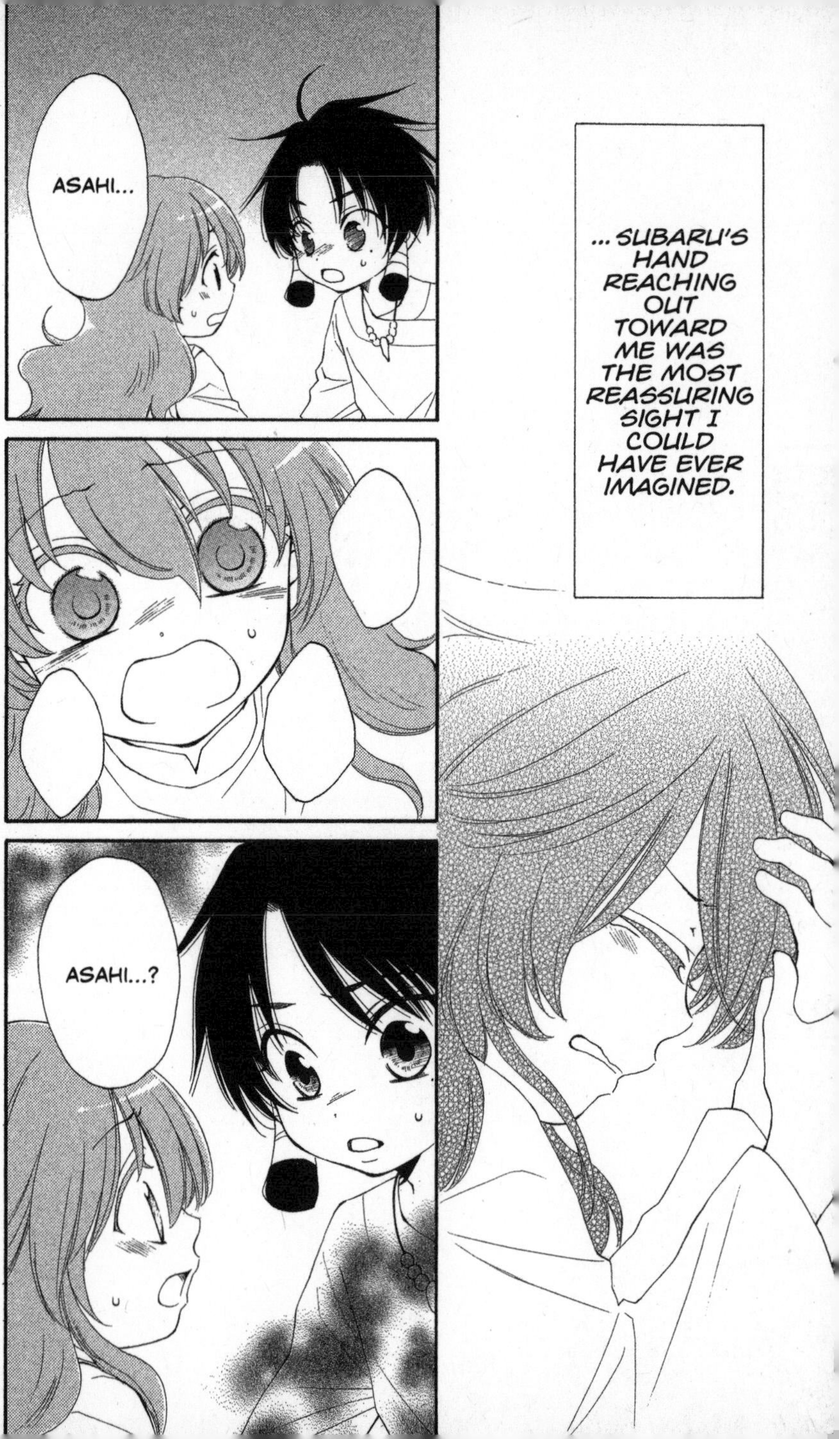
...SUBARU'S HAND REACHING OUT TOWARD ME WAS THE MOST REASSURING SIGHT I COULD HAVE EVER IMAGINED.
ASAHI...
ASAHI...?

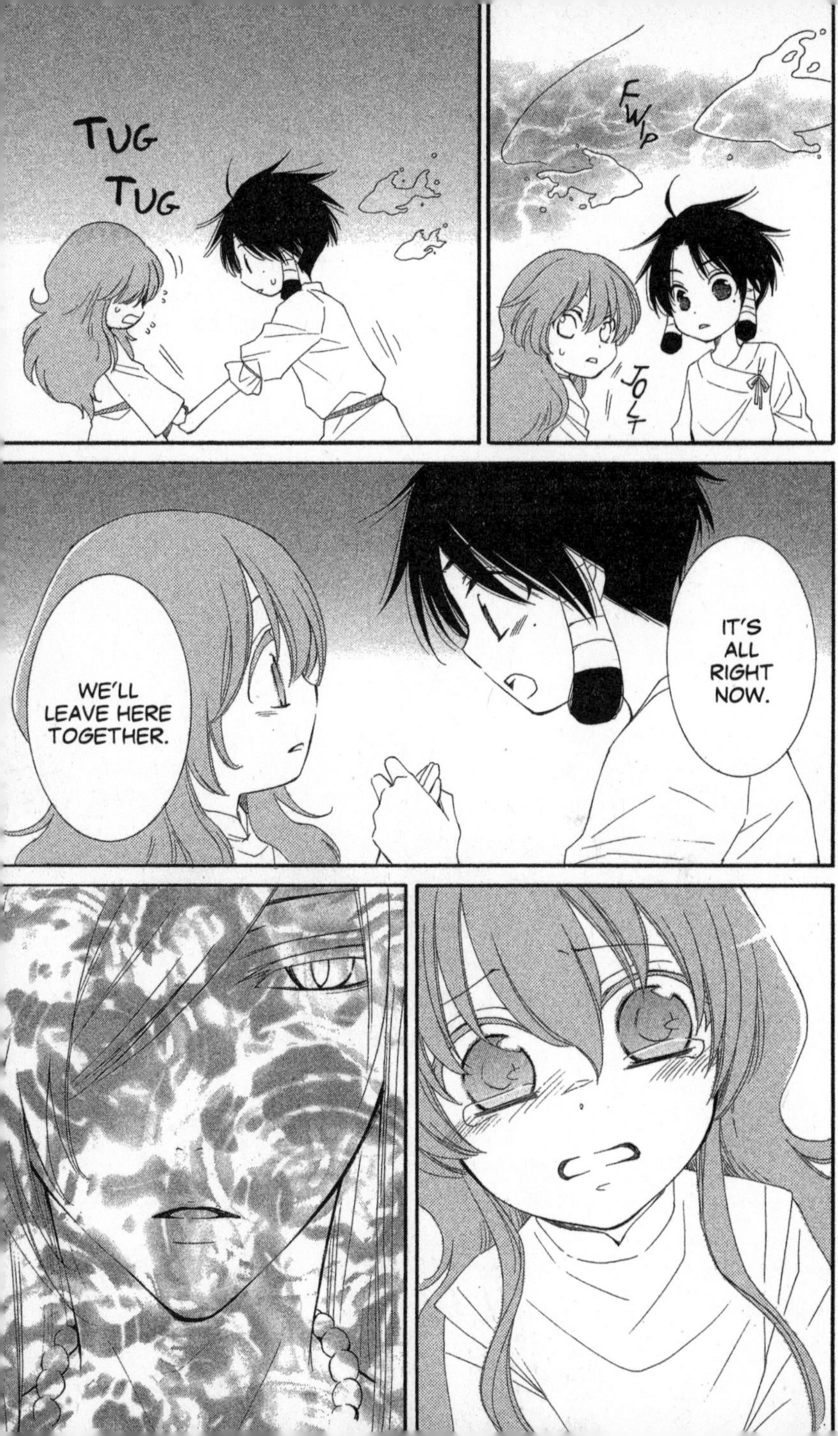
FWIP
JOLT
TUG TUG
IT'S ALL RIGHT NOW.
WE'LL LEAVE HERE TOGETHER.

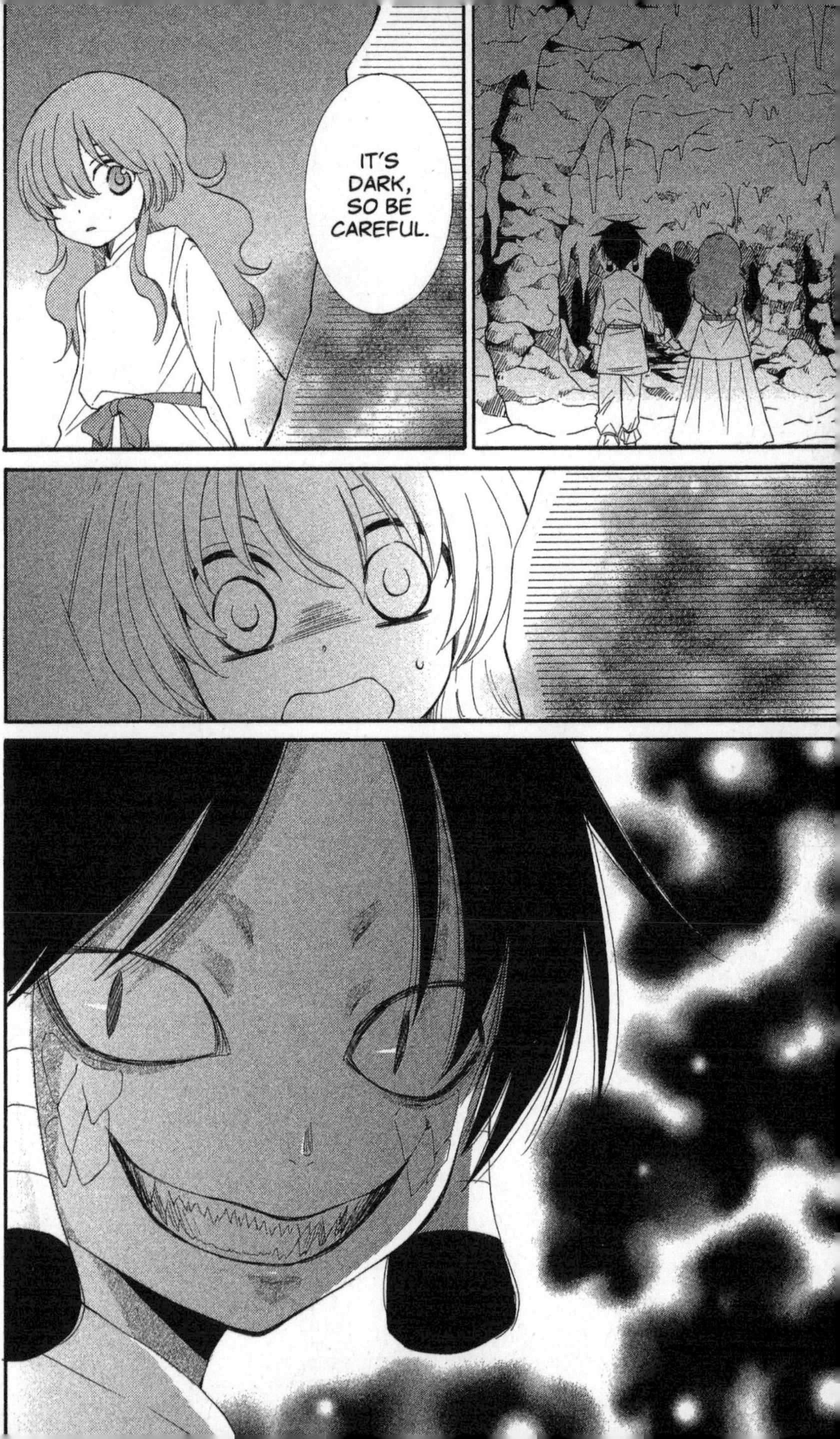
IT'S DARK, SO BE CAREFUL.

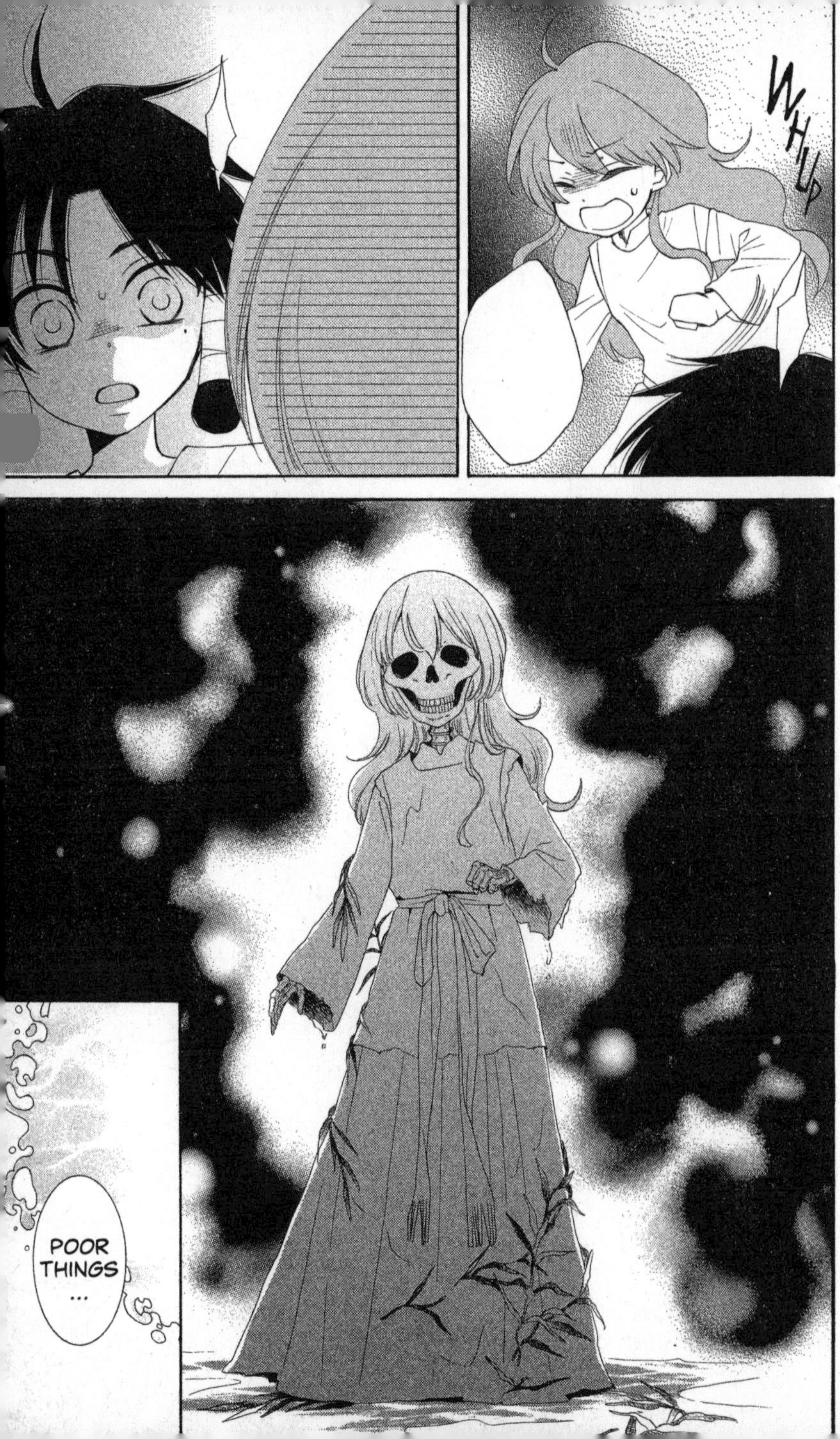
WHUP
POOR THINGS ...

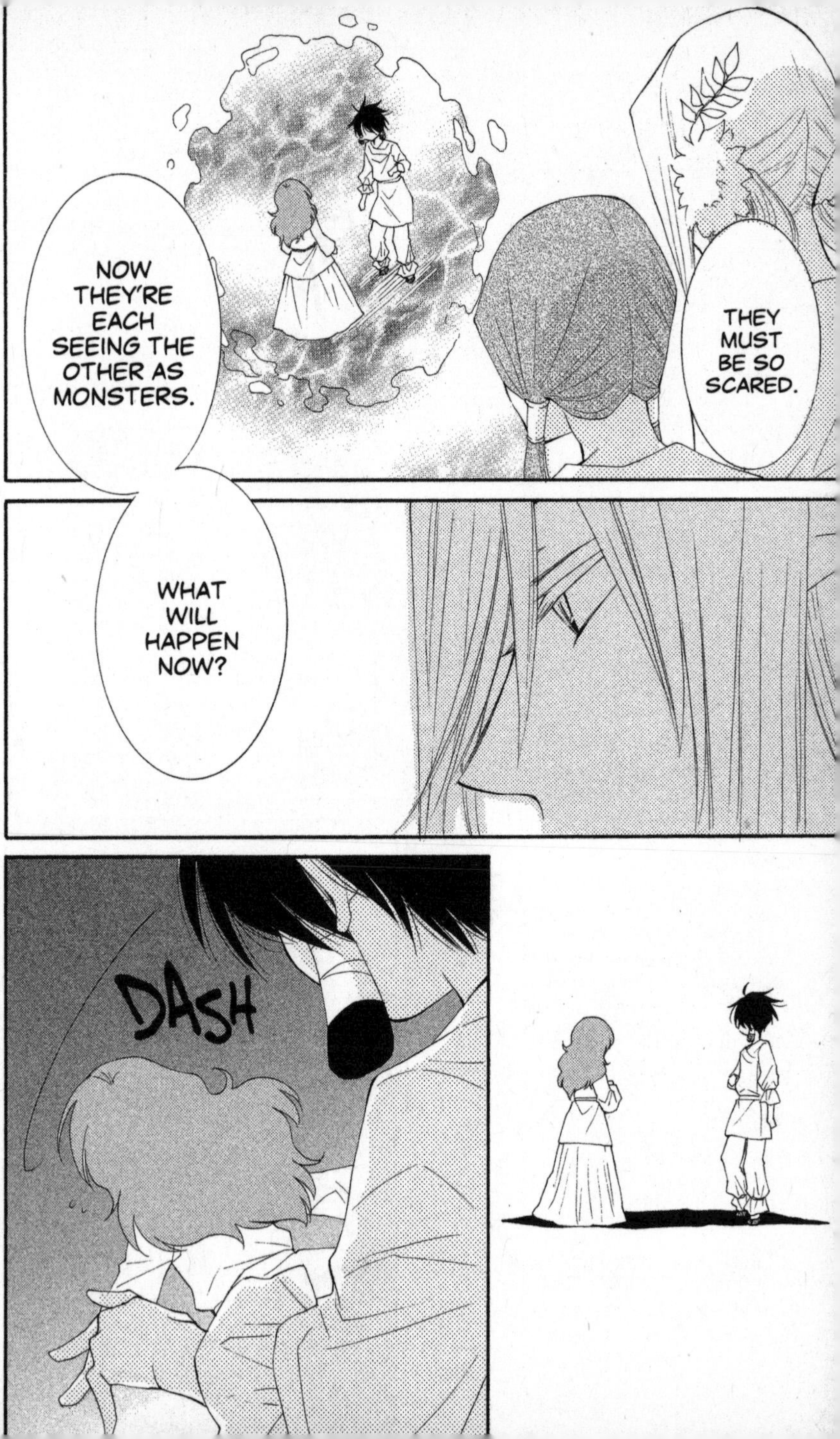
THEY MUST BE SO SCARED.
NOW THEY'RE EACH SEEING THE OTHER AS MONSTERS.
WHAT WILL HAPPEN NOW?
DASH

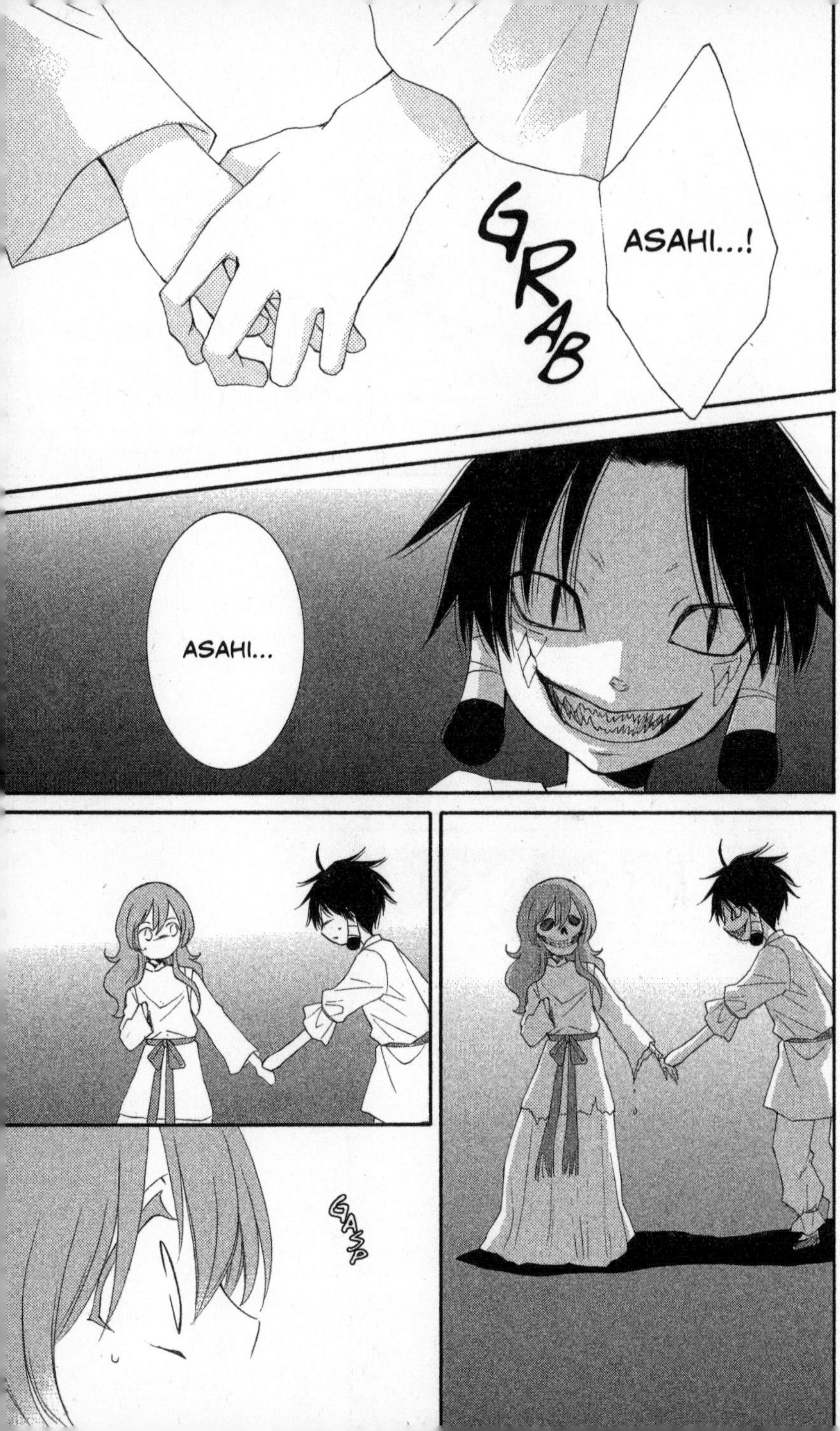
ASAHI...!
GRAB
ASAHI...
GASP

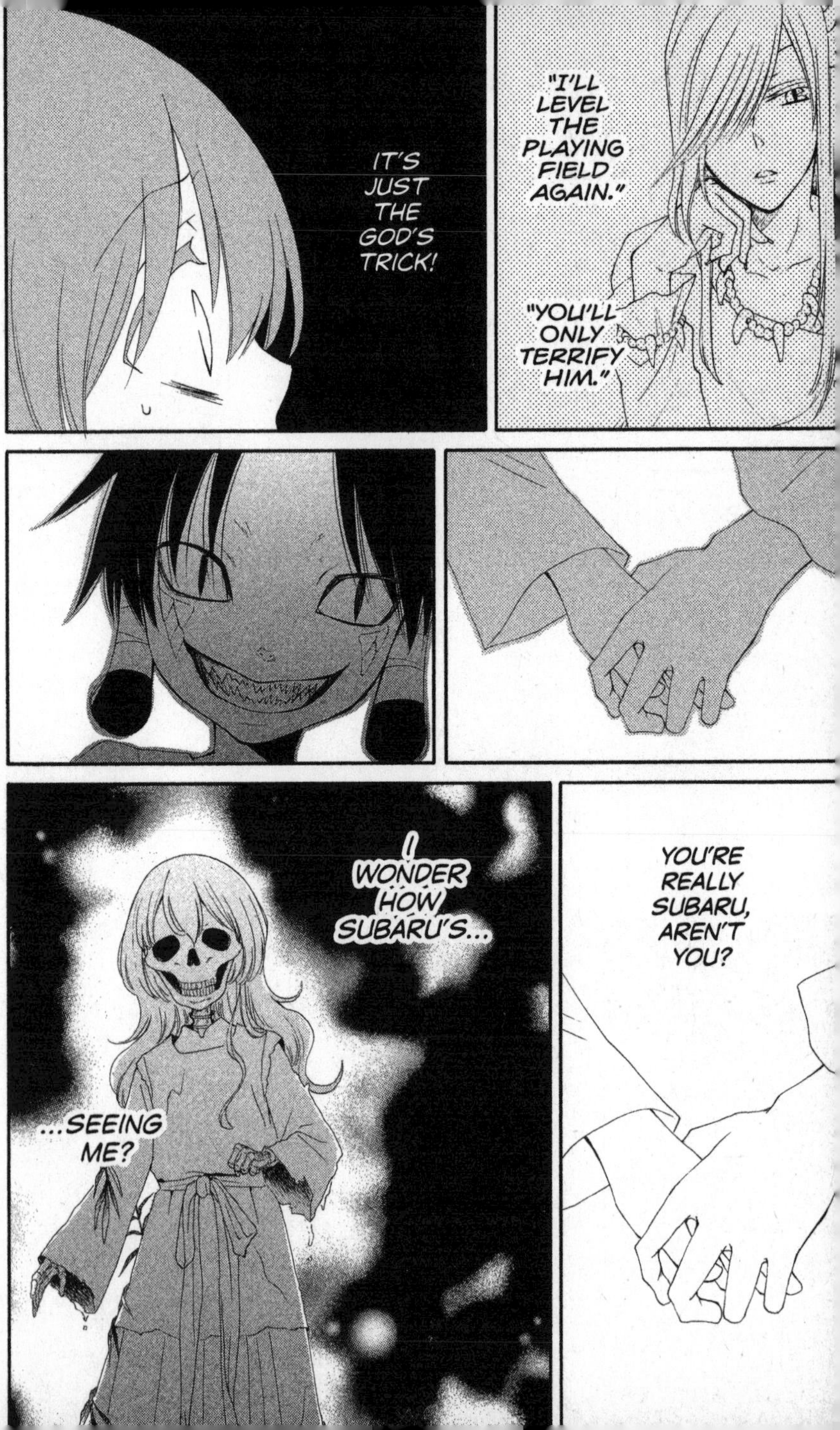
"I'LL LEVEL THE PLAYING FIELD AGAIN."
"YOU'LL ONLY TERRIFY HIM."
IT'S JUST THE GOD'S TRICK!
YOU'RE REALLY SUBARU, AREN'T YOU?
I WONDER HOW SUBARU'S...
...SEEING ME?

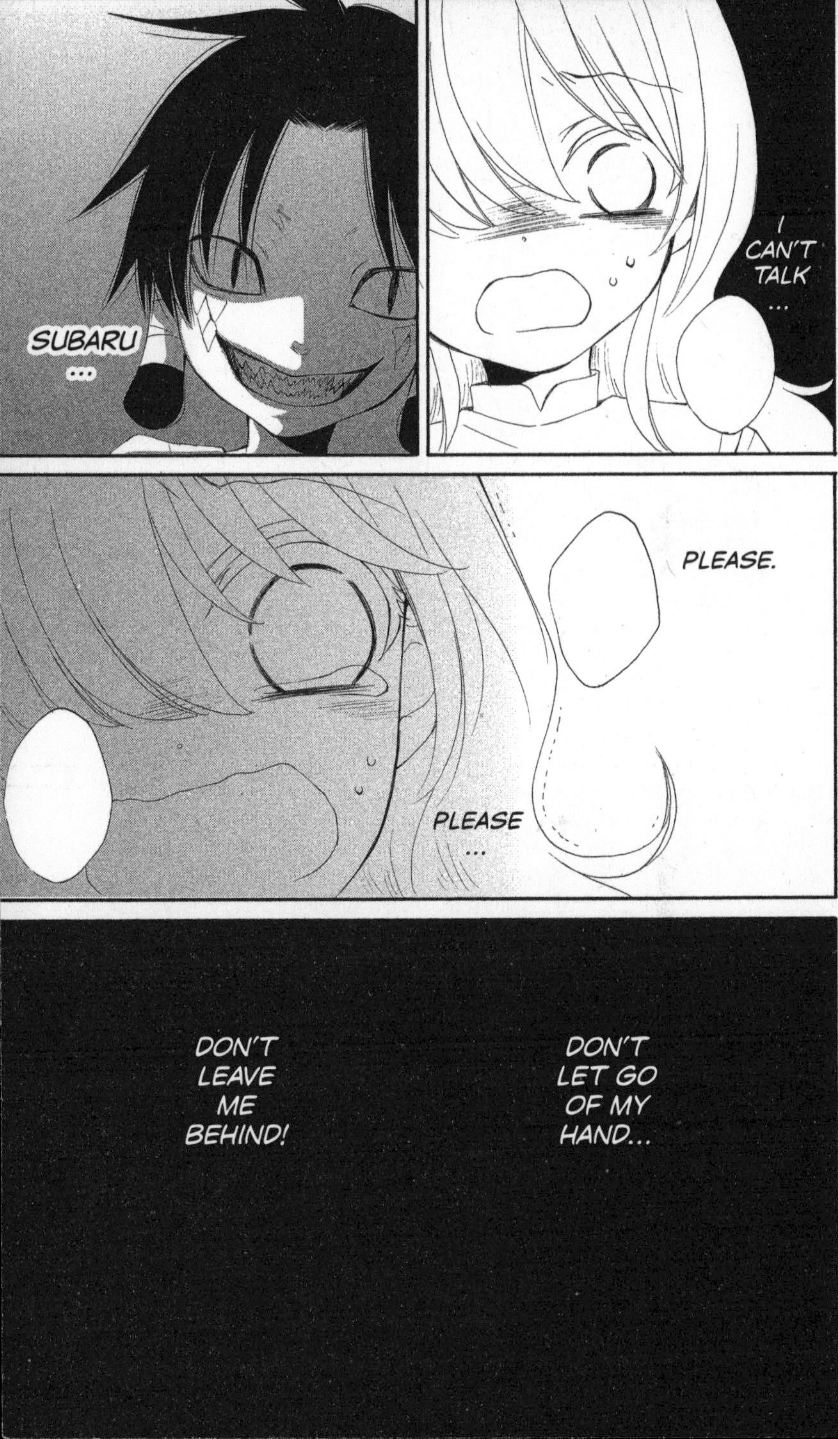
I CAN'T TALK ...
SUBARU ...
PLEASE.
PLEASE ...
DON'T LET GO OF MY HAND...
DON'T LEAVE ME BEHIND!

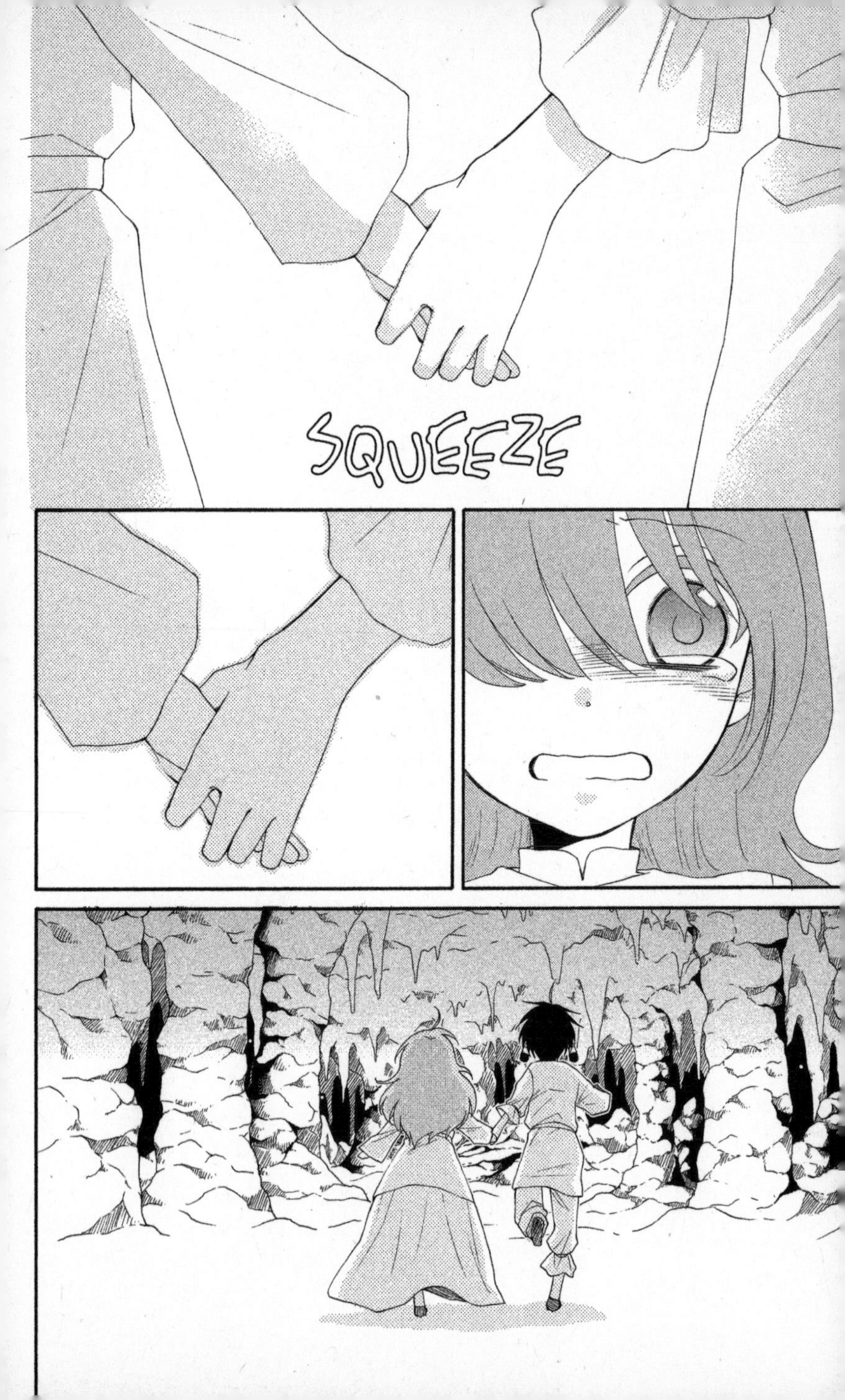
SQUEEZE

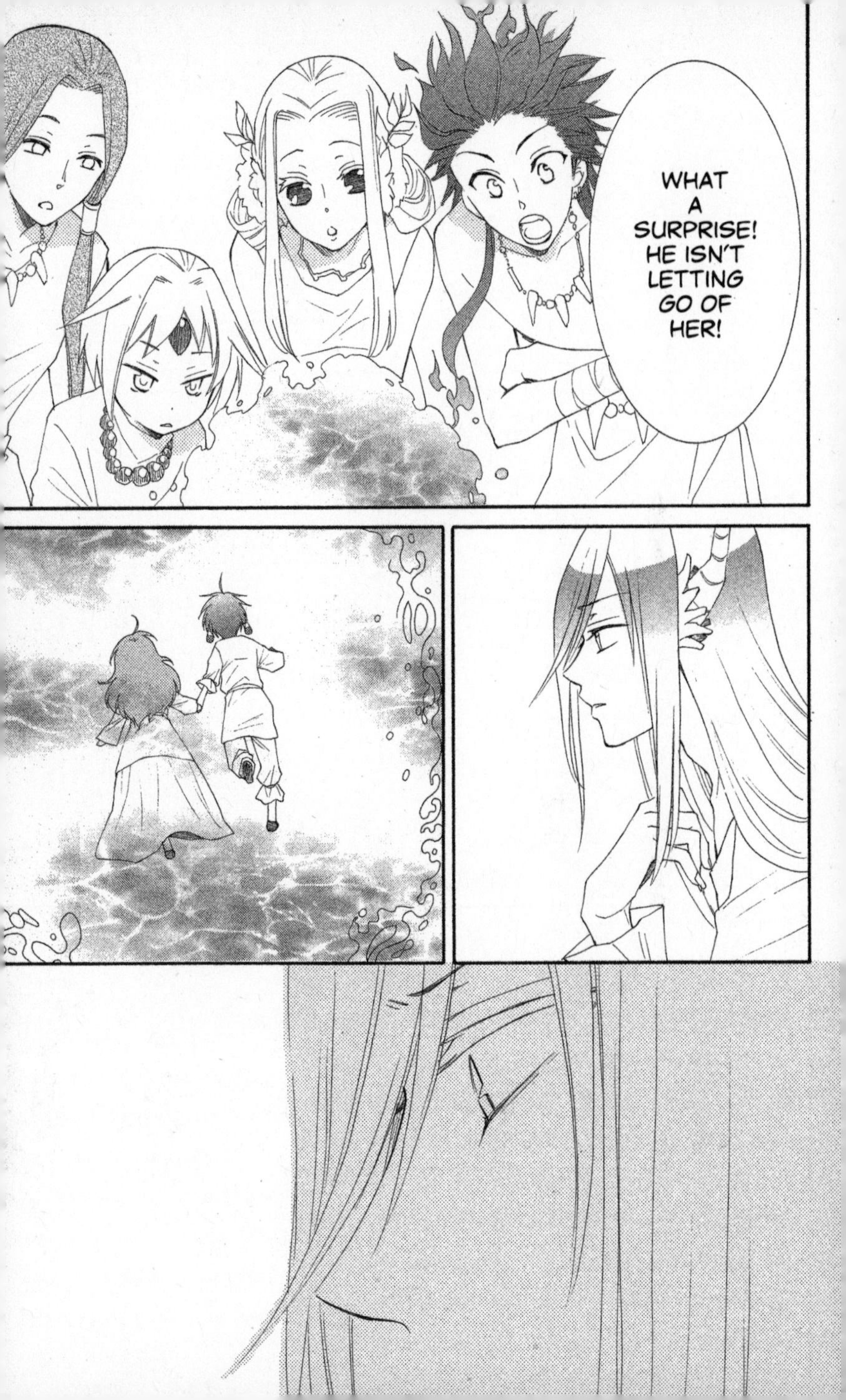
WHAT A SURPRISE! HE ISN'T LETTING GO OF HER!

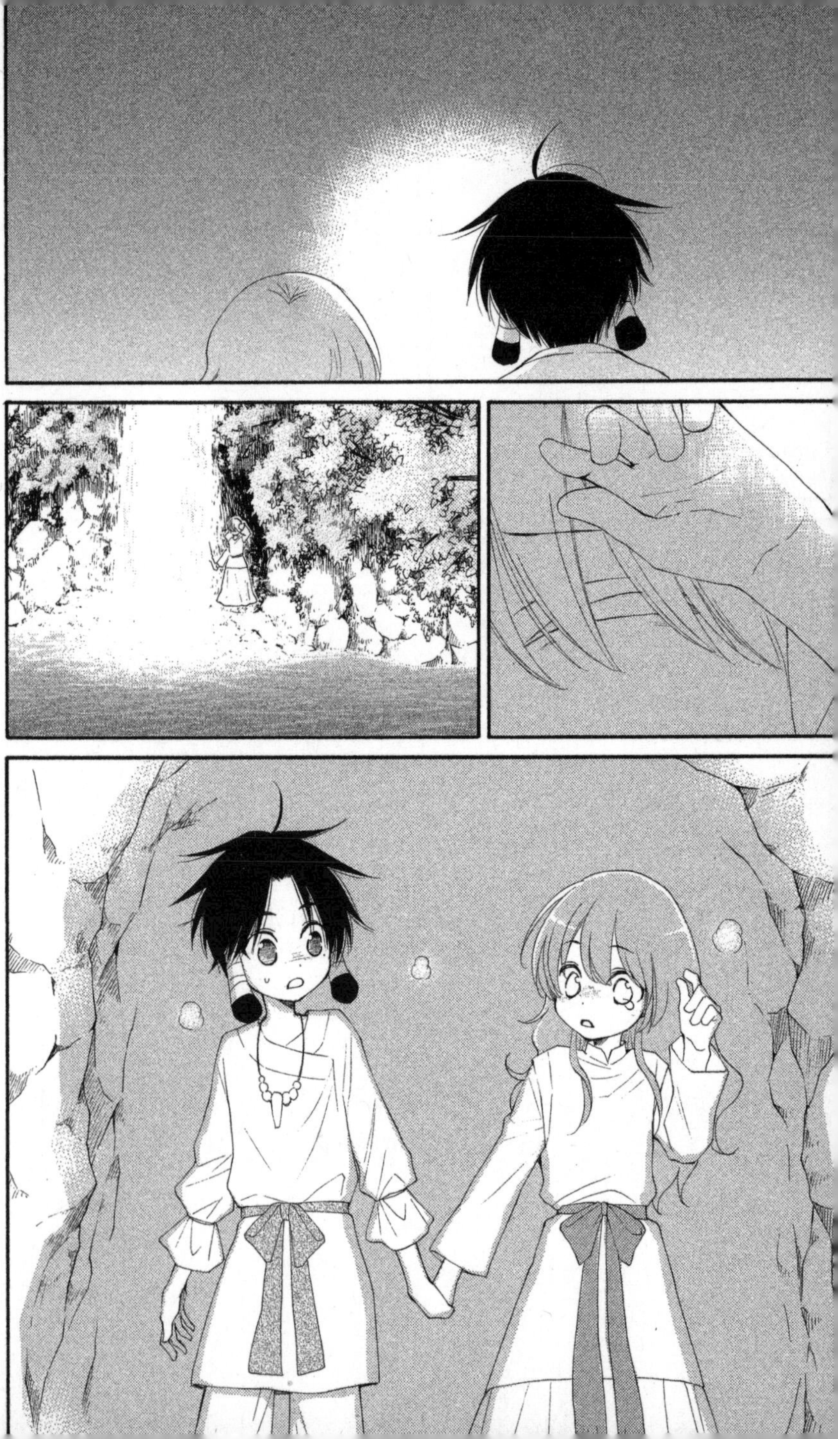

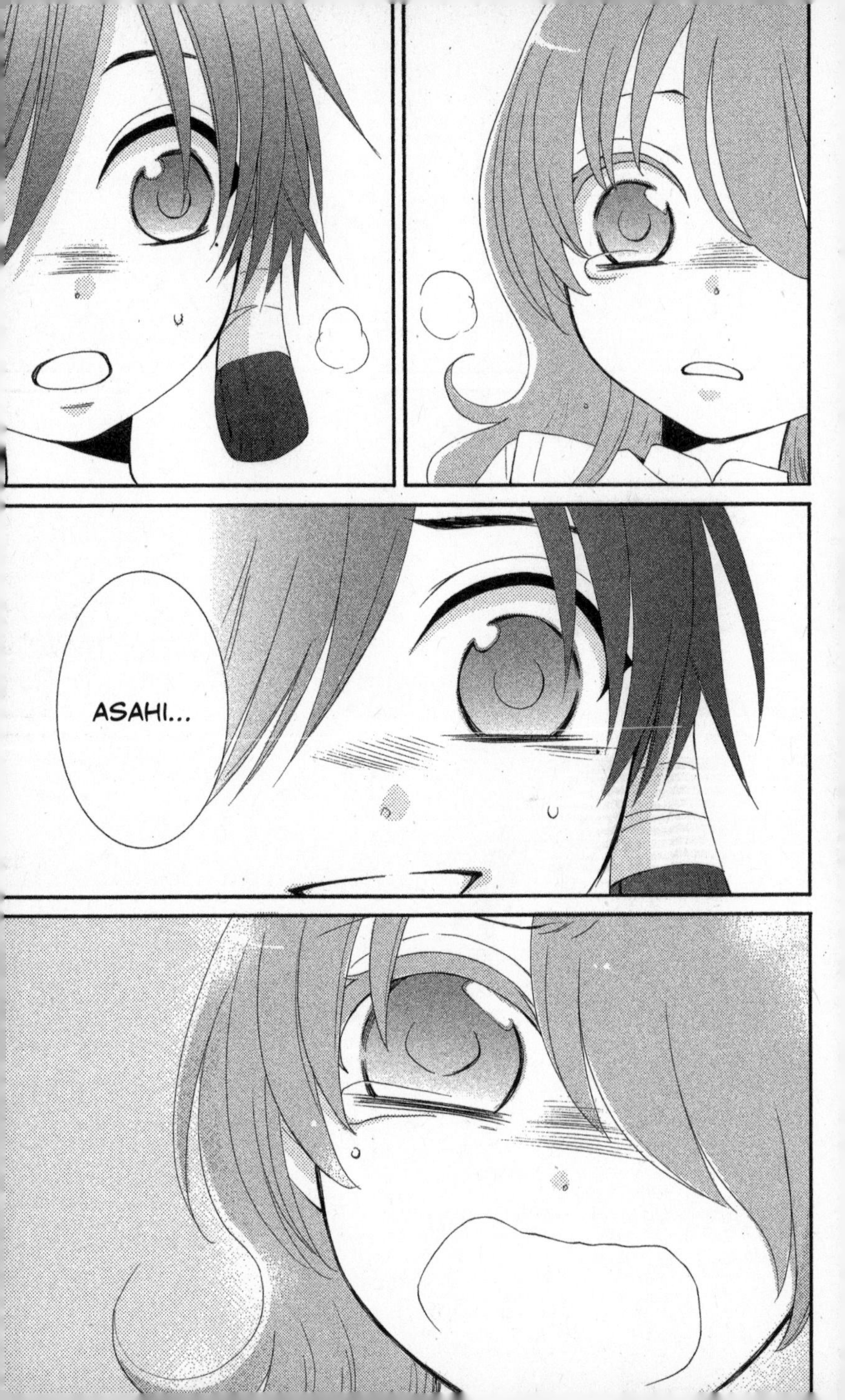
ASAHI...

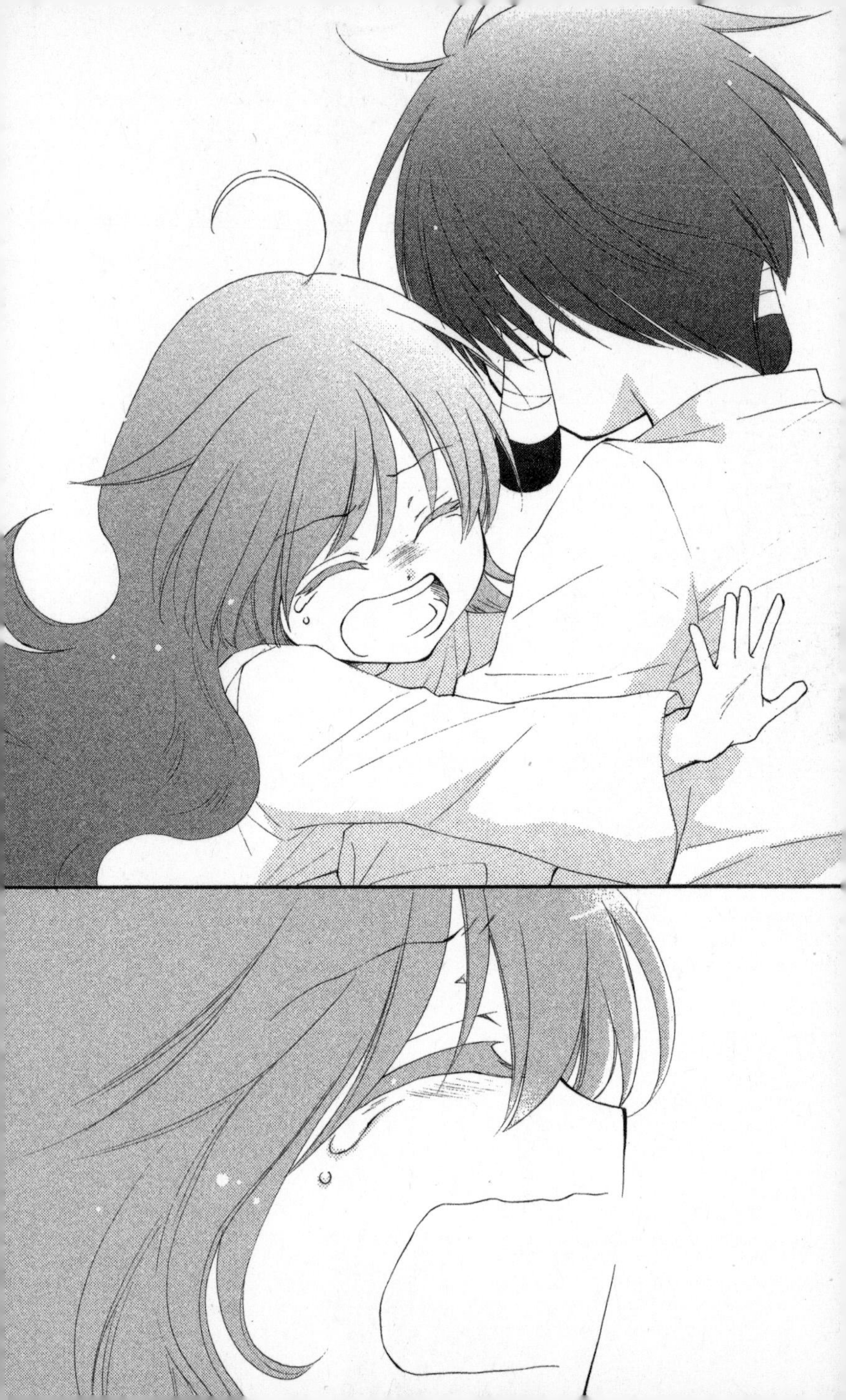

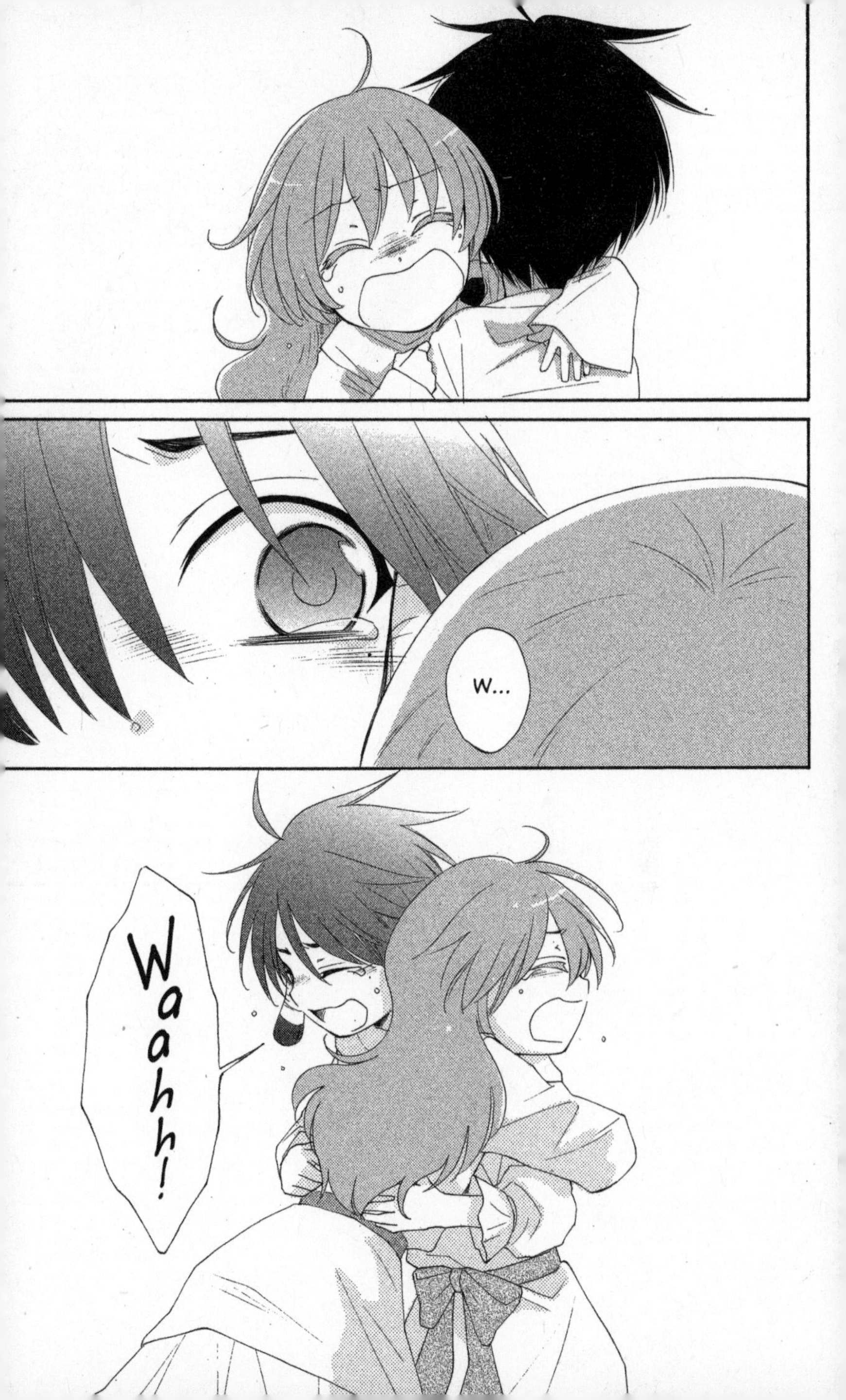
W...
Waahh!

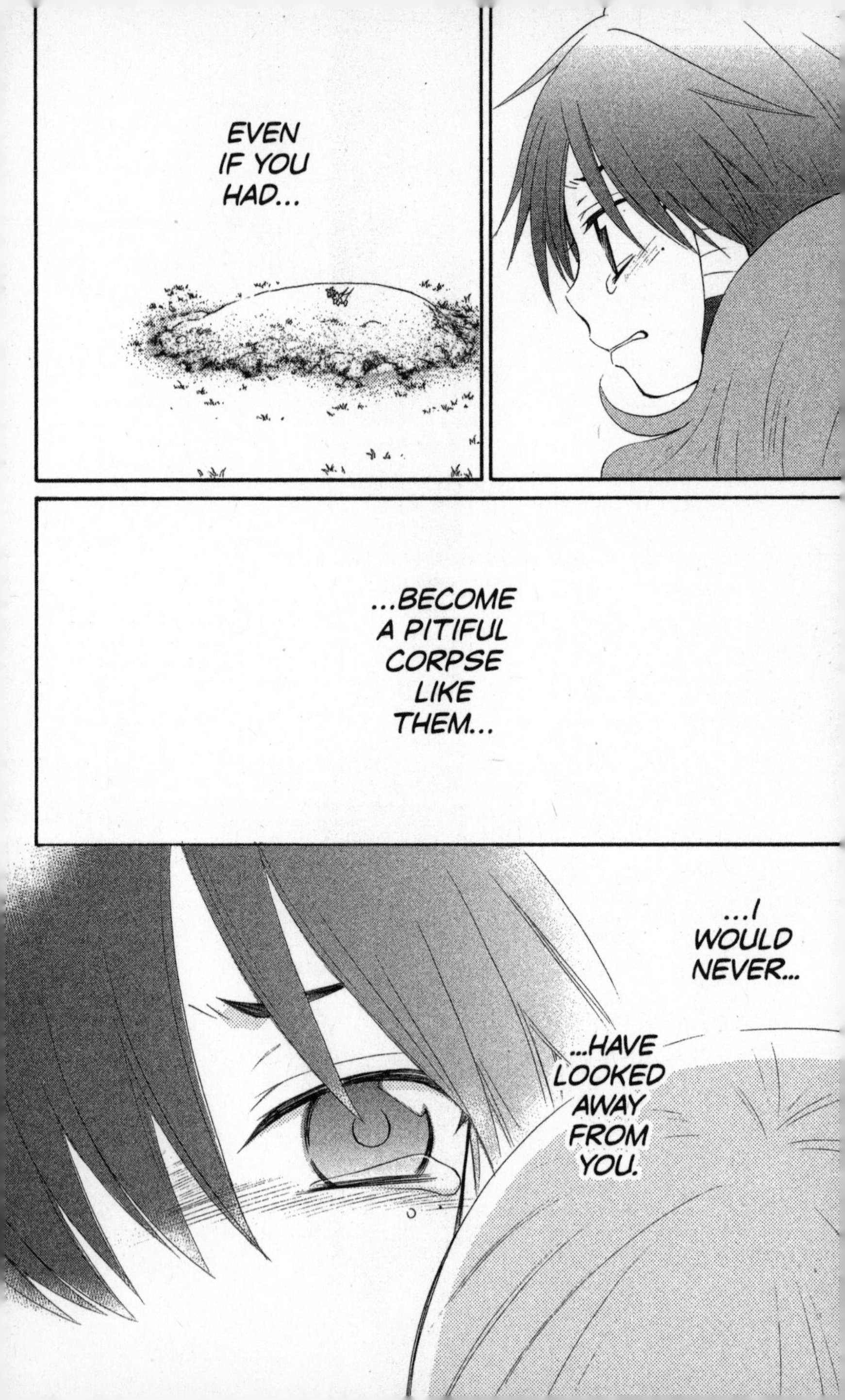
EVEN IF YOU HAD...
...BECOME A PITIFUL CORPSE LIKE THEM...
...I WOULD NEVER...
...HAVE LOOKED AWAY FROM YOU.

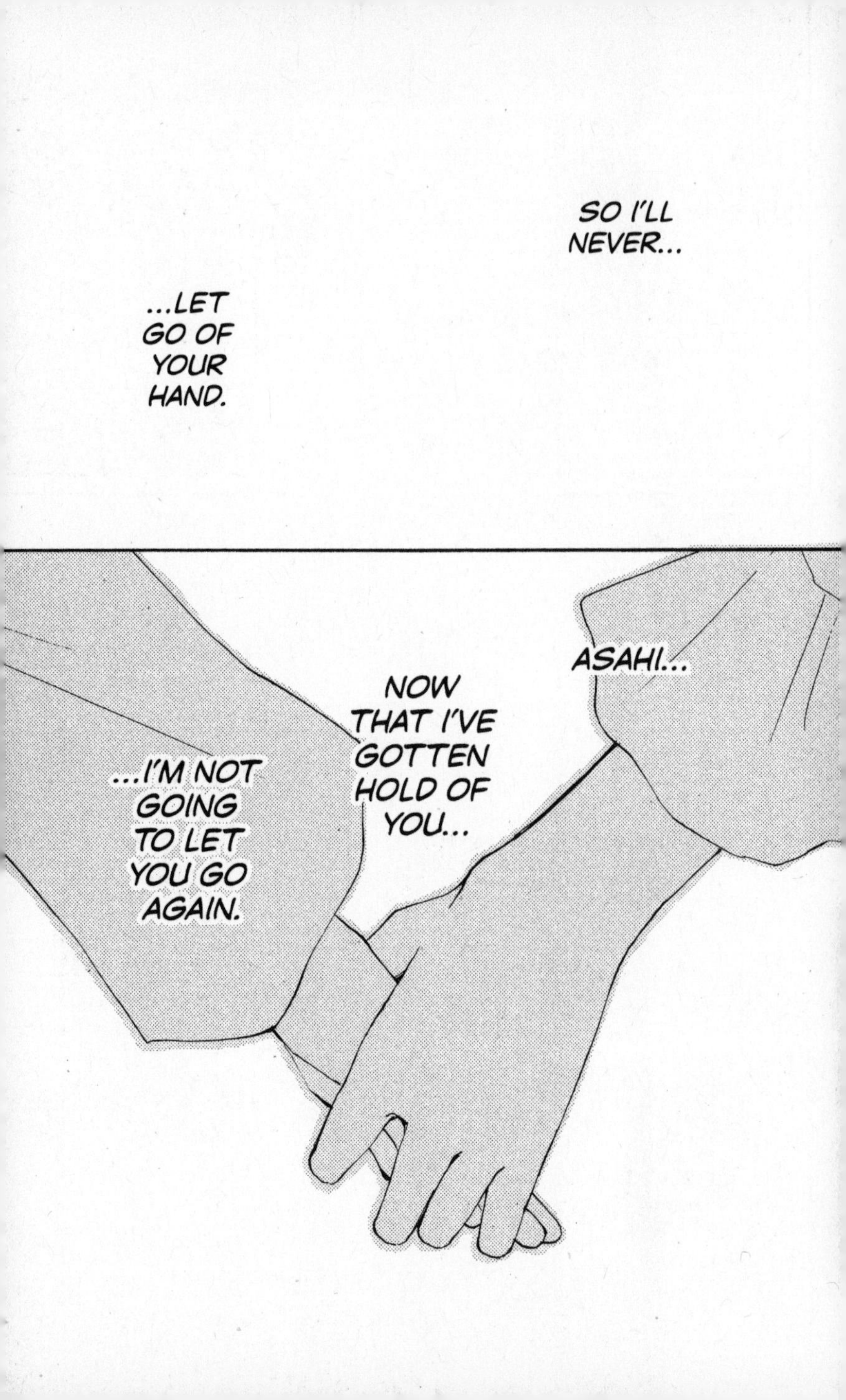
SO I'LL NEVER...
...LET GO OF YOUR HAND.
ASAHI...
NOW THAT I'VE GOTTEN HOLD OF YOU...
...I'M NOT GOING TO LET YOU GO AGAIN.

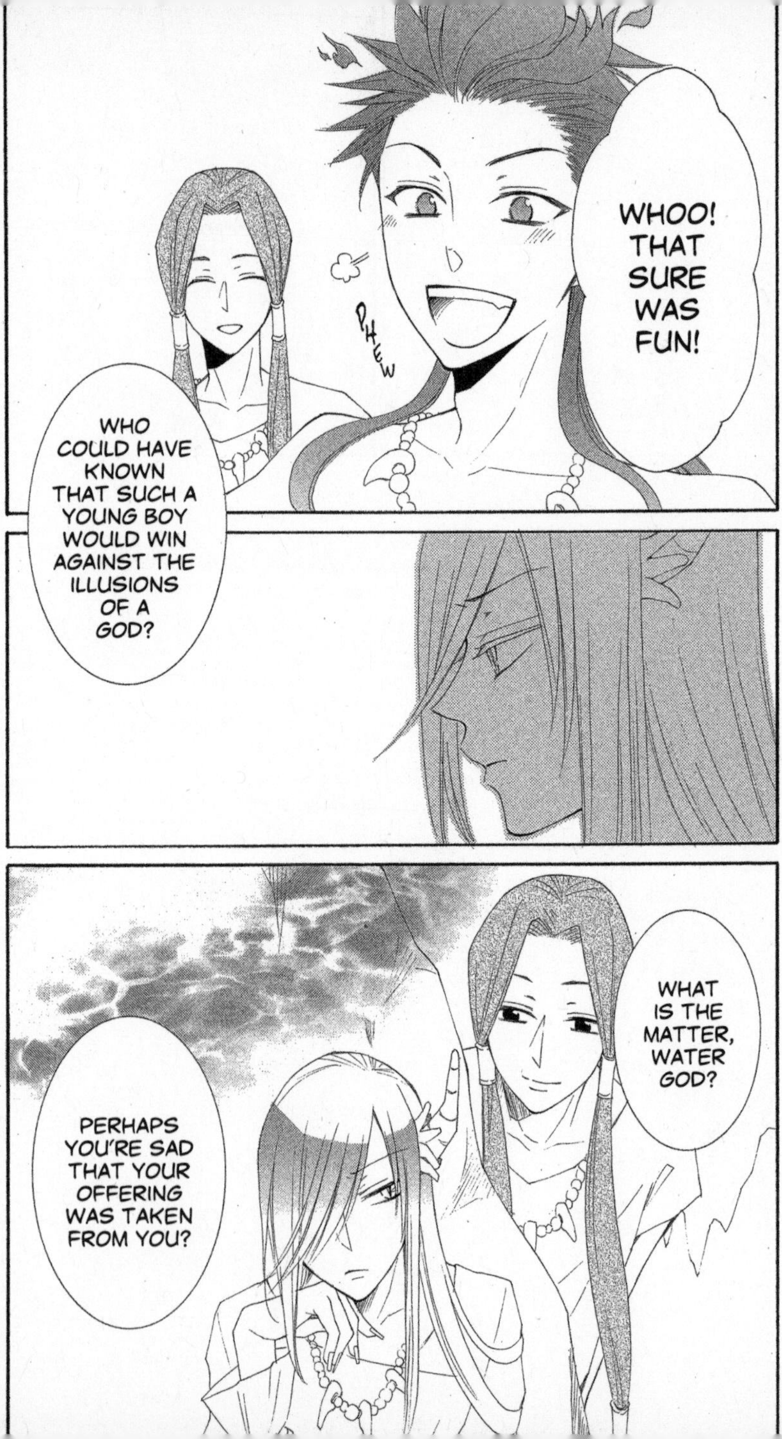
WHOO! THAT SURE WAS FUN!
PHEW
WHO COULD HAVE KNOWN THAT SUCH A YOUNG BOY WOULD WIN AGAINST THE ILLUSIONS OF A GOD?
WHAT IS THE MATTER, WATER GOD?
PERHAPS YOU'RE SAD THAT YOUR OFFERING WAS TAKEN FROM YOU?

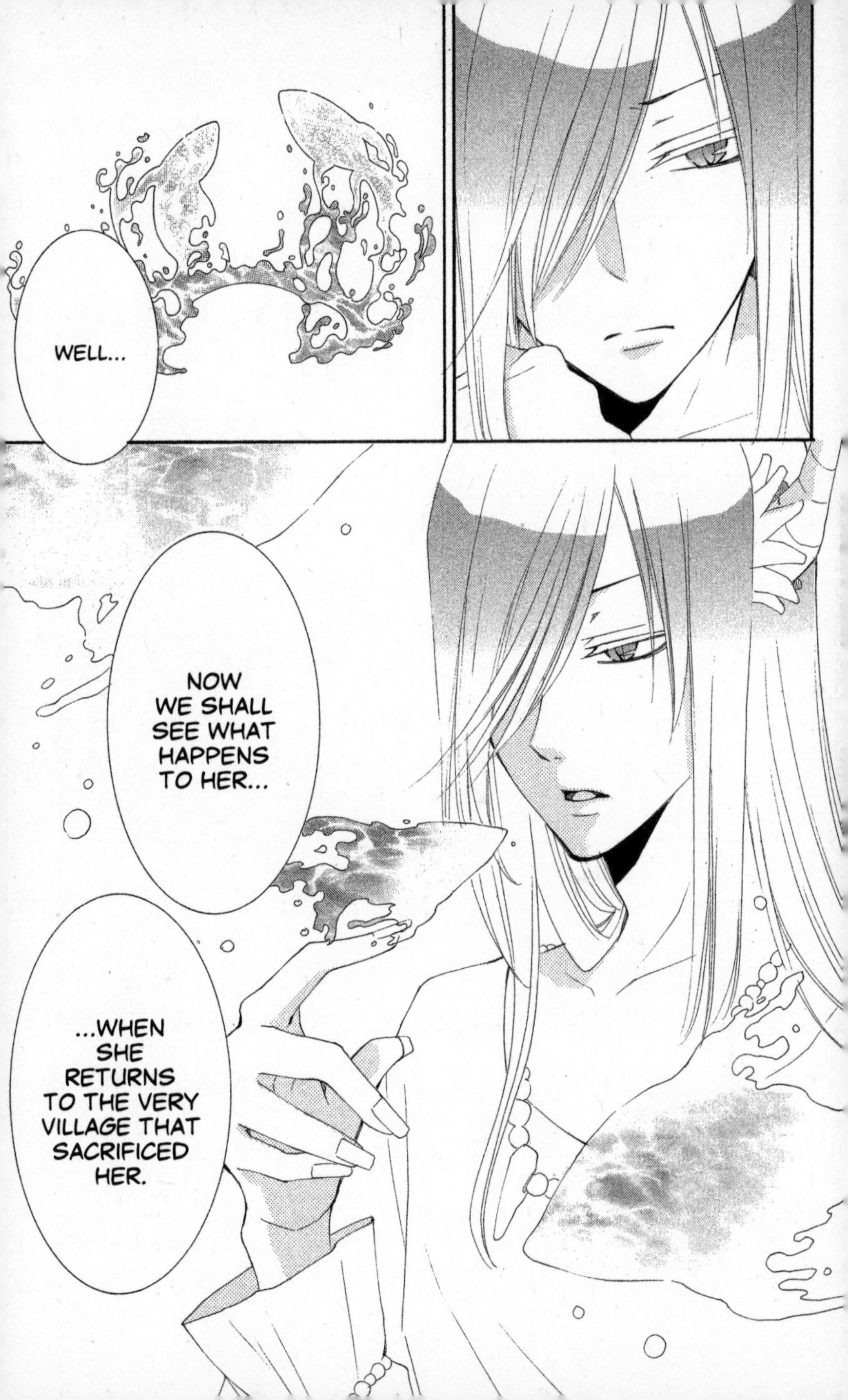
WELL...
NOW WE SHALL SEE WHAT HAPPENS TO HER...
...WHEN SHE RETURNS TO THE VERY VILLAGE THAT SACRIFICED HER.

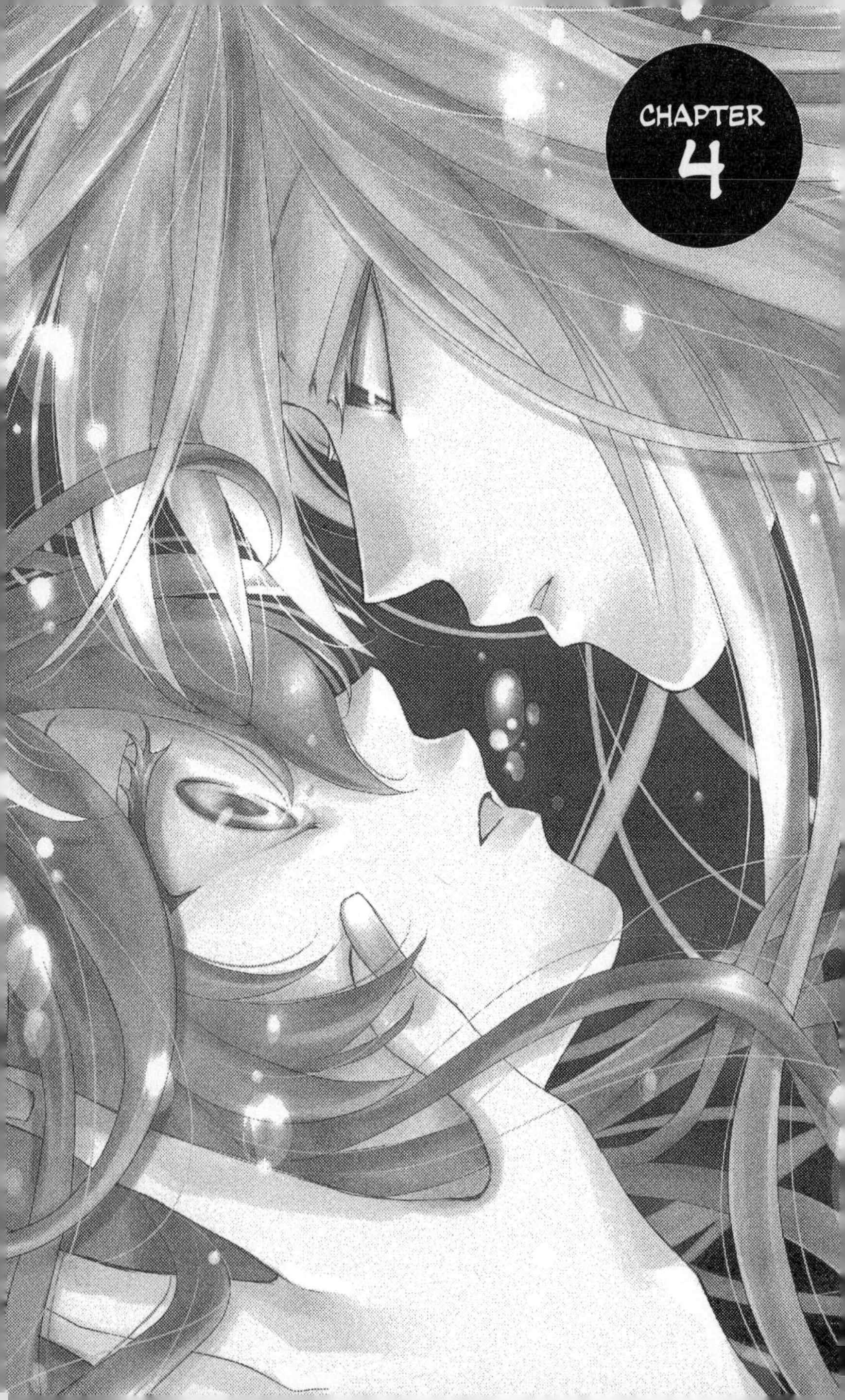
CHAPTER
4

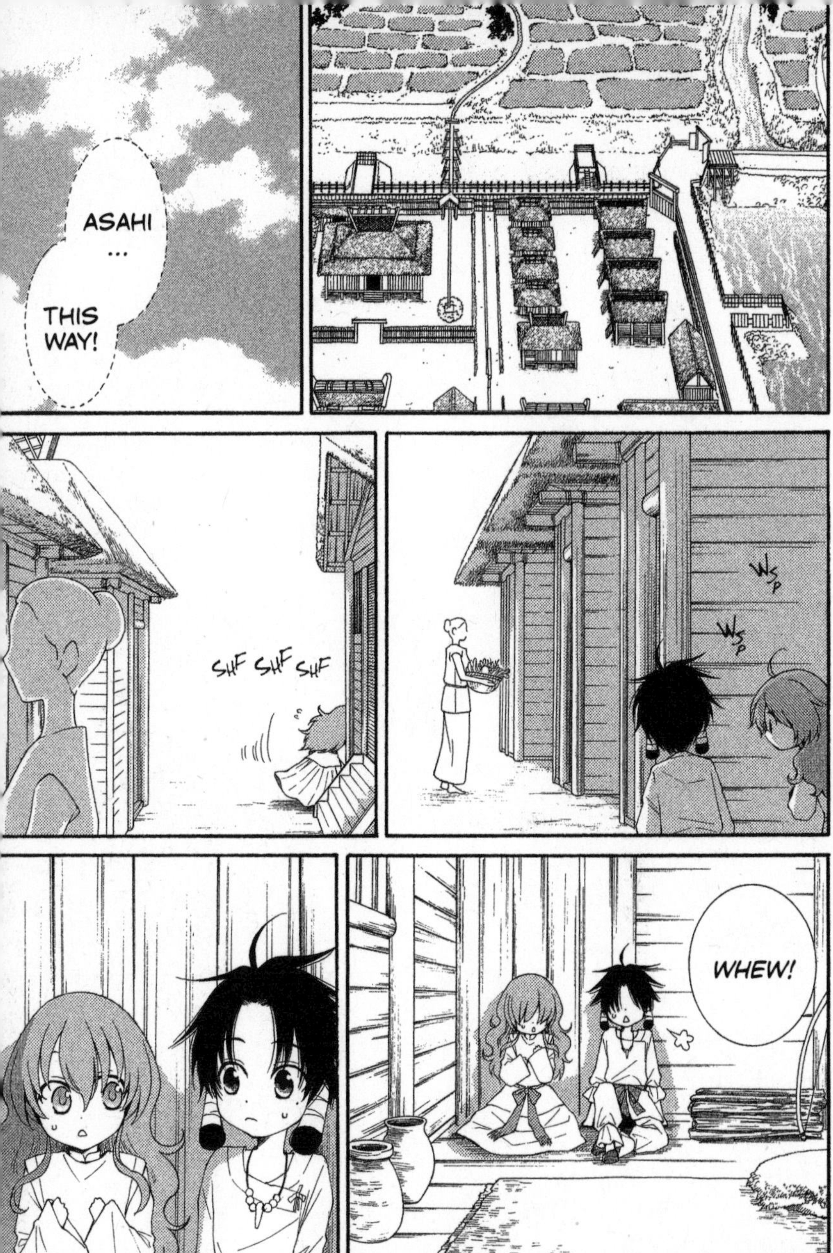
ASAHI ... THIS WAY!
WSP
WSP
SHF SHF SHF
WHEW!

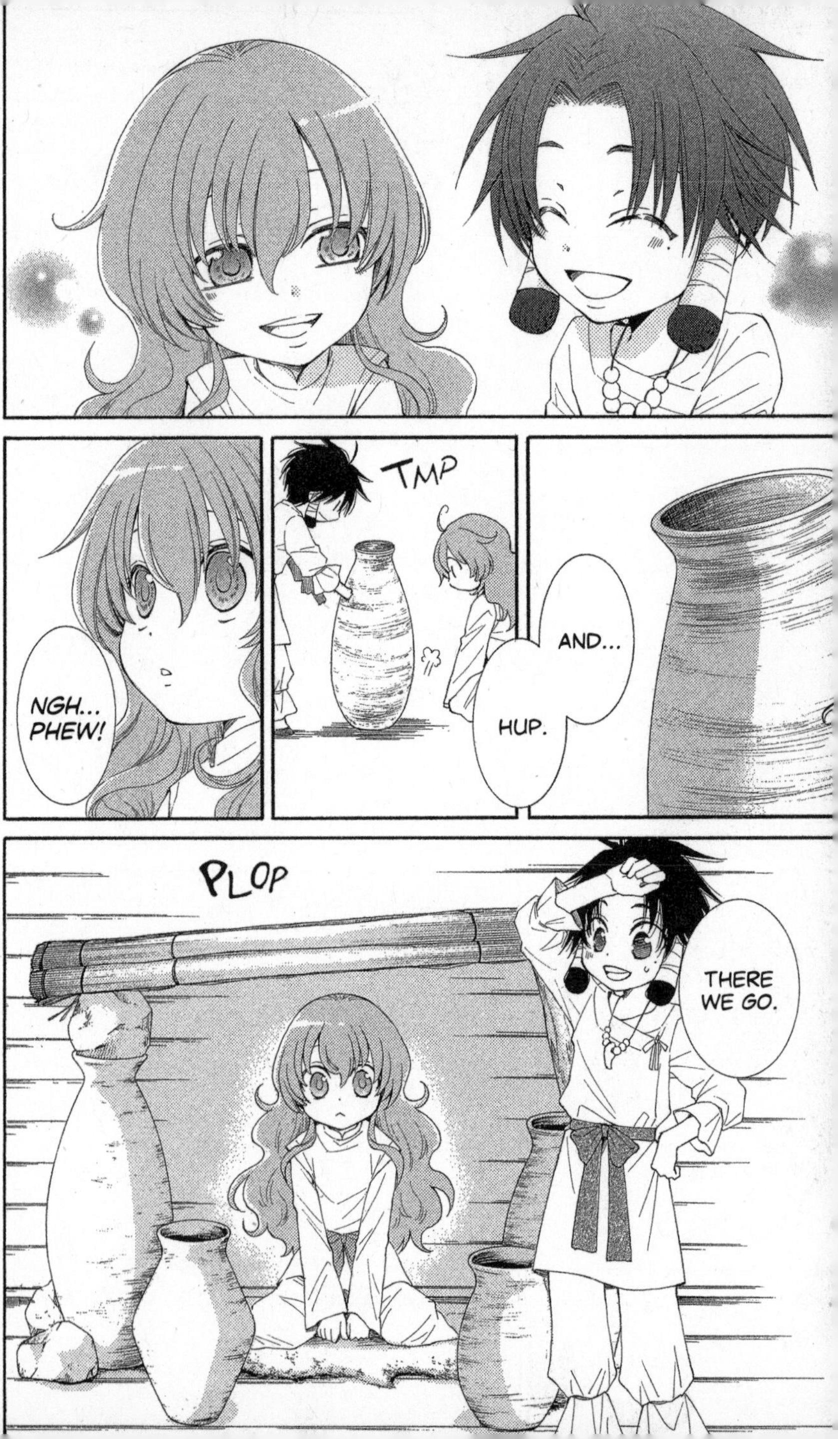
AND...
HUP.
TMP
NGH... PHEW!
PLOP
THERE WE GO.

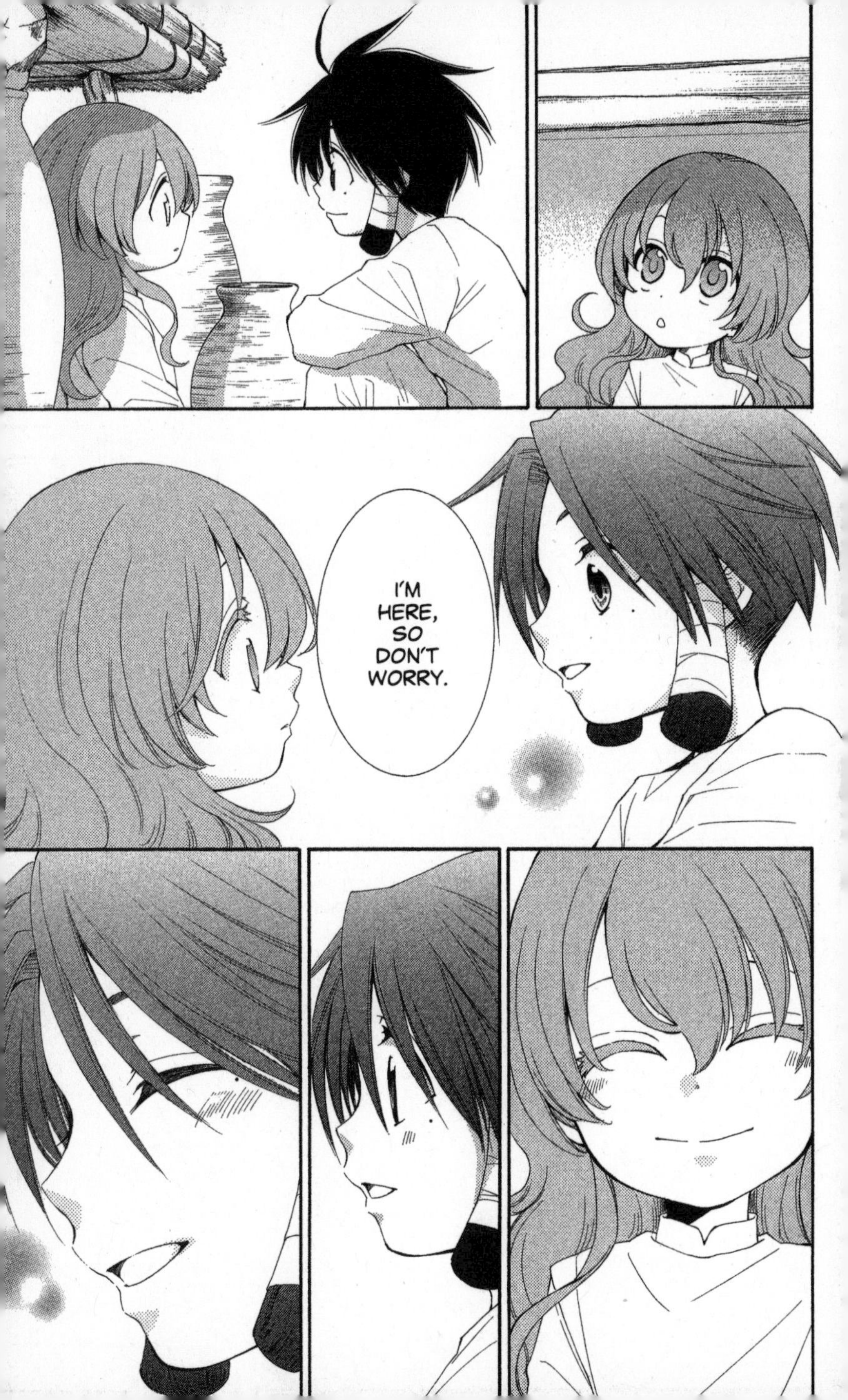
I'M HERE, SO DON'T WORRY.

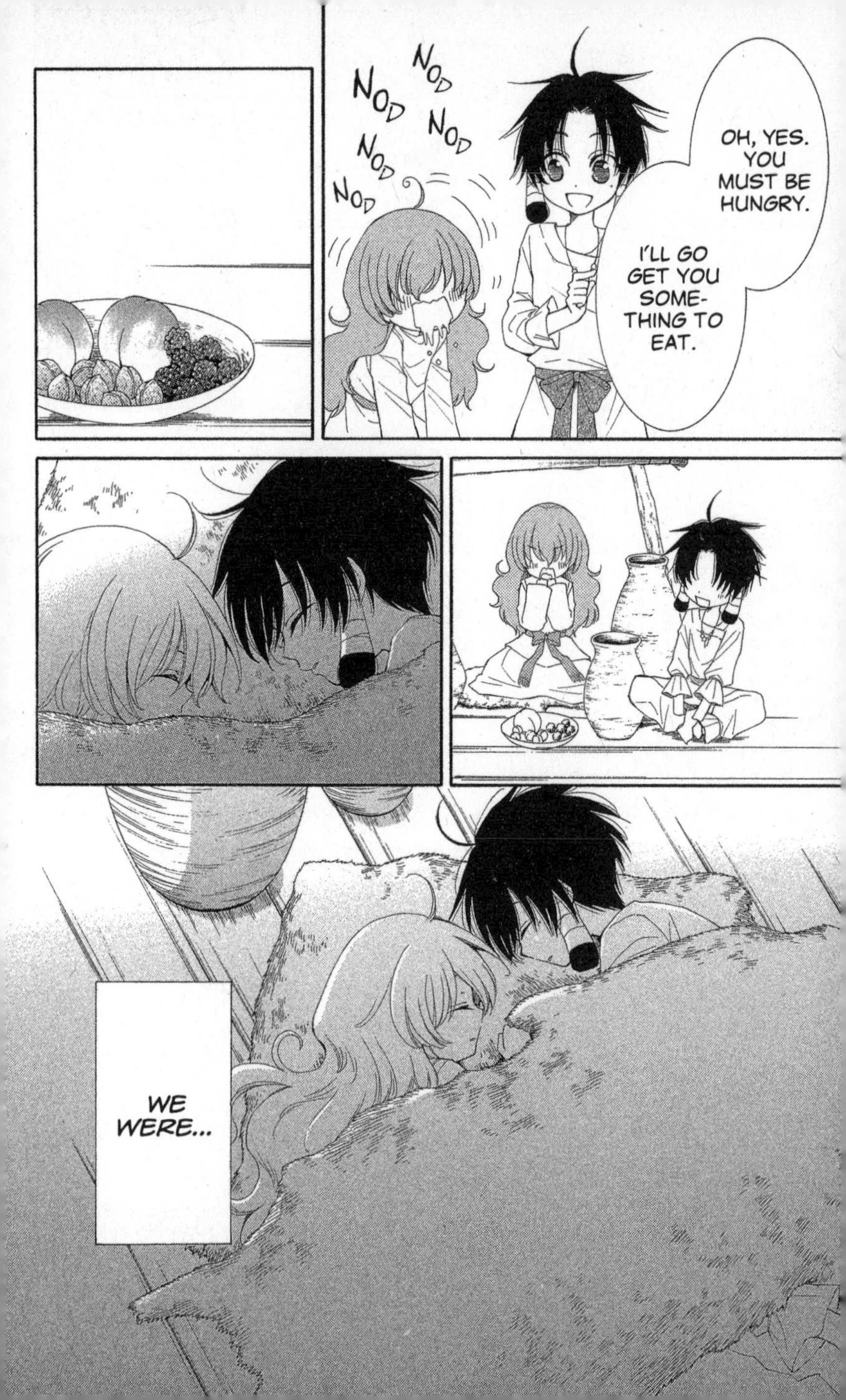
OH, YES. YOU MUST BE HUNGRY.
I'LL GO GET YOU SOME-THING TO EAT.
NOD NOD NOD NOD NOD
WE WERE...

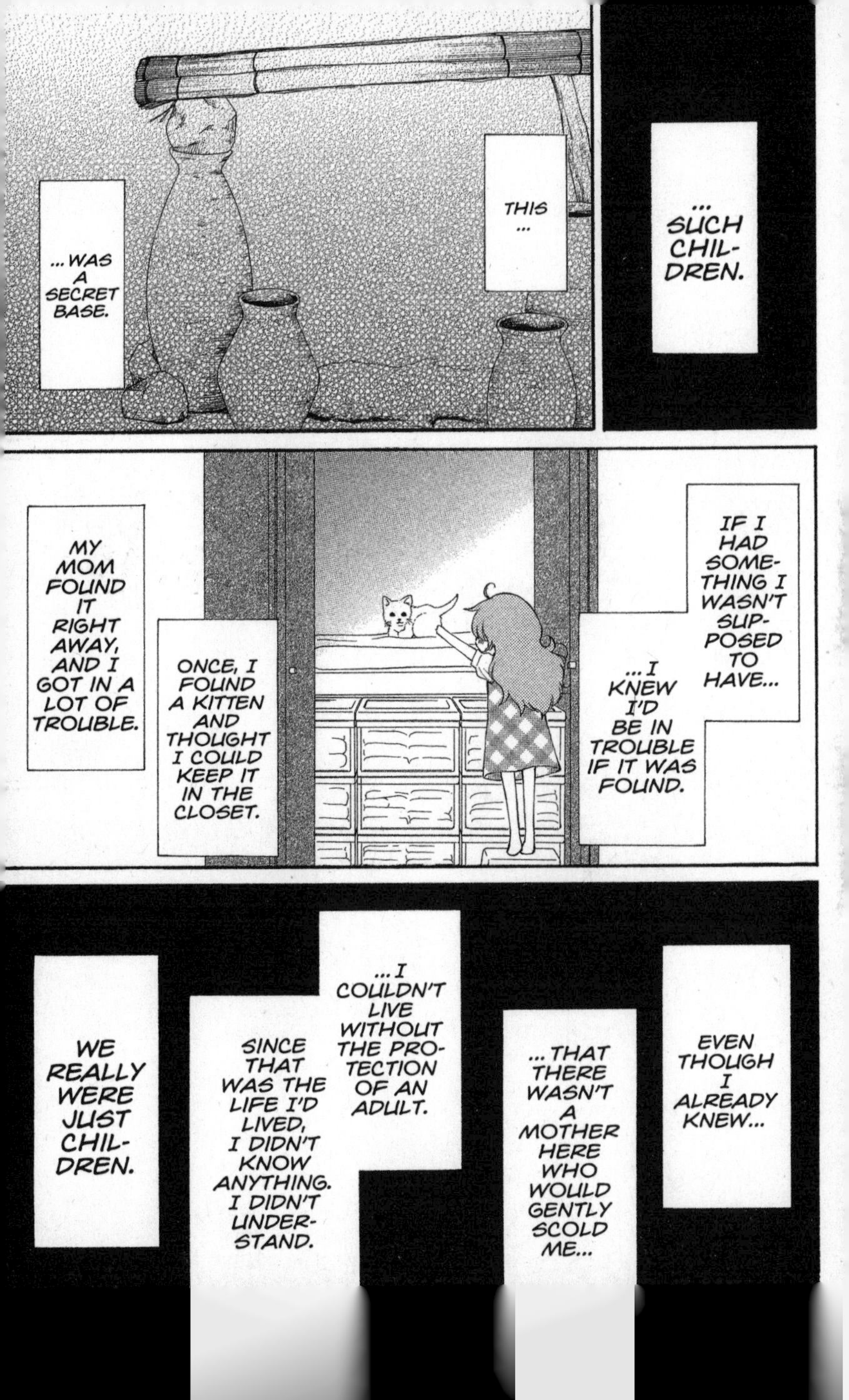
...SUCH CHIL-DREN.
THIS...
...WAS A SECRET BASE.
IF I HAD SOME-THING I WASN'T SUP-POSED TO HAVE...
...I KNEW I'D BE IN TROUBLE IF IT WAS FOUND.
ONCE, I FOUND A KITTEN AND THOUGHT I COULD KEEP IT IN THE CLOSET.
MY MOM FOUND IT RIGHT AWAY, AND I GOT IN A LOT OF TROUBLE.
EVEN THOUGH I ALREADY KNEW...
...THAT THERE WASN'T A MOTHER HERE WHO WOULD GENTLY SCOLD ME...
...I COULDN'T LIVE WITHOUT THE PRO-TECTION OF AN ADULT.
SINCE THAT WAS THE LIFE I'D LIVED, I DIDN'T KNOW ANYTHING. I DIDN'T UNDER-STAND.
WE REALLY WERE JUST CHIL-DREN.

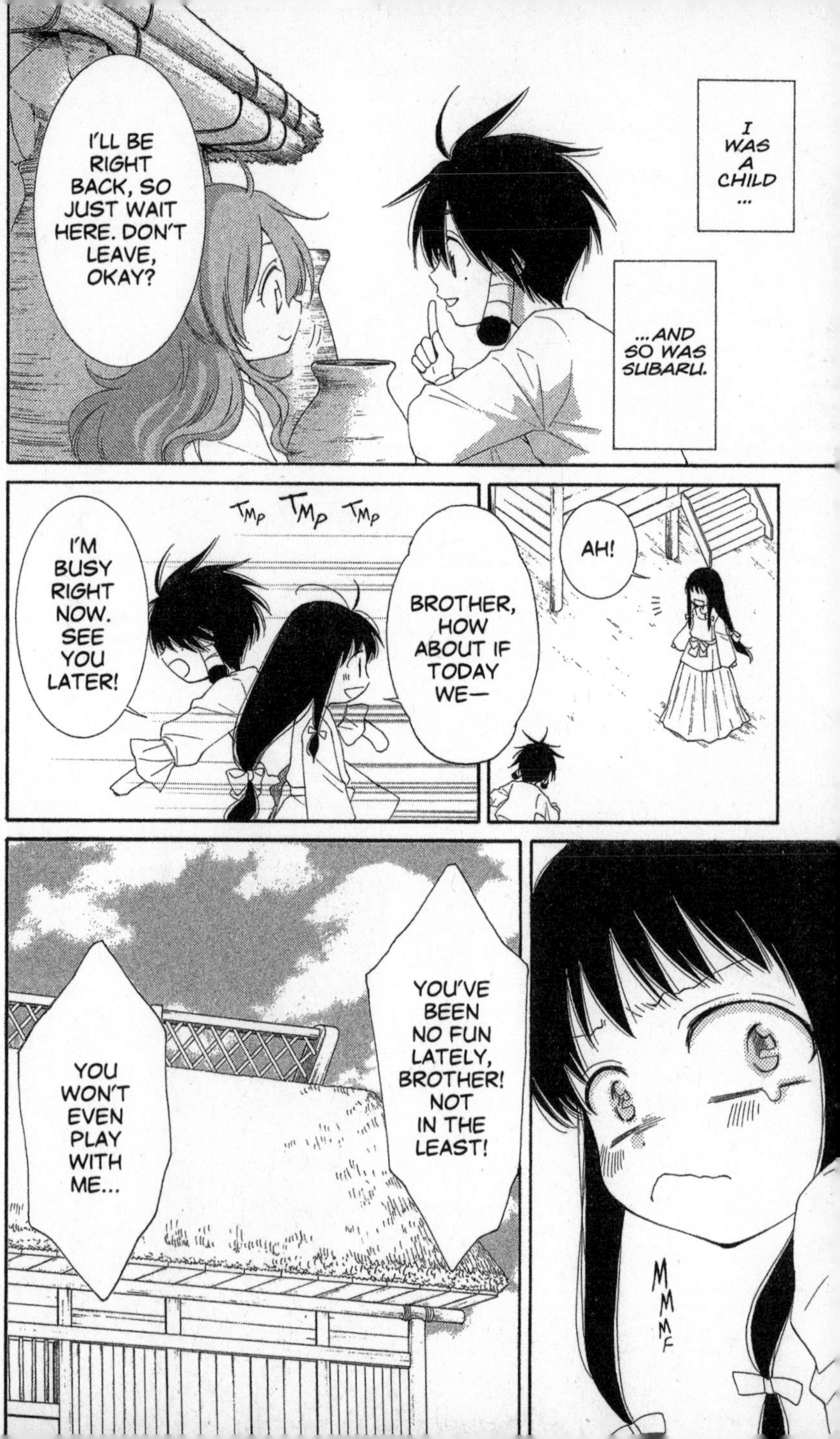
I WAS A CHILD...
...AND SO WAS SUBARU.
I'LL BE RIGHT BACK, SO JUST WAIT HERE. DON'T LEAVE, OKAY?
AH!
TMP TMP TMP
BROTHER, HOW ABOUT IF TODAY WE—
I'M BUSY RIGHT NOW. SEE YOU LATER!
MMMF
YOU'VE BEEN NO FUN LATELY, BROTHER! NOT IN THE LEAST!
YOU WON'T EVEN PLAY WITH ME...

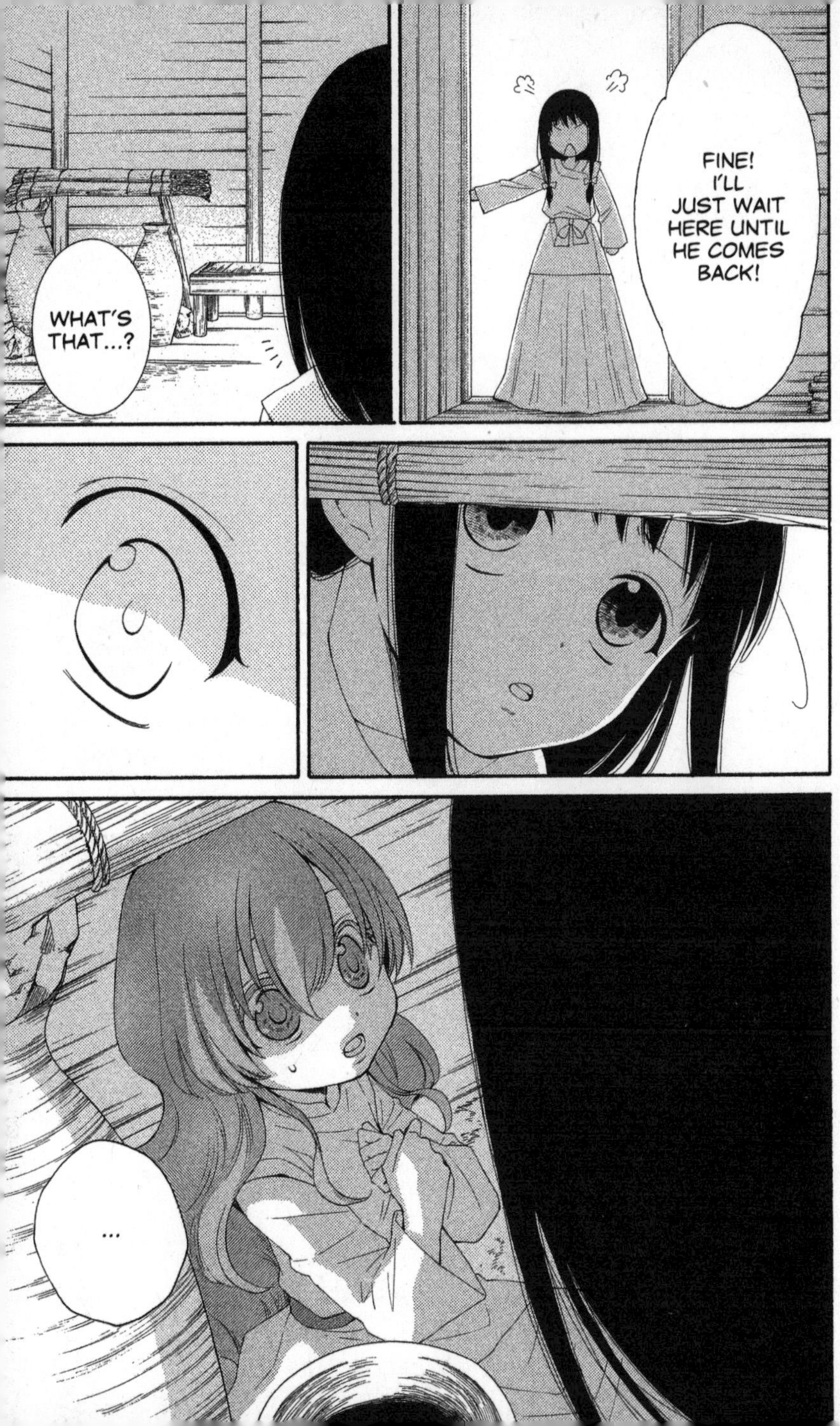
FINE! I'LL JUST WAIT HERE UNTIL HE COMES BACK!
WHAT'S THAT...?
...

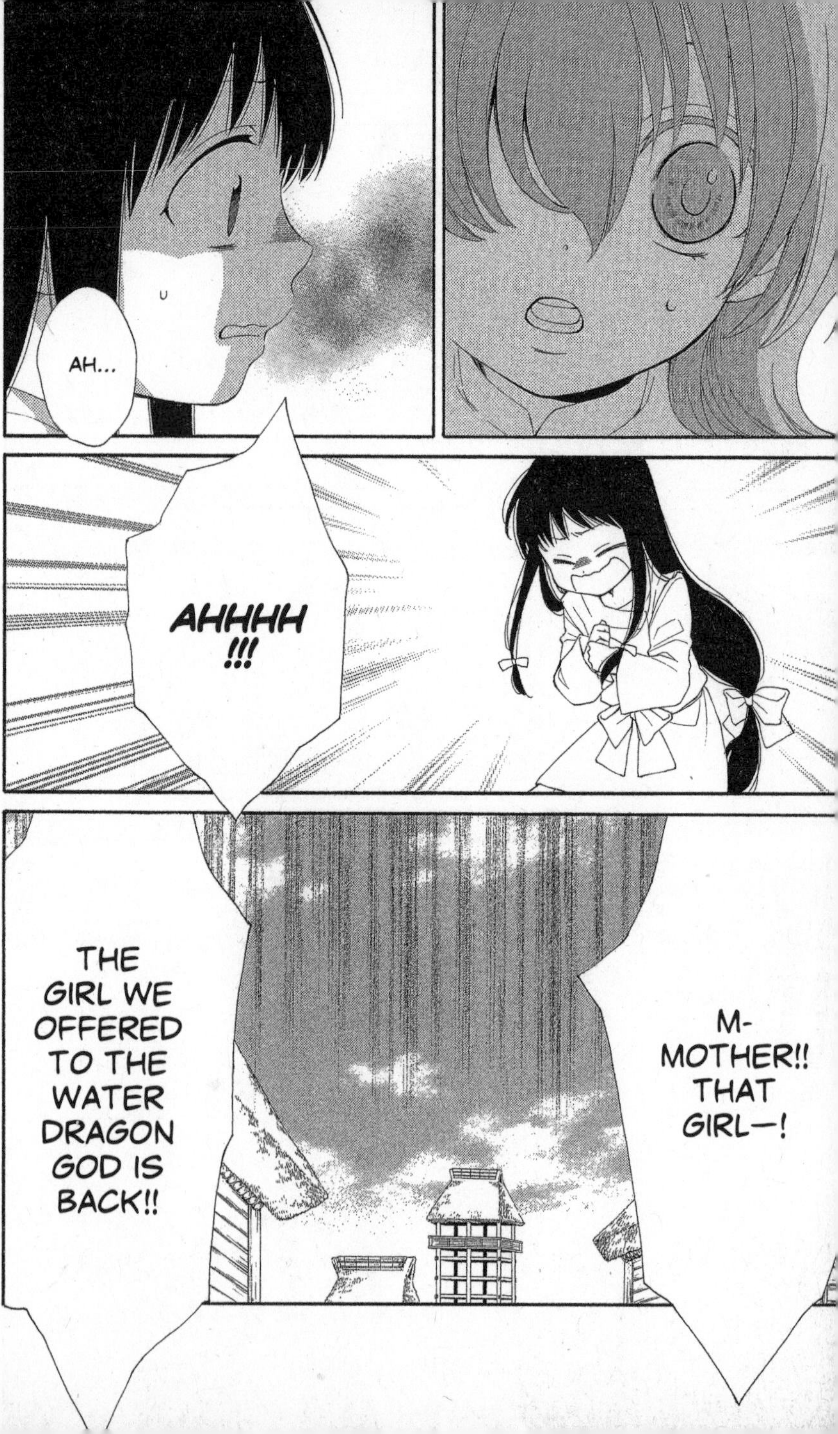
AH...
AHHHH !!!
M- MOTHER!! THAT GIRL—!
THE GIRL WE OFFERED TO THE WATER DRAGON GOD IS BACK!!

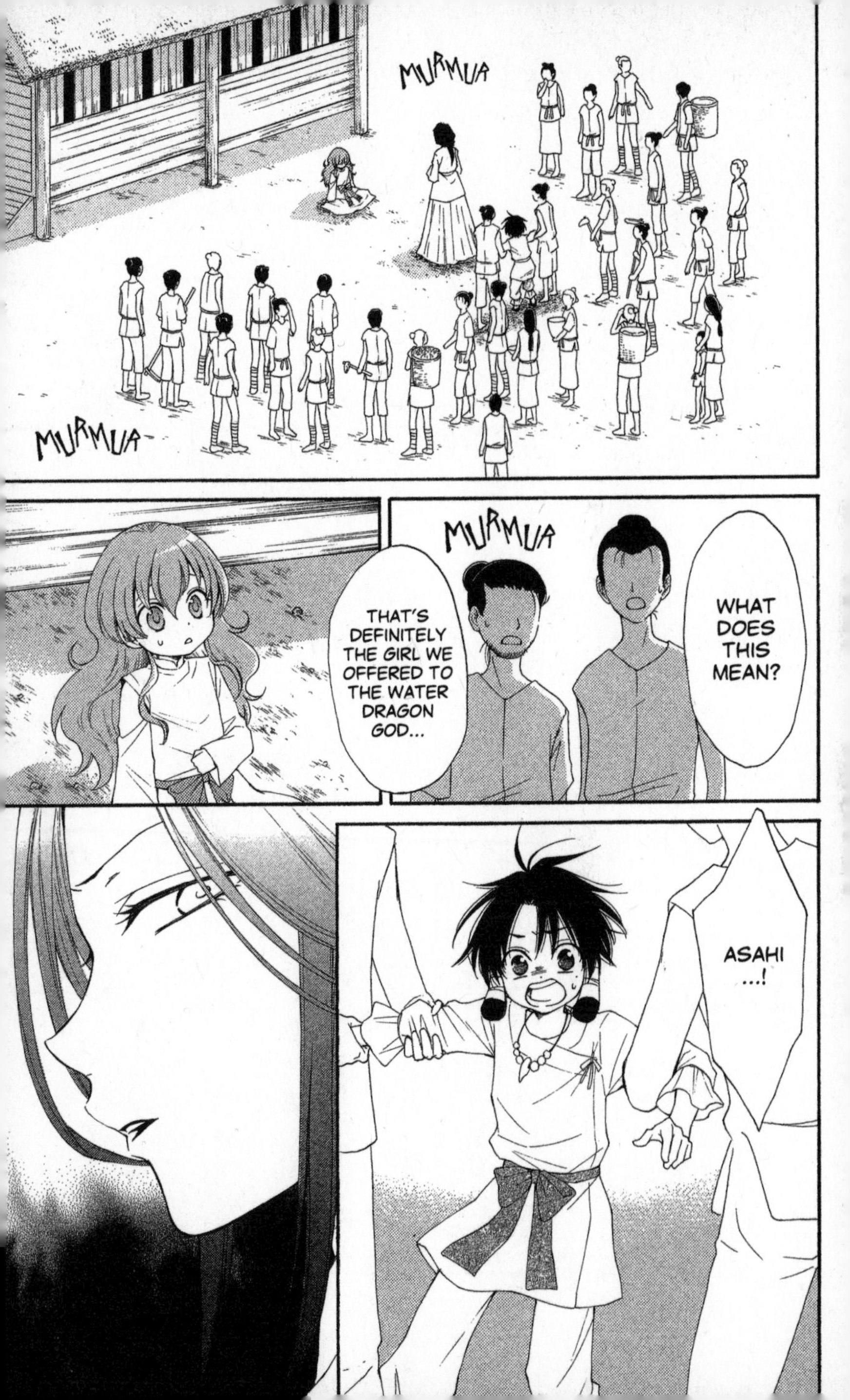
MURMUR
MURMUR
MURMUR
WHAT DOES THIS MEAN?
THAT'S DEFINITELY THE GIRL WE OFFERED TO THE WATER DRAGON GOD...
ASAHI ...!

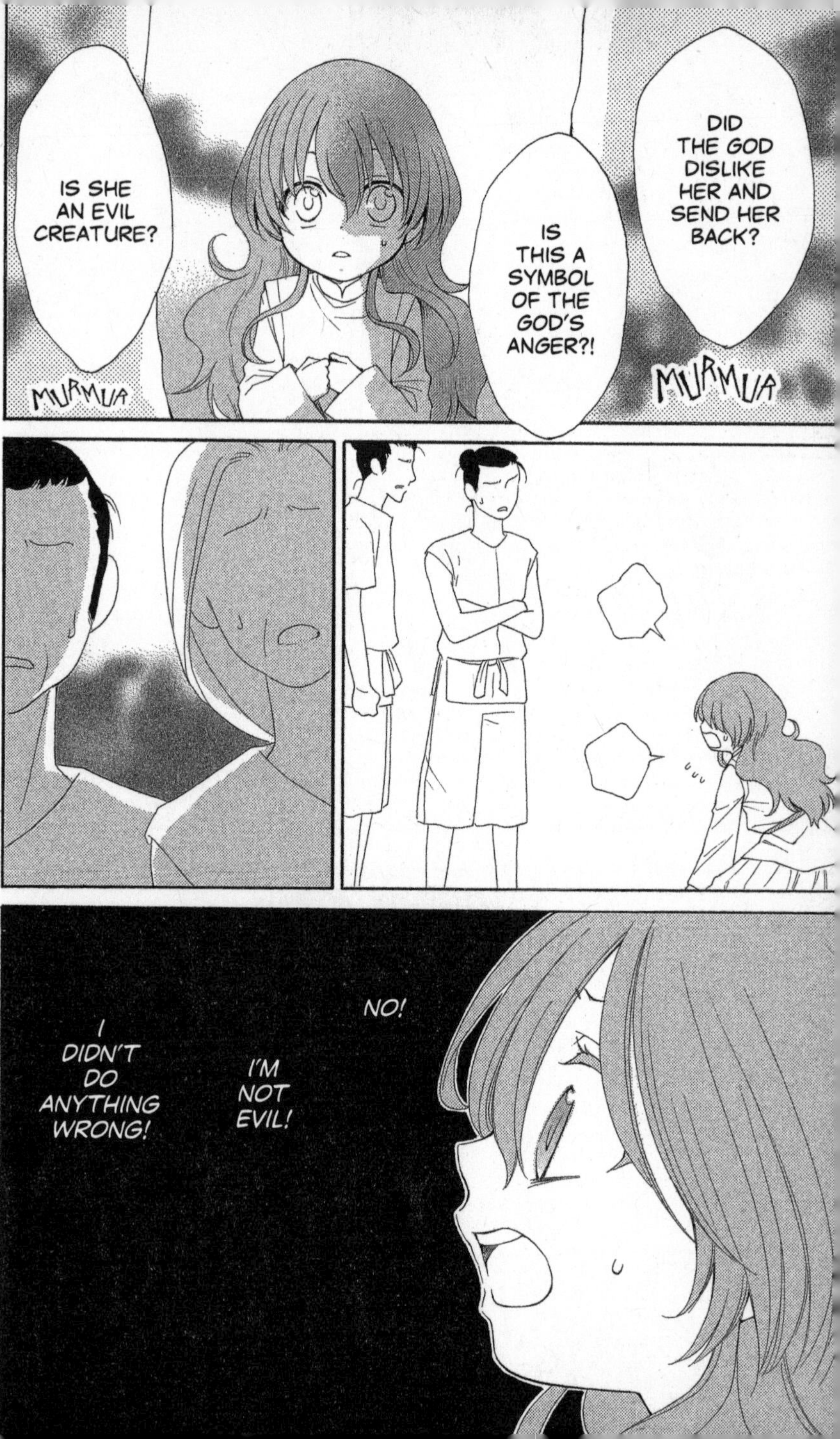
DID THE GOD DISLIKE HER AND SEND HER BACK?
MURMUR
IS THIS A SYMBOL OF THE GOD'S ANGER?!
IS SHE AN EVIL CREATURE?
MURMUR
NO!
I'M NOT EVIL!
I DIDN'T DO ANYTHING WRONG!

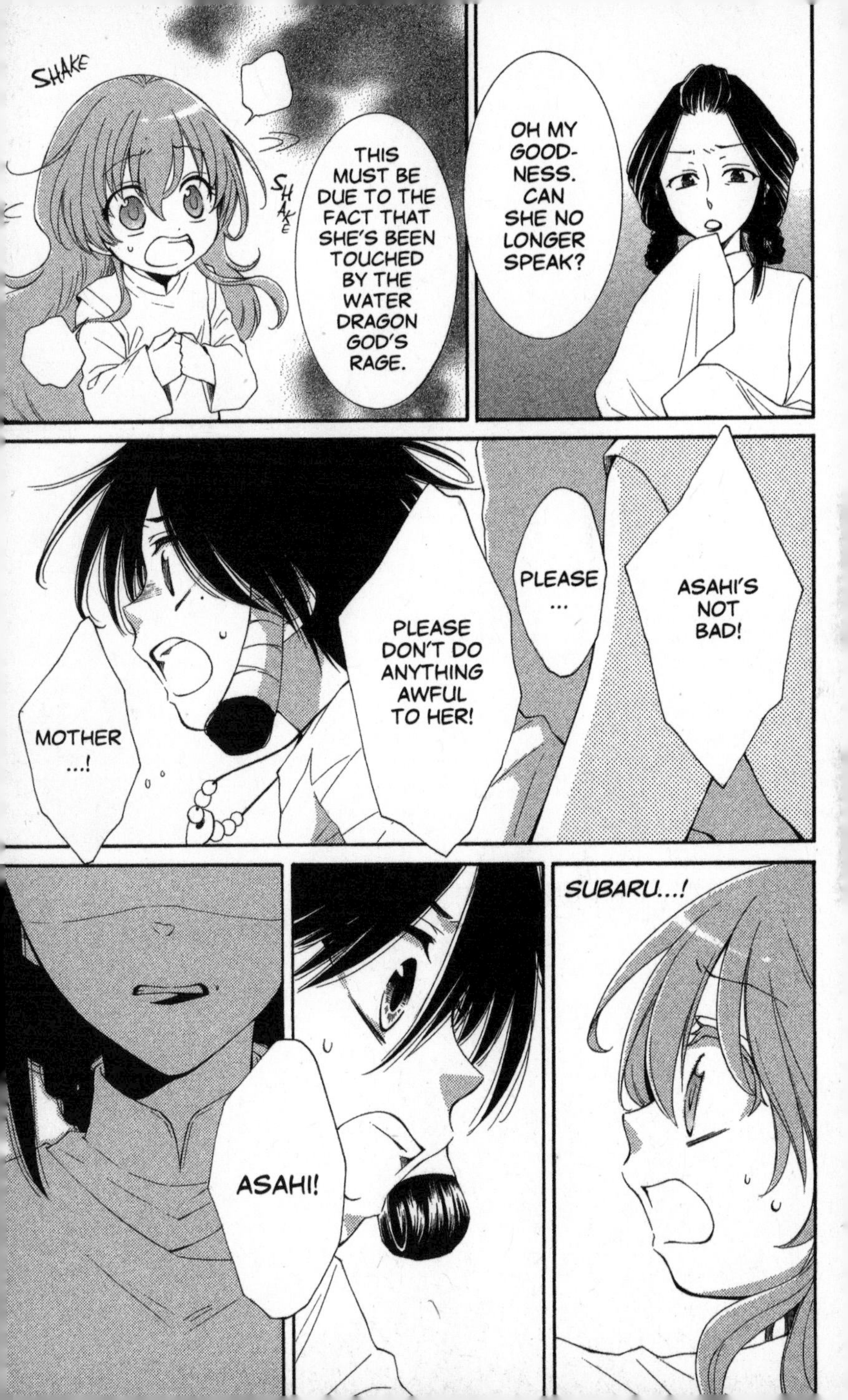
OH MY GOODNESS. CAN SHE NO LONGER SPEAK?
THIS MUST BE DUE TO THE FACT THAT SHE'S BEEN TOUCHED BY THE WATER DRAGON GOD'S RAGE.
SHAKE
SHAKE
ASAHI'S NOT BAD!
PLEASE...
PLEASE DON'T DO ANYTHING AWFUL TO HER!
MOTHER...!
SUBARU...!
ASAHI!

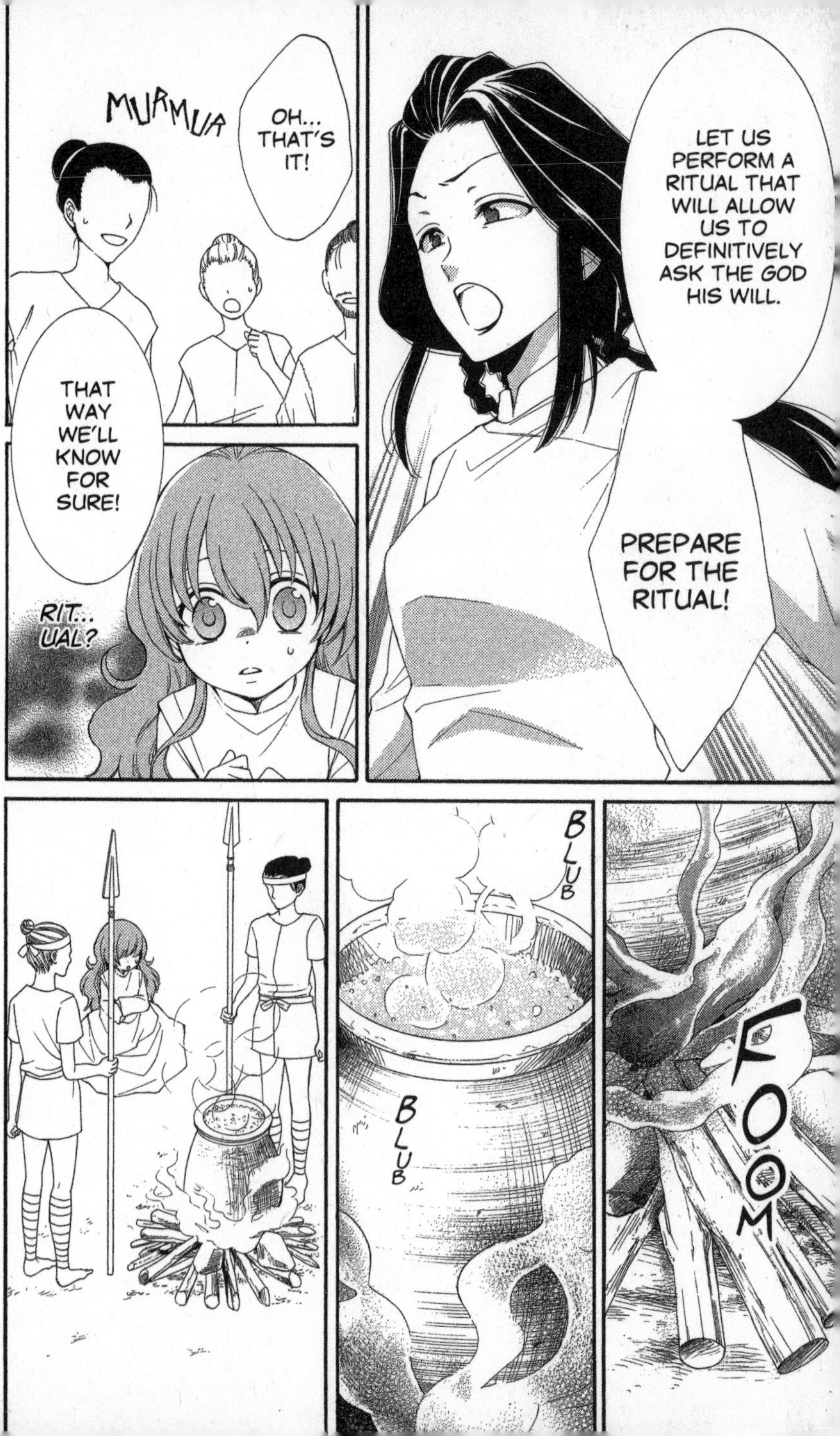
LET US PERFORM A RITUAL THAT WILL ALLOW US TO DEFINITIVELY ASK THE GOD HIS WILL.
PREPARE FOR THE RITUAL!
MURMUR
OH... THAT'S IT!
THAT WAY WE'LL KNOW FOR SURE!
RIT... UAL?
FOOM
BLUB
BLUB

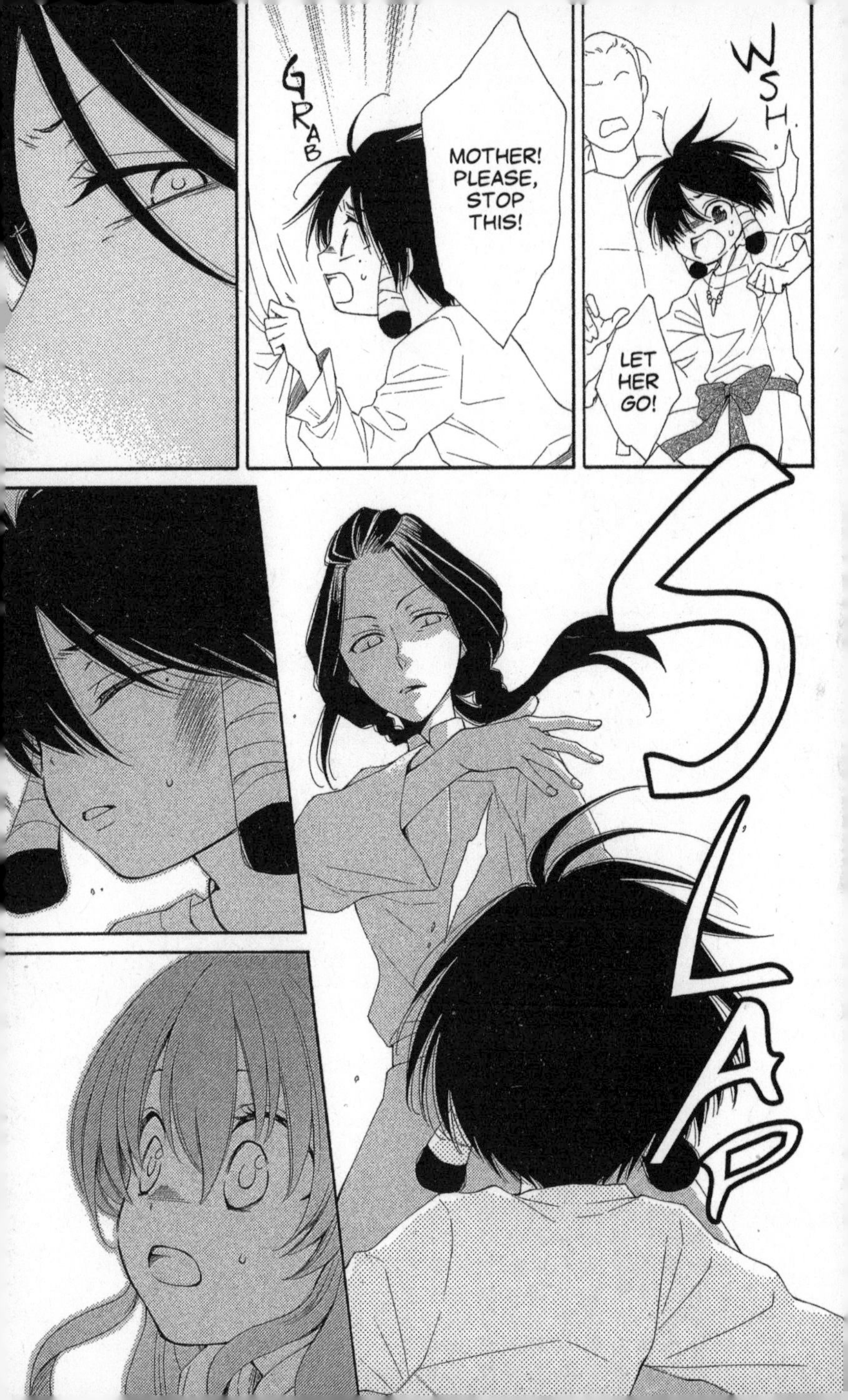
WSH
LET HER GO!
GRAB
MOTHER! PLEASE, STOP THIS!
SLAP

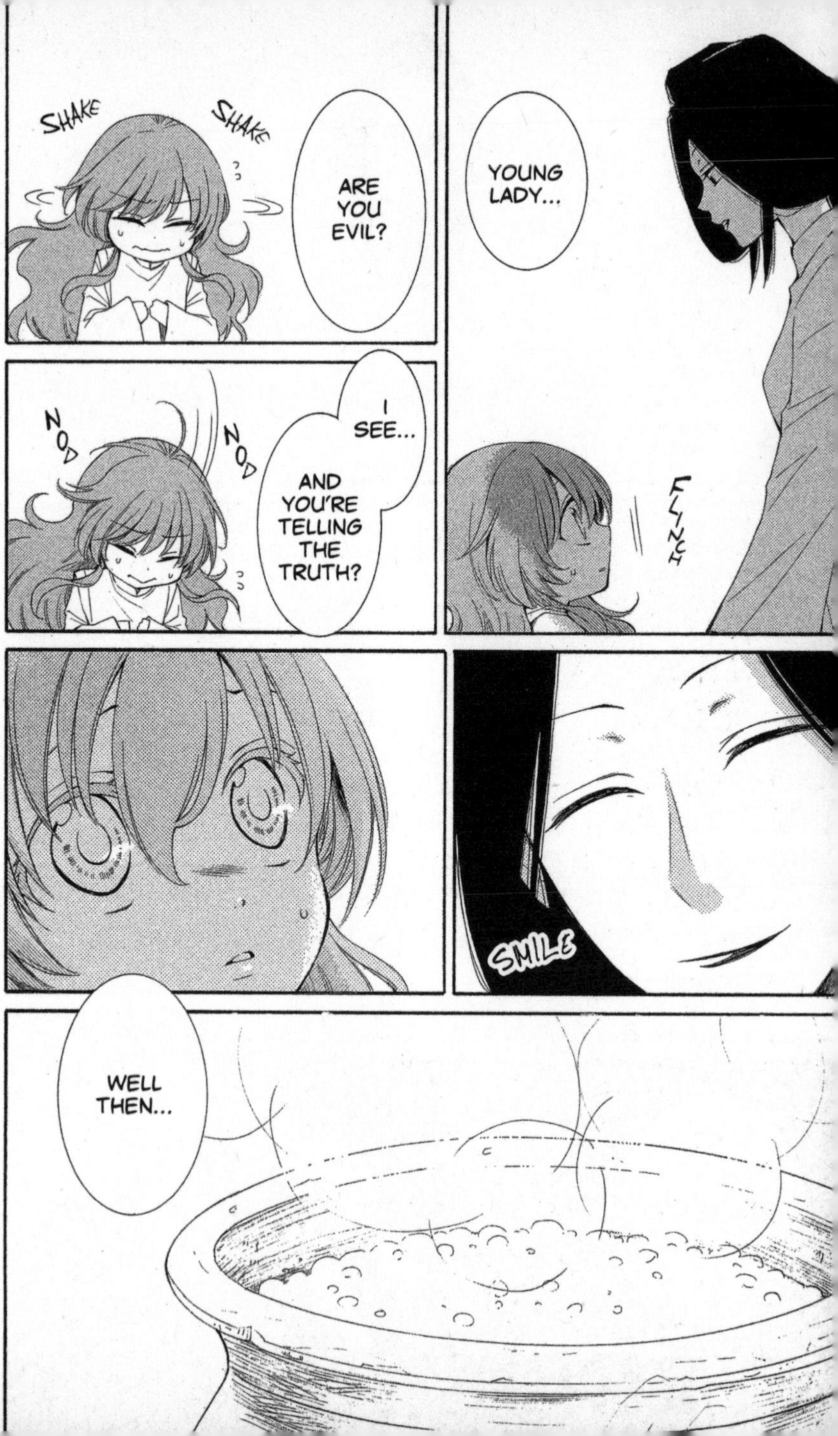
YOUNG LADY...
FLINCH
ARE YOU EVIL?
SHAKE
SHAKE
I SEE...
AND YOU'RE TELLING THE TRUTH?
NOD
NOD
SMILE
WELL THEN...

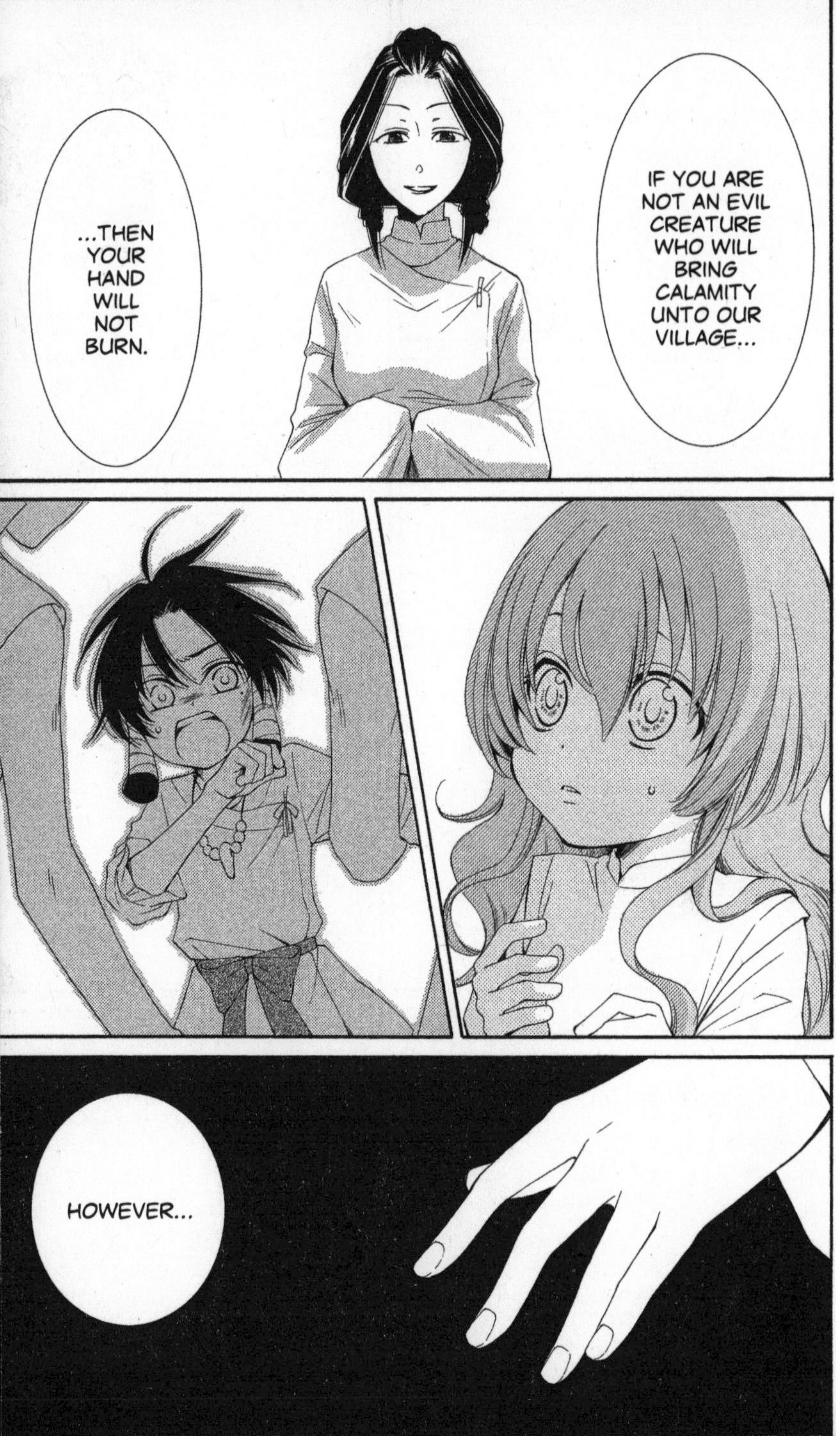
IF YOU ARE NOT AN EVIL CREATURE WHO WILL BRING CALAMITY UNTO OUR VILLAGE...
...THEN YOUR HAND WILL NOT BURN.
HOWEVER...

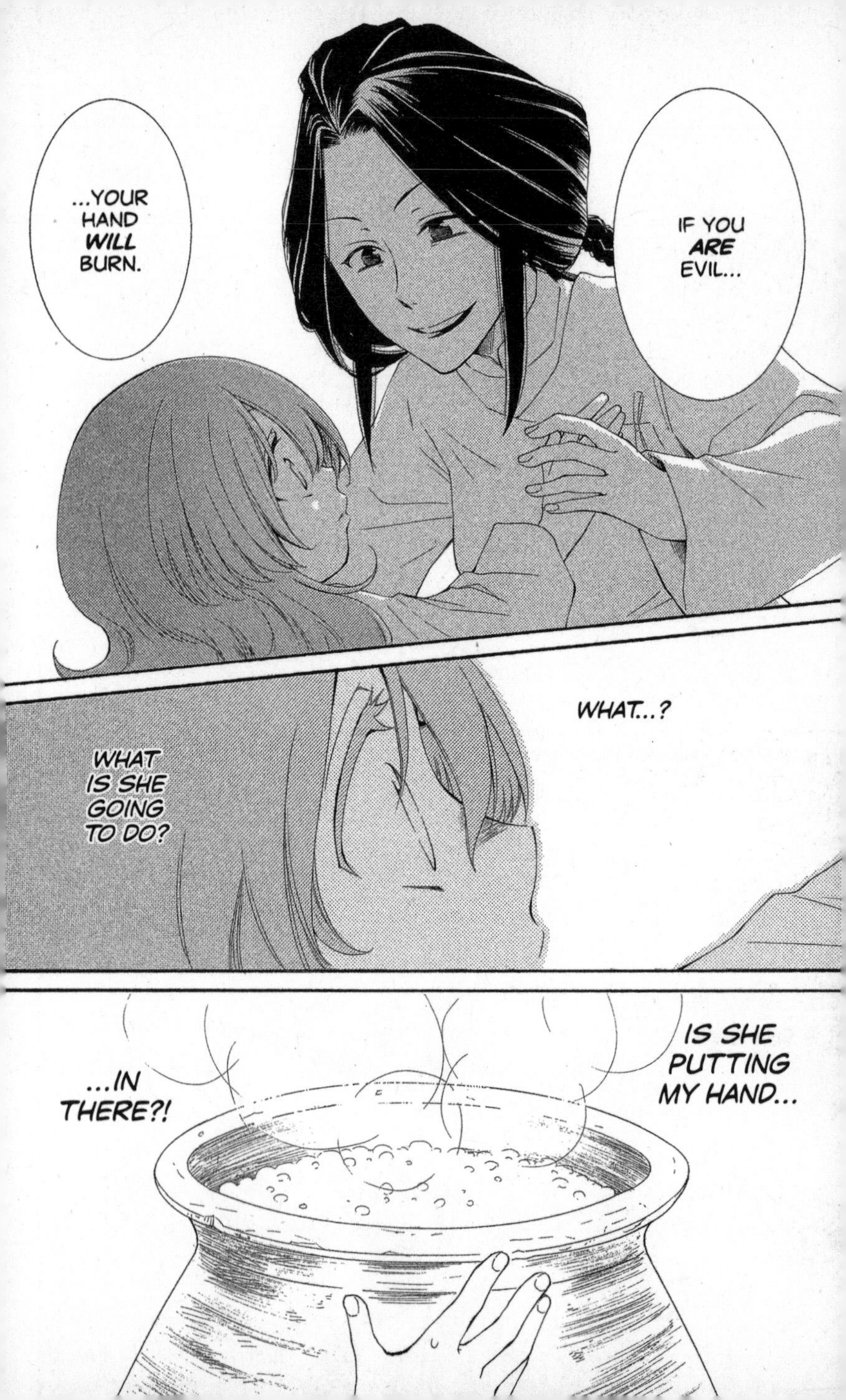
IF YOU **ARE** EVIL...
...YOUR HAND **WILL** BURN.
WHAT...?
WHAT IS SHE GOING TO DO?
IS SHE PUTTING MY HAND...
...IN THERE?!

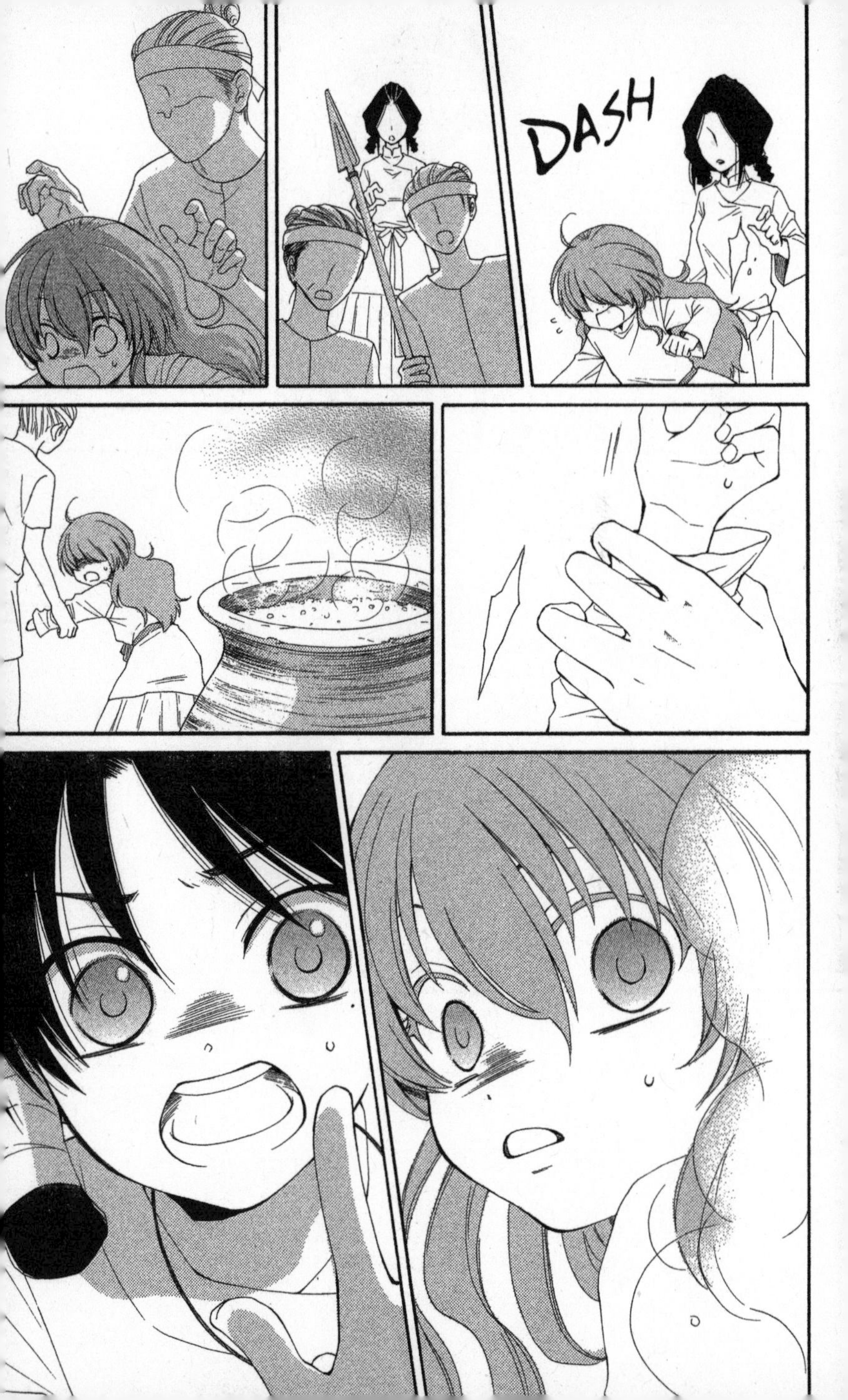
DASH

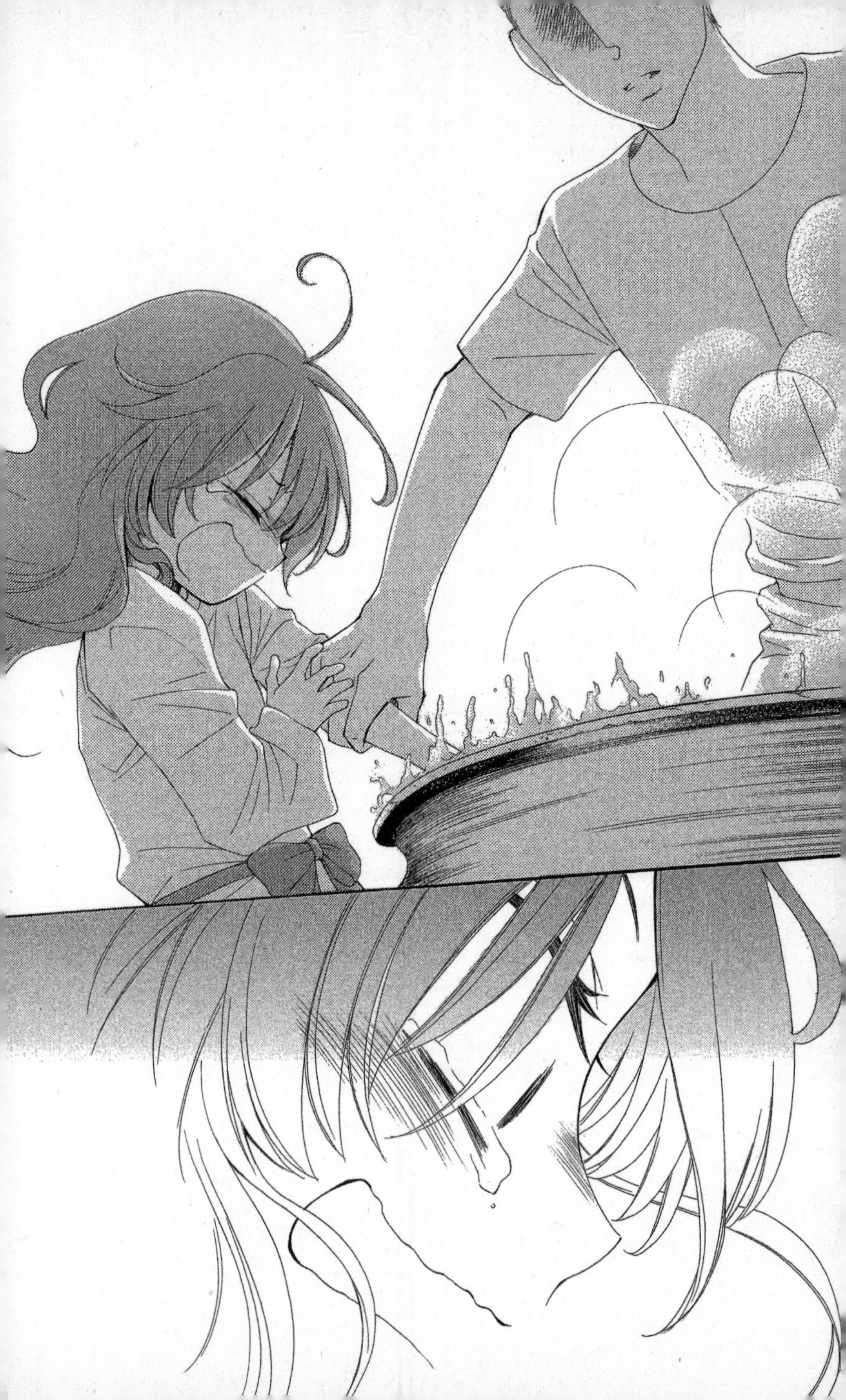

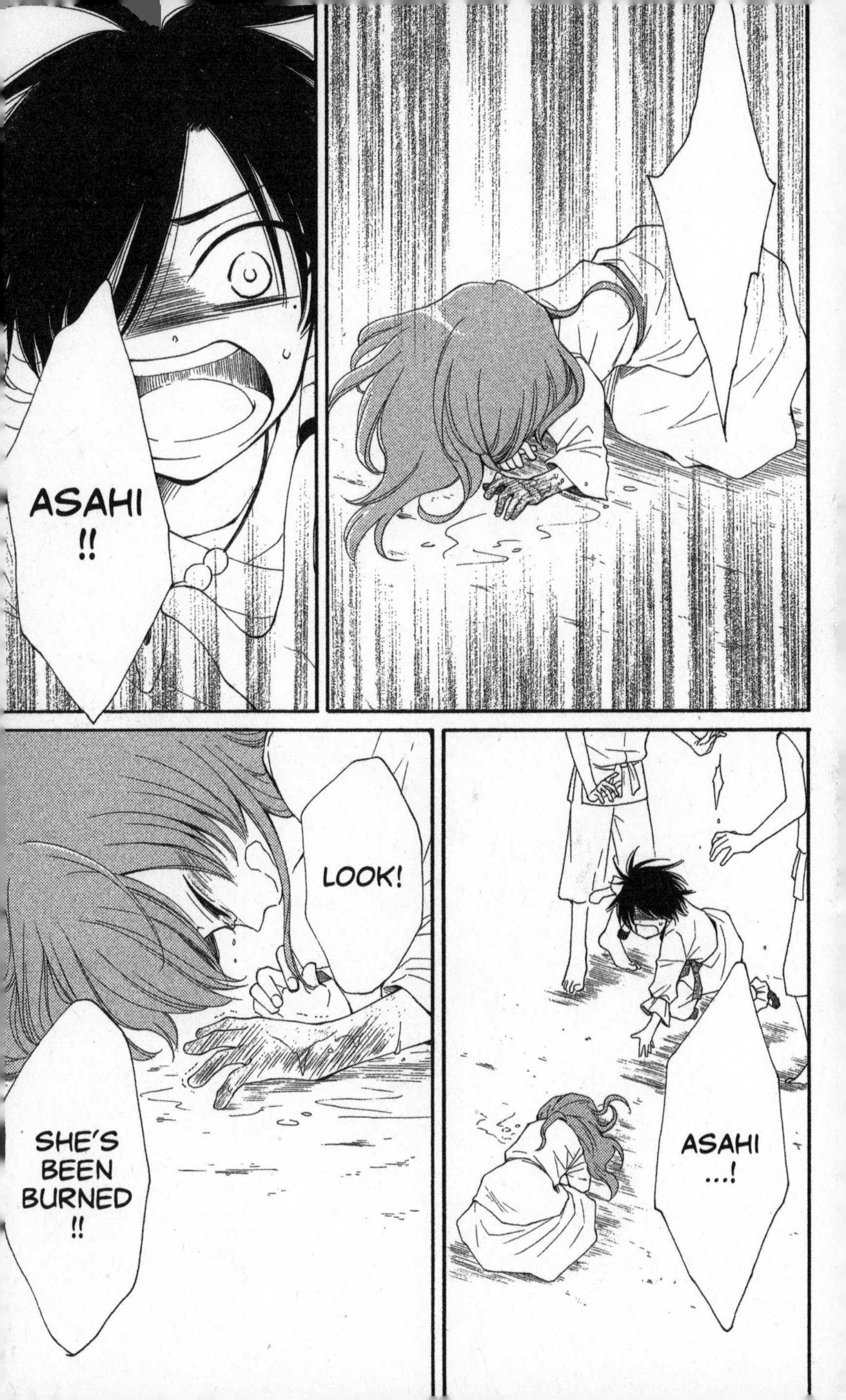
ASAHI !!
ASAHI ...!
LOOK!
SHE'S BEEN BURNED !!

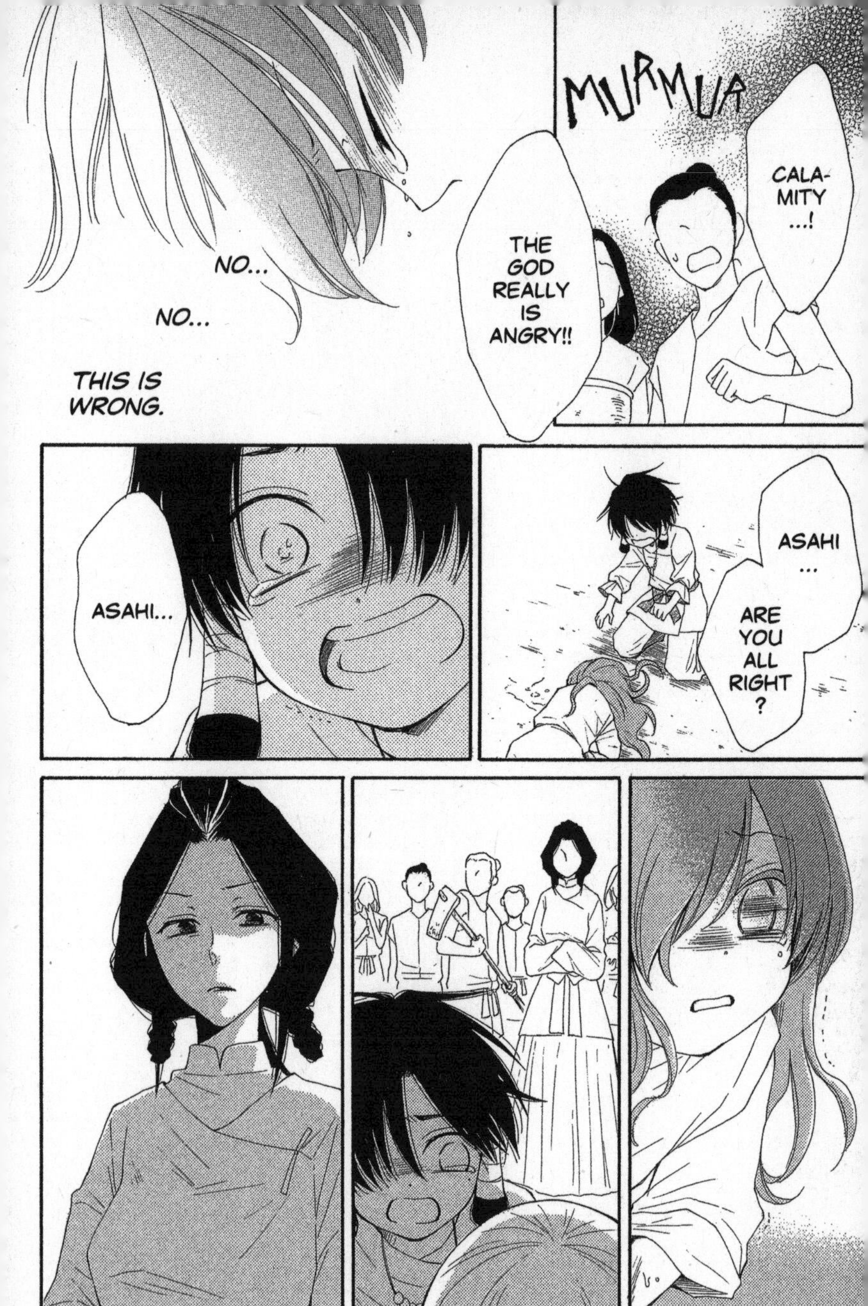
MURMUR
CALAMITY ...!
THE GOD REALLY IS ANGRY!!
NO...
NO...
THIS IS WRONG.
ASAHI ... ARE YOU ALL RIGHT?
ASAHI...

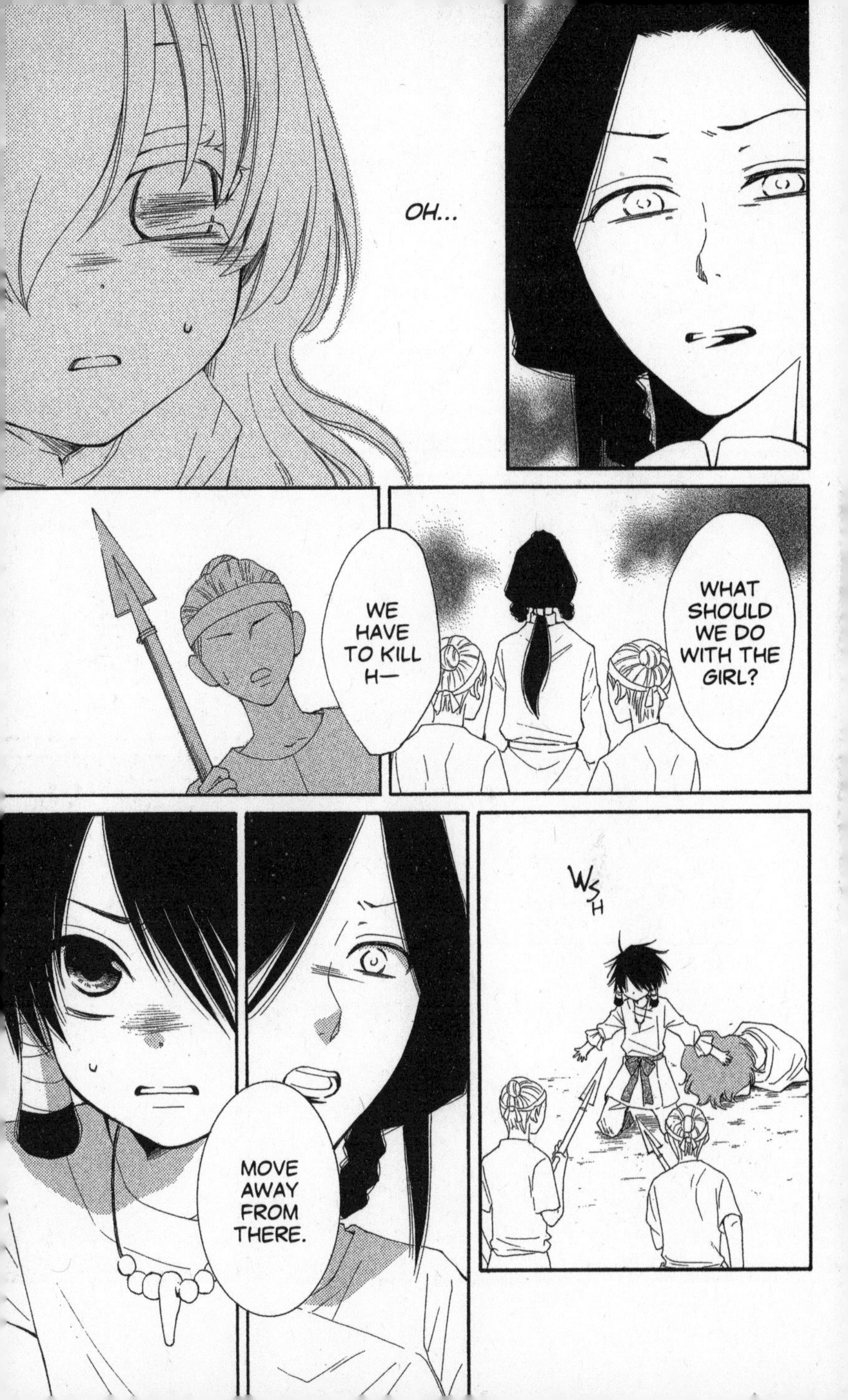
OH...
WHAT SHOULD WE DO WITH THE GIRL?
WE HAVE TO KILL H—
WSH
MOVE AWAY FROM THERE.

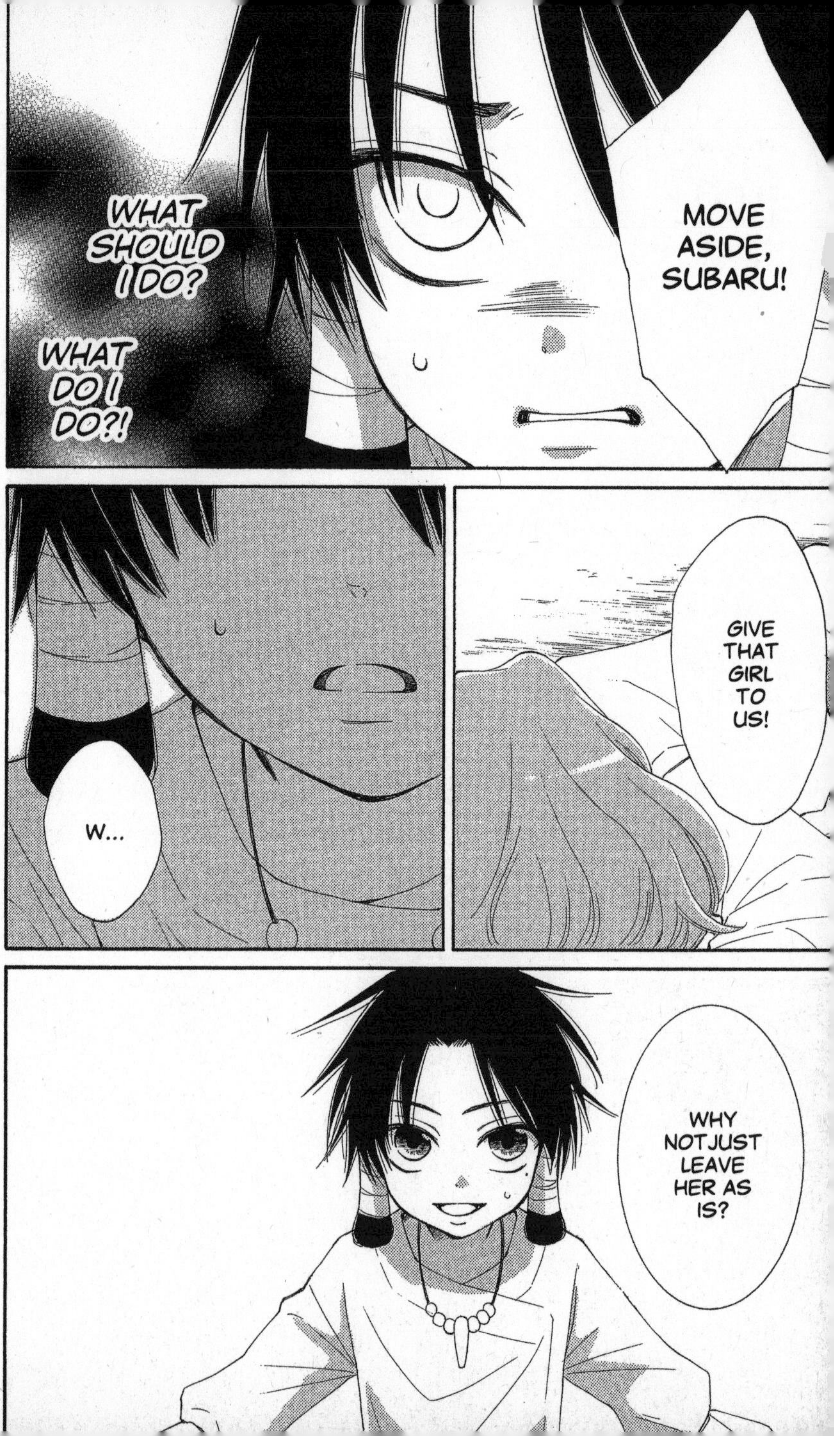
MOVE ASIDE, SUBARU!
WHAT SHOULD I DO?
WHAT DO I DO?!
GIVE THAT GIRL TO US!
W...
WHY NOTJUST LEAVE HER AS IS?

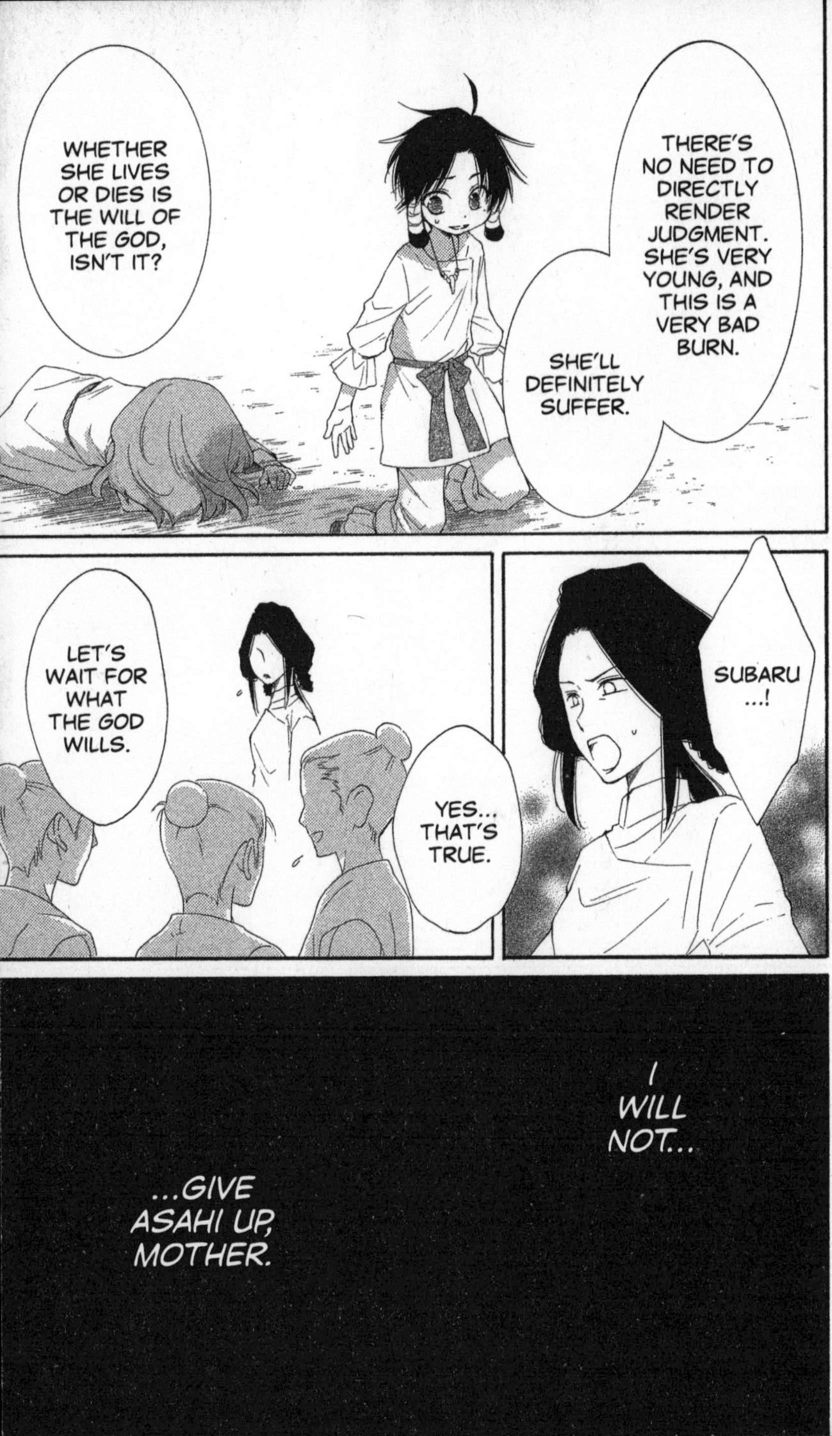
THERE'S NO NEED TO DIRECTLY RENDER JUDGMENT. SHE'S VERY YOUNG, AND THIS IS A VERY BAD BURN.
SHE'LL DEFINITELY SUFFER.
WHETHER SHE LIVES OR DIES IS THE WILL OF THE GOD, ISN'T IT?
SUBARU ...!
LET'S WAIT FOR WHAT THE GOD WILLS.
YES... THAT'S TRUE.
I WILL NOT...
...GIVE ASAHI UP, MOTHER.

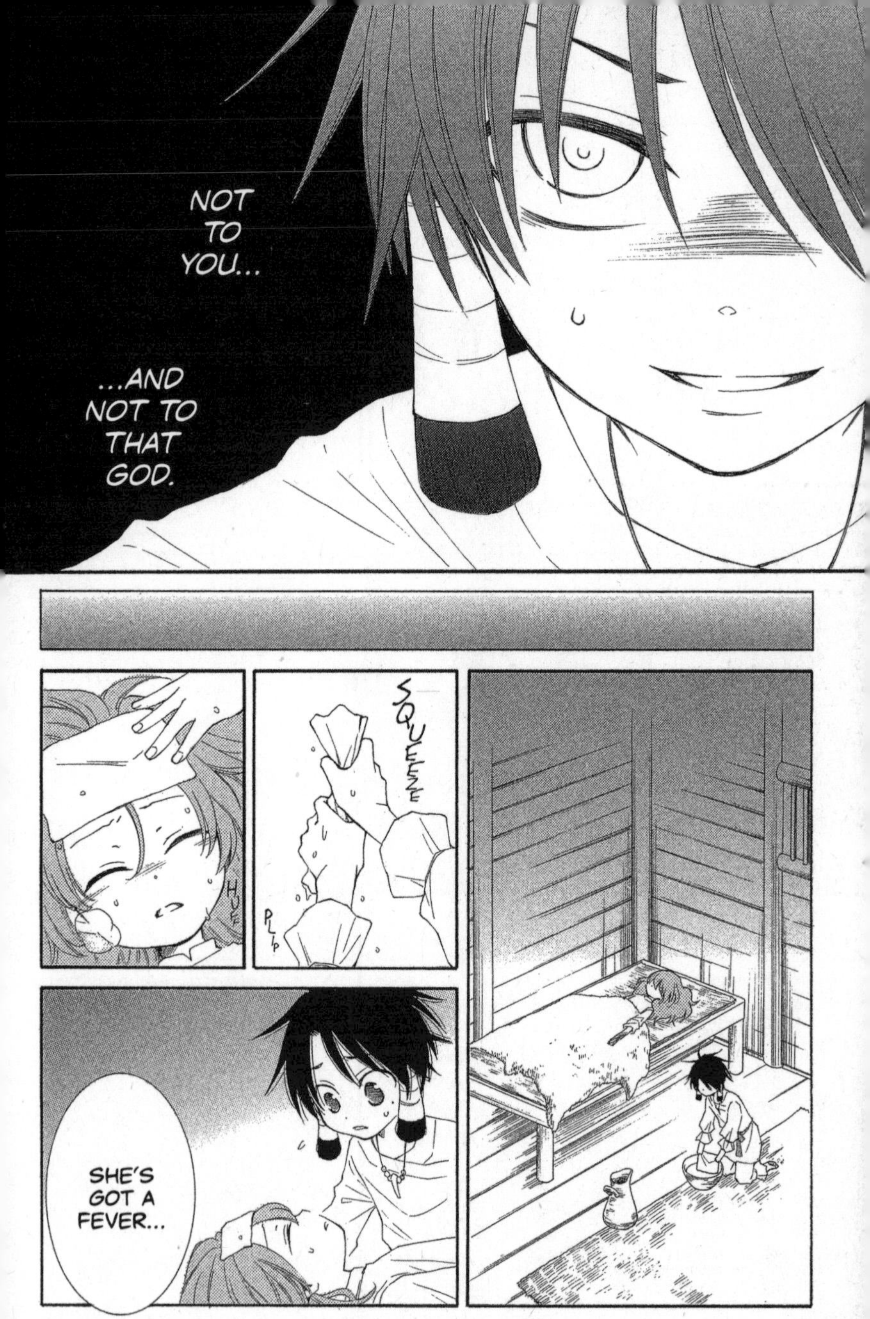
NOT TO YOU...
...AND NOT TO THAT GOD.
SQUEEZE
PLIP
HUF
SHE'S GOT A FEVER...

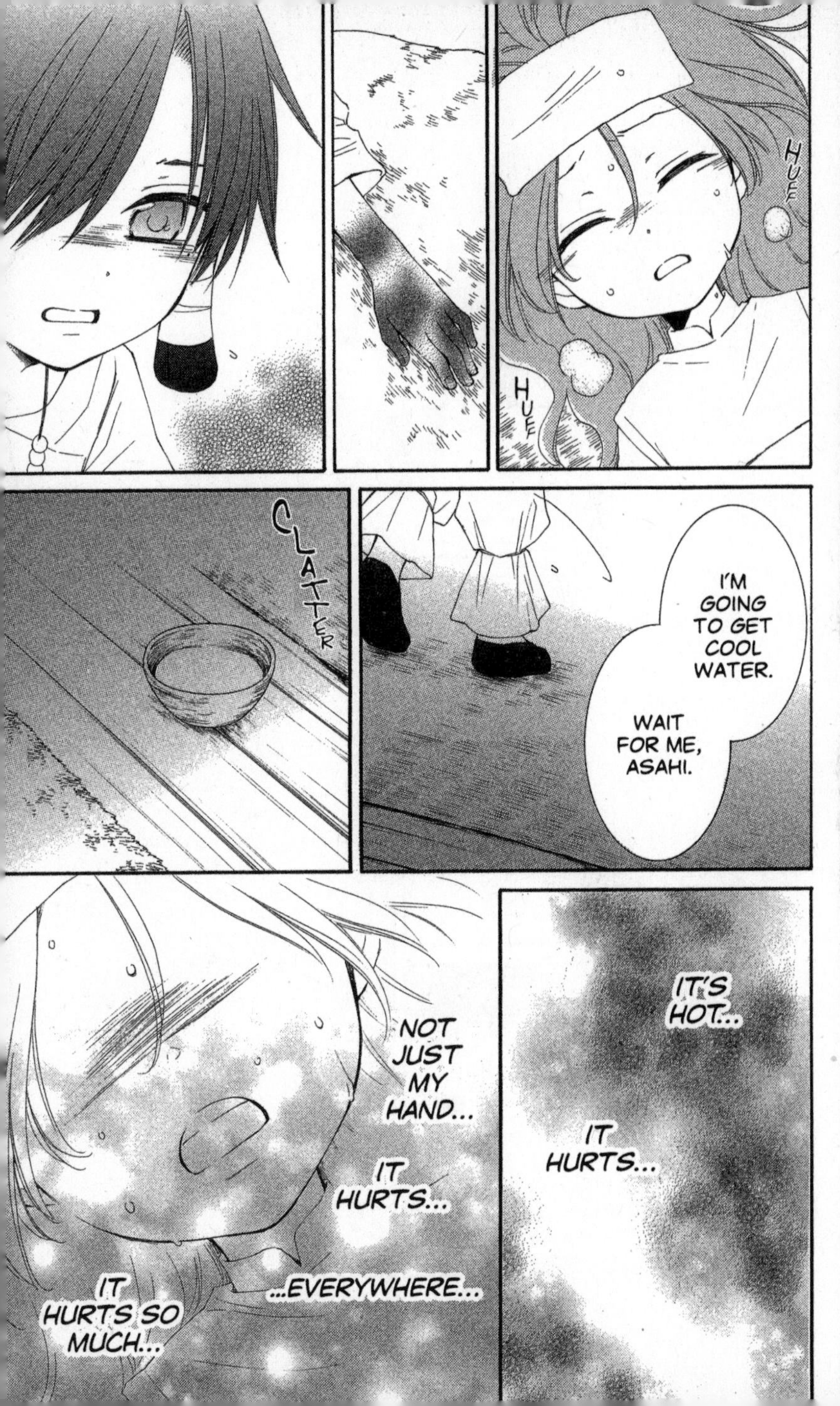
HUFF
HUFF
I'M GOING TO GET COOL WATER.
WAIT FOR ME, ASAHI.
CLATTER
IT'S HOT...
IT HURTS...
NOT JUST MY HAND...
IT HURTS...
...EVERYWHERE...
IT HURTS SO MUCH...

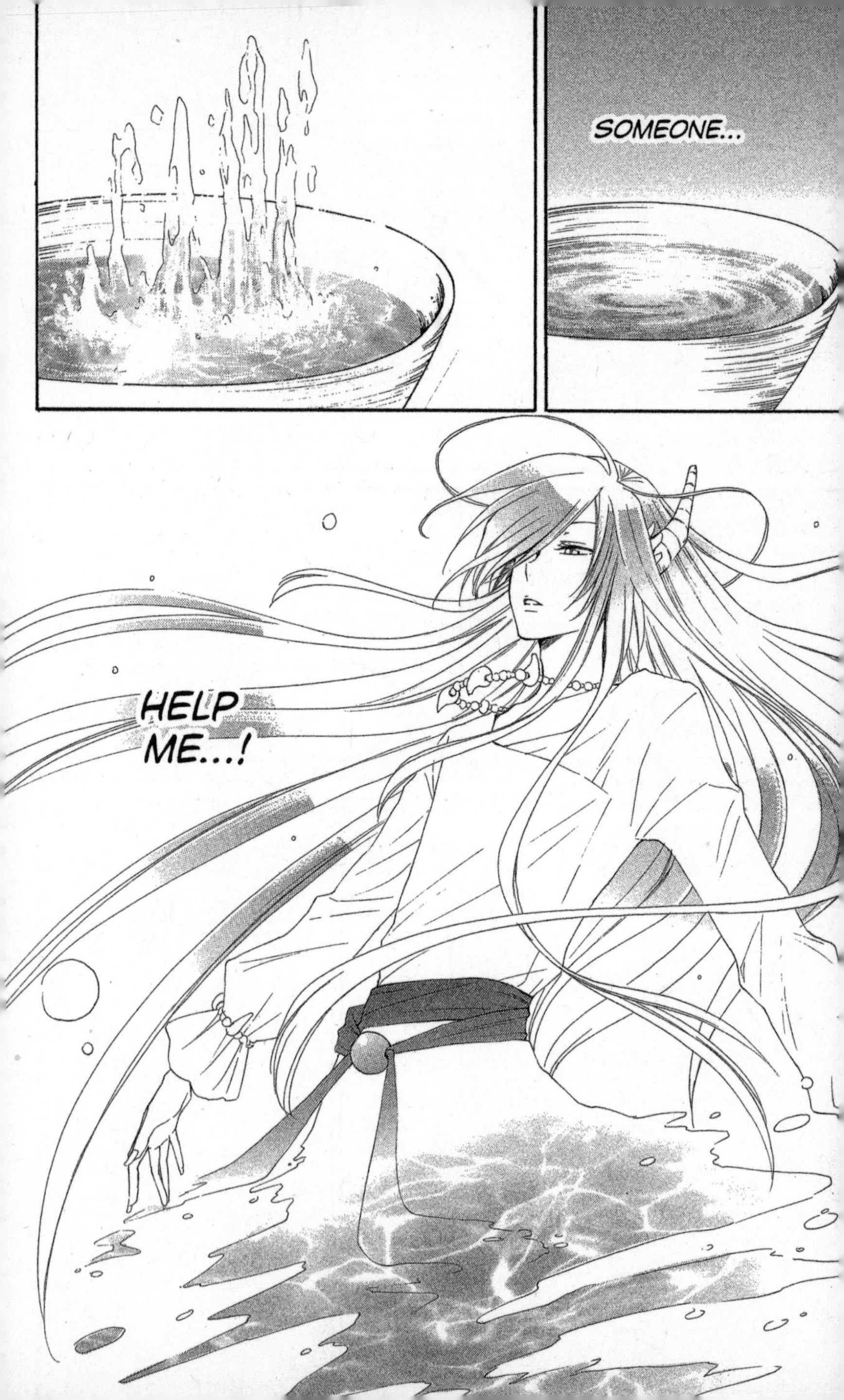
SOMEONE...
HELP ME...!

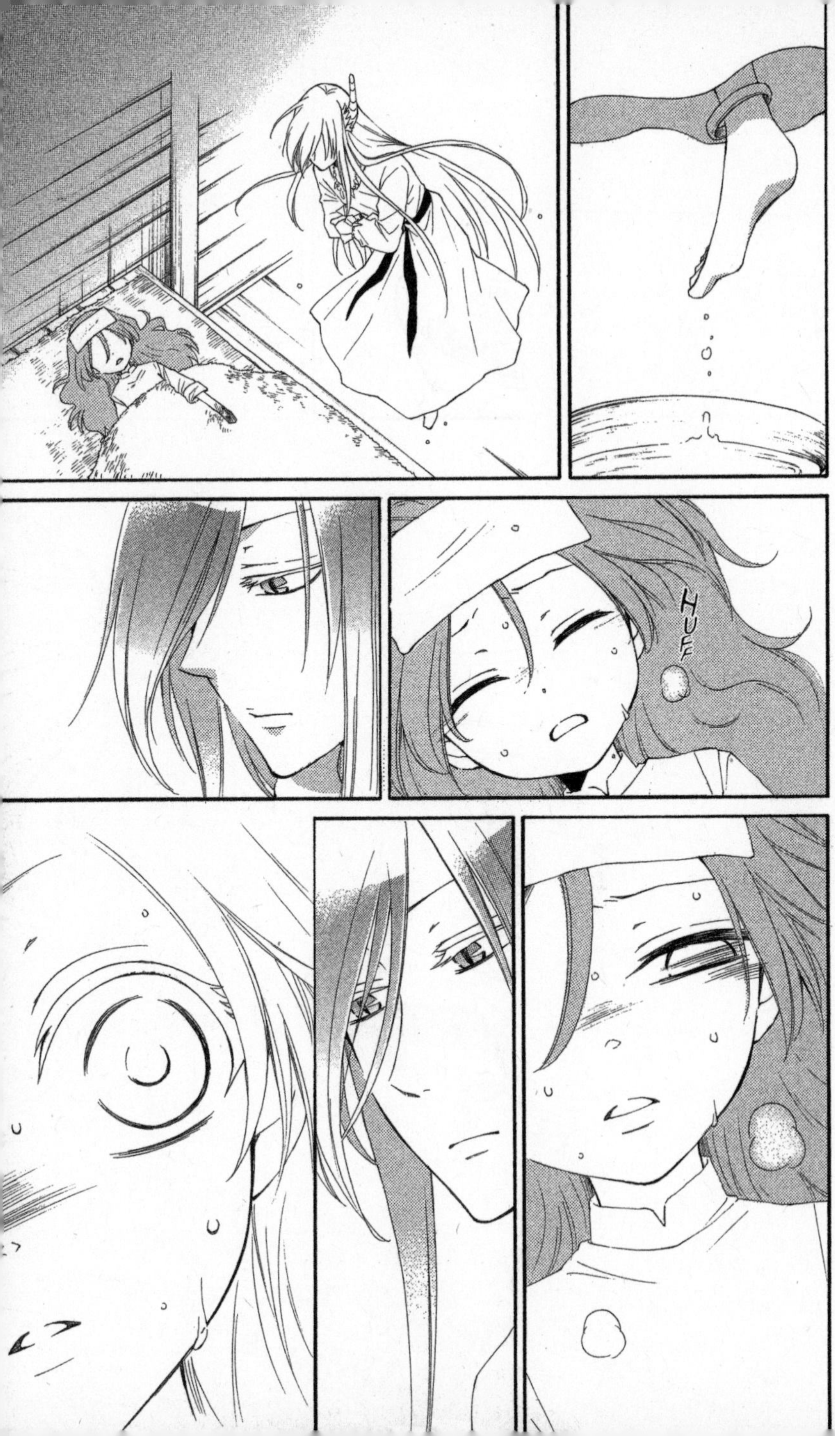
HUFF

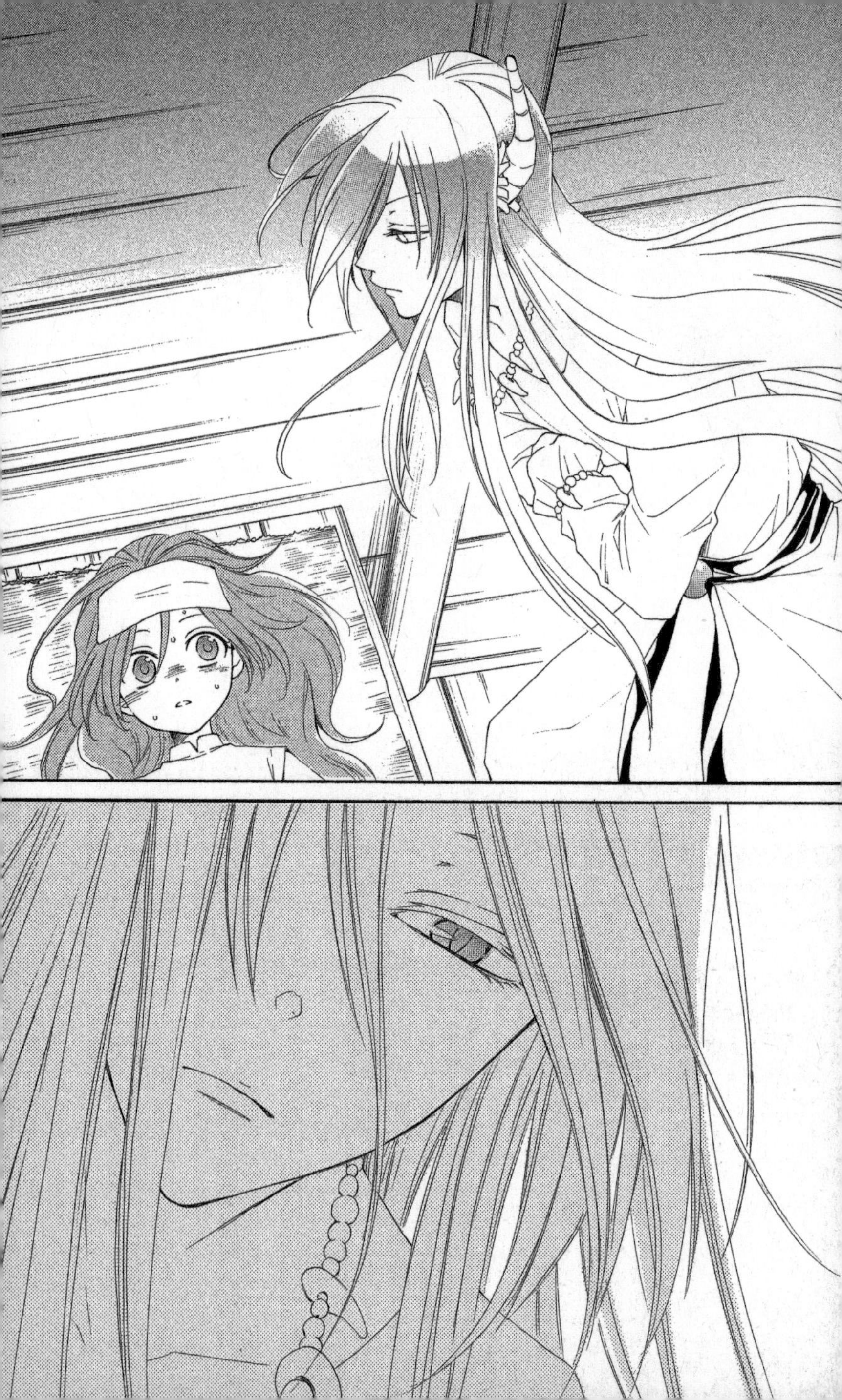

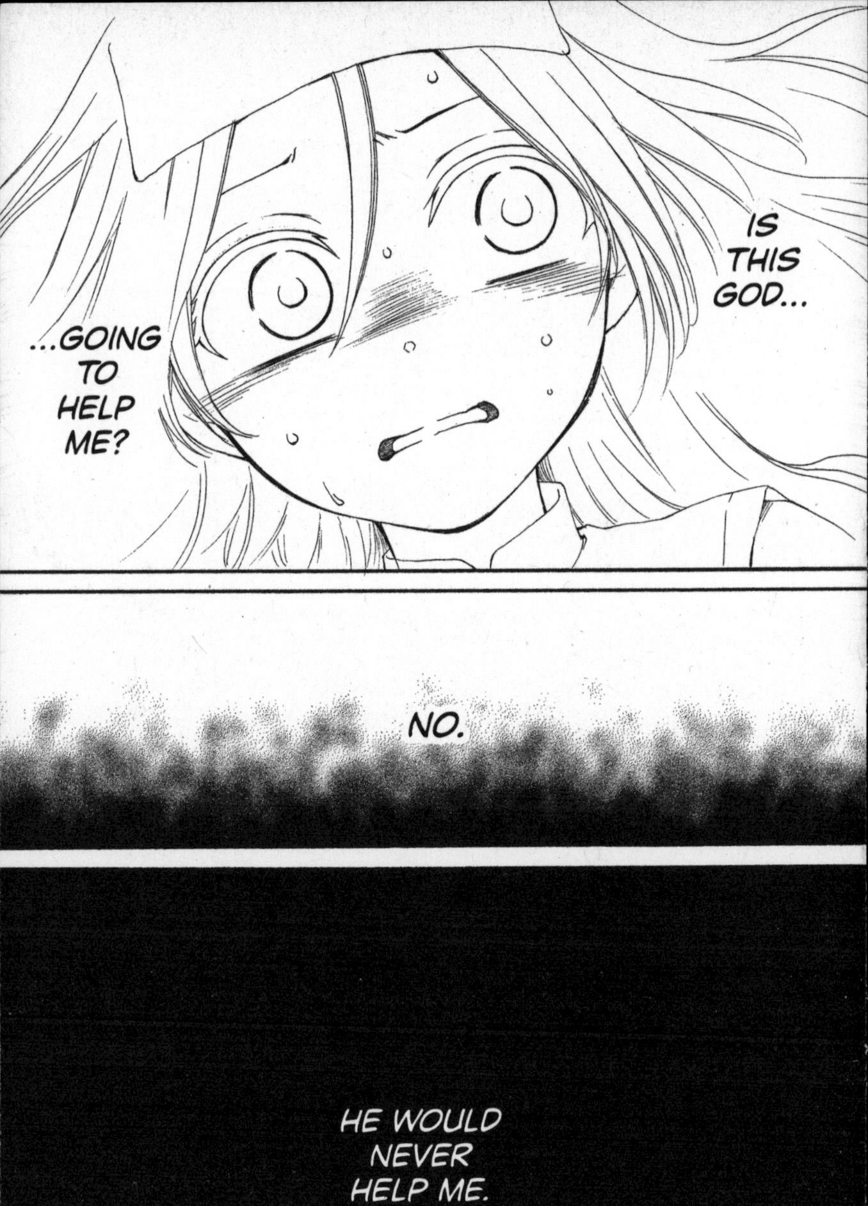
IS THIS GOD...
...GOING TO HELP ME?
NO.
HE WOULD NEVER HELP ME.

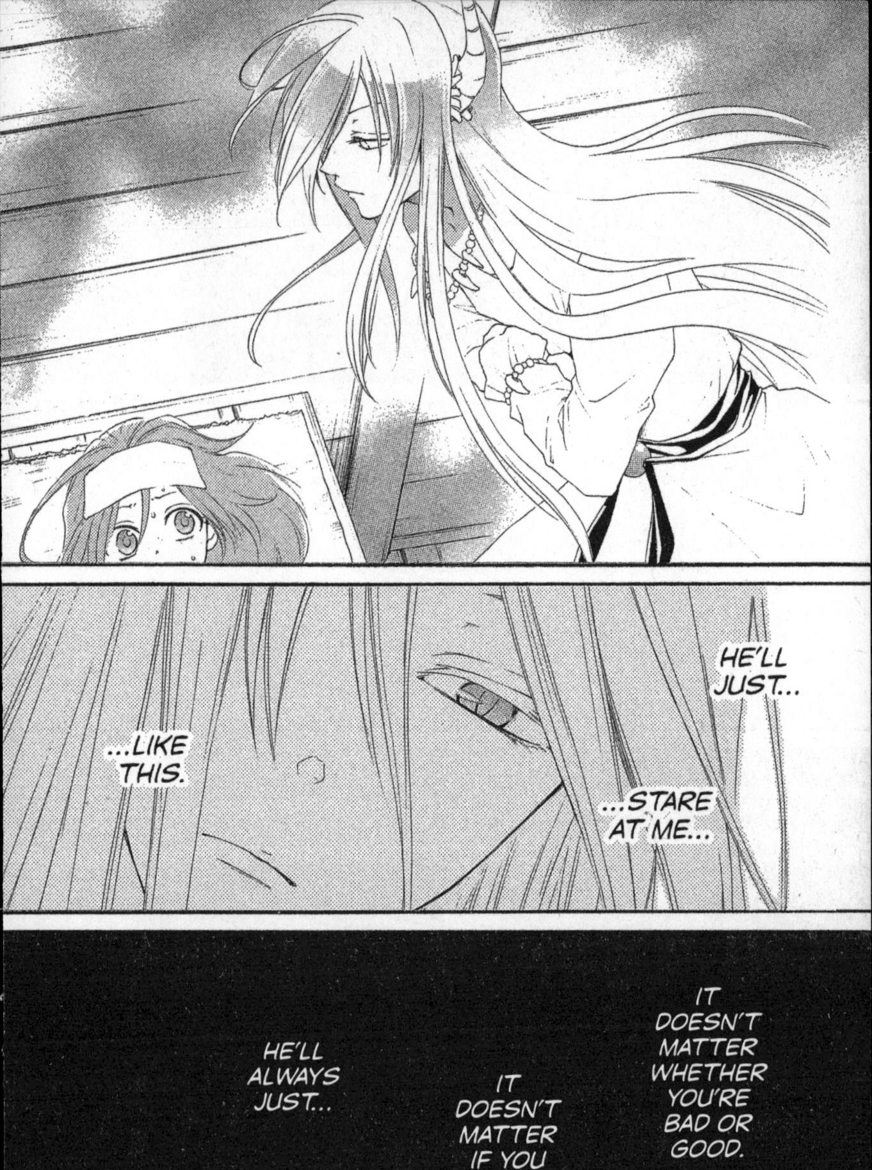
HE'LL JUST...
...STARE AT ME...
...LIKE THIS.
IT DOESN'T MATTER WHETHER YOU'RE BAD OR GOOD.
IT DOESN'T MATTER IF YOU
HE'LL ALWAYS JUST...

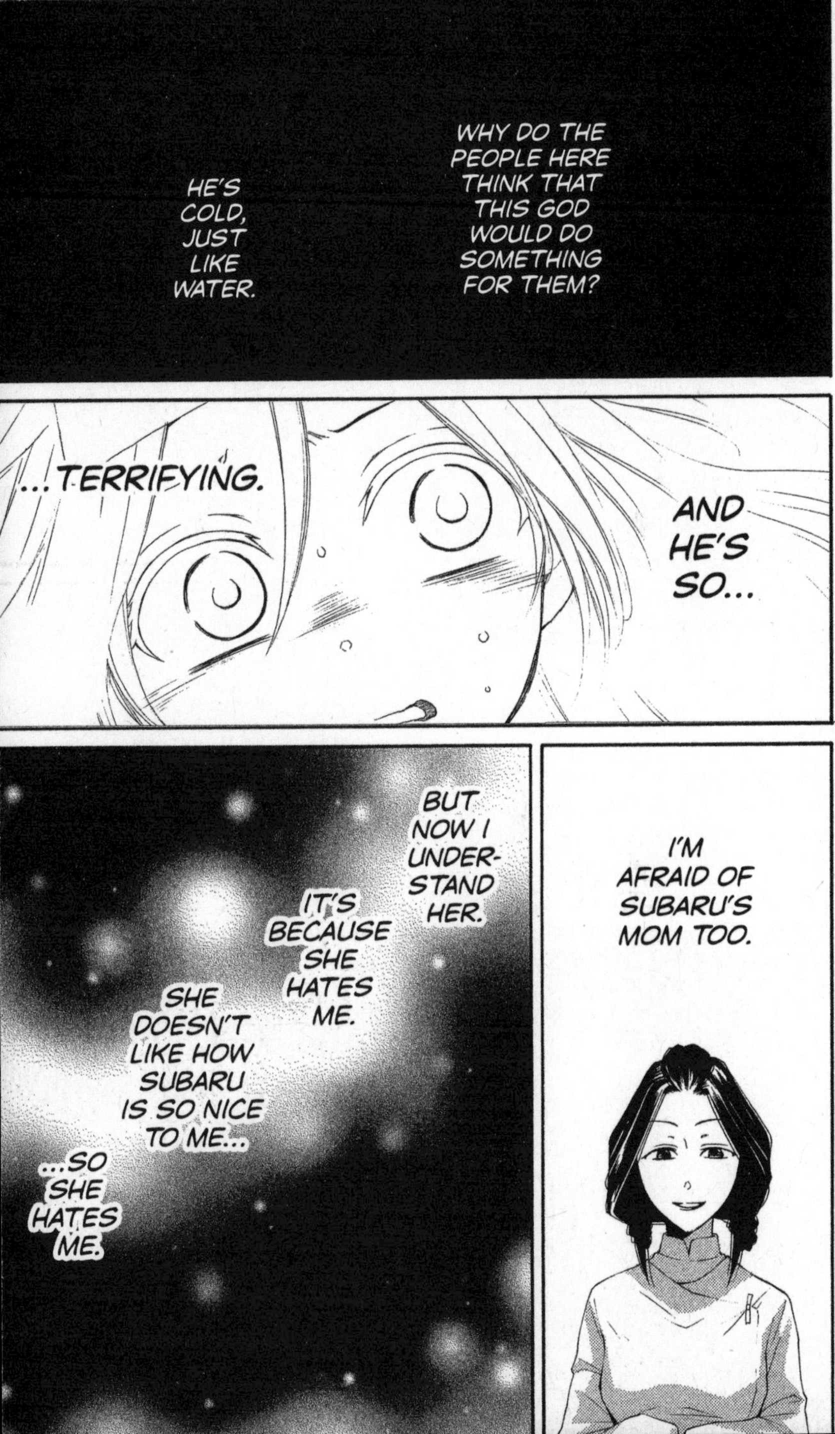
WHY DO THE PEOPLE HERE THINK THAT THIS GOD WOULD DO SOMETHING FOR THEM?
HE'S COLD, JUST LIKE WATER.
AND HE'S SO...
...TERRIFYING.
I'M AFRAID OF SUBARU'S MOM TOO.
BUT NOW I UNDER-STAND HER.
IT'S BECAUSE SHE HATES ME.
SHE DOESN'T LIKE HOW SUBARU IS SO NICE TO ME...
...SO SHE HATES ME.

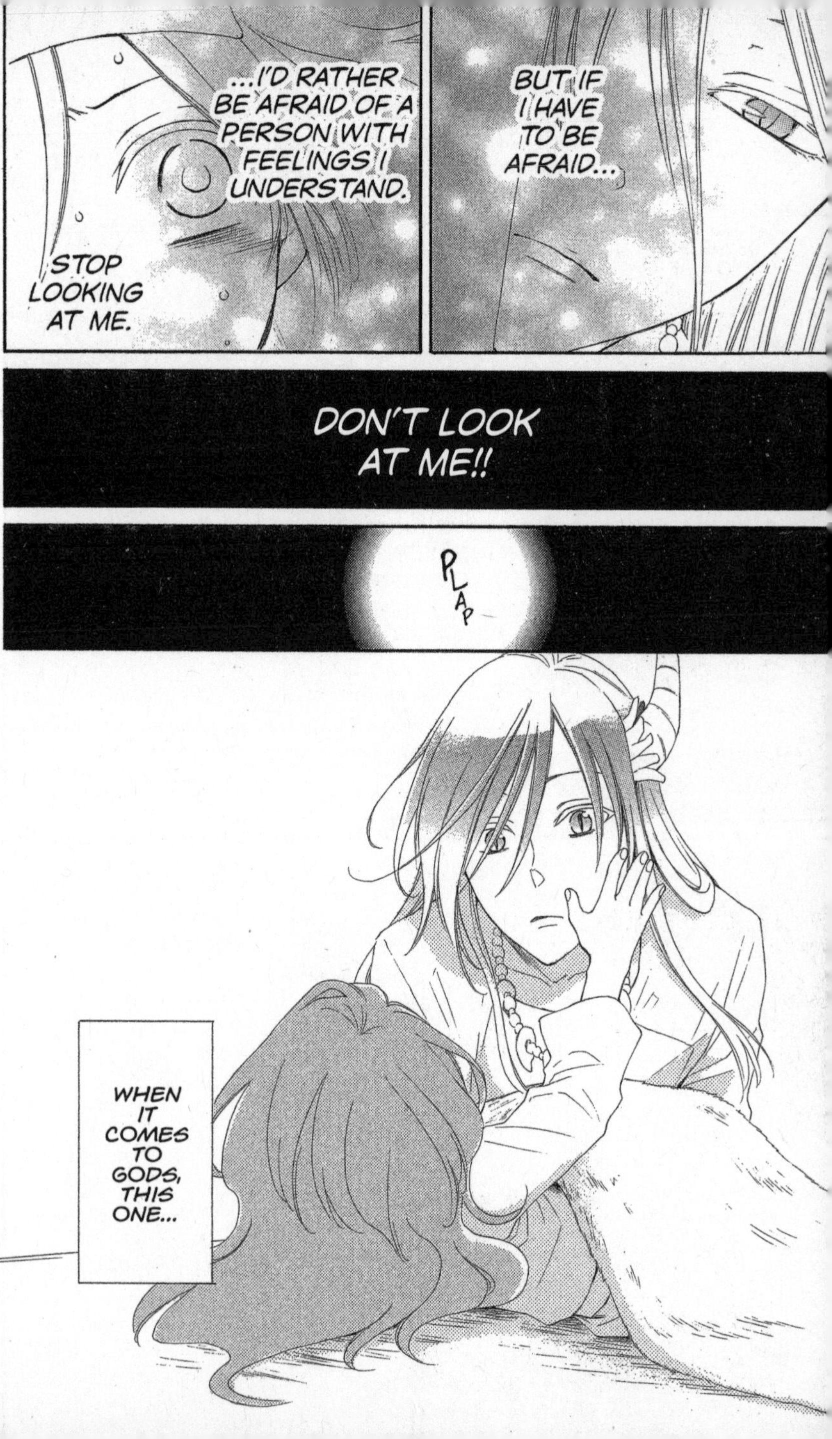
BUT IF I HAVE TO BE AFRAID...
...I'D RATHER BE AFRAID OF A PERSON WITH FEELINGS I UNDERSTAND.
STOP LOOKING AT ME.
DON'T LOOK AT ME!!
PLAP
WHEN IT COMES TO GODS, THIS ONE...

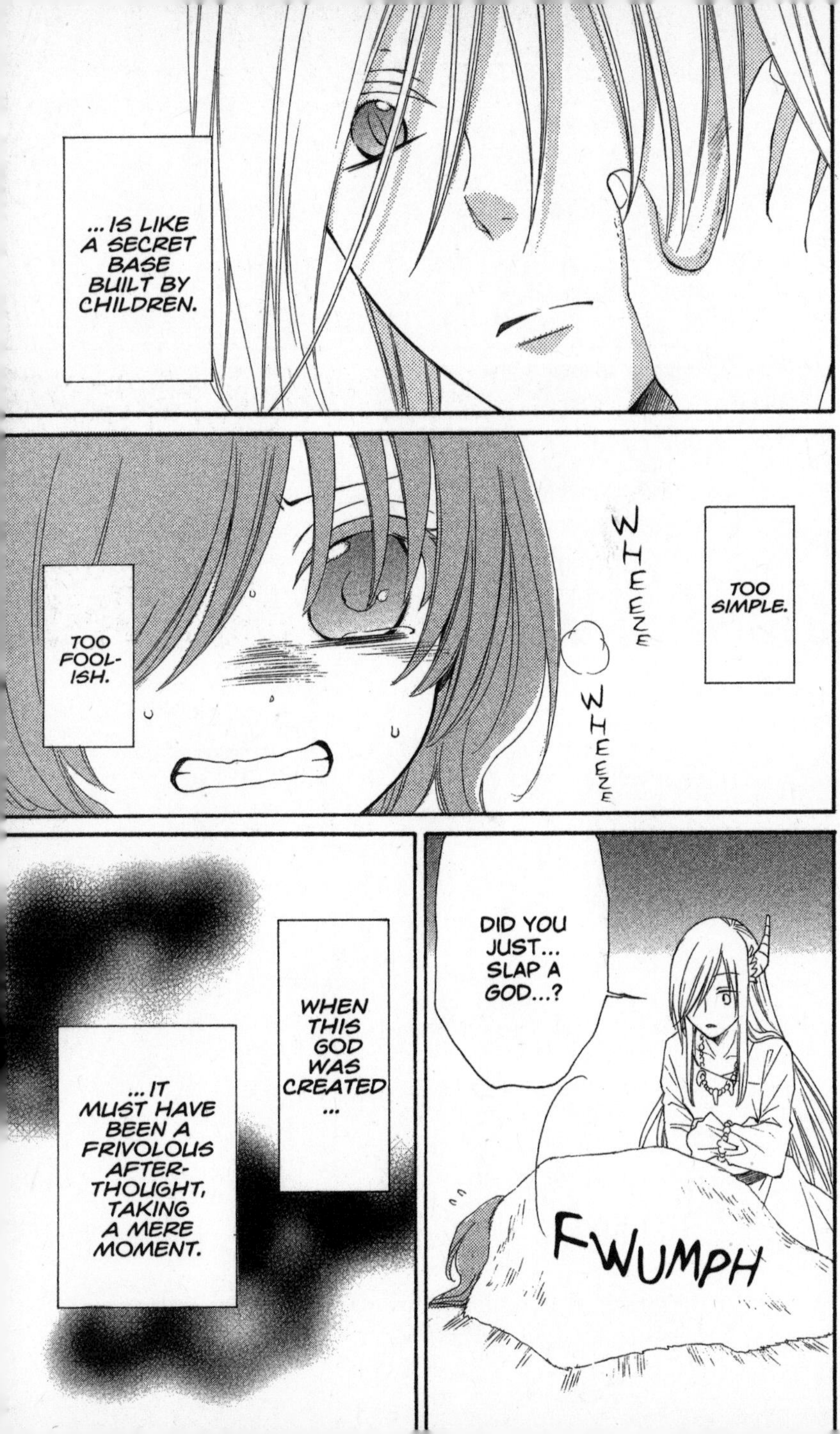
...IS LIKE A SECRET BASE BUILT BY CHILDREN.
TOO SIMPLE.
WHEEZE
WHEEZE
TOO FOOL-ISH.
DID YOU JUST... SLAP A GOD...?
FWUMPH
WHEN THIS GOD WAS CREATED...
...IT MUST HAVE BEEN A FRIVOLOUS AFTER-THOUGHT, TAKING A MERE MOMENT.

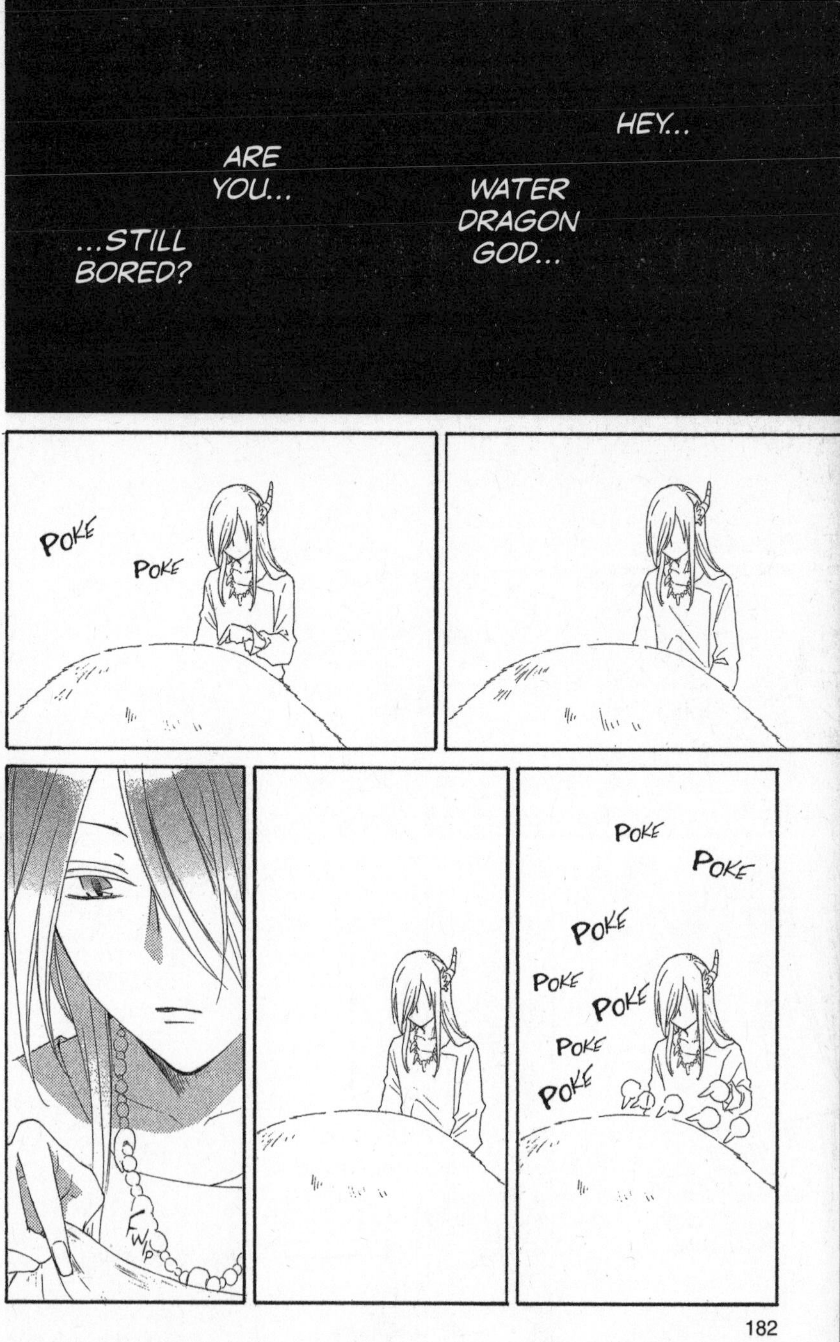
HEY...
WATER DRAGON GOD...
ARE YOU...
...STILL BORED?
POKE
POKE
POKE
POKE
POKE
POKE
POKE
POKE
POKE
FWIP

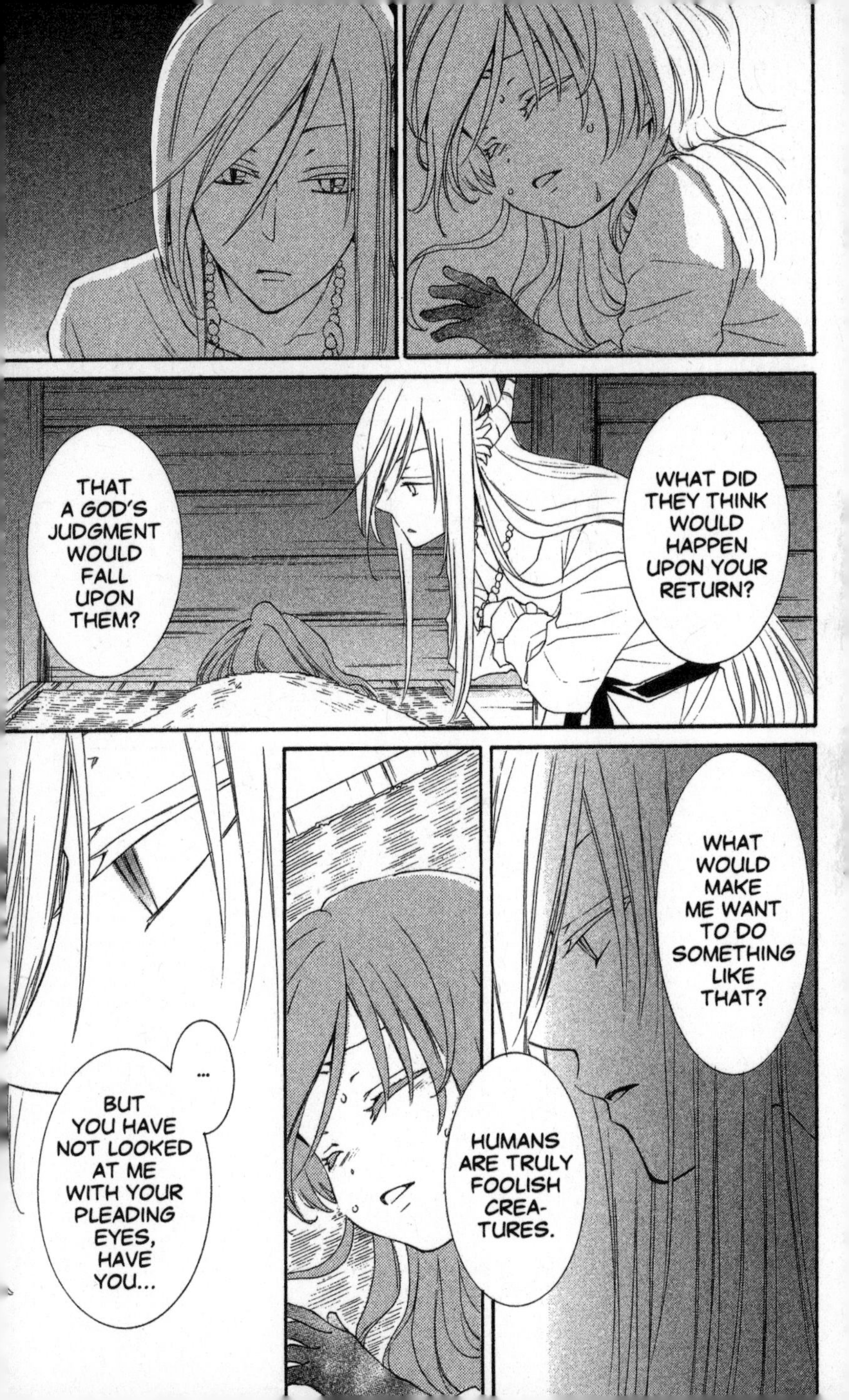
WHAT DID THEY THINK WOULD HAPPEN UPON YOUR RETURN?
THAT A GOD'S JUDGMENT WOULD FALL UPON THEM?
WHAT WOULD MAKE ME WANT TO DO SOMETHING LIKE THAT?
HUMANS ARE TRULY FOOLISH CREA-TURES.
...
BUT YOU HAVE NOT LOOKED AT ME WITH YOUR PLEADING EYES, HAVE YOU...

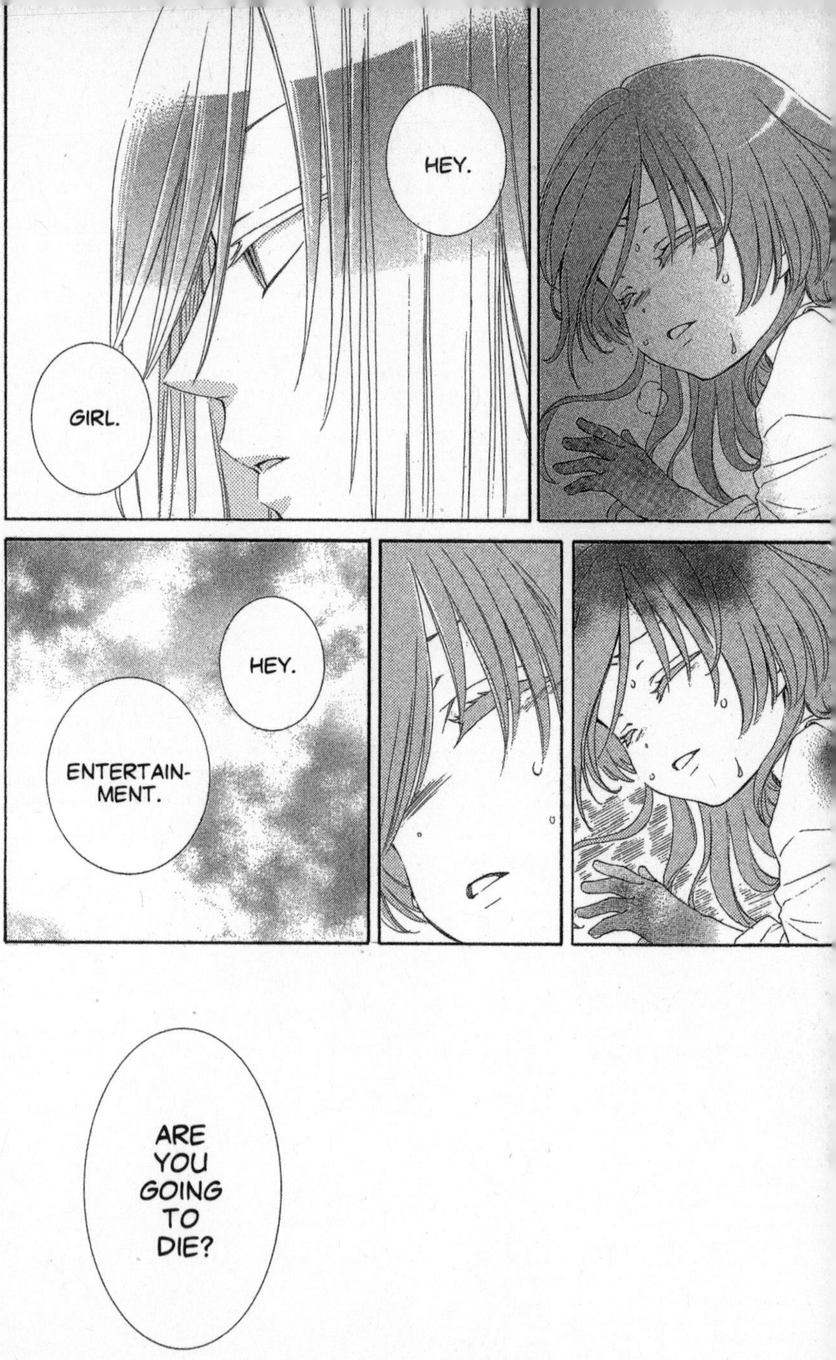
HEY.
GIRL.
HEY.
ENTERTAIN-MENT.
ARE YOU GOING TO DIE?

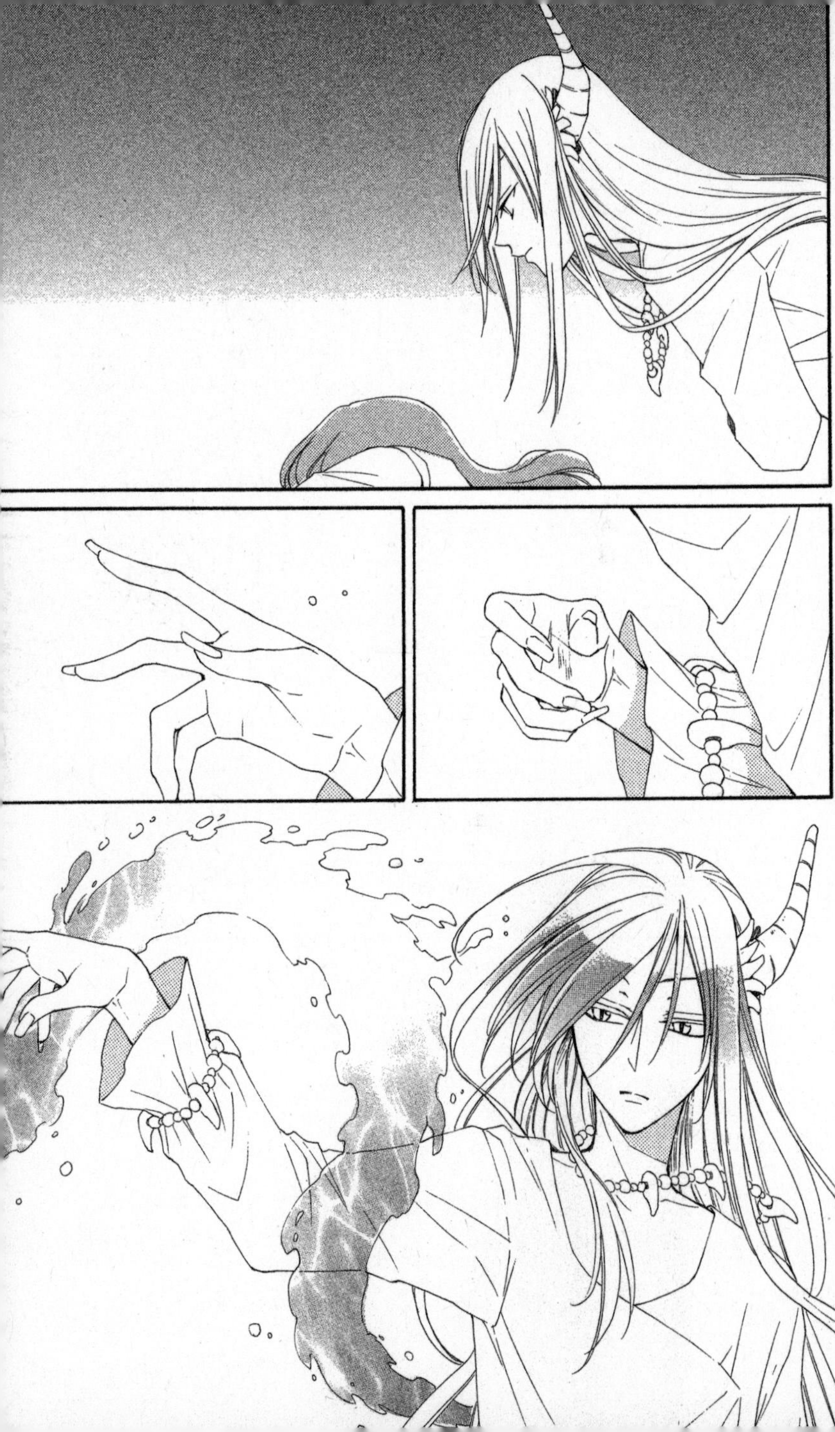

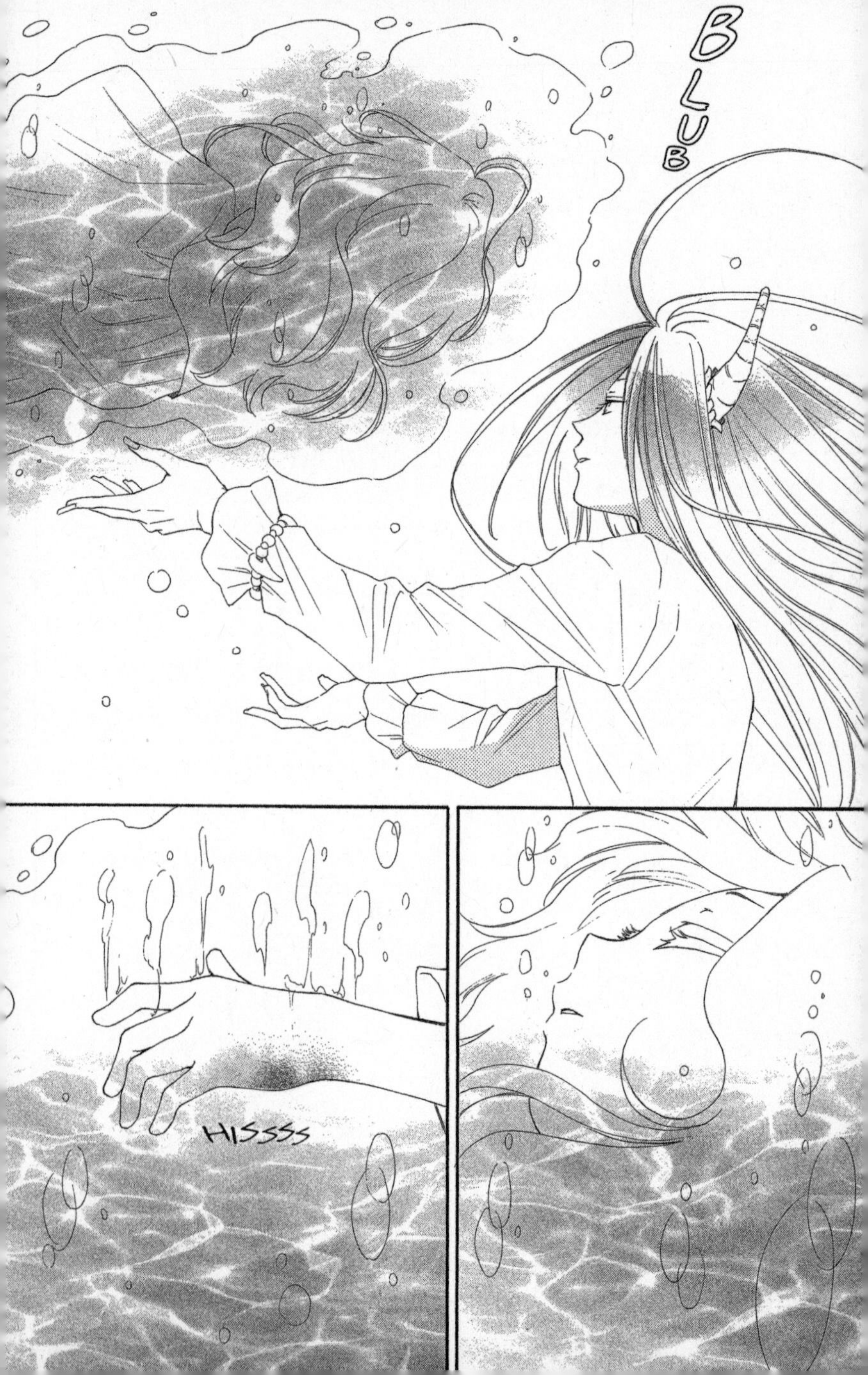
BLUB
HISSSS

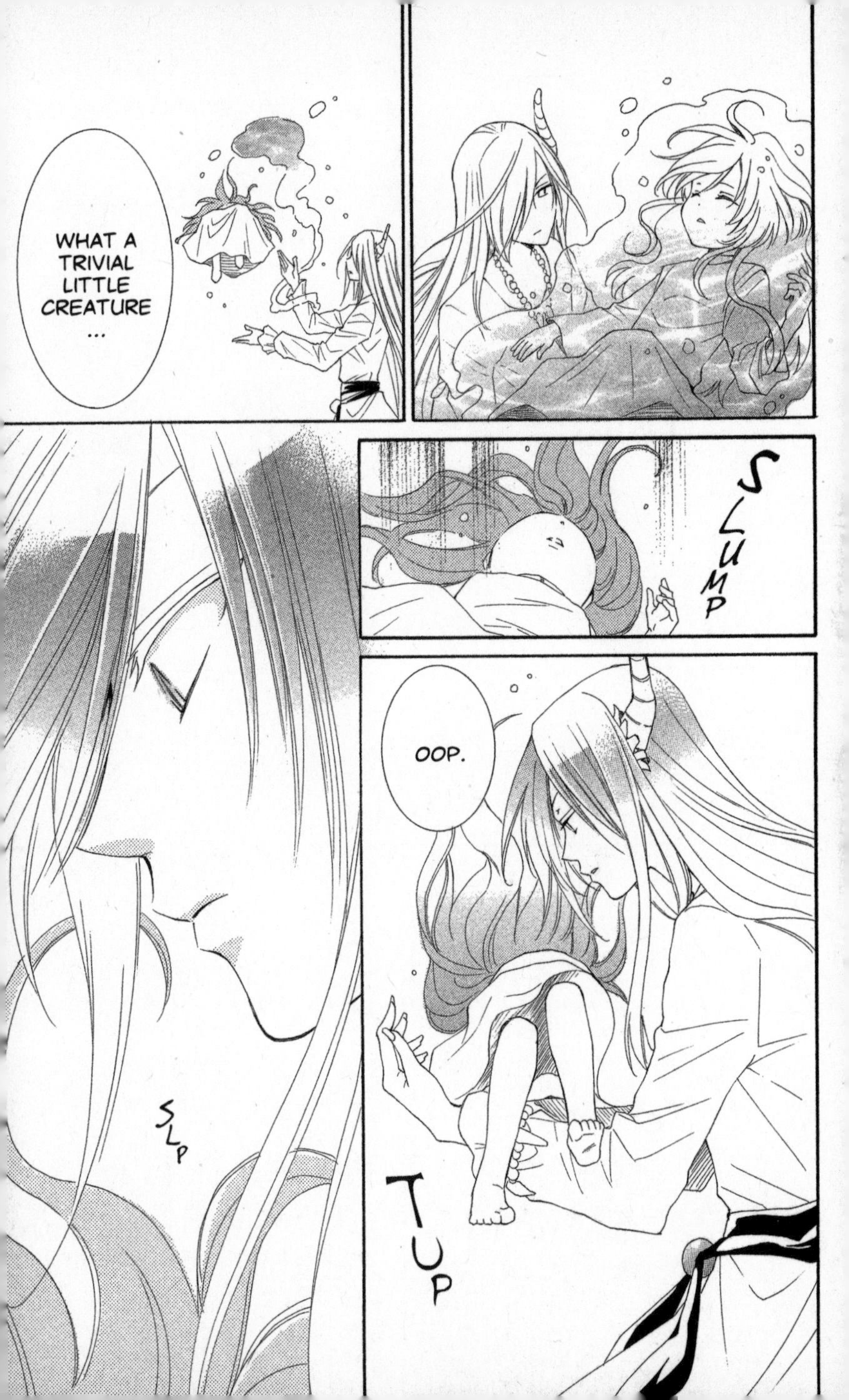
WHAT A TRIVIAL LITTLE CREATURE ...
SLUMP
OOP.
TUP
SLP

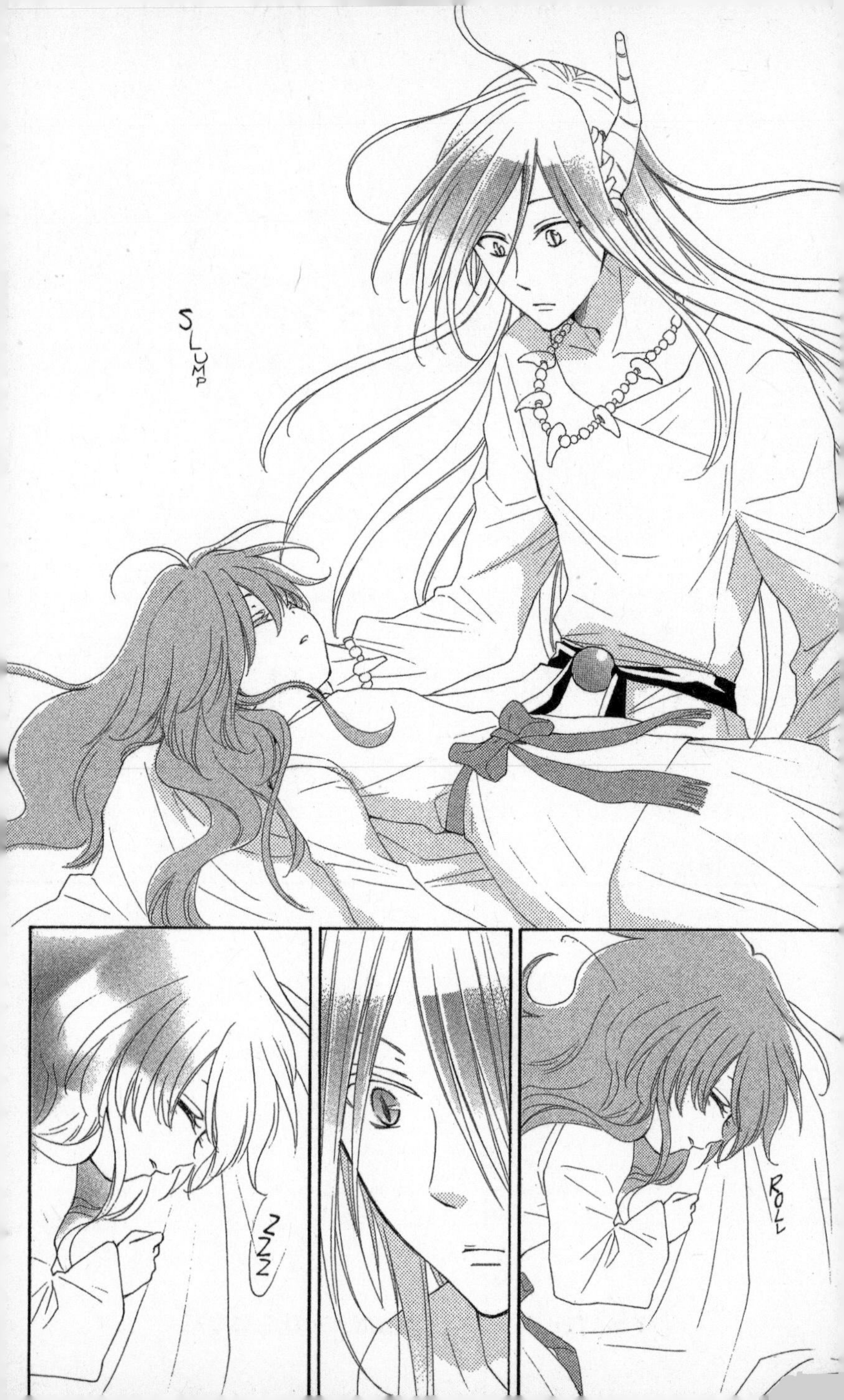
SLUMP
ROLL
ZZZ

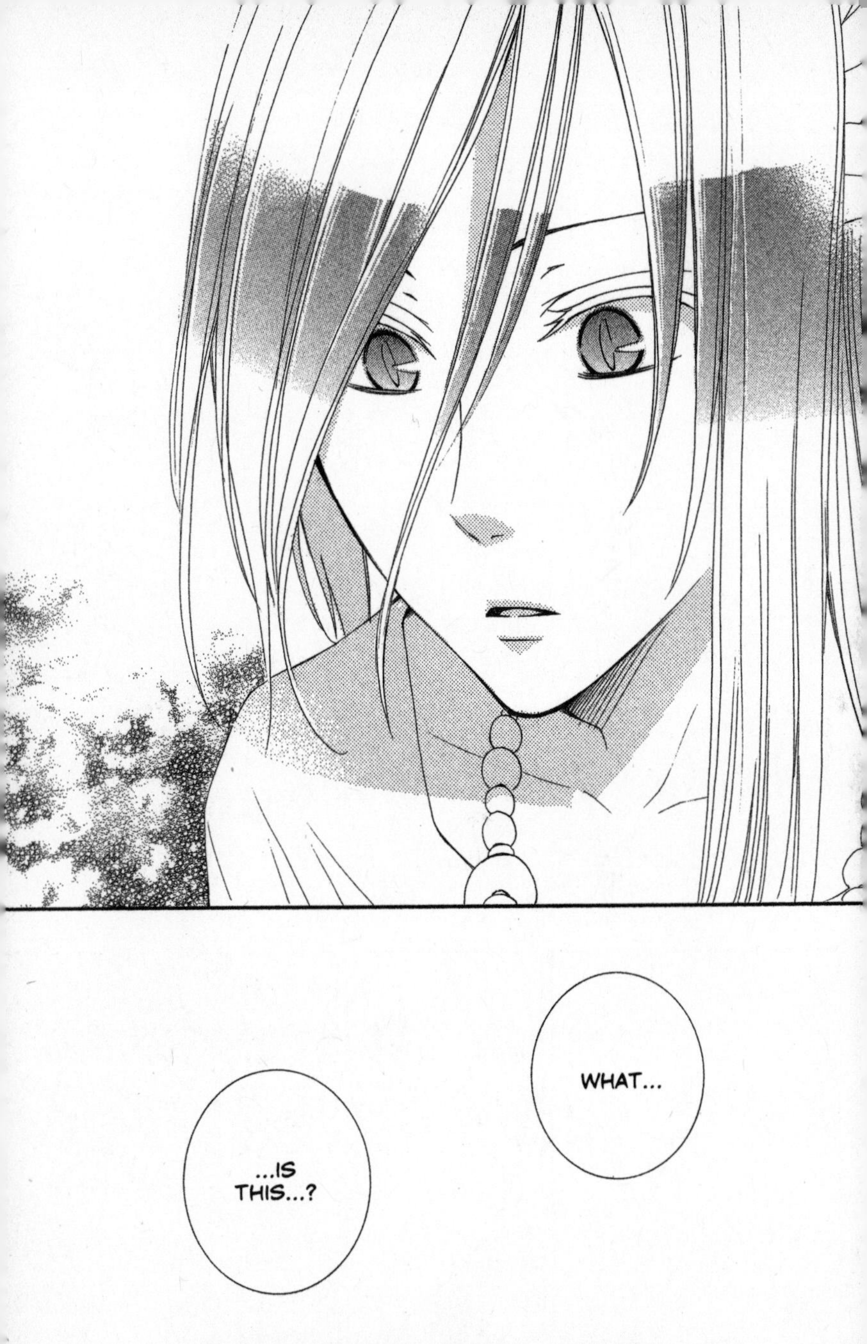
WHAT...
...IS THIS...?

THE WATER DRAGON'S BRIDE 1 – THE END –

This is the volume 1 graphic novel
of my new series!
It's a fantasy work again.
I'd be really happy if you enjoyed it!

– REI TOMA

Rei Toma has been drawing since childhood, and she
created her first complete manga for a graduation project
in design school. When she drew the short story manga
"Help Me, Dentist," it attracted a publisher's attention and
she made her debut right away. After she found success
as a manga artist, acclaim in other art fields started to
follow as she did illustrations for novels and video game
character designs. She is also the creator of *Dawn of the
Arcana,* available in North America from VIZ Media.

The Water Dragon's Bride
VOL. 1
Shojo Beat Edition

Story and Art by
Rei Toma

SUIJIN NO HANAYOME Vol.1
by Rei TOMA
© 2015 Rei TOMA
All rights reserved.
Original Japanese edition published by SHOGAKUKAN.
English translation rights in the United States of America,
Canada, the United Kingdom, Ireland, Australia and New
Zealand arranged with SHOGAKUKAN.

ORIGINAL COVER DESIGN/Hibiki CHIKADA (fireworks.vc)

English Translation & Adaptation **Abby Lehrke**
Touch-Up Art & Lettering **Monalisa de Asis**
Design **Alice Lewis**
Editor **Amy Yu**

The stories, characters and incidents mentioned in this
publication are entirely fictional.

Printed in the U.S.A.

Published by VIZ Media, LLC
P.O. Box 77010
San Francisco, CA 94107

10 9 8 7 6 5 4 3 2 1
First printing, April 2017

viz.com

shojobeat.com

You may be reading the wrong way!

In keeping with the original Japanese comic format, this book reads from right to left—so action, sound effects and word balloons are completely reversed. This preserves the orientation of the original artwork—plus, it's fun!

Check out the diagram shown here to get the hang of things, and then turn to the other side of the book to get started!

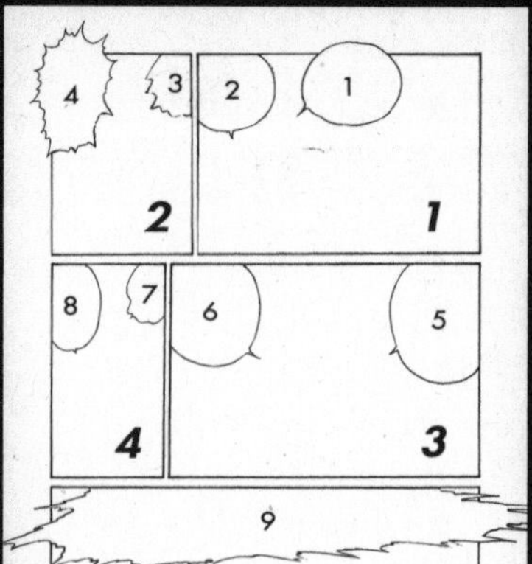
1
2
3
4
1
2
5
6
7
8
3
4
9
5
142

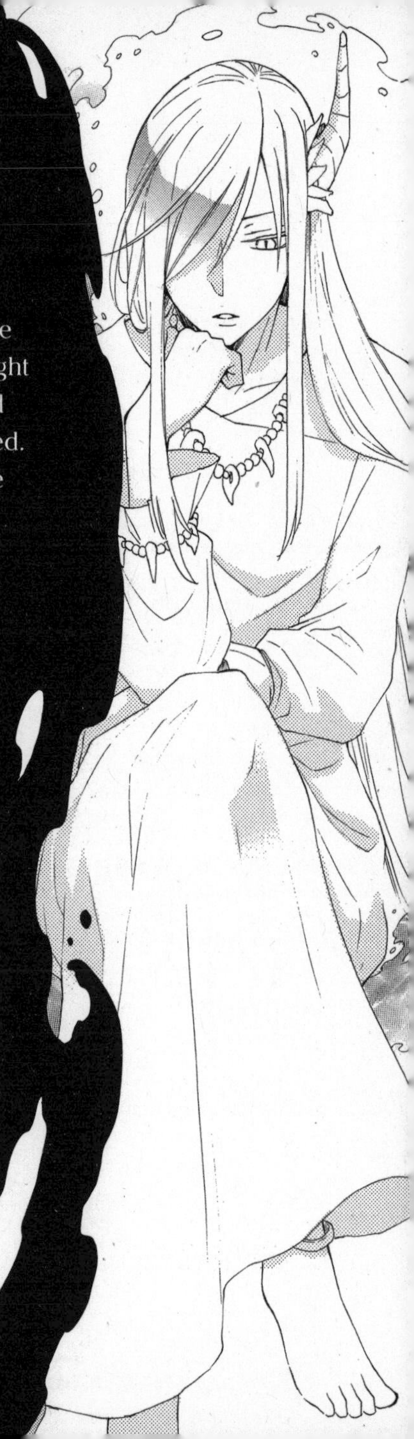

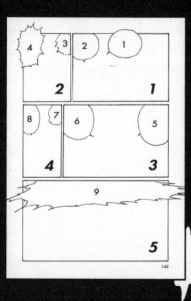